DOING DIGITAL METHODS

DOING DIGITAL METHODS

2nd Edition

RICHARD ROGERS

1 Oliver's Yard
55 City Road
London EC1Y 1SP

2455 Teller Road
Thousand Oaks
California 91320

Unit No 323-333, Third Floor, F-Block
International Trade Tower,
Nehru Place, New Delhi – 110 019

8 Marina View Suite 43-053
Asia Square Tower 1
Singapore 018960

©Richard Rogers 2024

First published 2019

Apart from any fair dealing for the purposes of research, private study, or criticism or review, as permitted under the Copyright, Designs and Patents Act, 1988, this publication may not be reproduced, stored or transmitted in any form, or by any means, without the prior permission in writing of the publisher, or in the case of reprographic reproduction, in accordance with the terms of licences issued by the Copyright Licensing Agency. Enquiries concerning reproduction outside those terms should be sent to the publisher.

Editor: Umeeka Raichura
Editorial Assistant: Hannah Cavender-Deere
Production editor: Nicola Marshall
Copyeditor: Tom Bedford
Proofreader: Sarah Cooke
Indexer: C&M Digitals (P) Ltd, Chennai, India
Marketing manager: Ben Griffin-Sherwood
Cover design: Shaun Mercier
Typeset by: C&M Digitals (P) Ltd, Chennai, India
Printed in the UK

Library of Congress Control Number: 2023938593

British Library Cataloguing in Publication data

A catalogue record for this book is available from the British Library

ISBN 978-1-5297-6433-8
ISBN 978-1-5297-6432-1 (pbk)

At Sage we take sustainability seriously. Most of our products are printed in the UK using responsibly sourced papers and boards. When we print overseas we ensure sustainable papers are used as measured by the Paper Chain Project grading system. We undertake an annual audit to monitor our sustainability.

CONTENTS

ABOUT THE AUTHOR

Richard Rogers is Professor of New Media & Digital Culture, Media Studies, University of Amsterdam. He is Director of the Digital Methods Initiative, Amsterdam, known for the development of software tools for the study of online data. He is author of *Information Politics on the Web* and *Digital Methods* (both MIT Press) and is editor of *The Politics of Social Media Manipulation* (with Sabine Niederer) and *The Propagation of Misinformation in Social Media: A Cross-platform Analysis* (both Amsterdam University Press).

ACKNOWLEDGEMENTS

The Digital Research Methods course, upon which this book is based, has a particular working model and rhythm. The model and rhythm are akin to a 'sprint', where participants undertake a research project (encapsulated in each chapter of this book) in a single, pressure-packed week. In a flipped classroom approach, the initial tool training is video tutorial homework. Students are required to watch the video tutorials which are software walkthroughs, a common video genre on the web, and itself a digital method (Light, 2018). Subsequent hands-on training takes place through actual project work in a lab setting, with moveable tables and laptops, rather than in a 'computer room' or a tiered lecture hall.

Having read the chapter and viewed the tutorial, to kick off the lab session, groups of students pitch project ideas, in the form of five slides – introduction to subject matter, research questions, methods, expected outcomes and 'why is it interesting?' The groups of students (no more than four) work at the same table, and teachers are on hand during the sessions where data are being collected and analysed, and nitty-gritty questions may be posed about software, such as 'what does this setting do?'

Students write research reports weekly (or bi-weekly if one would like to dedicate a week to discussing related academic literature). After they have handed in their research report, they are given the next chapter and video tutorials for the following week's assignment. The course finishes with a week-long data sprint, where there is a theme (e.g., migration crisis or pandemic) and the students apply whichever methods they have learned that best fit the research questions they pose.

Issue or subject matter experts are often brought in to the sprints and asked to (1) explain the state of art of their field, (2) their current analytical needs and (3) what web or social media data may add. These subject matter expert pitches form the basis for the sprint projects from which participants may choose.

The city government of Amsterdam made inquiries about Airbnb which led to a project on the hotelization of private apartments, as was found through Airbnb image analysis. Greenpeace International were interested in how their campaigns resonated during a UN climate summit, which resulted in a critique of 'issue celebrities' and their symbolic power (Couldry, 2001), given the attention paid to their appearance at the summit, rather than to NGO campaigns. These are only two prompts that led to compelling projects, but the model has been applied across digital methods and sprint-oriented courses elsewhere, too (Laursen, 2017; Venturini et al., 2018). It also explains in part the issue-oriented focus found throughout the cases and sample projects in the book (see also Rogers et al., 2015).

I now would like to turn to the digital methods projects that comprise this book and acknowledge their origins and mention the projects and those involved who honed the techniques. Making a screencast documentary of an archived webpage was inspired by Jon Udell's 'heavy metal umlaut' video on the coming into being of a Wikipedia article (2005). 'Google and the Politics of Tabs' (Rogers, Richard and Govcom.org, 2008), made on the occasion of Google's 10th year, was the first one of its kind that colleagues and I stitched together, with production by Menno Endt and Theun Hendrikx and research by Laura van der Vlies, Kim de Groot, Esther Weltevrede and Erik Borra, who developed the software to extract links from the Wayback Machine, automatically take screenshots and array them in order to play back the history of a webpage in the style of time-lapse photography. Emile den Tex created the latest version of the screenshot generator, which Stijn Peeters and Dale Wahl modified. Two compelling examples of video projects are discussed: the evolution of the *New York Times* online (nytimes.com) by Eelke Hermens, and that of theknot.com by Maya Livio, Jules Mataly and Mathias Schuh, where changes over the years to the wedding planner website show the commercialization of the web (and marriage). A previous edition of the chapter appeared in 2017 as 'Doing web history with the Internet Archive: Screencast documentaries', *Internet Histories: Digital Technology, Culture and Society*, 1(1/2), 1–13.

The Google critique chapter, which was written on the occasion of Google's 20th year online, ultimately leads to a project that audits or probes Google results. The approach benefits from a series of engine audits, including the early Issuedramaturg project (2007) where the results of the query '9/11' were captured daily and the rankings of websites displayed over time. The 'drama' occurred when a conspiracy website, long at the top of the returns, fell precipitously to 200th place in the rankings, and then out of the top 1,000, only to reappear at the top two weeks later. It leads to questions of ranking volatility. Given that scraping engine results is against Google's terms of service (for commercial reasons), it also raises questions of how to perform regular, critical engine audits to enable what is called 'platform observability' (Rieder and Hofmann, 2020). The auditing work discussed in the chapter is enabled by another piece of software, the Search Engine Scraper, developed by Stijn Peeters and Dale Wahl. It allows for cross-engine results comparison as well as cross-region Google analysis (discussed in the subsequent chapter). Other auditing work, of Google Autocomplete (as well as that of Yahoo! and DuckDuckGo), was part of a collaboration with Alina Leidinger, which appeared as 'Which stereotypes are moderated and under-moderated in search engine autocompletion?, *FAccT '23: Proceedings of the 2023 ACM Conference on Fairness, Accountability, and Transparency*, June 2023: 1049–1061. It was aided by discussions about Google autocompletion with Rosie Graham contained in her book *Investigating Google's Search Engine* (2023). One other auditing exercise, where we re-queried problematic Google results from the past, inquiring into the extent to which they have been remedied, had its first iteration during the Digital Methods Winter School 2022 and was published as 'Algorithmic probing: Prompting offensive Google results and their moderation', *Big Data & Society*, January-June 2023: 1-25. Taking part were Zoe Chan, Sarah Gralla, Alistair Keepe, Natalie Kerby, Goran Kusic, Barbara Matijasic, Leah Nann, Olga Parai,

Piet van den Reek, Miazia Schueler, Tatiana Smirnova and Liam van de Ven. The heart of the Google critique chapter appeared as 'Aestheticizing Google critique: A twenty-year retrospective', *Big Data & Society*, January–June 2018: 1–13.

The search as research chapter, originally co-written with Esther Weltevrede, benefits from the work undertaken on the Google Scraper and later the Lippmannian Device, developed during the MACOSPOL project, Mapping Controversies on Science for Politics, led by Bruno Latour. The Scraper itself, together with the DMI Firefox plug-in that allowed the scraping to be offloaded to the individual user's browser, was developed by Erik Borra and Koen Martins. The 'source distance' method that is built into the Google Scraper was developed at the first Digital Methods Summer School, where the project with Anne Helmond, Sabine Niederer, Bram Nijhof, Laura van der Vlies and Esther Weltevrede concerned how close to the top of the web are the climate change sceptics as well as which animals are most prominent in the climate change issue space. The 'Rights Types' project, undertaken with Vera Bekema, Liliana Bounegru, Andrea Fiore, Anne Helmond, Simon Marschall, Sabine Niederer, Bram Nijhof and Elena Tiis, makes use of an ambiguous query ('rights') in multiple languages in order to perform cross-cultural comparison. The triangulation tool for list comparison, developed by Erik Borra, received impetus from a project by Natalia Sánchez Querubín that compares the country origins of sources returned for the query, 'Amazonia'. The Craig Venter example derives from a workshop at Lancaster University with Adrian MacKenzie, and the technique of mapping the issue agenda of a movement or network (such as that of the global human rights network) benefited from collaboration with Charli Carpenter at the University of Massachusetts Amherst.

The observation that Wikipedia articles on the 'same' subject matter in different languages have 'cultural points of view' may be traced to the project comparing Srebrenica articles in Bosnian, Serbian and Dutch (among other languages), undertaken with Emina Sendijarevic and published as 'Neutral or national point of view? A comparison of Srebrenica articles across Wikipedia's language versions', Wikipedia Academy: Research and Free Knowledge: June 29 – July 1, 2012, Berlin. The tools for article comparison (such as the Wikipedia Cross-Lingual Image Analysis) were developed by Erik Borra. The Wikipedia categories scraper, which may be used for cross-lingual event analysis, was developed during the Digital Methods Summer School project comparing Brexit articles, with analysis by Viola Bernacchi, Carlo De Gaetano, Simon Gottschalk, Sabine Niederer, Warren Pearce and Mariasilvia Poltronieri. The comparison of Auschwitz articles (in German, Polish and Portuguese) was performed by students at the University of Mannheim, Nathalie Bielka, Helena Buhl and Monica dos Santos. They found that only the Polish article discussed the controversy surrounding the notion of 'Polish death camps'.

The title of the YouTube teardown chapter takes its inspiration from *Spotify Teardown: Inside the Black Box of Streaming Music* (2019), the book by Maria Eriksson, Rasmus Fleischer, Anna Johansson, Pelle Snickars and Patrick Vonderau, which hacks Spotify in a variety of manners to unbox its inner workings. The YouTube teardowns put forward here rely on the software, YouTube Data Tools, developed by Bernhard Rieder. The software suite sits atop the YouTube API and collects data for YouTube searches, individual channels and videos as well as related videos, among others, enabling the analysis of search volatility, influencer privileging, channel subscription networks as well as the carousel or rabbit hole one enters when following related videos. One may also study the comment space.

The Facebook analysis initially relied on Netvizz, the Facebook data extraction software by Bernhard Rieder which was retired after the so-called APIcalypse, a notion coined by Axel Bruns (2019), when Facebook discontinued its Pages API, shutting down a central data source for social media research. The most engaged-with content analysis technique was originally developed during the counter-jihadism winter school, 'What does the internet add? Studying extremism and counter-jihadism online', a collaboration with the London-based NGO, Hope not Hate. The analysis of the Facebook page, 'Stop Islamization of the World', which ushered in the most engaged-with content analysis technique (and its eventual visualization as a tree map), was conducted by Ana Crisostomo, Juliana Marques, Joe Mier and Despoina Mountanea. Since the shutting down of the Pages API, two forms of Facebook engagement analysis have emerged. One relies on a data journalism technique, originally employed by Craig Silverman in his seminal 'fake news' story in *BuzzFeed News*, where he found that imposter and hyperpartisan sources were outperforming mainstream news in the run-up to the 2016 US presidential elections. His data source was BuzzSumo, the marketing data dashboard that provides engagement scores for web URLs liked (or reacted upon), shared and commented upon on Facebook as well as other platforms. Meta, the company behind Facebook, Instagram, WhatsApp and other services, also grants access to its CrowdTangle marketing data dashboard to journalists and academics who meet their vetting criteria, though at the time of writing its future is clouded. The dashboard has provided access to Facebook and Instagram data (as well as Reddit and some Twitter data) and is useful for studying engagement and, among other entry points, the effectiveness of Facebook's (and Instagram's) content moderation. In the Facebook and platform studies chapter, I put forward a means to study the 'fake news' problem on Facebook, which builds on an article published as 'The scale of Facebook's problem depends upon how "fake news" is classified', *Harvard Kennedy School Misinformation Review*, 1(6), 2020.

The proposition of 'debanalizing' Twitter and turning it into a story-telling machine that recounts events on the ground and in social media is rooted in the #iranelection RT project conducted with Erik Borra, Marieke van Dijk, Sabine Niederer, Michael Stevenson and Esther Weltevrede, and shown at Arts Santa Mònica in Barcelona, together with the IP Browser, in the Cultures of Change exhibition curated by Josep Perelló and Pau Alsina. Arraying the top three retweeted tweets by day, in chronological order, is among the many modules built into DMI-TCAT, the Twitter Capture and Analysis Toolset, developed by Erik Borra, Bernhard Rieder and Emile den Tex. Among the other analytical modules discussed, particularly with respect to studying 'issue spaces' with the 'critical analytics' approach, are ranked @mention lists (for dominant voice analysis) and hashtag and co-hashtag lists (for analyses of matters of concern and commitment). Twitter, more recently known as X, once a relatively expensive data provider (for paid historical tweet data), has had an academic

API that allows for such queries, shut down at the time of writing. Alternatively, the data may be scraped via Zeeschuimer, a browser plug-in originally developed for gathering TikTok data. Once collected it may be fed into 4CAT, the wide-ranging social media data capture and analysis tool, spearheaded by Stijn Peeters and Sal Hagen.

The cross-platform analysis techniques, where Instagram and Tumblr tools make an appearance, benefit from a teaching unit created by Bernhard Rieder, where he compared digital objects across a series of social media platforms, suggesting how they may be made commensurable. The sample projects comparing content across platforms about Aylan Kurdi and the Cologne New Year's incidents were led by Marloes Geboers. An earlier rendition of the chapter appeared in 2018 as 'Digital methods for cross-platform analysis', in Jean Burgess, Alice Marwick and Thomas Poell (eds), *SAGE Handbook of Social Media*, London: Sage, pp. 91–110.

The TikTok chapter benefited from an algorithmic auditing course I developed at the University of Amsterdam, where in one unit we compared outputs of the same query in TikTok and Douyin, its domestic Chinese counterpart. The case concerned the November 2022 fire in a residential building in the Chinese city, Urumqi, where ten inhabitants perished. Their inability to escape from the building (and the hindrances faced by the fire-fighters) were attributed to the strict enforcement of official Covid-19 pandemic policies, sparking protests around the country. Videos of the protests were present on TikTok and absent on Douyin.

The Data Journalism chapter has been inspired by exchanges with Liliana Bounegru and Jonathan Gray, who together with Tommaso Venturini and Michele Mauri, compiled the *Field Guide to Fake News* (2018), where we also studied Russian disinformation campaigning through an analysis of websites that share the same Google Analytics and Ads IDs. Mischa Szpirt was instrumental in refining the Google Analytics ID network discovery technique. The EXIF camera data extraction technique was aided by software reworked by Emile den Tex in the Gezi Park (Istanbul) research project, a collaboration with Greenpeace International and Soenke Lorenzen. The painstaking work of identifying the cameras taking the iconic 'Lady in Red' and other pictures and looking up the cameras' retail prices (to study the grassroots 'pop-up media ecology') were performed by Federica Bardelli, Giulia De Amicis, Carlo De Gaetano, Saskia Kok, Sandrine Roginsky, Saya Saulière and Thijs Waardenburg.

The more conceptual chapters on positioning digital methods, query design as well as critical social media research had their forerunners. The positioning piece in an earlier form appeared in 2015 as 'Digital methods for web research', in Robert A. Scott and Stephen M. Kosslyn (eds), *Emerging Trends in the Behavioral and Social Sciences*, Hoboken, NJ: Wiley, pp. 1–22. It also has been translated into German and published as 'Digitale Methoden: Zur Positionierung eines Ansatzes', *Medien & Kommunikationswissenschaft*, 69(1), 2020. A previous version of the query design chapter appeared in 2017 as 'Foundations of digital methods: Query design', in Mirko Schaefer and Karin van Es (eds), *The Datafied Society: Studying Culture through Data*,

Amsterdam: Amsterdam University Press, pp. 75–94. The critical social media piece was developed upon an invitation by Sarah Lewthwaite to create an instructional video for the UK National Centre for Research Methods. It was published in the special issue, 'From big data in politics to the politics of big data' (2018), in the Italian journal, *Partecipazione and Conflitto* (PaCo), edited by Alice Mattoni and Elena Pavan.

The book was made possible by the students, participants, designers, programmers, teachers and staff taking part in the Digital Research Methods course as well as the Digital Methods Winter and Summer Schools at the University of Amsterdam. The information designers from Density Design, Milan, have been pivotal in the development and rendering of the research: Camila di Amicis, Guilherme Appolinário, Antonella Autuori, Elena Aversa, Matteo Azzi, Matteo Banal, Federica Bardelli, Andrea Benedetti, Matteo Bettini, Niccola Brignoli, Agata Brilli, Angeles Briones, Michele Bruno, Eleonora Capuccio, Gabriele Colombo, Giulia Corona, Giulia De Amicis, Carlo De Gaetano, Alessandra Del Nero, Serena Del Nero, Daniele Dell'Orto, Luca Draisci, Tommaso Elli, Andrea Fabres, Alessandra Facchin, Sara Ferrini, Elena Filippi, Giacomo Flaim, Emanuele Ghebaur, Beatrice Gobbo, Stefania Guerra, Michele Invernizzi, Irina Kasatkina, Giovanni Lombardi, Michele Mauri, Marco Mezzadra, Alessia Musio, Claudia Pazzaglia, Davide Perucchini, Camilla Pilotto, María Cristina Pita, Cristina Pita da Veiga, Chiara Piva, Mariasilvia Poltronieri, Jacopo Poletto, Andrea Pronzati, Alessandro Quets, Tommaso Renzini, Donato Ricci, Chiara Riente, Barbara Roncalli, Noemi Schiavi, Laura Swietlicki, Ginevra Terenghi, Marco Valli, Daniele Zanetti and Alice Ziantoni. Special thanks for the dedication on the part of the digital methods teachers as well as the organizers of multiple Summer and Winter Schools: Erik Borra, Liliana Bounegru, Jonathan Gray, Sal Hagen, Emilija Jokubauskaitė, Saskia Kok, Kamila Koronska, Sabine Niederer, Bernhard Rieder, Natalia Sánchez Querubín, Marc Tuters, Guillén Torres, Fernando van der Vlist and Esther Weltevrede.

BEFORE BEGINNING DIGITAL METHODS

Digital methods and methodologies

This book is an elaboration on the practice of collecting data online and undertaking contemporary research with digital methods. The digital methods described hereafter are often built into tools and are thus 'programmed methods' (Borra and Rieder, 2014). They evolve with the medium, meaning that they are updated when a web service changes or deprecated when it is discontinued. In between these states, there may be workarounds or manual alternatives. While digital methods may often make use of certain software tools, they do not solely depend on them, and thus also should be considered digital methodologies. These are more generalized ways and means of performing online research, often just with a (research) browser.

These generalized ways of performing online research include a keyword or hashtag list-building technique called 'associational snowballing', where one types two keywords (or two hashtags) into Google (or another engine), peruses the results for a third, related keyword (or hashtag) and iterates this routine until no new related keywords appear. It is one technique of 'query design', where one crafts a search engine query for research purposes (as opposed to informational or navigational searches). Other digital methods include compiling historical screenshots from the Internet Archive and narrating screen-cast documentaries about web, media and/or social history. This book introduces techniques for comparing the images, references and tables of contents of the 'same' Wikipedia article across different language versions, posing questions about cross-cultural comparison and the politics of memory. There are how-to's on performing single-platform and cross-platform analysis (with X/Twitter, Facebook, YouTube, Instagram, Telegram and others) in order to research dominant voice, concern, commitment and other 'critical analytics' for undertaking 'remote event analysis' or studying influencers. There are procedures to locate the content on Facebook and Instagram that has elicited the most engagement, inquiring at the same time into the formats that circulate well (such as memes) and the groups animated by them (such as the alt-right). There are visualization strategies discussed, including the concept of 'metapicturing', which seeks to combine close and distant reading techniques. A simple network mapping technique is introduced as a means to map relationships between images and reactions (or emoji) using Facebook data. Network mapping and 'visual network analysis' are further elaborated in techniques to create channel networks on YouTube, depicting (and labelling) subcultures online. Another network analysis technique is applied to TikTok data, where relationships between hashtags and sounds are mapped. Here we enquire into the extent to which users act like imitation publics, whereby trending sounds are used no matter the subject matter of the video. Finally, there are recipes for detecting trackers and other third-party elements on websites in order to show (for example) how 'fake news' purveyors often use off-the-shelf trackers compared to mainstream news providers who tend to have customized trackers. In another technique, one may also identify the owners – be they individuals or media groups – of websites purveying such news or undertaking disinformation campaigns. Digital methods thereby enter the realm of data journalism and open source intelligence and investigation.

Foundations of digital methods

The early chapters introduce two core skills – building keyword and source lists. Keywords may be part of programmes or anti-programmes, such as 'blood diamonds' and 'conflict minerals', respectively, or as the *New York Times* 1619 project had it, 'slave labor camps' in contrast to 'plantations'. Building lists of them (be they the keywords themselves or hashtags) enables one to undertake resonance research, a skill used in media monitoring and marketing research (on impact or 'buzz'). One learns how to design a query that answers research questions about the uptake and circulation of one campaign or initiative over another. Keyword and hashtag lists are also the seeds for creating collections of posts, an initial step in some X/Twitter, Instagram and TikTok analysis.

These keyword and source-building skills are applied when doing 'search as research', 'single-platform studies' (such as X/Twitter and Facebook) as well as 'cross-platform analysis' that also includes Instagram (and in passing Tumblr as well as YouTube), as touched on above. They can be used for platform comparison work, such as between TikTok and its Chinese counterpart, Douyin. They are also useful for building lists of junk news, disinformation or other thematically poignant sites and pages in order to discover who is behind them and which other sites belong to the same owners (through Google ID and Ad tracking), ultimately making journalistic accounts.

The other foundational chapter concerns critical social media research, where I enumerate issues with social media research data. For example, user engagement metrics, routinely deployed in research as an indication of interest or circulation, could be considered platform-driven, rather than expressions of user views. Certain posts (in the Facebook Feed, for example) are privileged over others. These posts are boosted for they are more liable to be engaged with, given that they have elicited angry reactions, as was detailed in the internal Facebook documents that a whistleblower made available to journalists (Merrill and Oremus, 2021). That ranking practice would privilege 'angertainment', which is one manner to audit Facebook's Feed, inquiring into the extent to which posts receiving angry reactions elicit more interactions than those that do not. Other issues discussed include such proprietary effects as company-held 'archives' and the treatment of marketing data dashboards as scientific data instruments.

The foundations of digital methods are the spine of the book, and throughout its pages the recurring themes are how to formulate a research question as well as how to tell a story of the findings or outcomes. One starting point for the formulation of a research question is to invert a current claim, be it from the academic literature or the intellectual or tech press, where many conceptual innovations in new media and digital culture originate (e.g., crowdsourcing and 'filter bubble') or claims arise (e.g., continuous partial attention (Stone, 2008)). Making findings and creating accounts of them are detailed initially in narrating a screencast documentary of the history of a web page and later in network story-telling techniques (in the YouTube Teardown chapter). Formulating research questions and telling stories with findings are also emphasized throughout the search engine, Wikipedia and the social media chapters, especially in the sample projects inquiring into the climate change sceptics, Srebrenica, Auschwitz, #iranelection, Aylan Kurdi, Russian influence campaigning, Chinese protests over pandemic-related restrictions and others.

By way of prefacing the book, I now would like to provide a series of insights about doing digital methods, including some admonitions as well as bright spots per methods chapter.

Screencast documentaries with the Internet Archive

The web history chapter employs screen-capturing software that utilizes the output of a scraper of Wayback Machine URLs to compile them into a movie, ready for recording a voiceover narrative. In other words, there are a few steps to creating a screencast documentary of the history of one webpage. Indeed, once one is able to compile and playback the screenshots in a movie, a couple of days of work may have been expended, only for the researcher to realize that creating and recording a voiceover narrative with a compelling storyline requires yet more time investment. Indeed, that project may be the most arduous, and oftentimes the most rewarding for its creative output.

Auditing Google

The first of two Google chapters concerns Google critique. Over the past twenty plus years of its existence a variety of concepts, some more well known than others, have been developed that capture critical points made about the engine (and company) such as 'semantic capitalism', 'filter bubble', 'Googlization' and others. It also has been dubbed a discriminatory machine, outputting racist, derogatory and shocking results which over time may have been patched or otherwise remedied. Google's biases, content moderation and privileging mechanisms may be explored through techniques called 'algorithmic auditing' or 'algorithmic probing'. Among the suggested projects is to formulate queries that examine the extent to which Google privileges its own properties, outputs offensive results or favours progressive or conservative sources for political queries. Another auditing technique is to examine whether the top ranked sites per query rely on search engine optimization rather than other marks of authority.

Repurposing Google

'Search as research' (with the Google Scraper) breaks Google's terms of service, for one is not allowed, in its so-called 'browse wrap' contract, to query Google outside of its search bar, save results, or create a derivative work from them. It would be worthwhile to work with alternative engines that do not have such restrictions or are less diligent in blocking non-standard uses, but given Google's dominance, both its study ('Google studies') as well as social research with Google are considered important enough to ask the engine (and company) for its forbearance. At issue, however, is the practicality of batch-querying Google, for it continues to block such practices by occasionally or frequently issuing a 'captcha' or other human-user verification checks which the researcher must overcome, in order for the work to continue. Thus, it is very much a semi-automated, small-scale data collection technique. A Search Engine Scraper tool (accessing and studying a longer list of engines) provides a workaround and offers the capacity for cross-engine studies.

Comparing Wikipedia language versions

Unlike commercial engines and platforms that block research and break tools with their 'updates', Wikipedia is remarkably stable and research friendly. Both the platform and the tools built upon it have a higher likelihood than others of remaining in place. The method described in the chapter – and the sample project on Srebrenica, also detailed in my previous *Digital Methods* book (Rogers, 2013b) – relies on a remarkable finding that upon reflection seems mundane: the 'same' articles in the various language versions of Wikipedia may have telling differences, worthy of study. Writing an account of these differences has proven to be one of the most compelling modules, however much by this point some may wish to lighten the subject matter, away from the Srebrenica massacre or the subtle differences between how the Polish and German Wikipedia language versions discuss 'Auschwitz', which are the sample project examples.

YouTube teardown

There is a series of methods put forward to 'tear down' YouTube, an exercise in platform studies where one may lay bare privileging mechanisms. YouTube recommends videos in at least three manners: when watching, there are videos in the carousel that are 'up next'. Lists are returned when one searches. Channels subscribe to other channels and feature other ones. Through capturing the outputs of each mode of watching, one can strive to break down how these recommendation systems work, and for whom. For which subject matters and queries are the native YouTubers (with high subscription counts), (junk) news channels or more establishment voices granted the authority and privilege to be viewed?

X/Twitter as story-telling machine

X/Twitter studies with digital methods begin by creating a tweet collection or making use of existing ones either from other researchers or from the platform itself. Twitter has had APIs, which have allowed researchers to make historical and contemporaneous queries, albeit with certain ceilings. More recently, the discontinuation of the academic API has occasioned researchers to scrape X/Twitter. One makes a tweet collection by querying one or more hashtags and/or keywords; capturing all tweets from particular accounts also may be of interest. Alternatively, one could import another research group's historical tweet collections by asking for a set of tweet IDs, and then recapturing them (otherwise known as 'rehydrating') from the APIs that the tweet collection software uses. In the recompilation, data from any deleted tweets or accounts would no longer be part of the tweet collection. Among the analytical procedures are arranging the tweets to tell the story of an event as well as making a co-hashtag network and deploying critical analytics to study issue and movement spaces.

Identifying engaging content on Facebook

Facebook allows for historical data collection, so one is able to collect the data from a Facebook page, or a curated set of pages, from their inception, unless it has been deactivated or deleted. There are broadly three methods for Facebook studies discussed. One compiles a list of pages (e.g., the Somali diaspora), asking questions about what animates the communities. The second queries Facebook posts, probing the platform's privileging mechanisms and enquiring into the extent to which it boosts 'angry' or other emotive posts. In an algorithmic probing or auditing technique, one asks to what extent Facebook could be dubbed an 'angertainment' machine. That technique may make use of CrowdTangle or its alternative (where one studies Facebook pages). A third method enquires into the extent to which Facebook returns misleading information (e.g., regarding the Covid-19 pandemic) or 'fake news'. The data are sourced from BuzzSumo, the content marketing tool employed in the seminal fake news article where web URLs (appearing in Facebook posts) are returned (Silverman, 2016). Earlier Facebook studies of friend networks and profile interests, or 'tastes and ties' work, are now improbable, given the removal of Facebook's API. Postdemographics research, the notion I put forth in the *Digital Methods* book, is the comparative study of a set of friends' interests, such as the interests of Joe Biden's and Donald Trump's Facebook friends, in order to make an inquiry into culture wars or other questions about the politics of media and preference. The work of collecting the interests of the top friends of opposing political leaders would have to be performed manually these days.

Metapicturing Instagram

Instagram is one in a class of visual social media platforms where images (and videos) are the primary content. The chapter first introduces Instagram studies, including two schools of thought, Instagramism and Instagrammatics. The one discusses the staging aesthetic prevalent on Instagram, where the other puts forward techniques that make use of the platform's affordances to study it, in the style of digital methods. The chapter subsequently puts forward an array of visual analysis techniques that revolve around the concept of the 'metapicture' or picture in a picture. It seeks to bridge close and distance reading. For close reading, it retains the images under study in the visualization (or metapicture), and arranges them, in distant reading, for critical reflection. Among the metapicturing methods that are enumerated are image reuse, image trends, image vernaculars, dominant image, image presence, image quality, image staining (or tarnishing), image circulation, image engagement, image–emoji associations, image removal and feed competition. They draw from Instagram data but also make use of Google Image Search, YouTube, X/Twitter, Facebook and 4chan.

Co-linked, inter-liked and cross-hashtagged content

Cross-platform analysis, such as querying the 'same' hashtag on X/Twitter as well as Instagram (e.g., #selfie), is less straightforward than it sounds, given distinctive platform cultures or vernaculars, and the differences in what the counts may mean. For example, on Instagram there are more hashtags used per post than on X/Twitter. The chapter on cross-platform studies provides examples of using the same digital object in two or more platforms and comparing their use across each platform, making findings on how to characterize a platform's relationship with news, for example. Apart from the specificity of platform cultures and the types of research questions one may pose, cross-platform studies are reliant on each of the single platform's APIs, unless scraping or manual work is performed.

TikTok as memetic infrastructure

TikTok, the short-form video platform, has burst upon the new media scene, growing in leaps and bounds since its founding in 2018, owing in part to the popularity or stickiness of its For You Page (FYP), which may be probed for what it privileges or boosts. One can also critique the rankings when querying for particular hashtags. As such one could treat TikTok as just another platform to be examined through an algorithmic audit or probe. TikTok, however, has certain native affordances that invite its analysis as a memetic infrastructure. One can navigate the platform, or app, by the sounds shared by videos, exploring their trendiness, given how its users have been characterized as imitation publics. Alternatively, do sounds mobilise movements or have politics? Using the Zeeschuimer browser extension or another tool, one would collect the hashtags associated with a set of sounds and perform a relational (or network) analysis between sounds and hashtags, demonstrating how sounds are distributed across interest areas (imitation publics) or amass around similar ones (hashtag publics).

Tracker analysis

Finally, the detection work behind tracker analysis and Google Analytics ID owner searches brings an investigative (and data) journalism spirit to digital methods training, where certain of the techniques are borrowed from open source intelligence and investigation. It also may be the case that both analytics companies and website owners implement new masking or cloaking techniques to conceal owner identities, thereby rendering certain fingerprinting and reverse look-up services less useful. The chapter also describes procedures to study the history of tracking per website or website type, employing the Tracker Tracker software (built atop Ghostery), and loading it with historical versions of webpages from the Wayback Machine of the Internet Archive. In comparison to the ever-evolving masking strategies of website owners, including the removal of Google Analytics IDs, using the Wayback Machine for the study of the history of surveillance is less susceptible to the effects of data ephemerality.

Doing digital methods in the contemporary situation

Behind the making of this book is a decade-long exploration of how to undertake research *with* the web, rather than just about it. The general digital methods approach may be historicized, for it shares an outlook and practice from a web whose data may be scraped, mashed up and outputted in visualizations that can make findings, tell a story or otherwise describe a current state of affairs. They are very much webby methods and techniques, built on and for the open web. With the rise of social media, and especially the API as a main data source, data collection has become in part API critique. Is there researcher access? How generous are the data limits? How does the API shape what may be researched? How does it obstruct research? How can research be undertaken when the API is shut down? Is digital methods research increasingly relying on marketing dashboards and scrapers?

The rise of the social web over the info-web (or social media over the open web) also has brought with it human subjects. Of course, human subjects were always present on the web, but in the info-web period one was apt to research organizational and issue networks rather than personal and social ones. Upon its arrival, social media heralded the prospect for social network analysis, and at the same time brought with it a palpable site for a heightened awareness of the ethics of internet research.

Online data is already public?

Critical studies on data ethics address two assumptions that often underlie research with social media data: first, that online data is already public, and therefore its collection for research purposes is supposedly not a delicate ethical matter; and second, that since the social media user agreed to the terms of service, the researcher can fall back on those terms and use them as cover.

Although online data is already public, and the terms have been agreed to, a social media user does not necessarily expect that their data will be used outside of the context in which it was originally posted, despite terms of service clearly stating that the data may be employed for academic research (as well as marketing purposes and in-house software improvement).

The social media platforms themselves have developed privacy settings as well as rules and guidelines that are oriented towards users and are of interest to ethics researchers. Facebook, for one, stopped supporting the harvesting of personal profiles and friend networks, making routine social network styles of analysis ('tastes and ties') less likely. The platforms also routinely block scrapers that may try to collect such data.

The newly typical research practised with Facebook pages consists of most engaged-with content (variously weighted sums of reactions, shares and comments), where the individual user generally is not identified, though a particularly popular post will be. In social issue-oriented work, the engaged-with posts are often from the press, governmental or non-governmental sources, but also may be from individuals or aliases (posting to pages) who are readily identifiable with some online discovery technique, beginning with search and extending to reverse lookups of available usernames, where one takes note of the use of an alias on other platforms, and hunts for real names or other identifiable material. Another, related issue is whether to cite these individuals and aliases as authors. They are not authors in the sense of those who have rendered a cultural product through the sweat of the brow, though an act of creation may be wrought in a mere few words. Does a high level of engagement constitute evidence of creative expression, making the 'data' into a quotable phrase? A single tweet someone has written could be found (through sentiment analysis, for example) to be the angriest or most joyful of all election-related tweets. Is it thus deserving of authorship, and cited, or should it be anonymized? Does it matter if it is posted by a readily identifiable individual who is not a public figure?

Indeed, if following guidelines that invite one to be 'ethics compliant', here it would be necessary to examine the analytical outputs for individual user traces, and redact the user upon publication, not to mention in any aggregated data set that would be made published or held for research use. Here a good compliance practice is to seek to redact individuals including aliases, while retaining public figures as well as organization names.

If one decides that online users posting content are not authors, one may seek a form of 'informed consent', which for small data sets could be undertaken through direct messaging. On a medium-sized data set, more elaborately, one also could consider using a research bot that would inform X/Twitter account holders that their user accounts (and selected tweets) would be stored or in the analytical output. Having given a description of those outputs and the accompanying research project, the researcher would invite the subject to opt out. An opt-in bot, or manual procedure, also could be developed at the outset of a project.

Data ethics philosophy

The European General Data Protection Regulation (GDPR) on personally identifiable information stipulates a set of guidelines that are tangible and useful for researchers in thinking through data collection, analysis, storage and publication, especially of online data from social media. But before considering a 'compliance' approach to the guidelines, touched upon above, researchers ought to think about the cultivation of a data ethics based on both an ethics of care and an understanding of contextual privacy. The GDPR provides an opportunity to supplement that overall awareness with rather concrete questions posed by the GDPR to the researcher. In the following both the overall philosophy behind the cultivation of such a data ethics philosophy as well as the questions arising from the GDPR are briefly sketched.

An ethics of care, together with an understanding of contextual privacy, are means by which to develop a data ethics sensibility. 'Care' is relational, meaning there is care given as well as taken. Thus, the researcher considers both how to care for the data subjects' needs, and the data subject should be open to receiving that care. An ethics of care is thus often described as relational, rather than based on an individual's moral sense, or the individual as moral agent, though it does not exclude the development and application of such sense. The researcher, first incipiently and perhaps over a longer term, has a relationship with the data subjects. At the outset he or she is concerned with demonstrating social responsibility through attentiveness (recognizing the other), competence (caring for others well) and responsiveness (to and by others). Such an awareness of the other's vulnerabilities and needs (together with the contexts in which the data arise) is continuously present and also endures throughout the project as well as its aftermath. As such it may be contrasted to an ethics programme that is based on obligation and a 'compliance check', e.g., at the project's start.

The other term, contextual privacy, has arisen specifically from online research. As touched upon above, contextual privacy refers to an understanding that a user posting data online does not necessarily expect that same data to be used in a different context, e.g., for commercial activities or research purposes not consented to or reasonably expected, even if the terms of service, agreed to by the user, appear to grant a wide range of data uses, including to third parties who have acquired that data through purchase or the proper use of the API. Researchers seeking only 'cover' through user terms agreements would not be respectful of contextual privacy concerns.

On top of the sensibility sketched previously, the GDPR provides a kind of flow chart or diagram for a research practice with a data ethics. The first stop concerns data collection. Is there a legitimate research interest in collecting personally identifiable data in the first place? Here one should consider where to draw the line with respect to data collection practices that are ongoing (or 'running' on a data collection server), when a particular research project or programme of research has yet to be formulated. Such a point applies to big data epistemologies, where one may be continuously collecting online data, often structured data with clear data fields containing individuals' identifiers, to be 'explored' at a later moment.

For the GDPR, one should be able to lay out the research questions as well as the expected results, including their domain of application and whether and how the research intends to affect the individuals behaviourally. Data control is also at issue, both during the research period as well as after project completion. Is the data secure, who has access, and how are these regulated and ensured? Data repositories such as Harvard's Dataverse and Zenodo consider such questions for they have elaborate infrastructures for securing access to data; they also aid in determining the sensitivity of the data by having the researcher reflect upon it. Does it fall into the GDPR category of 'extra sensitive' such as personal health records?

Another issue concerns whether it is desirable and possible to treat the data so that the data subjects are no longer personally identifiable. Anonymization would achieve that goal. It is considered so challenging, however, that aggregation techniques such as generalization and randomization or pseudonymization are often thought to be more practically viable to reduce (rather than remove) the prospect of re-identification. Here the question of data access is central, no matter how the data have been treated. There may be legitimate research interests in retaining personally identifiable information. The data obfuscation technique notwithstanding, the main point concerns whether personally identifiable information is retained on a personal laptop/tablet/phone or in a (secure) data repository.

Indeed, another question, pertaining to social media and other data, concerns whether the data being collected were made public already, and for what purpose. There are different degrees as well as contexts of making data public. Contextual privacy is a concern here; one who speaks publicly on X/Twitter may not have an expectation that the username appears on a network graph or map, published in an authoritative academic journal.

A case that could obviate the need for special data treatment concerns whether the user could be considered a public figure. Politicians, celebrities, performing artists and sports stars are considered as such, but the threshold may be lower than one expects. For example, in the data sets X/Twitter has made available to academics, users with over 5,000 followers are not pseudonymized through hashing or replacing the usernames with other characters.

Are there precautions being taken so that the data are not misused? Here the risks and harms to the individuals are paramount, to the extent to which the data could interfere with privacy, cause discrimination or impinge upon other fundamental rights. As mentioned above, these concerns have a bearing during but also after the conclusion of the project. How necessary is data retention after a project is finished? Will the data remain securely protected? Updating the security is also a matter of concern.

Could the research project be open and transparent about their data collection exercises, purposes and safeguards? One may briefly treat the consent question in this regard, together with care ethics. One could consider a spectrum of ways of informing the data subjects from directly informing and asking for consent, to creating a mechanism to opt out, to providing information on a continual basis on data collection and usage, for instance, on the project website. There are also temporal considerations, such as considering consent at the stage of collection, analysis or publication. In the event, every research project should provide the means to collect and respond to objections to the data collection, analysis and publication, however much aggregated or pseudonymized data may make it difficult for the project to re-identify those who have requested to be forgotten or wish to revoke their consent. If the publication of personally identifiable information is in the public interest, however, it may be plausible to disagree with the objection, carefully laying out the case one is making for having the data and the results of its analysis appear in public.

PART I

BEGINNING

DIGITAL

METHODS

POSITIONING DIGITAL METHODS

*Digital methods are research strategies
for dealing with the ephemeral and
unstable nature of online data*

Digital methods for internet-related research

Digital methods are techniques for the study of societal change and cultural condition with online data. They make use of available digital objects such as the hyperlink, tag, timestamp, like, share and retweet, and seek to learn from how the objects are treated by the methods built into the dominant devices online, such as Google Web Search. They endeavour to repurpose the online methods and services with a social research outlook. Ultimately the question is the location of the baseline, and whether the findings made may be grounded online.

Digital methods as a research practice are part of the computational turn in the humanities and social sciences, and as such may be positioned alongside other recent approaches, such as cultural analytics, culturomics, webometrics and altmetrics, where distinctions may be made about the types of data employed (natively digital or digitized) as well as method (written for the medium or migrated to it). The limitations of digital methods are also treated. Digital methods recognize the problems with web data, such as the impermanence of web services, and the instability of data streams, where for example APIs are reconfigured or discontinued. They also grapple with the quality of web data, and the challenges of longitudinal study, where for instance X/Twitter accounts and Facebook pages are deleted just as researchers are beginning to study the reach of Russian disinformation campaigning during the US presidential election (Albright, 2017). The politics of account deletion is also of interest. A far greater percentage of Pro-Brexit Twitter accounts, compared to those campaigning to remain in the European Union, were deleted after the referendum (Bastos, 2021).

When one raises the question of the web as a site for the study of social and cultural phenomena, a series of concerns arises. Web data are problematic. They have historical reputational issues, owing to the web's representation and study as a medium of self-publication as well as one of dubious repute, inhabited by pornographers and conspiracy theorists (Dean, 1998). This was the cyberspace period, with an anything-goes web, where it often was treated analytically as a separate realm, even a 'virtual society' (Woolgar, 2003). Later, the web came to be known as an amateur production space for user-generated content (Jenkins, 2006). Nowadays the web is becoming a space for more than the study of online culture. Indeed it has become a site to study a range of cultural and social issues, charting for example 'concerns of the electorate' from the 'searches they conduct', and 'the spread of arguments… about political and other issues', among other questions concerning society at large (Lazer et al., 2009: 722; see also Watts, 2007). Of course, it also remains a site to study online culture and undertake medium research. Digital methods are approaches to studying both, a point I return to when taking up the question of whether one can remove medium artefacts (such as manipulated search engine results or bots) and have a purified subject of study. The point to be made is that the carrier or medium should be studied alongside its content.

Scrutinizing web data

As indicated, however, the web has had the general difficulty of meeting the standards of good data (Borgman, 2009). As such, web data are also candidates for a shift, however slight, in methodological outlook. If web data are often considered messy and poor, where could their value lie? The question could be turned around. Where and how are web data handled routinely and deftly? Digital methods seek to learn from the so-called methods of the medium, that is, how online devices treat web data (Rogers, 2009a). Thus, digital methods are, first, the study of the methods embedded in the devices treating online data (Rieder, 2012). How do search engines (such as Google) treat hyperlinks, clicks, timestamps and other digital objects? How do platforms (such as Facebook) treat profile interests as well as user interactions such as liking, sharing, commenting and liking comments?

Digital methods, however, seek to introduce a social research outlook to the study of online devices. 'Nowcasting' (however newfangled the term for real-time forecasting) is a good example and serves as a case of how search engine queries may be employed to study social change (Ginsberg et al., 2009). The location and intensity of flu and flu-related queries have been used to chart the rising and falling incidence of flu in specific places. The 'places of flu' is an imaginative use of web data for social research, extending the range of 'trend' research that engines have been known for to date under such names as Google Trends, Google Insights for Search, Yahoo Buzz Log, Yahoo Clues, Bing Webmaster Keyword Research, AOL Search Trends, YouTube Keyword Tool, YouTube Trends and the Google AdWords Keyword Tool (Raehsler, 2012; US Centers for Disease Control and Prevention, 2014). It is also a case where the baseline is not web data or the web, but rather the (triangulated) findings from traditional flu surveillance techniques used by the Centers for Disease Control and Prevention in the United States and its equivalents in other countries. Search engine query data are checked against the offline baseline of data from hospitals, clinics, laboratories, state agencies and others. The offline becomes the check against which the quality of the online is measured.

For those seeking to employ web data to study social phenomena, the webometrician, Mike Thelwall, has suggested precisely such a course of action: ground the findings offline. Given the messiness of web data as well as the (historical) scepticism that accompanies its use in social research (as mentioned above), Thelwall et al. (2005: 81) relate the overall rationale for a research strategy that calls for offline correlation:

> One issue is the messiness of Web data and the need for data cleansing heuristics. The uncontrolled Web creates numerous problems in the interpretation of results… Indeed, a sceptical researcher could claim the obstacles are so great that all Web analyses lack value. One response to this is to demonstrate that Web data correlate significantly with some non-Web data in order to prove that the Web data are not wholly random.

Online groundedness

Digital methods raise the question of the prospects of online groundedness. When and under what conditions may findings be grounded with web data? One of the earlier cases that pointed at the prospects of web data as having a 'say' in the findings is journalistic and experimental. In the long-form journalism in the *NRC Handelsblad*, the Dutch quality newspaper, the journalist asked the question whether Dutch culture was hardening, given the murders and the backlash to them of the populist politician, Pim Fortuyn, and the cultural critic, Theo van Gogh in the mid-2000s (Dohmen, 2007). By the 'hardening of culture' is meant becoming less tolerant of others, with even a growing segment of radicalizing and more extremist individuals in society. The method employed is of interest to those considering web data as of some value. Instead of embedding oneself (e.g., among hooligans), studying pamphlets and other hard-copy ephemera, and surveying experts, the research turned to the web. Lists of right-wing and extremist websites were curated, and the language on the two types of sites was compared over time, with the aid of the Wayback Machine of the Internet Archive. It was found that in time the language on the right-wing sites increasingly approximated that on the extremist sites. While journalistic, the work provides a social research practice: charting change in language over time on the web, in order to study social change. The article also was accompanied by the data set, which was unusual for newspapers, and heralded the rise of data journalism. The journalist read the websites, in a close reading approach; one could imagine querying the sources as well in the distant reading approach which has come to be affiliated with the computational turn and big data studies more generally (Moretti, 2005; boyd and Crawford, 2012).

Another project that is demonstrative of digital methods is the cartogram visualization of recipe queries, which appeared in the *New York Times* (Ericson and Cox, 2009). All the recipes (on allrecipes.com) queried the day before Thanksgiving, the American holiday and feast, were geolocated, showing the locations whence the search queries came. For each recipe, the map is shaded according to frequency of queries by state (and is statistically normalized), where one notes differences in recipe queries, and perhaps food preference, across the United States. It presents, more broadly, a geography of taste. Here the question becomes how to ground the findings. Does one move offline with surveys or regional cookbooks, or seek more online data, such as food photos, tagged by location and timestamped? Would Flickr or Instagram provide more grounding? Here the web becomes a candidate grounding site.

Online data have been employed to study regional differences. One case in point is the classic discussion of language variation in the use of the terms 'soda', 'pop' and 'coke' in the United States. Geotagged tweets with the words 'soda', 'pop' or 'coke' are captured and plotted on a map, displaying a geography of word usage (see Figure 1.1). In the project the findings are compared to those made by another web data collection technique, a survey method migrated online, also known as a 'virtual method', discussed below. A webpage serves as an online data collection vessel, where people are asked to choose their preferred term (soda, pop, coke or other) and fill in their hometown, including state and zip code (see Figure 1.2). The resulting map shows starker regional differentiation than the Twitter analysis. Chen, while not confirming the earlier findings, reports 'similar patterns', with pop being a Midwestern term, coke Southern and soda Northeastern (2012; Shelton, 2011).

The natively digital and the digitized

Digital methods may be situated as somewhat distinctive from other contemporary approaches within the computational turn in the social sciences and the digital humanities (see Table 1.1). First, like other contemporary approaches in the study of digital data, they employ methods based on queries and have as a research practice what may be called search as research. They differ, however, from other approaches in that they rely largely on natively digital data and online methods as opposed to digitized data and migrated methods.

Two approaches in the digital humanities that may be compared to digital methods are culturomics and cultural analytics. While digital methods study web or natively digital data, culturomics and cultural analytics have as their corpuses what one could call digitized materials, which then are searched for using either words (in culturomics) or formal material properties (in cultural analytics). Culturomics queries Google Books and performs longitudinal studies concerning the changes in use of language from the written word, inferring broader cultural trends. For example, American spelling is gradually supplanting British spelling, and celebrity or fame is increasingly more quickly gained and shorter-lived (Michel et al., 2011). Cultural analytics is a research practice that also queries, but at a lower level in a computing sense; it queries and seeks patterns and changes not to words but to formal properties of media, such as the hue, brightness and saturation in images.

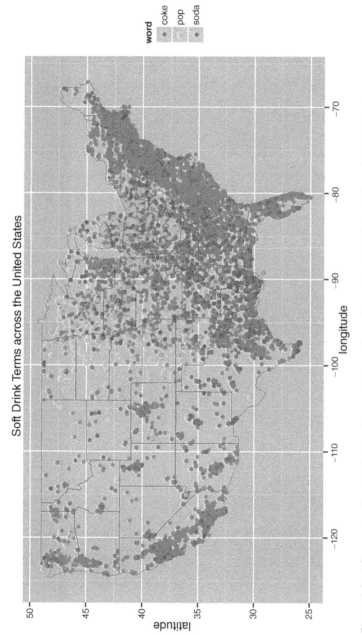

Figure 1.1 US map showing distribution of usage of terms (in geotagged tweets in Twitter) for soft drinks, 2012.

Source: Chen, 2012.

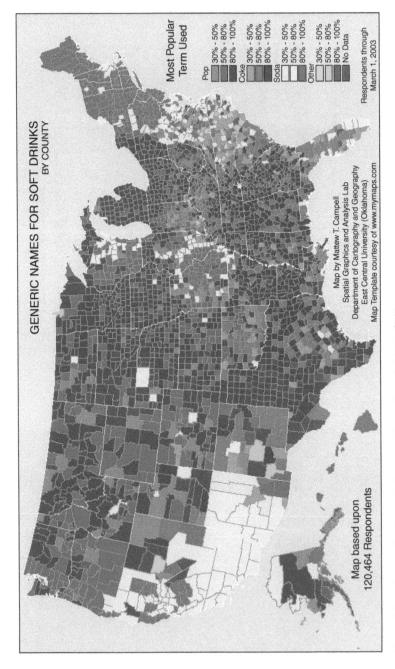

Figure 1.2 US map of self-reported usage of terms for soft drinks, 2003.

Source: Campbell, 2003.

Table 1.1 Situating digital methods among other approaches in the computational turn in the humanities and social sciences, according to their use of natively digital or digitized data and methods.

		METHOD	
		DIGITIZED	**NATIVELY DIGITAL**
DATA	**DIGITIZED**	▶ Culturomics* ▶ Cultural analytics*	
	NATIVELY DIGITAL	▶ Webmetrics ▶ Altmetrics	▶ Digital methods

*Uses 'search as research'
Source: Adapted from Rogers, 2014.

Digitized data are often considered better than web data, as mentioned. Both culturomics and cultural analytics have to their advantage the study of what has been described as 'good data'. For culturomics the queries are made in a large collection of historical books, which the researchers describe as the study of millions of books, or approximately '4% of all books ever printed' (Michel et al., 2011: 176). For cultural analytics, the preferred corpus is the complete oeuvre of an artist (such as Mark Rothko) or the complete set of covers of a magazine (such as *Time*). In those cases, the data are good because they exist or have been captured from the beginning, cover long periods of time, and are complete, or mostly so. One knows the percentage of missing data. With the web much of the data is from a recent past, covers a short period of time and is incomplete, where there is often a difficulty in grasping what complete data would be.

Two approaches in the social sciences also may be compared to digital methods: webometrics and altmetrics. Both are scientometric or bibliometric approaches of studying reputation or impact, applied to web data. As such they migrate citation analysis to the web, albeit in distinct ways. Webometrics studies hyperlinks and derives site reputation or impact from the quantity and quality of links received. It uses natively digital objects (hyperlinks) and digitized method (bibliometrics). Altmetrics is similar, employing social media metrics (natively digital activities such as retweeting) to assign an 'attention' score to a published academic article (digitized method). The score increases depending on the quantity of mentions across online sources. Mentions in the news and in blog postings weigh more heavily than on Reddit, for example.

Virtual and digital methods compared

Indeed, the difficulties of moving methods and collecting data online are the subject of a social science approach, in the computational turn, called virtual methods. While digital methods seek to make use of the methods of the medium, virtual methods migrate the social science *instrumentarium* online, such as online surveys. The transition of the methods online varies in smoothness. Virtual ethnography has been able to define communities, enter them and observe and participate (Hine, 2005). For other techniques virtual methods seek to overcome some difficulties inherent in the web as a site of study and data collection realm. When surveying, the question is how to find the respondents, and whether one knows a response rate. For sampling, similarly, there are questions about whether one can estimate the population of websites or Facebook pages on a given topic. The migration of methods online could be said to raise questions about the fit between the method and the medium.

Digital methods, contrariwise, strive to make use not only of born-digital data but also the methods that are native to the medium. 'Native' is meant not in an ethnographic or anthropological sense. Rather it is applied in the computing sense of that which is written for a particular processor or operating system, rather than simulated or emulated. Native here is that written for the online medium, rather than migrated to it.

A third type of digital object may be discussed, beyond the natively digital and the digitized. The reborn digital object is that which was once born in the medium, archived and 'reborn' as an archived object in a digital library (Brügger, 2012). Thus, the study of web archives would be the study not only of the natively digital materials, but also of the effects of the archiving as well as the archive as institution or regime. For example, the Library of Congress's Twitter collection, when it is eventually made accessible to researchers, begins with Jack Dorsey's first tweet in March 2006, but has certain gaps (such as user profiles only from September 2011 onwards), and researchers likely will have to take account of the fact that Twitter's terms of service changed a number of times (Osterberg, 2013). There are also certain Twitter policies about the user's intent that the archive would be expected to follow (such as not allowing access to deleted or suspended tweets, even if available). The completeness of the collection is finite; the Library of Congress announced that the Twitter archive would end as of 2018. Special tweet collections still may be made, though at the time of writing none is listed. Making tweet collections, and to what research ends, is also a subject of this book.

Digital methods have a general research strategy, or set of moves, that have certain affinities with an online software project, mashup or chaining methodology. First, stock is taken of the available digital objects, such as hyperlinks, tags, retweets, shortened URLs, Wikipedia edits, anonymous user IP addresses, timestamps, likes, shares, comments and others. Subsequently it is asked how the devices online handle these objects. How may we learn from online methods? Here the social research outlook enters the purview. How to repurpose the online methods and the devices so as to study not online culture or the virtual society, but cultural condition and societal change? At that point, the question of triangulation and benchmarking arises. How to ground the findings made with online data?

Must we step offline to do so, may we combine online and offline data and methods, or can the findings be grounded in the online?

Digital methods as a research practice

How may certain devices or platforms (e.g., the Internet Archive, Google Web Search, Wikipedia, YouTube, Facebook, X/Twitter, Instagram, TikTok and others), be studied for social research purposes? It should be said at the outset that digital methods are often experimental and situational, because they develop in tandem with medium conditions and occasionally are built on top of other devices. They may be short-lived, as certain services are discontinued. They may fall victim to changes made by a platform, such as when a service is discontinued, advanced search in social media is removed, or if an API is discontinued. When there are such changes, research may be affected or perhaps discontinued; longitudinal studies are affected. Here, adding to Thelwall above, the researcher sceptical of the value of web data becomes wary of the instability of the infrastructure that provides it. Critique, especially of commercial search engines and social media platforms, arises. Search engines and social media platforms may deny legitimate research use of engine results or other post data, for it may not be part of a business model to serve researchers at least as a distinctive user group.

In the following the Internet Archive, Google Web Search, Wikipedia, YouTube, Facebook, X/Twitter, Instagram and TikTok are each taken in turn for the opportunities afforded for social research purposes, *à la* digital methods. For each the question is what digital objects are available, how are they handled by the device, and how one can learn from the medium method, and repurpose it for social research. The question of medium effects is also treated, or the study of how the medium affects the data extracted from it.

Internet Archive

The interface on the Internet Archive, the Wayback Machine, has as its main input a single URL. One is returned the stored pages of that URL since as far back as 1996. One also may have uniques returned. One research practice that has been developed follows from the Wayback Machine's single-site focus, parlaying it into single-site histories. Changes to the interface of a homepage are captured, screengrabbed, placed in chronological order, and played back, in the style of time-lapse photography. A voiceover track is added, where the suggested approaches (among others) concern how the history of a single website can tell the history of the web, the collision between old and new media (such as the history of an online newspaper), or the history of an institution (such as whitehouse.gov). Making a single-site history as a movie builds on particular, well-known screencast documentaries, especially the seminal 'Heavy Metal Umlaut', on the evolution of the Wikipedia article of that same name, in a sense telling the story of Wikipedia's editing culture (Udell, 2005). Here one tells the story of a platform or crowdsourcing through the history of a single

Wikipedia article. The first example of a single-site history screencast documentary, made from screenshots taken from the Wayback Machine of the Internet Archive, is 'Google and the Politics of Tabs' (Rogers and Govcom.org, 2008). By examining the changes to the search services privileged (as well as relegated) by google.com on its interface over time, the story is told of the demise of the human editors of the web (and the web directory), and the rise of the algorithm and the back-end taking over from the librarians.

Google Web Search

Google Web Search has been critiqued for its privileging mechanisms and the hierarchies it returns. For example, does it privilege the powerful, personalized results, SEO'd websites and/or its own properties? For some time now it also has been scrutinized for another result type: the derogatory or offensive return. Beginning as long ago as 2004, when the query for 'Jew' returned an anti-Semitic site at the top of the returns, the study of offensive returns reached a height with the publication of Noble's *Algorithms of Oppression* (2018), which documents racist and other offensive results across multiple Google products and services. The documentation technique could be described as algorithmic auditing or probing, where through prompting queries the extent of problematic results is captured and measured. Does Google Autocompletion contain stereotypes about women and older people, for example?

Google Web Search has become so familiar that it requires some distancing efforts to consider its potential as a social research tool over its everyday value as a consumer information appliance. Google treats such digital objects as hyperlinks, clicks, and date stamps (freshness). It is a ranking and also status-authoring machine for sources per keyword, based on algorithmic notions of relevance. Relevance increasingly relies on users' clicks and the page's freshness over

Figure 1.3   Source cloud. Presence of a climate change sceptic in the top Google results for the query ['climate change'], July 2007. Output by the Lippmannian Device, Digital Methods Initiative, Amsterdam.

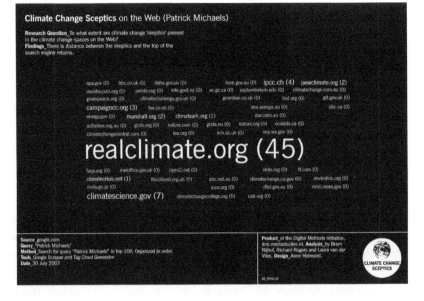

how sites are linked, as in the past. Thus one could view the results of the query 'climate change' as a list of websites, mainly organizations, ranked according to relevance. Once one has a list of the 'top sources' for climate change, one could query each source for the names of climate change sceptics, noting how close to the top of engine returns each appears (and with what frequency). 'Source distance' is the name given to this two-step method which seeks to measure distance from the top of the web for a given name or sub-issue, in a larger issue space (Rogers, 2013b). It is the web equivalent of studying the top of the news (see Figure 1.3).

Apart from a ranking machine, Google is also a massive indexing machine, meaning, for the user, that the contents of websites may be queried, not only for single terms but also multiple ones, so as to gain a sense of which words appear more frequently than others. One may make use of such single-site indexing to study an organization's concerns. For example, Greenpeace.org is queried for all its campaigns, individually, to gain a sense of which campaigns have greater internal resonance than others, at least according to the number of mentions on its website (see Figure 1.4). Given Google's presentism, it would deliver recent concerns, though with date range queries one could begin to gain a sense of changes in concern, or what could be called commitment. One may also query multiple websites for single terms, or for numerous terms. For example, one could query human rights websites for different sorts of terms – such as campaigns and sub-issues – to gain indications of the significance of each across the range of organizations. One could imagine seeking to begin the study of the agendas of the global human rights network in such a manner. This is precisely the purpose of the Lippmannian Device (another use case of the Google Scraper described above in the source distance work). The Device allows the user to create source clouds (which sources mention which issues) and issue clouds (which issues are mentioned by the given sources).

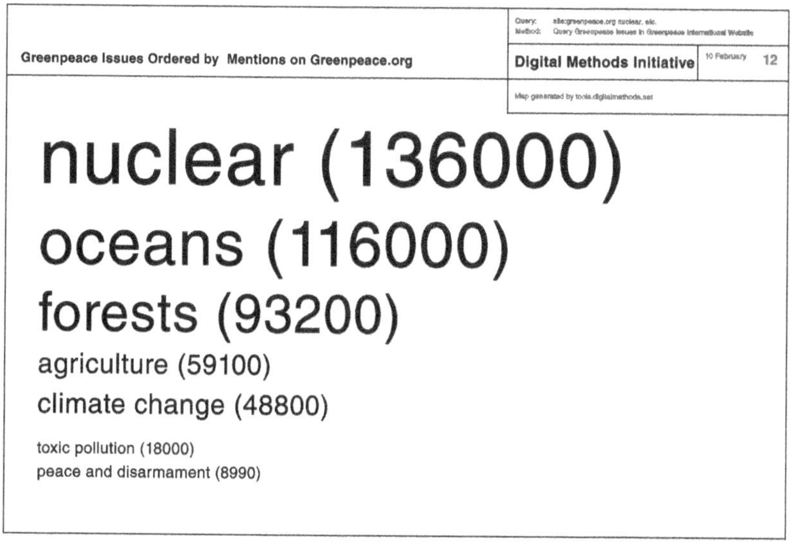

Greenpeace Issues Ordered by Mentions on Greenpeace.org

Query: site:greenpeace.org nuclear, etc.
Method: Query Greenpeace Issues in Greenpeace International Website

Digital Methods Initiative   10 February   12

Map generated by tools.digitalmethods.net

nuclear (136000)
oceans (116000)
forests (93200)
agriculture (59100)
climate change (48800)

toxic pollution (18000)
peace and disarmament (8990)

Figure 1.4 Issue cloud. Greenpeace campaigns mentioned on Greenpeace.org's website, February 2012. Output by the Lippmannian Device, Digital Methods Initiative, Amsterdam.

Wikipedia

Wikipedia, the online encyclopedia, has a series of principles which its editors follow in order to have its articles achieve and retain 'encyclopedia-ness', namely, neutral point of view, no original research, and source verifiability. It is also routinely returned in the top results of Google for substantive queries (compared to navigational and transactional ones), making it a highly visible source of reference for its users. How would a digital methods researcher approach it? When examining its affordances, Wikipedia also has language versions, and each article has links to its other language versions ('interwiki links'), so that the researcher can view the collection of articles on the one subject across language Wikipedias. If the articles are not (recently) translated, then they are available for cross-cultural (or cross-linguistic) analysis. What may be compared? Each article has a series of digital objects such as anonymous edits with the IP address of those editors, whose location can be looked up. Thus, one can study the places of edits. It also has a revision history and a discussion history (talk pages), so one can study the intensity of editing as well as of debate. Furthermore, there are the article's title, editors (including bots), table of contents, images and references. All may be compared. Projects such as Manypedia and Omnipedia have automated means of comparison of Wikipedia articles across language versions, which the former calls LPOV, or language points of view. Instead of a reference work, Wikipedia becomes the source of study for cultural reference, or even national or cultural points of view. One case in point is the Srebrenica massacre, which is how it is titled in the Serbian version, the Srebrenica genocide (Bosnian) and the Fall of Srebrenica (Dutch). This is a comparison of three significant parties to the events of July 1995, when some 6000–8000 (Serbian version), 8000 (Bosnian), or 7000–8000 (Dutch) Bosnians were killed (Rogers and Sendijarevic, 2012). The Bosnian entry has distinctly different images, including a 13-year-old boy's grave, which, given that he was not of fighting age, would be evidence of genocide (see Figure 1.5). The Dutch version emphasizes the military side of the story, and the Serbian, once similar in that respect to the Dutch, is alone in

> **Content Warning**
> Please note that this example contains content relating to genocide which you may find distressing.

Figure 1.5   Wikipedia as the study of cultural points of view. Comparison of images present on the Srebrenica article in the Dutch, English, Bosnian, Croatian, Serbian and Serbo-Croatian Wikipedia language versions, 20 December 2010. Output by the Cross-Lingual Image Analysis Tool, Digital Methods Initiative, Amsterdam.

providing a section on the events according to the Republika Srpska, the part of Bosnia and Herzegovina where the town of Srebrenica is located. The articles also do not share references, or editors. The differences between the articles, not to mention the differences in locations of the edits as well as the activities of the editors, provide materials for the study of cultural memory as well as controversiality, which has prompted scholars to encourage home-grown articles over translations from the English-language Wikipedia (Callahan and Herring, 2011).

YouTube

The earliest archived YouTube page shows a dating site from which to 'broadcast yourself', but the platform quickly became associated with amateur content, and more generally the user-generated content and creativity implied in the notion of participatory culture (Jenkins, 2009). While critique arose about the 'cult of the amateur' and the value of such material as 'Charlie bit my finger', lament followed with the platform's commercialization, witnessed by the overtaking of user-created videos by commercial content (e.g., music) on the most viewed video lists. A more recent period of YouTube studies has concentrated on the labour put in to become a YouTuber, or native micro-celebrity or influencer, in a wide range of subject areas, including those where the utterance of extreme speech is prevalent. Another concern lies in the 'rabbit hole' thesis, which purports that users are being fed more and more extreme content so that they remain on the platform, while at the same time being affected adversely by the bingeing. There is also the question of the extent to which platform performers (or influencers) are taking over from other (otherwise authoritative) actors in the content served. The digital methods approaches are critical diagnostics of the workings of the recommendation systems and device or ranking cultures. Is it the amateur, the commercial video or the YouTuber who is recommended 'up next' and in search results? In an approach borrowed from Swedish researchers investigating Spotify, the 'tear down' of YouTube critically examines the output of its various recommendation systems, investigating how it ranks, and who benefits. It also provides means to map channel and other networks.

Facebook

The digital objects much studied on Facebook were once ties (friends) and tastes (interests listed in user profiles) (Lewis et al., 2008a, 2008b). Using its Pages API and the application Netvizz or FacePager, for example, one could perform ego network research, pulling in the available data from yourself and your friends. Facebook's other digital objects include the profile, which provide the opportunity to study what I refer to as postdemographics – the media preferences and tastes of sets of social media users. In experimental work employing the advanced search of MySpace, compatibility comparisons were made of the interests of John McCain's friends and those of Barack Obama, prior to the 2008 US presidential elections where the two faced off (see Figure 1.6). Here the profiles are repurposed to inquire into the so-called culture wars, considering the extent of the polarization between red (Republican) and blue (Democratic) supporters according to their respective interests.

PROFILE BASED ON OBAMA		COMPATIBILITY	PROFILE BASED ON MCCAIN	
General	, barack obama, reading, music, writing, history, politics, movies, traveling, friends, bob marley, peace, family guy, chicago, books, democrats, photography, harry potter, as a u, running, the producers, jon stewart, the daily show, art, senator, macs, napoleon dynamite, conan o'brien, sleeping, guinness, italy, the beatles, psychology, cats, dancing, shopping, summer, poetry, democracy, voting, gay rights, obama, mythology, coffee, borat, concerts, george orwell, david sedaris, icons, buddhism, ingrid chavez, pink floyd, piano	17%	General	yes, sometimes, edwin mccain, friends, reading, music, swimming, concerts, piercings, shopping, com, movies, metal, get paid to take surveys!, create your own!, (8), death metal, art, what?, soemtimes, laguna beach, jj mccain, john mccain, the beach, fugazi, freya, from autumn to ashes, full blown chaos, from first to last
Music	radiohead, belle and sebastian, the beatles, the roots, pearl jam, sufjan stevens, bob dylan, swervedriver, the smiths, cat power, nina simone, amy winehouse	0%	Music	the shins, corn, the bravery, coldplay, evanescence, guster, blink 182, dido, green day, taking back sunday, the used
Movies	little miss sunshine, american beauty, goodfellas, alice in wonderland, amelie, a clockwork orange, archangel, secretary, memento, magnolia, lost in translation, rushmore	0%	Movies	love actually, old school, garden state, kill bill, pirates of the caribbean, napoleon dynamite, shawshank redemption, big fish, princess bride
Television	the office, arrested development, weeds, the daily show, lost, heroes	16%	Television	family guy, project runway, top chef, america's next top model, csi, desperate housewives, lost
Books	atlas shrugged, books, alice in wonderland, gone with the wind, harry potter, 1984, america: the book, catch-22, josef mengele, gravity's rainbow, the baroque cycle (quicksilver, being written before obama decided on a political career it offers an honest introspective look that few other politicians could ever have offered:	0%	Books	to kill a mockingbird, corn, me talk pretty one day, 'sneaking into the flying circus, it's just enough to get the blood pumping!
Heroes	my mom, , johnny cash	0%	Heroes	haha, kat von d, john lennon, barry goldwater

Figure 1.6   Aggregated profiles of the interests of the top 100 friends of Barack Obama and John McCain, MySpace.com, September 2008. Analysis and output by Elfriendo.com, Govcom.org Foundation and Digital Methods, Initiative, Amsterdam.

Since the 'ethics turn' in social media research, arguably prompted by Michael Zimmer dean-onymizing Harvard College students who were the subject of the tastes and ties research discussed above, Facebook changed its API, no longer allowing the study of friends and profiles (Zimmer, 2010a; Rieder, 2015a). Only Facebook pages (and groups) were available to the researcher, using the API. (Later closed groups, even when joined, were no longer open to data analysis.) Thus, on Facebook the operative digital objects for analysis became the page and the open group, together with what a user may do there: like or react, share and comment. Pages can like other pages. In a digital methods technique, an 'inter-liked page network' could be produced (with one or two degrees of separation). It could be analysed through a network story-telling approach and/or by examining 'most engaged-with content', techniques described below. A researcher also could curate a set of pages related to a particular subject matter, such as a diaspora or a social movement, and study the content that most animates the users of those pages. On Facebook one has access to the data set of post engagement per page, also longitudi-nally. One can determine which content (and which content types) has elicited engagement (including which types of engagement). CrowdTangle, made available to researchers through Facebook's Social Science One project, became a primary data source for engagement data, though data journalists and researchers also have repurposed BuzzSumo, the marketing data dashboard, studying, for example, the extent and persistence of the 'fake news' problem on Facebook (and Instagram) (Silverman, 2016; Rogers, 2020). When studying engagement, it is important to recall the insights that resulted from a Facebook whistleblower, who revealed that Facebook optimizes content that elicits stronger emotions or more commentary. Producers are also optimizing content by monitoring its performance with analytics. Thus engagement measures are driven in part by optimization strategies. Inquiring into sensitive or underground matters may require other approaches. In a pioneering technique, researchers put up ads in right-wing groups, inviting members to participate in a project, thereby being transparent as well as gaining consent (Bartlett et al., 2011).

Twitter (now X)

In the early study of Twitter tweets were categorized as either banal or having pass-along value, which eventually would be codified by its users as RT (retweets), or those tweets of such interest that they should be tweeted again (Rogers, 2013a). The retweet was joined by other digital objects fashioned by its users, especially the hashtag, which would group content by subject, such as an event. Retweeted tweets per hashtag became a means of studying significant tweets of the day, such as the Iran elections and their aftermath in June 2009. How to repurpose the stream? In an effort to 'debanalize' Twitter, one digital methods approach has been to invert the reverse chronological order of Twitter and place the most significant retweets per hashtag in chronological order, so as to tell the story of an event from Twitter (see Figure 1.7). Here the key question remains the relationship between what is happening on the ground and in social media – a debate that was led by Evgeny Morozov, who quotes Al Jazeera's head of new media as saying that during the Iran election crisis there were perhaps six Twitter users tweeting from the ground in Tehran (Morozov, 2011).

Twitter, the company, began to recognize, as its co-founder Jack Dorsey related, that it does 'well at natural disasters, man-made disasters, events, conferences, presidential elections' (Sarno, 2009b). It changed its slogan in 2009 from 'What are you doing?' to 'What's happening?',

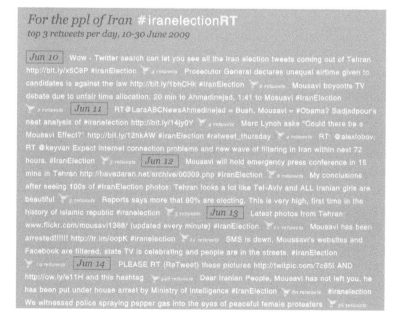

Figure 1.7 Top three RTs per day with #iranelection hashtag, 10–30 June 2009, in chronological order, telling the story of the Iran election crisis from Twitter. Data collection at rettiwt.net. Digital Methods Initiative, Amsterdam, 2009.

indicating a shift from Twitter as a friend-following tool (for ambient or remote intimacy) to a news medium for following events, especially elections and disasters. Here Twitter becomes a data set not only of commercial but also historical value, indicated by the significance of the Library of Congress's embracing Twitter as a digital archival project. Routines to build tweet collections and to output them as event chronologies for 'remote event analysis' are among the scholarly uses and the specific digital methods developed and discussed below. One also may make a tweet collection of an 'issue space', such as global health and development or human rights. Once demarcated, the space of actors posting campaigns, event announcements, resources, story links and other formats to do the issue (so to speak) may be studied with a variety of techniques, including 'critical analytics'. These are engagement metrics that seek to research dominant voice, matters of concern, commitment, positionality and alignment. They are critical in two senses. First, they provide an alternative to 'vanity metrics', or brute follower counts often boosted by paying for better numbers, which allows one to show off. Second, they demonstrate whether the space marginalizes certain participants and issues, at the same time scrutinizing the dominant actors for issue trend-following and other commitment critiques.

Instagram

Instagram, the platform that gained popularity through its photo filters, has evolved over the years from one associated with selfies to all manner of lifestyle influencers and finally to a site for the study of 'fake followers' as well as misinformation. Early selfie research, exemplified by the Selfie City project, relied on the Instagram API (later discontinued), whereby one could query a hashtag as well as geo-coordinates (such as the five 'selfie cities' Los Angeles, Rio, Tokyo, Berlin and Moscow), inquiring into city mood or sentiment through the facial expressions on the selfies from those places. Influencers and digital nomads, with their seemingly luxurious or otherwise enviable lifestyles, it was found, depended on 'visibility labour' (Abidin, 2016) on the production side as well as 'relational labour' (Baym, 2018) to build an active fan base. Where the former relates to creating a particular staging aesthetic, referred to as 'Instagramism' (Manovich, 2017), the latter relates to how one remains authentic, relatable, approachable or otherwise 'insta-friendly'.

Digital methods approaches to Instagram, summed up in the term Instagrammatics, rely on the available digital objects (such as hashtags, geo-coordinates, filters) and, after querying either scrapers or CrowdTangle, concern themselves largely with engagement, asking for example whether Instagram influencers or subject matter experts are returned at the top of queries for the pandemic, Covid-19 or vaccine. Are the influencers at the top propagating conspiracy theories or debunking them? Here the question relates to the social responsibility of the platform performers, a question that may be put to other social media, too. The market for 'fake followers' on Instagram is also of interest, since it was found that celebrities across multiple sectors (politicians, sports stars, musicians, etc.) purchased them (Confessore et al., 2018). How to determine the authenticity of followers and the kind of symbolic power accrued when having masses of inauthentic ones?

TikTok

Since its launch in 2018, TikTok, the platform that contains short videos whose style originated from recordings of people singing or lip-syncing to popular songs on Musical.ly, has attracted scholarly attention for its user culture, or vernacular, particularly how 'audio memes' emerge (Abidin, 2021; Hautea et al., 2021). Content creators appropriate popular songs from other videos, thereby creating a collection of videos unified by a TikTok sound. Users also can navigate the platform by song, watching videos that contain the same one. TikTok has other 'native' features such as stitching and dueting where a new video contains elements of another video or is set side-by-side the other video in a split screen. These navigational and editing features invite imitation trends, which has prompted scholars to dub TikTok users 'imitation publics' (Zulli and Zulli, 2022). The digital methods approach put forward here explores these publics, using relationships between sounds and hashtags for their study. To what extent do these publics follow sound trends, no matter the subject matter? Or do sounds have politics, which can be construed by the hashtags associated with them?

Beyond single-platform studies

Single-platform studies have come into being largely owing to API-driven (and accompanying tool-driven) research. Rather than being researcher led, the social media company also dictates the data available, and the terms of accessibility. 'Transmedia' and cross-media scholars often lament the focus on the single platform, both conceptually and empirically, as I relate below (Jenkins, 2011). The story of an event or issue space (including campaigns and their effectiveness) may unfold across multiple platforms, and actors readily employ more than a single platform to do their issue work. Hyperlink analysis software (such as the Issuecrawler or Hyphe) could provide insights into the key platforms (as well as websites) of relevance to a subject matter, and also point to which platforms may be worthy of study. Each could be studied in isolation, but, as I elaborate, strategies for undertaking cross-platform analysis benefit from a comparison of the data points of each platform (e.g., likes on Facebook and X/Twitter, hashtags on X/Twitter and Instagram, web links and keywords on most platforms). Also of importance is an appreciation of how the platforms differ (e.g., hashtag inflation on Instagram compared to X/Twitter). Performing cross-platform analysis thus is also the study of distinctive platform use cultures or 'platform vernaculars'.

Digital methods' repurposing outlook

Digital methods begin with an observation concerning the ontological distinction between objects born in the medium and those migrated to it. The observation is extended subsequently to methods. There are those methods that could be described as 'of the medium' and those that have been ported onto it. While not absolute (or absolutist), the differentiation between the natively digital and the digitized (in terms of both content and method) prompts reflection on how to approach the medium for research purposes. Rather than lament data ephemerality and medium instability and conclude that web data are not good data, could one begin with asking what is available? Can one learn from the methods built in, and repurpose them for research?

'Repurposing' in digital methods shares a lineage or outlook with such approaches as reverse engineering and unobtrusive measures. It also draws most readily from new media practice with the open web, also known as mashup or remix culture, albeit applied to research.

With reverse engineering one develops an understanding of a system (and specs it out, so as to imitate or emulate it) 'without the original drawings' (Chikofsky et al., 1990: 14). In a similar manner, without knowing the contents of the proverbial black box, one learns from the medium and redeploys that knowledge. How do the engines and platforms recommend content, and how could one learn from such workings? With engines one reads the trade press (including the search engine optimization (SEO) literature) and saves engine results; with platforms one also examines the API as well as the data dashboard noting the (changing) data fields available to the researcher. 'Reversing' is also part of other techniques put to use. Above, mention was made of reverse look-up software, for example, when identifying the multiple websites associated with a single Google Analytics or AdSense ID. 'Reverse image search' is another case in point, where one looks up which websites contain a particular image facsimile or approximation.

The repurposing approach also has affinities with the study of residuals, otherwise known as unobtrusive measures. With such an approach one obtains data through 'non-reactive' means, eschewing the survey and questionnaire for a focus on traces (Webb et al., 1966). What may be observed and learned from the traces left by users online? For example, 'shares' in social media not only are means of post placement and boosting (as we learn from platform methods), but also could be said to be indicators of the content that animates groups. Perhaps traces are no longer the preferred term, for one is often conducting research with logged (rather than left) activities on the basis of what once was called 'registrational interactivity'. Users are also prompted (or primed) by platforms as they recommend content that is more likely to draw out engagement, though users should be considered 'active' rather than platform 'dummies' or 'dopes' clicking whatever is served up. The study of engagement is therefore a mix of what the platform and producers optimize, together with what the users decide to interact with.

Digital methods, finally, should be viewed as a webby project of 'putting things on top of other things', as the net artist Heath Bunting once described new media. Web cartographers also describe the early mashups (or 'web application hybrids') as such (Woodruff, 2011). 'Repurposing' also speaks to other new media 're-' words, such as remixing (in the creative output sense used by Lawrence Lessig, 2004). Practically speaking, one takes stock of the digital cultural landscape for the objects on hand, asks how they are treated by online devices, and considers how that stock-taking and device-learning could be put to a productive research use. Hyperlinks connect webpages but can be indications of reputational value; retweets are content-sharing gestures but can be viewed as content valuations; and likes are social bonding as well as animation indicators. More specifically, shared Google Analytics and AdSense IDs show common ownership, but when mapped could also make visible influence networks or media group strategies. Indeed, throughout this book one takes note of how online objects and methods may be recombined and reused.

STARTING WITH QUERY DESIGN

On formulating research questions as queries

When words are keywords

Query design is a term that refers to curating collections of data in a way that suggests research projects or even builds in research questions. There are two essential components to query design: making keyword as well as source lists. In this chapter I present a general strategy for keyword list building; they may be terms, but they may be other substantive digital objects such as hashtags. How does one go about making lists of keywords and to what ends? One method of query design that I discuss at some length is the programme/anti-programme approach, where one builds competing lists of keywords.

Subsequently, I discuss source list building, especially a technique referred to as associative query snowballing. Here Google or another search engine is queried iteratively in order to make lists of URLs; Facebook Pages; X/Twitter, Instagram and TikTok hashtags; or other substantive digital objects. (These engine queries may be supplemented with platform searches.) Ultimately, one fuses these two techniques: querying keywords in the curated source lists or in platforms more broadly.

The question of what constitutes a keyword is the starting point for query design, for that is what makes querying and query design practically a part of a research strategy. When formulating a query, one often begins with keywords in order to ascertain who is using them, in which contexts and with what spread or distribution over time. In the following a particular keyword query strategy or design is put forward, whereby one queries competing keywords, asking whether a particular term is winning favour and among whom.

The keyword has its origins in the notion of a 'hint' or 'clue'. The *New Oxford American Dictionary* calls it 'a word which acts as the key to a cipher or code'. In this rendering, keywords have not so much hidden but rather purposive meaning that enables an unlocking or an opening up. Relatedly, Raymond Williams, in his book *Keywords*, discusses them in at least two senses: 'the available and developing meanings of known words' and 'the explicit but as often implicit connections which people are making' (1975: 13). Therefore, behind keywords are both well-known words (elucidated by Williams's elaborations on the changing meaning of 'culture' over longer periods of time, from the high/low distinction to an ethnographic sense of 'everyday life') or neologistic phrases such as concerns surrounding 'blood minerals' or the more defused 'conflict minerals' mined and built into mobile phones. The one has readily available yet developing meanings and the other are new phraseologies that take positions.

For the query design I am proposing, the purposive meaning of keywords is captured by Williams most readily in his second type (the new language that positions). The first type may apply as well, as in the case of a new use or mobilization of a phrase, such as 'new economic order' or 'land reform'. The question then becomes what is meant by it this time.

Query design with the 'programme' and 'anti-programme' approach

Concerning how deploying a keyword implies a side-taking politics, I refer to the work of Madeleine Akrich and Bruno Latour (1992) and others, who have discussed the idea that, far from having stable meanings (as Williams also related), keywords can be parts of programmes or anti-programmes. The term 'programme' refers to efforts made at putting forward and promoting a particular proposal, campaign or project. Conversely, anti-programmes oppose these efforts or projects through keywords. Following this reading, keywords can be thought of as furthering a programme or an anti-programme. There is, however, also a third type of keyword I would like to add, which refers to efforts made at being neutral. These are specific undertakings made not to join a programme or an anti-programme. News outlets such as the BBC, the *New York Times* and the *Guardian* often have dedicated style guides that advise their reporters to employ certain stance-free language and avoid laden terms. For example, the BBC instructs reporters to use generic wording for the obstacle separating Israel and the Palestinian Territories:

> The BBC uses the term 'barrier', 'separation barrier' or 'West Bank barrier' as an acceptable generic description to avoid the political connotations of 'security fence' (preferred by the Israeli government) or 'apartheid wall' (preferred by the Palestinians). (BBC Academy, 2013)

When formulating queries, it is pertinent to consider keywords as being parts of programmes, anti-programmes or efforts at neutrality, as this outlook allows the researcher to study trends, commitments and alignments between actors. In a sense, the query design pits keyword campaigns against one another, inquiring into which one is finding favour and with whom. To this end (and in contrast to discourse analysis), one does not wish to have equivalents or substitutes for the specific issue language being employed by the programmes, anti-programmes and the neutral programmes. For example, there is a difference between using the term 'blood minerals' or the term 'conflict minerals', or using 'blood diamonds' or 'conflict diamonds', because the terms are employed (and repeated) by particular actors to *issuefy*, or to make into a social issue, forced and often brutal mining practices that fuel war (blood diamonds or minerals) or to have industry recognize a sensitive issue and their corporate social responsibility (conflict diamonds or minerals). Therefore, they should not be treated as equivalent and grouped together, when one is seeking to study who favours which terms.

Here it is useful to return to the point that one should use quotation marks around key-words when querying, in order to return exact matches. Without quotation marks and thus exact keyword queries, Google, for one, returns equivalents. Mobile phone and cell phone are examples of equivalents. Indeed, one should treat 'conflict minerals' and 'blood miner-als' as separate because, as parts of specific programmes, they show distinctive commitments and can help to draw alignments. If someone (often a journalist) begins using a third term, such as 'conflict resources', it probably constitutes a conscious effort at being neutral and not joining the programmes using the other terms. Those who then enter the fray and knowledgeably employ what have become keywords (in Williams's second sense) can be said to be taking up a position or a side or avoiding one.

A programme and an anti-programme on display

To demonstrate the notion of programmes, anti-programmes and efforts at neutrality further, the Palestinian–Israeli conflict, alluded to above, presents a compelling case for studying posi-tioning as well as (temporary) alignment. There are two famous recorded exchanges that took place at the US White House: firstly, between President George W. Bush and the leader of the Palestinian Authority, Mahmoud Abbas; and, secondly, between President Bush and the Prime Minister of Israel, Ariel Sharon (see Figure 2.1). These exchanges, from the time when the barrier was under construction, show the kinds of positioning efforts that are made through the use of particular terms and thus the kind of specific terminology that one should be aware of when formulating queries. They also reveal temporary alignments that put diplomacy on display, with the US President using the Palestinian and then the Israeli preferred terminology in the company of the respective leaders, but only partly, thereby never fully taking sides.

The first exchange between President Bush and the Palestinian leader, Abbas, begins with a discussion in which Bush refers to the barrier as a 'security fence', which is the official Israeli term. Abbas then makes an attempt to correct this keyword by replying with the term 'separation wall', thereby using a very different adjective – separation instead of security – to allude to the interpretation of the purpose of the barrier as separating peoples and not securing Israel, as well as a poignant noun, wall. The word 'fence', as in the Israeli 'security fence', connotes a lightweight, neighbourly fence. By calling it a 'wall', however, Abbas connotes the Berlin Wall. The third person in this exchange, the journalist, then steps in with the term 'barrier wall' in an effort not to take sides, though at the moment 'wall' actually gives the Palestinian position some weight. Following this exchange, Bush, being diplomatic, realizes when talking to Abbas that the word 'wall' is being used, so he switches terms and concludes by using, albeit without an adjective, the term 'wall', which would validate Abbas and clash with the official Israeli term.

Four days later, the Israeli Prime Minister, Sharon, visits the White House to talk to President Bush, and he begins by using 'security fence', the official Israeli term. A journalist steps in and seems not to have read any newspaper style guides on the matter, because he

"When words are keywords"

U.S.-Palestinian Exchange, 25 July 2003

PRESIDENT BUSH: Israel will consider ways to reduce the impact of the security fence on the lives of the Palestinian people.?(...)

PRIME MINISTER ABBAS: [T]he construction of the so-called separation wall on confiscated Palestinian land continues (...).

[T]he wall must come down.?(...)
[JOURNALIST] QUESTION: Would you like to see Israel (...) stop building this barrier wall??

PRESIDENT BUSH: Let me talk about the wall. I think the wall is a problem, and I discussed this with Ariel Sharon. It is very difficult to develop confidence between the Palestinians and the Israel – Israel – with a wall snaking through the West Bank.

U.S.-Israeli Exchange, 29 July 2003

PRIME MINISTER SHARON: [A] number of issues came up: the security fence, which we are forced to construct in order to defend our citizens against terror activities (...). The security fence will continue to be built, with every effort to minimize the infringement on the daily life of the Palestinian population.?

[JOURNALIST] QUESTION: Mr. President, what do you expect Israel to do in practical terms in regarding the separation fence that you call the wall? Due to the fact that this is one of the most effective measures against terrorism, can you clarify what do you oppose – the concept of the separation fence, or only its roots??

PRESIDENT BUSH: I would hope, in the long-term a fence would be irrelevant. But, look, the fence is a sensitive issue, I understand. (...) [W]e'll continue to discuss and to dialogue how best to make sure that the fence sends the right signal that not only is security important, but the ability for the Palestinians to live a normal life is important, as well..

Exchanges between US. President G.W. Bush and the Palestinian and Israeli leaders, Rose Garden, White House, 2003. Source: "The Divide," Exhibition, Gallery Centralis, Budapest, Hungary, 2004.

Figure 2.1   The use of keywords by US, Palestinian and Israeli leaders, showing (temporary) terminological alignments and diplomacy. Exchanges between the leaders at the Rose Garden, US White House, 2003.

first says, 'separation fence' and then 'wall'. The journalist, moreover, does not use 'security fence' and, therefore, the question he poses, while critical, also seems one-sided for it was preceded by quite some Palestinian language (separation, wall). Bush concludes by being diplomatic once again to both parties involved: he is tactful to Sharon by using the word 'fence', but he does not use any adjective so as to be wary of Abbas, his recent visitor.

Wall and fence talk in the Middle East, of course, is very specific conflict terminology, but it does highlight a particular programme ('security fence'), an anti-programme ('separation wall') as well as an effort at being neutral ('barrier wall'). It also shows how temporary alignments, often only partial ones, are made with great tact, providing something of a performative definition of diplomacy.

Issue spaces can be analysed with this sort of keyword specificity in mind. A related example in this regard concerns the United Nations Security Council's debates on the barrier between Israel and the Palestinian Territories, which took place in 2003 and 2005 when it was first being constructed (Rogers and Ben-David, 2010). The terms used by each country participating in the debates were lifted directly from the Security Council transcripts. The resultant issue maps, or bipartite graphs, contain nodes that represent countries, clustered by the term(s) that each country uses when referring to the barrier (see Figures 2.2 and 2.3). The network clearly demonstrates the specificity of the terminology put into play by the respective countries at the table as well as the terminological alignments that emerge. When countries utter the same term, groupings or blocs form, to speak in the language of international relations. For example, the largest surrounds 'separation wall', and mention of other terms ('expansionist wall', 'racist wall', 'security wall', 'the barrier', 'the fence', 'the wall', 'the structure', 'separation barrier' and so forth) make for smaller groupings or even isolation.

In 2003 a majority of countries come to terms around 'separation wall' or 'the wall', both Palestinian side-taking keywords, and there is a smattering of more extreme terms, such as 'racist wall'. On the other side of the divide, the term 'security fence', the official Israeli nomenclature, is only spoken by Israel and Germany, showing terminological alignment between the two countries. Two years later, in 2005, the next UN Security Council debate on the barrier took place, and a similar pattern of terminology use emerged, albeit with two distinct differences. Neutral language has found its way into the debate, with 'the barrier' enjoying support. And this time, Israel is alone in using the term 'security fence' and is thereby isolated.

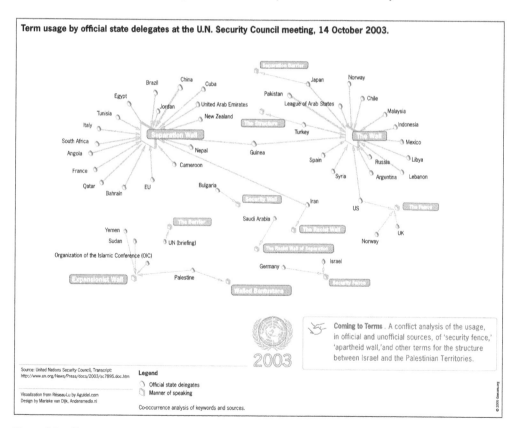

Figure 2.2   Cluster graph showing co-occurring country uses of terminology for the structure between Israel and the Palestinian Territories, UN Security Council meeting, 2003. Visualization by ReseauLu and Marieke van Dijk.

Source: Rogers and Ben-David, 2010.

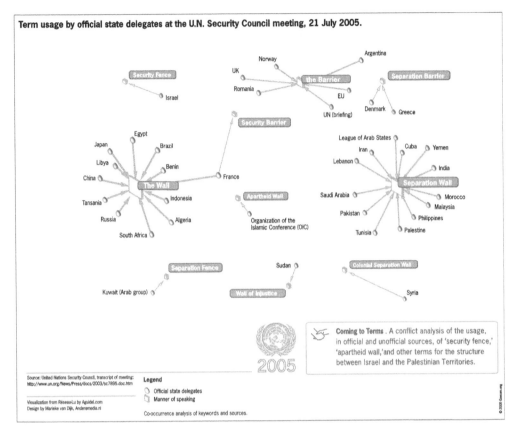

Term usage by official state delegates at the U.N. Security Council meeting, 21 July 2005.

Figure 2.3 Cluster graph showing co-occurring country uses of terminology for the structure between Israel and the Palestinian Territories, UN Security Council meeting, 2005. Visualization by ReseauLu and Marieke van Dijk.

Source: Rogers and Ben-David, 2010.

Countries are 'linked' or isolated by terminology. They settle into positionings by subscribing to programmes, anti-programmes and efforts at neutrality, together with light gestures towards the one side or another (e.g., by using just 'wall' or 'fence'). In some cases, there are evident language blocs. Each bloc shows alignment in that countries (over time) come to terms with other countries by means of using the same language. It is precisely this alignment of actors to programmes, anti-programmes or efforts of neutrality that one seeks to build into query design from the outset.

ASSOCIATIVE QUERY SNOWBALLING

How to build a list of websites to be queried (in a search engine) for keywords in order to answer a research question about which programme/anti-programme is winning favour or, in another research strategy, which matters of concern are in ascendancy? How to curate lists of

X/Twitter, Instagram or TikTok hashtags or Facebook Pages in order to query either a demarcated subset of a platform and the platform more globally? Several social media research strategies that follow in the chapters (e.g., remote event analysis, segmented audience analysis and antagonistic hashtag publics) begin with curating such lists. In the following the associative query snowballing technique is detailed; it is a method, or heuristic, to build a list of URLs, hashtags or Facebook Pages using a search engine. Subsequently, I discuss social media and search engine research strategies that make use of them.

The example of list building below is for webpages of the 'extreme right' in Spain; however, much of the process is the same for any list of groups or hashtags in any country or across multiple ones. After the step-by-step instructions to create a list of webpages, I note how to apply the technique to create a list of hashtags as well as Facebook pages, which relies on other query design.

1   Open the Google search engine in the browser. If undertaking country-specific list making, use the appropriate 'region' setting in Google's interface. Design a broad query that will output extreme right groups in Spain. For example, use [Grupos de extrema derecha en España] (translation: 'Extreme right groups in Spain').

2   After performing the query, the user is returned a set of results, some of which are lists. 'List' is meant in a broad sense. For example, a news article that reviews the most influential extreme right-wing groups usually will name a number of them across the article. One might find that the article refers to parties or groups not only from the country in question but also to other international groupings. From the pages and articles extract the names of the groups that correspond to the country in question, and also find the URLs and include them in a spreadsheet. Suppose in this first step two main groups have been found: España 2000 and Plataforma per Catalunya.

3   Return to Google, using the same settings. Enter the names of the groups found in the previous search results as a query using quotation marks: ['España 2000' 'Plataforma Catalunya']. The fresh set of results returned contain ideally not just the two groups used in the query but also new ones that will be associated with them (associative snowballing). Comb through the results, select the names of the new groups and add them to the spreadsheet. For example, the first result contains the new name, 'Democracia Nacional'.

4   Enter the two initial groups (España 2000 and Plataforma per Catalunya) together with the new group (Democracia Nacional) in the search box, using quotation marks around each group. Again, one will receive results in which the three groups may be associated with other groups. Add the new ones, including their URLs, to the spreadsheet.

5   Repeat until either the same results continue to be returned or no new groups are found. For the purposes of robustness, one may wish to make queries that contain new combinations of fewer groups.

6   As a note, the last groups to make the lists could be thought of as marginal or historical. It is advisable, as a last step, to query the marginal groups separately, which ideally will return a new set of even more marginal groups, though these also could be from other countries. Repeat until no new country-specific results are found.

(*Continued*)

The next step, which is optional, entails finding expert lists, compiling them and adding them to the web list, which then constitutes the final list.

1   Search for academic literature that mentions the extreme right in Spain. Academic articles and grey literature case studies usually have their own collections of names. One may use Google Scholar to query in the original language or in English, again employing broad search terms: [extreme right-wing Spain]. From the results explore and choose approximately three or more articles that you have detected containing lists. Recall that lists do not always look like lists.

2   Extract the names of the groups, and search for the groups' URLs, if (as is often the case) they are not included. Make a list of all groups and URLs. This is the expert list.

3   Compare the web list (from the associative query snowballing technique) with the expert list. There is a list comparison tool, 'triangulation', at https://tools.digitalmethods.net/beta/triangulate/. It shows the URLs unique to each list as well as those that are common.

4   Take note of the groups or other entities that are unique to the expert list or to the web list. Query the unique groups' names in the search engine and ascertain whether it has one or more URLs. Retain those groups on the expert lists that have a web presence, that is, one or more associated URLs claiming to represent or give significant voice to the group.

5   Concatenate the URLs from the web list and the expert list.

Finally, one may take note of what the web yields in comparison to the expert. One may compare epistemologies (how lists are made) as well as ontologies (types of lists). Expert lists (including Wikipedia's) are often exhaustive and alphabetical, and include historical actors, while web lists outputted by search engines are in the main hierarchical and fresh.

For hashtag lists, use Google or another search engine and insert a query of one or more hashtags. The hashtags should be in quotation marks, as without quotation marks the engine may treat them as keywords. For the query, '#blacklivesmatter', one may note that it co-occurs with other hashtags such as '#blm'. When querying the two together, the yield becomes richer, with additional hashtags. Such a list, built in this manner, could be considered a programme. If, however, one would like to study counter-hashtags or counter-hashtag publics, either separately or symmetrically, the research strategy would be different; there are reactionary, anti-programme hashtags such as #bluelivesmatter as well as #alllivesmatter. One scholar has called them a 'post-racial rhetorical strategy' (Orbe, 2015). If one would like to study the debate, the query would be: '#blacklivesmatter' '#alllivesmatter'. For the anti-programme only, the query of only #alllivesmatter could lead to related ones such as #PoliceLivesMatter and #BlueLivesMatter.

The query design for building a list of Facebook Pages (to analyse the posts that most engage them) is a two-step procedure, where one first queries Google or another search engine for facebook.com and a keyword, such as Somali diaspora. More formally one can employ a site query with the keyword: site:www.facebook.com Somali diaspora. Quotation marks return Facebook Pages (and Groups as well as Events) with that exact phrase. The absence of quotation marks yields a broader trawl.

Designing ambiguous and unambiguous queries

If one peruses the search engine literature, there are mentions of navigational queries, transactional queries and informational queries, among other types. Yet, on a meta level, we can broadly speak of two kinds of queries: unambiguous and ambiguous. The original strength of Google and its PageRank algorithms lay in how it dealt with an ambiguous query that matches more than one potential result and thereby is in need of some form of 'disambiguation'. An example that was often used in the early search engine literature is the query 'Harvard'. It could refer to the university, a city (in Illinois, USA) or perhaps businesses near the university or in the city. It also could refer to the man who gave the university its name. By looking at which sites receive the most links from the most influential sites, PageRank would return Harvard University as the top result because it would presumably receive more links from reputable sources than a dry-cleaning business near the university, for example, called Harvard Cleaners. The outputs depend on a disambiguating mechanism (Google's PageRank) that places Harvard University at the top. The ability to disambiguate is also thereby socio-epistemological or one that reveals and stabilizes social hierarchies. Harvard University is at the top because it has been placed there through establishment linking practices.

More recently, the inlink has been supplemented as an authority marker by other so-called signals such as user clicks and freshness, as discussed in the Search as Research chapter.

Suffice it to say, the social researcher may take advantage of how the search engine treats ambiguous queries. As a case in point, the ambiguous keyword 'rights' is queried in a variety of local domain Googles (e.g., google.co.jp, google.co.uk), in order to create hierarchies of concerns (rights types) per country (or Google country), thereby employing Google as a socio-epistemological machine.

Contrariwise, an unambiguous query is one in which it is clear which results one is after (e.g., 'Harvard University'). If we return to the cluster maps of countries using particular terms for the barrier between Israel and the Palestinian Territories, recall that precise terms are used. By putting these terms in quotation marks and querying them, Google would return an ordered list of sources that use those specific terms. If one forgoes the use of quotation marks in the query, Google, as mentioned, 'helpfully' provides the engine user with synonyms or equivalents of sorts.

It is instructive to point out a particular form of annotation when writing about queries. When noting down the specific query used, Google's own recommendation is to use square brackets as markers (Cutts, 2005). Therefore, a query for 'apartheid wall' with exact match quotation marks included would be written, ['apartheid wall']. Oftentimes, when a query is mentioned in the literature, it will have only quotation marks without the square brackets. A reader is often left wondering whether the query was in fact made with quotation marks or whether the quotation marks are used in the text merely to distinguish the term as a query. To solve this problem, the square brackets annotation is employed. If one's query does not have quotation marks they are dropped but the square brackets remain.

Research browser

There are two preparatory steps to take prior to doing search as research. The first is to install a research browser. This means installing a separate instance of one's browser, such as Firefox, or creating a new profile in which you have cleaned the cookies and otherwise disentangled yourself from Google. The second is to take a moment to set up one's Google results settings. If saving results for further scrutiny later (including manual interpretation as in the Rights Types project discussed below), set the results from the default 10 to 20, 50 or 100. If one is interested in researching a societal concern, one should set geography in Google to the national level – that is, to the country-level 'regional' setting and not to the default city setting. If one is interested in universal results only, consider obfuscating one's location. In all cases one is not logged into Google.

One example of research conducted using unambiguous queries concerns the Google image results of the query for two different terms for the same barrier: ['apartheid wall'], which is the official Palestinian term for the Israeli–Palestinian barrier mentioned previously, versus the Israeli term, ['security fence'] (see Figure 2.4). The results from these two queries present

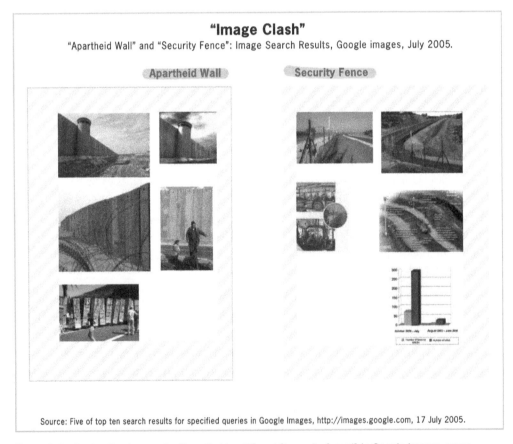

"Image Clash"

"Apartheid Wall" and "Security Fence": Image Search Results, Google images, July 2005.

Apartheid Wall   Security Fence

Source: Five of top ten search results for specified queries in Google Images, http://images.google.com, 17 July 2005.

Figure 2.4   Contrasting images for ['apartheid wall'] and ['security fence'] in Google Images query results, July 2005.

images of objects distinct from one another. The image results for ['apartheid wall'] contain graffitied, wall-like structures, barbed wire, protests, and people being somehow excluded, whereas with ['security fence'] there is another narrative, one derived through lightweight, high-tech structures. Furthermore, there is a series of images of bomb attacks in Israel, presented as justification for the building of the wall. There are also information graphics, presenting such figures as the number of attempted bombings and the number of bombings that met their targets before and after the building of the wall. In the image results we are thus presented with the argumentation behind the building of the fence. The two narratives resulting from the two separate queries are evidently at odds, and these are the sorts of findings one is able to tease out with a query design in the programme/anti-programme vein. Adding neutral terminology to the query design would enrich the findings by showing, for example, which side's images (so to speak) have become the neutral ones. Studying the politics of neutral or generic images also may be undertaken with Getty Images, the stock image company, where for example the number one image sold for [woman] has changed over time from one lightly clad in bed to mountain hiker, or 'from sex object to gritty woman', as the *New York Times* phrased it (Miller, 2017).

Search engine artefacts

When doing search as research as above, the question is often raised whether and under what circumstances to remove Google artefacts and Google properties in the results. Wikipedia, towards the top of the results for substantive queries, is ranked highly in the results for the query ['apartheid wall'] yet has as the title of its article in the English-language version an effort at neutrality in 'West Bank barrier'. (The article, as one may expect, includes a discussion of the various names given to the barrier.) While a Google artefact, Wikipedia's efforts at neutrality should be highlighted as such rather than removed. A more difficult case relates to a Google artefact in the results for an underspecified query [rights] in google.com, discussed in more detail below. At the time of the analysis, the non-governmental organization R.I.G.H.T.S. (rightsforartists.com) was returned highly in the results, owing more to its name than to its significance in the rights issue space. Here again the result was retained, and footnoted (or highlighted) as a Google artefact, which in a sense answers questions regarding the extent or breadth of artefacts in the findings. Here the research strategy is chosen to highlight rather than remove an artefact, so as to anticipate critique and make known media effects.

The last example is a project using an ambiguous query that takes advantage of Google's social sorting. In this case we undertook a project about rights, conducted by a large group of researchers who spoke some 30 languages among them. Using this abundance of diverse language skill, we set about determining what sorts of rights are held dear to particular cultures relative to others. In the local languages we formulated the query for [rights], and we ran the query in all the various local domain Googles per language spoken, interpreting the results from google.se as Swedish concerns, .fi for Finnish, .ee for Estonian, .lv for Latvian, .co.uk for British and so forth. With the results pages saved as HTML (for others to check), the researchers were instructed to work with an editorial process where they manually extract the first ten unique rights from the search results of each local domain Google. Information designers visualized the results by creating an icon for each rights type and a colour scheme whereby unique rights and shared rights across the languages (or local domain Googles) are differentiated. The resultant infographic graphically shows rights hierarchies per country as well as those rights that are unique to a country and those shared among two or more countries. One example of a unique right is the case of Finland, in which the 'freedom to roam' is high on the list (see Figure 2.5). Far from being a trivial issue, this right implies that one can walk through someone's backyard, whereas in other countries (e.g., the UK) ramblers make great effort lobbying for the right to ramble and walk the ancient pathways. Another example is in Latvia, where pension rights for non-citizens are of particular importance.

Figure 2.5 Rights types in particular countries, ranked from Google results of the query [rights] in the local languages and local domain name Googles (google.se, google.fi, google.ee and google.lt), July 2009. Black indicates a unique right (on the graphic).

Source: Rogers, 2013b.

Conclusions: Query design for search as research

Digital methods have been developed as a distinctive strategy for internet-related research where the web is considered both unstable and an object of study for more than digital culture only. As a part of the computational turn in social research, digital methods may be considered as a counterpart to virtual methods, or the importation of the social scientific *instrumentarium* onto the web, such as online surveys (Rogers, 2009a). Digital methods, as an alternative, strive to employ the methods of the medium, imagining the research affordances of engines and platforms, and repurposing their methods and outputs for social (and medium) research.

The above is foundational in the sense of outlining certain premises of digital methods but also the nitty-gritty of doing online analysis. In conclusion, I would like to return to the premises of doing digital methods with Google Web Search in particular as well as to the finer points of query design, which underpins 'search as research' as an approach distinctive from other analytical traditions, such as discourse analysis.

First, in the digital method of search as research, Google is repurposed from its increasing use as a consumer information appliance, with personalized results that evermore seek to anticipate consumer information needs (such as with autosuggest or the erstwhile service, Google Instant, which populated the results page as one typed a query). Rather, with digital methods, Google is relied upon as an epistemological machine, yielding source hierarchies and dominant voice studies (through its ranked results for a keyword query) as well as individual actor commitment (through its quantitative counts for a single or multiple site query). Transforming Google back into a research machine (as its founders asserted in the early papers on its algorithms) these days requires disentangling oneself from the engine through the installation of a clean research browser and logging out. Once in use, the research browser is not expected to remove all Google artefacts from the output (e.g., Google properties, SEO'd results); rather they become less obfuscated and an object of further scrutiny (medium research), together with the social research one is undertaking with repurposed online methods.

Query design is the practice behind search as research. One formulates queries whose results will allow for the study of trends, dominant voice, positioning, commitment, concern and alignment. The technique is sensitive to keywords, which are understood as the connections people are currently making of a word or phrase, whether established or neologistic, leaning on Raymond Williams's second definition of a keyword. Indeed, in the query design put forward above, the keywords used could be said to take sides, and are furthermore conceptualized as forming part of a programme or anti-programme, as developed by Madeleine Akrich and Bruno Latour. I have added a third means by which keywords are put into play. Journalists, and others conspicuously not taking sides, develop and employ terms as efforts at neutrality. 'West Bank barrier' is one term preferred by BBC journalists (and the English-language Wikipedia) over 'security fence' (Israeli) or 'apartheid wall' (Palestinian). Querying a set of sources (e.g., speeches at the UN Security Council debates) for each of the terms and noting use as well as common use (co-occurrence) would show positioning and alignment, respectively.

For digital methods practice, I would like to emphasize that for query design in the conceptual framework of programme/anti-programme/efforts at neutrality, one retains the specific language (instead of grouping terms together), because the exact matches are likely to show alignment and non-alignment. Furthermore, language may also change over time. Therefore, if one conducts an analysis over time, one can determine whether or not certain actors have, for example, left a certain programme and joined an anti-programme by changing the language and terms they use. Some countries may have become neutral, as was noted when contrasting term use in the 2003 and 2005 Security Council debates on the barrier. As another example, one could ask whether there has been an alignment shift signified through actors leaving the 'blood minerals' programme and joining the 'conflict minerals' programme.

While the discussion has focused mainly on unambiguous queries, search as research also may take advantage of ambiguous ones. As has been noted, if we are interested in researching dominant voice and commitment as well as showing alignment and non-alignment, an unambiguous query is in order. Through an ambiguous query, such as [rights], one can tease out differences and distinct hierarchies of societal concerns across cultures. Here a cross-cultural approach is taken which for search as research with Google implies a comparison of the results of the same query (albeit in each of the native languages) of local domain Google results.

Finally, query design may be viewed as an alternative to forms of discourse analysis (and topic modelling), which may have labelled category bins with keywords (and associated items) tossed into them. Google's helpful 'equivalents' would fall into this category. In query design, however, specificity of the language matters for it differentiates rather than groups. Moreover, it allows one to cast an eye onto the entire data set, making as a part of the analysis so-called long tail entities that previously might not have made the threshold to qualify as a label. One studies it all without categorizing and without sampling, which (following Akrich and Latour), allows not only for the actors to speak for themselves and for the purposes of their programme, anti-programme or efforts at neutrality, but – following Lev Manovich's (2007) cultural analytics – provides opportunities for new interpretive strategies. That there arise new computational hermeneutics which combine close and distant reading could also be seen as the work ahead for the analytical approach.

Query design

1   General rationales for query design

- Measure success or 'impact' (e.g., buzz of a brand or mentions of leader's name in the news). For example, the European Commission (Directorate-General for Communication) has a daily query set up for its president so as to monitor mentions in the news.
- Measure circulation, resonance or salience of a claim (e.g., climate change is human-induced).
- Measure competition between 'programme' and 'anti-programme' as well as 'efforts at neutrality'. For example, the structure between Israel and the Palestinian Territories is a 'fence' or a 'wall'. It is for 'security' or 'apartheid'. An effort at neutrality could be 'barrier'.
- Show keyword diplomacy and slighting. In an act of diplomacy, leaders may use 'wall' when in the presence of Palestinian leaders, but not wish to use both the official adjective and noun ('apartheid wall') so as to appear to endorse positioning or policy. A diplomatic slight would be to use 'fence' or even 'security fence' in their presence. How are keywords deployed in specific settings?
- Document keyword avoidance and resistance. Employees may have been instructed not to use particular language, such as 'evidence-based' (in the case of the Department of Health's Centers for Disease Control and Prevention during the Trump administration). Has the Centers for Disease Control's website been cleansed of keywords? Has such cleansing spread to other agencies and even larger departments? Can one document resistance to the keyword policing?

2   Guidelines for keyword list building and querying demarcated source sets

- Identify and retain specific 'issue language' per actor.
- The collection of terms is inclusive, so as to include all actors' issue language (multiple terms for programme, anti-programme, neutrality efforts).
- Design queries (with quotation marks) so as to study resonance of each actor's or each programme's specific issue language.
- Consider actors' terminological innovation (repositioning).
- Note which issue language is successful (and less successful) with particular actors through greater (and lesser) resonance over time.
- Watch actors adopting or distancing themselves from old and new programmes through analysis over time.

PREPARING FOR CRITICAL SOCIAL MEDIA RESEARCH

Contemporary critiques of social media platforms and their data

Issues with social media research data

Social media data as source for empirical studies regularly come under scrutiny, be it for the widespread deletion of Russian disinformation pages by Facebook or the suspension of the then President Donald Trump's account by Twitter (later reinstated). Deleted data is one issue, compounded by the fact that the 'archives' (if one may use the term) are also owned by the companies. Questions also revolve around the extent to which corporate data collected for one purpose (e.g., advertising) could be employed by social science for another (e.g., political or social engagement). Social media data could be said to be far from 'good data', since the platforms not only change and introduce new data fields ('reactions' on Facebook), but also increasingly narrow what is available to researchers for privacy reasons. Profound ethical issues were put on display during the Cambridge Analytica scandal – Facebook's sizeable data breach orchestrated by a Cambridge University researcher – as science became implicated in the subsequent 'locking down' of social media data by the corporations. How to approach social media data these days?

The purpose of the following is to introduce contemporary critiques of social media research, as they have gathered steam following the scandal as well as the 'fake news' debacle, which I come to. These are not social media or platform critiques per se, such as platformization which refers to how the web is becoming enclosed and overwritten by social media (Helmond, 2015). Embedded in the research critique is some discussion of Facebook policy as well as Twitter rules, but that is not the main effort here. Rather, the point is a larger academic one that discusses issues related to social media research, both concerning the use of the platforms for research generally as well as the data they collect. What are the implications for doing political and social research these days when employing social media platforms and their data? When one is studying (political and social) engagement online, as much digital research does, how to conceptualize platform effects?

Behind these questions is a digital methods approach to studying social media that revolves around the notion of 'repurposing'. Digital methods as an idea are built on the notion of using existing online data left behind, or collected for other purposes, and then repurposing it for research such as 'tracing the spread of arguments, rumors, or positions about political and other issues' (Lazer et al., 2009: 722; see also Watts, 2007). The data could be described as 'traces', as in that which was left behind like footprints in the snow. Social media data analysis thereby becomes akin to unobtrusive measures (Webb et al., 1966). Or, more aptly, the data could be thought of as 'interactions' expressly collected by the platforms. An early term that encapsulates platforms' collecting user interactions is registrational interactivity (Jensen, 1998). As the user 'likes' or otherwise interacts with posts, their activities are registered. They then are 'industrialized' by the platforms, or made productive use of, for commercial as well as socio-epistemological purposes, in a manner similar to how hyperlinks are construed as valuation practices, and their measure may be transformed into commercial product (Brin and Page, 1998; Turow, 2008; Helmond, 2013).

Recently, repurposing has been questioned, largely because of the current emphasis placed on how platforms capture user data, and how they encourage greater exposure of the self. Whether discussed as an ensnaring or an extractive practice, the platforms' models of interaction and user experience also enable it to offer fine-grained 'audience segmentation' to those who wish to purchase ads, such as on Facebook. In the infamous case of the US presidential elections in 2016 (but likely in many other cases, too), the ad systems were used to spread so-called hyperpartisan 'fake news', disinformation and other transgressive or malevolent content (Chen, 2015; Commons Select Committee, 2018a, 2018b). The use of traces and interactions for spreading fake news, especially to those with particular personality profiles, has prompted introspection in social media research, including calls for unplugging as well as developing alternative scientific *instrumentarium* for data collection (Venturini and Rogers, 2019). The question now reads, how could political and social researchers continue to use Facebook data to study engagement, when these systems are both normatively dubious in their data collection practices, and are being deployed for partisan, political ends?

In the following, the discussion of social media research critique has five entry points: good data, human subjects, proprietary effects, repurposing and alternatives. The first concerns how social media have oftentimes been criticized for not being 'good data' at least in the sense that the fields in the databases are unstable over time, and that the introduction of new ones leads to interactive complexity. For example, on Facebook the 'reactions' that were introduced in 2016 interfered with the stability of 'likes', given the new choices in how to react to a post. The critique extends beyond the data fields. Even the metrics used by the corporations evolve, such as the definition of reach on Facebook's CrowdTangle, as a researcher found after publishing findings on Russian disinformation pages on Facebook (Timberg, 2017).

The second issue – social media users as 'human subjects' – is part of an ethics turn in social media research and the so-called coming 'crisis' in computer science and online research more generally (Metcalf and Crawford, 2016). Regarding the crisis, it has been argued that unlike other disciplines computer science has not had the 'reckoning' that chemistry had after dynamite and poison gas, physics after the nuclear bomb, human biology after eugenics, civil engineering after bridge, dam and building collapses, and so forth (Zunger, 2018). The point is that the Cambridge Analytica affair could become such a reckoning. In the affair, a psychometrics researcher at the University of Cambridge delivered 80 million profiles to a political marketing firm intent on undertaking a 'psyops-style' political influence campaign on Facebook users, delivering 'dark posts' of hyperpartisan 'fake news' to those whose personality profile had been determined to have a high degree of 'openness' and 'neuroticism' (Commons Select Committee, 2018a). In the terms of service of the app that collected the personality profile data, the researcher did not indicate that individuals' answers would be deployed in such a manner, which captures the 'ethics divide' or 'discontinuities between the research practices of data science and established tools of research ethics regulation' (Commons Select Committee, 2018b; Metcalf and Crawford, 2016: 1).

The third issue – proprietary effects – has been present in the background of research based on social media data for some time. Social media platforms as proprietary platforms have different goals from science, though such a distinction may be blurred given that there are behavioural and data scientists working and publishing academically at these companies. It could be said that data are being collected for dual purposes, advertising foremost, and research secondarily. Nevertheless, one of the main differences between two data collection means and ends is the reflexivity involved. In digital sociology (and sociology more generally), the effects of collecting and analysing data anticipate societal impact, rather than experiment with it (Marres, 2018). Online software users are not unknowingly part of living labs run by social media companies.

The fourth point concerns the repurposing issue touched upon above. Given that social media data have been gathered primarily for the purposes of selling ads, and that system interactivity and user experience are aimed primarily at furthering social media consumption by the users and granting more exposure of oneself in order to provide still more data, repurposing faces the issue of medium or platform effects. One may not straightforwardly separate activity on social media with activity in the wild. Liking may be overdetermined by the platform rather than an unfettered expression of feeling or preference.

The fifth discussion point concerns alternatives to API-driven research or considering little data over big. The rationale for pursuing alternatives, or post-API research, comes on the heels of the cessation of Facebook's Pages API, 'replaced' with the Social Science One project that curates data sets for researchers. Instagram shut down its API years ago, so projects such as Lev Manovich's Selfie City no longer can be undertaken, unless one scrapes data (which can be done with such browser extensions as Zeeschuimer). Twitter has disabled certain data fields such as tweet time zone, thereby making it unlikely the Australian Twittersphere can continue to be mapped, to take just one example. There is an API graveyard, and those discontinued services were once the starting point of both social research as well as social media critique. There is a great deal of missing data as well, because the aforementioned Russian disinformation pages and many others have been removed, through so-called account or channel purges, as took place after the Capitol riots of January 2021. What to do? There are at least five pathways emerging: the return of scraping data and the concomitant discussions around breaking terms of service; user data dumps and crowdsourced data donations; small data digital ethnography and what were once called 'virtual methods'; social media 'counter-archiving' practices; and API critique. With the alternatives, there is often a call for the study of the 'user's view' (or what is recommended or fed to the user) rather than the 'developer's view', which is what an API provides. It is a research mode switch where one is concerned with effects of personalization as well as privileged content, such as those Facebook posts boosted because they were tagged with 'angry' reactions (Merrill and Oremus, 2021). The Facebook papers or files, the trove of internal company documents made available to journalists by a whistleblower, revealed how user posts are scored and subsequently privileged in the news feed on the basis of their potential to invite engagement.

Good data?

A starting point in the critique of social media research is that social media platforms are not instruments set up for the purposes of doing research, e.g., for tracking social discourse or 'social listening', a term often used in this regard, imported from the business and marketing literature (Balduini et al., 2013; Cole-Lewis et al., 2015). The platforms are not the equivalent of specially crafted sensors for collecting carbon dioxide levels in the air, for example, as the Mauna Loa Observatory in Hawaii has undertaken since the 1950s. The data the platforms do collect (whether traces or registered interactions) are also not to be considered good data in the sense of data that is collected at the beginning of a phenomenon, is complete and remains stable over time (Borgman, 2009). Rather, certain fields disappear, and other ones appear. When they do, there is what could be called 'interactive complexity' in the data (to borrow a term from technological systems theory), as certain data from the fields that were collected previously (e.g., 'likes') are then affected by new data fields that are introduced (e.g., 'reactions') (Perrow, 1984). If one examines 'likes' over time (as a proxy for feeling or preference), dips may be platform-dependent rather than an indicator of a change of heart. Moreover, the set of 'signals' used to privilege posts can change or be weighted differently. As mentioned above, 'angry' or other emoji reactions on Facebook may carry more weight than likes.

Not only are the data fields and privileging mechanisms unstable or unknown, but so are the data themselves as well as the inbuilt metrics. The journalism researcher, Jonathan Albright, brought to light in October 2016 how Facebook deleted Russian disinformation pages from CrowdTangle, Facebook's social media monitoring tool. Albright had captured the engagement counts from six Russian disinformation pages (Blacktivists, Heart of Texas, United Muslims of America, Being Patriotic, Secured Borders and LGBT United), and published his findings as a data visualization (Albright, 2017). The engagement as well as reach numbers

Albright published, which were drawn from Facebook's CrowdTangle dashboard, were much larger than Facebook had originally indicated in Congressional testimony. After Albright published his findings, Facebook 'wiped' the Page data from CrowdTangle, arguing that the Pages should not have been available any longer because they were 'inactive', the term for suspended, or accounts that broke Facebook rules (Timberg and Dwoskin, 2016). To Albright and others, the 'public interest data' was removed for public relations reasons, and researchers have no recourse (Timberg, 2017). After all, Facebook owns its data as well as its CrowdTangle 'archive' that once held the content of interest. Albright also found that Facebook changed the inbuilt metrics. The second of CrowdTangle's two metrics ('total engagement' and 'total people shared to') was renamed to 'total followers'. To Albright, that semantic change implies that 'the thousands of propaganda posts (with tens of millions of shares) were not shared to 'people', but rather to 'accounts', which lowers the perceived impact' (2018).

Holes in the data may be created for a variety of reasons, the most common of which are set country restrictions, but they also occur when data are shared. Twitter is a case in point. For example, the German authorities may ask Twitter to 'withhold' far right extremist tweets to users, and Twitter likely would comply for the location Germany, as has been the case on numerous occasions including tweets not only by German extremists but British ones, too (Kulish, 2012; Cox, 2017). The tweets may be unavailable in Germany, but they are still available in the Netherlands (and elsewhere for that matter). Routine data collection of German extremist tweets may thus be better performed outside the country, in order to plug the holes.

Another occasion where data sets are depleted occurs through sharing data. One may not share a tweet collection proper, but rather only a collection's tweet IDs. These tweet IDs may be recompiled as a collection by querying for them via one of Twitter's APIs, but those tweets that have been withheld or deleted would be cleansed from the 'rehydrated' data set by Twitter. Twitter also asks tweet collectors to obey Twitter's Rules and be a 'good partner' by routinely removing from one's tweet collections those that have been withheld or deleted. It becomes a debatable norm when Twitter purges accounts that a researcher feels are worthy of study, such as Russian disinformation trolls or alt-right figures, to name two examples. As one scholar points out in the study of missing Brexit Twitter data, the public record has been altered (Bastos, 2021). The third category of data hole that is created arises from privacy settings. Facebook Pages, for example, can have country and age restrictions set, and depending on where one collects the data or who collects it, some may be missing without the researcher having any knowledge of it.

Human subjects

Are researchers 'covered' by the fact that users have signed on to platforms' terms of service, which indicate clearly (and, in the case of X/Twitter, repeatedly) that their data may be used not only for the improvement of the software but also for marketing research and other research purposes, including academic endeavours? If one acquires historical data from X/Twitter, for example, is one able to use it for research purposes as one sees fit? The particular idea that researchers may use as cover platform terms of service or purchased data has come under scrutiny, not only in the debates that ensued from the 'outing' by Michael Zimmer of the (weakly) anonymized Facebook data set used in the taste and ties research at Zimmer (2010a), which is one marker in the ethics turn in social media research. The idea that 'the data are already public' (and users have agreed to share it) are points of departure in the debate surrounding notions of contextual privacy and contextual integrity, which puts forward the contrary position (Nissenbaum, 2011). Respect for 'contextual privacy' implies an understanding that a user posting data online does not expect that same data to be used in a different context, e.g., for commercial activities or research purposes not knowingly consented to or reasonably expected, even if the terms of service, agreed to by the user, appear to grant a wide range of data uses, including to third parties who have acquired that data through purchase or the proper use of the API.

Data ethics in the context of internet-related research (as espoused by the Association of Internet Researchers' guidelines and elsewhere) would have as its point of departure that care be taken with 'data subjects' who are not 'objects' in a database but rather human subjects (Markham and Buchanan, 2012). An ethics of care approach, which would consider establishing and maintaining a relationship with the data subjects, however, could be seen as incompatible with big data research, for its impracticality given the sheer number of subjects involved. When consent is not explicitly sought, one should publicize one's research and invite opt-out.

The third point concerns treating social media users as not only human subjects but also as authors. Is one using the subject's data, or is one citing and/or quoting them? The question of a tweet or a Facebook post as 'authored' work conventionally would consider if they are worthy forms of creative expression. An authored work is often considered as such owing to its originality or because it is the product of the sweat of one's brow (Beurskens, 2014). These benchmarks are considered when imparting copyright and other authors' rights. One case in point would be a particularly impactful tweet from an analytical point of view, such as one that was found (through emotion analysis) to be the angriest tweet on the night of the US presidential elections. That tweet could be considered a citable work by researchers.

'Proprietary effects'

The question of the impact of proprietary data or operations on research normally would begin with the observation that social media data increasingly have been commodified, meaning that the media companies are in the advertising as well as in the data business (Puschmann and Burgess, 2014). Such a state of affairs does not necessarily interfere with one repurposing the data for social research, if one can still acquire it. But the amount and quality of free data (especially on YouTube) have gradually declined. Researchers have been coming to grips for some time with the consequences of relying on commodified APIs, starting with the disclosure that in-house data scientists (at Twitter) have higher quality data than those on the outside (boyd and Crawford, 2012). There is a 'data divide' between those researchers with access to data pipelines and those making do with narrow ones that are choked by rate limiting. X/Twitter charges for data. Some time ago, a 'complete' 'climate change' (hashtag and keyword) Twitter data set I estimated with the aid of a Texifter tool at $54,000. (That tool was subsequently blocked by Twitter.) Accompanying the rise of the proprietary data is a price tag, or else the amount and quality are reduced.

When the company holding the data is charging handsome sums for it, one could consider consulting the archives. For some time there was the prospect that the US Library of Congress would continue to hold all of Twitter's archive, and eventually make it available with query machines, but the December 2017 announcement put paid to associated research plans (Osterberg, 2017). The Library related that it would cease collecting the entire Twitter archive, bravely reporting that it has its first 12 years (as text), which itself is a worthy collection. From thenceforward the Library would create special collections, and though it remains to be seen of which type, the plans would be to continue with its web collection policy, where there has been a preponderance of collections concerning disasters and elections (and transitions such as the papal or presidential) (Rogers, 2018b). When one is accustomed to querying a Twitter API (or scraping the platform) for whichever keywords and hashtags and is now confronted with limited, curated data sets on special subject matters, research agendas are affected, certainly ones that explore wide-ranging contemporary social issues with approaches that seek competing hashtag publics, for example.

More to the point, the social media archives are now held solely by the companies, and these archives are 'updated' from time to time, given that the companies make accounts inactive, or suspended, as in the case of the Russian disinformation Pages on Facebook or the alt-right accounts on Twitter. As Jonathan Albright has pointed out, this data has been removed, and there is no public archive that holds them for academic and other public research purposes.

Facebook has come under renewed criticism for its data supply through the publication of its 'transparency' report, Widely Viewed Content. It is a list of web URLs and Facebook posts that receive the greatest 'reach' on the platform when appearing on users' news feeds. Its publication came on the heels of Facebook's well catalogued 'fake news problem', first reported in 2016, as well as a well-publicized Twitter feed that lists the most-engaged with posts on Facebook (using CrowdTangle data). In both instances those contributions, together with additional scholarly work, have shown that dubious information and extreme right-wing content are disproportionately interacted with. Facebook's transparency report, which has been called 'transparency theatre', demonstrates that it is not the case. How to check the data? For now, 'all anybody has is the company's word for it' (Zuckerman, 2021).

Facebook's data sharing model is one of an industry-academic 'partnership' (Gonzalez, 2018; King and Persily, 2019). The Social Science One project, launched when Facebook ended access to its Pages API, offers big data – '57 million URLs, more than 1.7 trillion rows, and nearly 40 trillion cell values, describing URLs shared more than 100 times publicly on Facebook (between 1/1/2017 and 2/28/2021)' (King and Persily, 2020). To obtain the data (if one can handle it) requires writing a research proposal and if accepted compliance with Facebook's 'onboarding', a research data agreement. Ultimately, the data is accessed (not downloaded) in a Facebook research environment, the Facebook Open Research Tool (FORT). Meta reserves the right to review drafts for any confidential data, which prompted at least one research team to cancel its project (Murgia et al., 2021). A data access ethnography project, not so unlike one written about trying to work with Twitter's archive at the Library of Congress, may be a worthwhile undertaking (Zimmer, 2015).

The last proprietary effect to be mentioned here concerns researcher treatment by social media companies, especially Facebook. As noted above, researchers have access to curated data sets (including Twitter's Covid one), and social media APIs do not differentiate between academic researchers and marketing companies or potential data resellers. All are customers. If one strives to configure a system for more comprehensive data collection (using multiple accounts, funneling all data collected into one repository), one is treated as a spammer or reseller, blocked and actively worked against. Researchers become spammy users, breaking terms of service, or not regarded as a 'good partner'.

Since the Cambridge Analytica scandal of 2018 (and the fake news debacle that accompanied it), researchers with tools sitting atop Twitter's APIs or running native apps on Facebook have been asked by the companies to reapply for accounts and permissions. The Facebook application form (with a five-day deadline) is particularly worthy of study, since it seeks to determine whether there were ethical lapses in one's prior data collection.

'Repurposing'

Recently 'repurposing' social media data for social research has been critiqued along normative and analytical lines (Marres, 2018). As discussed above, platforms are not scientific instruments for collecting societal trend data, but rather are in the business of data extraction for the purposes of segmenting audiences and selling advertising. One queries keywords in the Facebook ad interface and an audience is returned. The company would like to increase the amount of data points per user so that the audience becomes ever more differentiated (segmented).

More critically, it is argued that social media companies, like natural resource firms before them, are the new extraction industries. They do not so much crowdsource as crowd-fleece (Scholz, 2016a). That researchers would rely on data that has been 'fleeced' from the crowd is normatively problematic. At bottom, the companies also operate outside of the norms of science, whether Mertonian, Kuhnian or otherwise.

Moreover, data extraction requires interface and interaction engineering that invites users to expose themselves further and interact often with the system. When one is studying social media data, one could just as well be studying the success of engineered user inter-action rather than 'genuine' behaviour (liking or endorsing), where for example measures of value, reputation or preference could be derived. On the contrary, so goes the argument, when one is studying social media data, one is primarily learning about social media con-sumption. In other words, the platform is so built to extract data from users in order for others to advertise to ever finer grained segmented audiences, rather than for other reasons such as to create community or enhance public debate.

Alternatives

By way of conclusion, I would like to discuss briefly the question of alternatives, both to API-driven research as well as to studying and using the dominant social media platforms. Scraping has been a method of online data collection that through the rise of the API became associated with breaking terms of service or 'partnership' guidelines (Marres and Weltevrede, 2013). Rather than collect data through scraping, researchers complying with the terms have witnessed an array of changes to the APIs of the dominant platforms and have been asked on several occasions to reapply for developer access as well as permission to deploy a research tool. On one specific occasion in 2016, applications made to Instagram (for the 'visual hash-tag explorer') failed (Rieder, 2016). Others in 2018 have been highly time-sensitive, such as Facebook's multiple-page reapplication form due in five days, as recounted above. Still others have been only cumbersome, such as Twitter's demand in 2018 to reapply for developer keys. Apart from calls to drop the API and return to digital ethnography, user studies and other small data research practices, reactions to such obstacles erected by social media companies more in line with digital methods include continuing technical fieldwork as well as API cri-tique. How is research affected by the latest API version, and what kind of tool development could (still) result in valuable social research? What do the platforms' updates imply for research both about and with social media data?

One alternative to API-driven research (and critical API vigilance) that has emerged is the data donation, originally put into service in the 'datenspende' project by Algorithm Watch, where in the run-up to German federal elections users were asked to install a plug-in and donate their search engine results. Here the questions concerned the level of personaliza-tion of (Google search) engine results and the engendering of any accompanying polarizing filter bubbles. Algorithm Watch's add-on technique, also employed by scholarly research-ers, was the subject of a stern warning by Facebook, after users installed an add-on which would store their Instagram feeds for further analytical scrutiny. Among the research ques-tions was one that concerned whether the feeds prompted users to post 'pictures that fit specific representations of their body' (Kayser-Bril, 2021). Instagram, it was found, has a 'skin bias' (Duportail et al., 2020).

When discussing alternatives more broadly, one also may begin with the observation made by Tim Berners-Lee (the web's co-inventor) that the 'open web' is in decline, and one of the major reasons (apart from the rise of surveillance) he listed is the growth of the social media platform, walling in users and content. As the Internet Archive has demonstrated, even public Facebook Pages are challenging to archive (and few have been retained); web 'recording' is one small-scale alternative. 'Counter-archiving' Facebook is another. In one project, crowdsourced screenshots of political ads on Facebook just prior to the Israeli elections resulted in a rebuke of one candidate's data collection tactics (Ben-David, 2020).

There has been a series of proposals put forward to change the social media landscape, including ones at an ownership level. Trebor Scholz's call for 'platform cooperativism' is a discussion about 'cloning the technological heart' of sharing economy platforms, whilst basing the co-ops on principles of solidarity and innovation for all rather than the few (2016a: 14).

The amount of scholarly output using Facebook and Twitter data is vast compared to that examining alternatives. But it is not just researcher interest in the dominant platforms over 'secondary social media'; it is also researcher use of such sharing platforms as researchgate. net, academia.edu and ssrn.com that is of interest here (Matthews, 2016). The Scholarly Commons is an alternative, implemented by universities as part of their domain such as scholarlycommons.law.northwestern.edu or repository.upenn.edu. These systems tend to highlight a university or department's output, rather than aggregate across universities. Another (at the demo phase) is ScholarlyHub, which (as Scholz calls for) emulates much of the functionality of academia.edu or researchgate.net but emphasizes scholarly sharing over ranking and scorekeeping.

PART II

DOING

DIGITAL

METHODS

WEBSITE HISTORY
Screencast documentaries with the Internet Archive

Doing web history with new media
methods and techniques

Web history, media history and digital history

The chapter is dedicated to investigating the history of the web, or history with the web, as may be undertaken using the platform that organizes it most palpably to date, the Wayback Machine of the Internet Archive. Among the research opportunities afforded by the Wayback Machine is the capacity to capture and 'play back' the history of a webpage, most notably a website's homepage. Created with special techniques and software tools, these playbacks assume the form of screencast documentaries, or narrated histories of websites. While the technique remains stable – screen-capturing archived webpages, loading them into a deck and playing them back in the style of time-lapse photography – there are at least three kinds of histories that may unfold: 'web history', 'media history' and 'digital history', the last one referring to recounting the past with (mainly) digital sources (Cohen and Rosenzweig, 2006). In other words, the researcher may recast the evolution of the web (as seen through a decade of changes to Google's homepage, for example), the history of media (as seen through the online transformations of the *New York Times* or the *Guardian*), or the history of an institution (from the substantive edits to the homepage of the US White House, especially during the transition from one president to the next). More generally, the screencast documentary is one technique to unlock the archive, and brighten it with uses, which is a concern for the digital humanities as more and more materials are digitized or, as is the case with the archived web, 'digitally reborn' (Brügger, 2012).

In the following, common use cases for web archives are put forward from legal, bibliographical and historiographical discourses. In those deliberations, there emerges digital source criticism of web archives. Are archived webpages to be considered accurate duplicates as well as valid and referenceable sources? Did the archived website ever appear in the wild in the same form and substance as it now does in the archive? Has the archive added to or subtracted material from the website?

Thereafter I discuss web historiography, and a number of approaches to archiving and accessing the web of the past, with the Internet Archive's Wayback Machine being only one manner of doing archiving. Alongside the biographical (or single-site histories) from the Wayback Machine, there are also event-based, national and autobiographical traditions. Each is built into collection and access routines (or the absence thereof) and shapes the histories that may be written.

The particular approach introduced in this chapter, the single-site history, is rendered practicable with a technique called the screencast documentary. It builds upon Jon Udell's pioneering screen-capturing work retelling the edit history of a Wikipedia page (discussed below). It also rests on the digital method of the 'walkthrough' (Light, 2018). Screen-capturing and narrating the use of software (as a means to provide instructions of use), video and computer game 'cheating' (showing how to level up) and even unboxing videos on YouTube of how to put together and play with toys are all common forms of online walkthroughs (Kücklich, 2007; Marsh, 2016). In employing the screen-capture and playback technique that walks us through the history of a webpage, I also discuss overarching strategies for narrating histories of the web as seen through the changes to a single page, in order to undertake web history, media history or digital history (or some combination).

The value of web archives

The Internet Archive as well as the web archives of national libraries are increasingly thought of as sources for 'digital history', which refers to history-writing with digital materials (Rosenzweig, 2003; Cohen and Rosenzweig, 2006; Brügger, 2012). The creation and maintenance of web archives often are justified for digital history purposes, considering the wealth of online materials not only compared to other media but also because they encompass them. The argument for the specificity of web archives thus lies in the growth of 'born-digital' materials, in contrast to digitized ones of media archives. It also rests especially upon their use by future historians, when they come to write the history of particular periods, such as the 1990s. The value of the archived web is thus often thought to lie in its special contents that are otherwise unavailable elsewhere and in its future use by historians, as Milligan (2016: 80) notes: 'Imagine a history of the late 1990s or early 2000s that draws primarily on print newspapers, ignoring the [internet] technology that fundamentally affected how people share, interact, and leave historical traces behind'.

Web history, on the other hand, may be distinguished from digital history, as it concerns employing the web to tell its own story, in the tradition of medium history (Hay and Couldry, 2011). While there are exceptions, web archives are not as often justified as sources for specific web or media histories (Ben-David, 2016; Stevenson, 2016; Goggin and McLelland, 2017). Moreover, broader internet histories may be written largely without them

(Abbate, 2000; Ryan, 2011). Indeed, be it for digital, media or web history, actual historian use of web archives remains limited (Brock, 2005; Dougherty et al., 2010; Hockx-Yu, 2014).

How to reconsider and further accrue value to web archives? The point of departure here is to build upon 'website history', a term put forward as an alternative use of web archives other than digital history (Brügger, 2008). That is, the screencast documentary approach, discussed below, is both an approach to studying website histories and a means to stimulate researcher use of web archives, which itself is understudied (Dougherty et al., 2010). It takes advantage of the organization of the Internet Archive, and especially the interface and query machine built on top of it to access its contents: the Wayback Machine.

While it recently has added a keyword search, for over a decade now the Wayback Machine has had as its primary (and default) input field a single URL. Using digital methods, or tool-based methods to extract and analyse web data and objects for social and cultural research, the screencast documentary approach put forward here captures the outputs of the Wayback Machine (list of archived pages with dates), screenshots the unique ones, and arrays them in chronological order so as to play back the history of the website in the style of time-lapse photography (Rogers, 2013b).

Narrations or particular goals for telling the history of a website are put forward. They offer means to study the history of the web (as seen through a single website or webpage like Google Web Search), the history of the web as media (such as how a newspaper has grappled with the new medium) as well as the history of a particular institution (such as marriage, as seen through a leading wedding website). Arguably, the first is a form of web (or medium) history, the second media history, and the third digital history, however much each also blends the approaches and blurs the distinctions.

It should be pointed out that the Wayback Machine of the Internet Archive is itself a web-historical object. In a sense it also tells the story of the web, or at least a particular period of it, through the manner in which it primarily grants access to websites. By the default means by which it is queried and also how archived webpages are interlinked, the Wayback Machine of the Internet Archive has organized a surfer's web of the 1990s rather than a searcher's web of the 2000s or a scroller's of the 2010s (with a smartphone).

Here, it is argued that the Wayback Machine also lends itself to a particular historiography that is embedded in the screencast documentary approach, namely a single-site or site-biographical method of recounting history. Having developed that argument in brief, the chapter concludes with how to put to use the Wayback Machine of the Internet Archive to tell single-site histories with screencast documentaries.

The Wayback Machine: Surf the web as it was, or use the Internet Archive as source

The Wayback Machine of the Internet Archive, with its original slogan 'surf the Web as it was', was conceived and presented in part as a solution to the 404 problem, the response code signifying that the file or webpage is not found. With the Alexa toolbar installed in a browser (in the late 1990s; see Figure 4.1), the web user confronted by a 404 error message would receive a flashing WayBack icon on the toolbar that indicates that the missing page is in the Internet Archive. If the button did not flash, there was no archived version, and the page had been lost. In return for Alexa's solution to the 404 problem as well as the content at the Internet Archive, the user would aid in populating the archive. That is, when downloading the toolbar, permission would be given to have his or her browsing activity logged, and webpages or sites that a user visited would be sent to Alexa. If a site was not yet in the archive, a crawler would visit it. Thus grew the Internet Archive. Later, high-traffic and other significant sites would be earmarked for regular archiving.

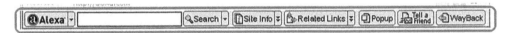

Figure 4.1 Alexa toolbar, with WayBack icon to access the Internet Archive, December 2004.

The Wayback Machine's architecture, designed in the mid-1990s, aimed to furnish an ideal surfer's experience, frictionless and without dead ends. Once onto a website in the archive, clicking links takes the surfer to the page closest in time, and, if unavailable, to the page on the live web. The surfer jumps through time as if in an atemporal hyperspace, one of the earliest web metaphors or structuring devices for a document universe without directories or search engines. The Wayback Machine thus sacrifices temporal matching for smooth navigation, and as such embeds a period in web history, in an experience that could be described as more living museum of a surfer's space than historian's meticulous archive.

Apart from the 'way it was' experience, the Wayback Machine is also suggestive of particular research practices and ultimately historiographical approaches. With respect to the research practices there are largely two afforded by the interface. At archive.org the input field invites a single page URL so as to summon its history. At the outset, in other words, one is asked to submit a URL and pursue its history through two outputs, one of which shows minute changes to the contents of the pages in the archive (additions and deletions), and another that suggests the exploration of a fuller arc, where one can click backward and forward arrows through larger chunks of the page's history, month by month.

In the original results page, asterisks next to date stamps indicate changed content on the webpage. One may thus peruse a webpage's history to spot the crucial, detailed change (or 'diff' in computational language). As a research output one perhaps would wish to put two or more pages side to side, highlighting the specific, telling diff, such as an infringement of one's intellectual property, which is a common use case of the Wayback Machine in the legal arena, discussed in more detail below.

> [I]n *Telewizja Polska USA, Inc. v. Echostar Satellite Corp.*, the plaintiff alleged that the defendant was using the plaintiff's trademark name in violation of its

intellectual property rights. In response, the defendant introduced the print-out of the defendant's archived webpage dated before the plaintiff received the trademark of its brand. (Gazaryan, 2013: 221)

The form of output navigation for exploring the fuller arc of history is the timeline (see Figure 4.2). Instead of pouring over the detailed changes, with the timeline, one makes a sweep through the interface and content of a webpage over the years with an eye towards the broader themes, such as the introduction and subsequent locking down or removal of comment spaces and other interactive features on websites that once made new media new.

Figure 4.2 Wayback Machine banner accompanying the archived webpage loaded in a browser. The example is Myspace.com, indicating the date it changed from a social networking to a music-oriented social entertainment site.

Source: http://web.archive.org/web/20101116021305/www.myspace.com/.

The interface to the Internet Archive thus creates at once a surfer's experience from a particular period in web history while also affording modes of historical work that privilege focusing on the minute as well as the sweeping change to a single page.

Digital source criticism

Seen from the perspective of digital history (history-writing with web materials), the Wayback Machine also could be said to invite the user to seek a specific source and scrutinize it for its veracity because it is a web source. Here, with the Wayback Machine, one brings the web, and its pages, into the evidentiary arena of source criticism. There are at least three sets of questions or aspirations for the 'digitally reborn' sources online now that they appear as web.archive.org URLs rather than in their original name space state (Brügger, 2012). Once captured and put back online, the archived webpages face tests, from a series of overlapping scholarly discourses, before they may be employed as proper sources. In legal studies do they count as duplicated sources, in the social sciences (and elsewhere) as valid and in history as sufficient substitutes for missing materials? From the start one of the more popular use cases for the Internet Archive, apart from the 404 error while surfing, has been as evidence (Howell, 2006). One could go back in time to a website for evidentiary purposes, checking for trademark and intellectual property infringements, as was the case with its first-time deployment in US courts in 2003 when printouts from the Wayback Machine were introduced as exhibits (Eltgroth, 2009). Here the questions concern the extent to which one can treat the archived page as a duplicate of the original no longer online, or in a lesser test, at least warrant through testimony that it represents accurately the material the site owner put online. In the event, the archived website need not be a duplicate in code and data to be admissible; rather it need only be an accurate representation. It also need not have archived all of the page. As a US court wrote in 2016: '[T]he fact that the Wayback Machine does not capture everything that was on those sites does not bear on whether the things that were captured were in fact on those sites. There is no suggestion or evidence… that the Wayback Machine ever adds material to sites' (Bychowski, 2016). Here accuracy is defined in part as the absence of addition.

Apart from its authenticity in legal arenas, a webpage faces scrutiny as a source for scholarly referencing purposes, in order to anchor an account of events, for example. In the very first place, the challenge put to the web as source may rest upon its overall (historical) reputation problem, as a medium of pirates, pornographers, conspiracy theorists and self-publishers (Dean, 1998). As the fake news scandals surrounding the US presidential campaigns of 2016 pointed to anew, it is a space with and without professional editors, and has been subject to the question of its quality, even as the web further domesticated, in its nearly 30 years of use (Thelwall et al., 2005; Marres, 2018).

More to the point is the question whether (presumably unstable) URLs should be referenced at all as sources, and if offline, whether a Wayback URL could stand in sturdily. Apart from the reputation problem, it is often argued that the web's ephemerality, or perhaps its uneven maintenance, disproves its worthiness as source. Referenced URLs break, as links rot (Veronin, 2002; Klein et al., 2014). In this context the Wayback Machine may be viewed as a set of well-tethered (rather than broken) source links. The Internet Archive thus becomes an early attempt at providing permanence to ephemeral web sources, in a lineage of such attempts from both the tradition of hypertext (permalinks in blogs and edit history retention in wikis) to that of library science (DOI numbers). Once accepted as not only references but referenceable, web sources that break and are reborn in the Internet Archive face further tests. Are the archived ones 'valid'? Such a determination relies, among other things, on whether the date stamps of archived webpages, including new archived versions, match the dates of the webpages when online, an issue studied by a series of authors (Murphy et al., 2007; Dougherty et al., 2010; Dougherty and Meyer, 2014). In the event, the Internet Archive has met validation challenges concerning webpage (and thus content) age, despite the atemporal surfing experience it affords.

For referencing, a Wayback URL supplements rather than replaces an original URL. According to the Modern Language Association (MLA) style guide, even (original) broken URLs should be referenced, with access date, for the reader may be able to 'evaluate the credibility of the site that published the source or locate the source under a new URL' (Gibson, 2016). In all the MLA recommends adding the Wayback URL to the reference after the broken URL, rather than pruning the citation through the use of the archived URL only (Internet Archive, 2016).

For historians, a further test concerns whether a reborn website in the archive was ever online as such in the first place (Brügger, 2012). Websites reconstituted by the archiving appear to be damning critiques of their value as historical sources (Russell and Kane, 2008). Newspapers especially, as proverbial first drafts of history, are susceptible to hotchpotch archival reconstructions, where certain plugged-in content is saved at another time than the front page of the newspaper, and when one recombines it in the archive the 'digitally reborn source' becomes a novel artefact of its archiving process. Even given the missing original, the question steps beyond whether the incomplete, archived source is acceptable, in the spirit of save what one can. When writing digital history, or using the web as historical source, being a scholar of the history of the web (and dynamic websites) together with the history of its archiving (and the treatment of dynamic websites) becomes crucial.

Web historiographies in brief

As discussed above, the architecture of the Wayback Machine of the Internet Archive invites website or webpage histories, given that one fetches the history of a URL through the interface, and peruses it looking for minor changes with the aid of the asterisks in the classic interface, or with a broad sweep, forward clicking month by month, examining the larger thematic changes to the life and times of the site.

Before introducing examples of website histories, in the style of Jon Udell's pioneering recounting of the edit history of the 'heavy metal' Wikipedia article, it is instructive to mention that the biographical (in which a website history would fall) is among at least four dominant traditions of web archive collection, access as well as usage. The second tradition is of a special collection, where typically elections, disasters and changes of power or transitions are archived, such as US presidential elections and the installation of a new pope (Schneider and Foot, 2004). Here the approach to web historiography is event-based. In the archiving there is an attention cycle to consider, both the run-up to an election and transition as well as its aftermath. Archiving agility (especially for a sudden disaster) is also called for.

A third type of web historiographical approach is embodied in the efforts by national libraries to demarcate and save 'national' webs, beginning with the preservation of the official public record and continuing often with a carefully considered definition of a website of relevance to national heritage (Jacobsen, 2008; Rogers et al., 2013). For example, the Danish national librarians, pioneers in web archiving, define a relevant national website as having at least one of four properties: in the top-level country.dk domain, written in Danish, about a Danish subject matter (e.g., the author Hans Christian Andersen) or material of relevance to the Danish or Denmark, the last type of which expands the material to such an extent that it becomes a matter of editorial selection, bringing the librarians back into web content curation (after the demise of the online directories and the rise of the algorithm and the automated back-end).

A fourth, the autobiographical, is the most recent, and concerns web properties that are essentially no longer considered websites, at least as we have known them to be as accessible without a password and residing for the most part on an open web. Whether they are social media platforms or smartphone apps, they are difficult to collect and preserve, and

Figure 4.3 'Amalia Ulman: Excellences
& Perfections', @amaliaulman, Instagram
artwork in the autobiographical tradition,
2014. See Rhizome, 2014.

improbable to make accessible at any scale, owing to the fact that they are personal, behind
user logins, or have other novel social and technical constraints. Facebook pages of public
figures, organizations and events may be stored. For example, Archive-It, the Internet
Archive service, has a default user on Facebook (Charlie Archivist, without friends or a
profile) who is logged in and captures sets of pages that a web archivist enters into the
software interface. For social media and the mobile web, there are additional approaches,
such as capturing just the data rather than the HTML (e.g., through an API or by individuals requesting personal data dumps from Facebook) or by videorecording a user interacting
with her mobile phone. The collections become social media data sets, or a user video
together eventually with the smartphone itself. Relatedly, at Rhizome, the digital arts collective, the 'webenact' technique, put online as webrecorder.io, has been developed to
capture or record a social media user's pages so as to re-enact them or play them back. The
work was developed on the heels of the critically acclaimed performance piece of the
Instagram user, Amalia Ulman (Figure 4.3; see Rhizome, 2014).

Web history, media history, digital history

From the standpoint of web historiography, a website history or single-site biography may
be understood as the unfolding of the history of the website, and with it a variety of stories
may be told. First, the history of a website could be seen to encapsulate the larger story of the
history of the web. In one example discussed in detail below, the history of the changes to the
front page of google.com (in particular the tabs or menu items) may be read as the history

of the demise of the human editors of the web, and the rise of the back-end, of the algorithm, taking over from the librarians. From the history of a website, secondly, one also may tell the story of the history of media, such as how a newspaper, a radio station, or a television channel grappled with the web, over time (Bødker and Brügger, 2017). Has the old media form, so called, embraced new media features, only to settle back into a digitized version of its original self? How have newspapers domesticated the blog, or tamped down the comment space where readers can talk back to the institution referred to historically as gatekeepers?

In a screencast documentary of the history of nytimes.com, the newspaper has experimented repeatedly with new media forms, beginning as a separate entity from the print version, without any reference to the print version or to subscriptions (Hermens, 2011). It was directed at a web-only audience with such features as 'cybertimes' and forums. Often these special new media forms would be jettisoned, though some have remained such as a curated comment space as well as novel newspaper navigation through 'most emailed', 'most viewed' and 'recommended for you'.

A third strategy is telling the history of an idea, individual, organization, institution or other entity to which a website has been dedicated, also known as digital history (or history-telling with digital sources). Examining the evolution of the contents of the 'issues' tab at whitehouse.gov shows at a glance how the priorities of the US presidential administration have changed, sometimes abruptly; after the 9/11 attacks on the World Trade Center and the Pentagon in 2001, almost all issues on whitehouse.gov included the word 'security', only gradually to broaden their scope in the years to come (Rogers, 2013b). In another case, examining the history of theknot.com over a ten-year period, researchers found how a simple advice and registry site became a complex wedding planner, multiplying expenses and product placements, concluding that nowadays for weddings 'no expense should be spared' (Livio et al., 2012). Thus one view on the evolution of the institution of marriage, reconstructed through a single-site history, is its commercialization (together with the company's expanding efforts at monetizing its web offerings).

Techniques for making screencast documentaries of the history of a webpage

There are practical aspects to creating a screencast documentary of the history of a webpage. At the Digital Methods Initiative, colleagues and I have created tools and techniques to compile the archived versions of a webpage and assemble them chronologically as a movie. There are four steps: make a list of the archived pages, capture or download them, load them in a movie-maker and record a voiceover. In the first step, to make a list of the archived pages, one may use the Internet Archive Wayback Machine Link Ripper. One enters the URL to be captured from the Wayback Machine (e.g., www.google.com), and the tool creates a list of links of its archived pages, removing duplicates by default, and providing options concerning the capture interval (e.g., daily or monthly). To study minute changes to the webpage over time, one chooses daily snapshots, and for a fuller arc of history, monthly. Other selection strategies of 'halving' and 'zooming' are mentioned below. In the second step the Wayback Machine URL list (a text file) is subsequently inputted into a screenshot generator (such as a browser extension or a dedicated digital methods tool). Screenshots are made of each archived webpage. The pages need to load in the browser for the screenshot to be made, so it is advisable to fine-tune the amount of time between screenshots so as to make sure the pages have arrived before the screenshots are taken. The third step is to load the screenshots into an image viewer such as iPhoto and make a project in movie-making software such as iMovie. Finally, the voiceover is recorded, and the movie is ready for playback.

Figure 4.4　Screenshot from Jon Udell's 'Heavy Metal Umlaut', screencast documentary, 2005, discussion of graffiti defacing a Wikipedia article.

For the voiceover consideration should be made of the narrative strategy. In 'Heavy Metal Umlaut' Jon Udell (2005) establishes the literary and social value of the (webpage) screencast documentary, previously known for software instructions of use and video game walkthroughs. In the screencast, Udell deploys a simple narrative strategy that could be employed as a starting point. He opens with an overview of his subject matter, the revision history of the Wikipedia article on the heavy metal umlaut. Through a 'quick flight' of the changelog (speeding up the chronological loading of the pages) he shows the growth and occasional vandalism of the article, speaking with awe about Wikipedians' vigilance (see Figure 4.4). Subsequently he introduces four themes and treats them one by one. The Spinal Tap theme concerns the typographical as well as factual question of the n-umlaut (or heavy metal umlaut). In the vandalism piece, he is impressed by the dedication shown by the Wikipedians, cleaning the graffiti and reverting other offensive edits only minutes after they have been made. He spends time talking about the organization of the article, and how the table of contents matures over time. (The focus on the changes to the table of contents led us to build a tool, the Wikipedia TOC scraper, that captures a Wikipedia article's table of contents, and with the use of the slider, shows its changes over time.) Finally, Udell mentions issues of cultural sensitivity, and in particular how the look of the font and the n-umlaut is no longer associated with Nazism (as it was initially in the article), but rather is described as Germanic. Without summarizing the four themes, Udell concludes the screencast documentary by returning to the first edit and jumping to the last, making mention of the achievement of a 'loose federation of volunteers', in this new type of content creation, otherwise known as the wisdom of the crowd (Surowiecki, 2004). In the edit revision history of a single Wikipedia article, it is as if web history was made. The screencast captures the birth of user-generated content.

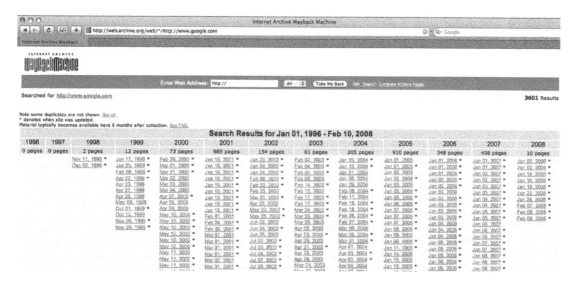

Figure 4.5 Original output of Wayback Machine for the query, www.google.com, August 2008, with asterisks indicating unique pages, compiled for screencast documentary, 'Google and the Politics of Tabs'. See R. Rogers and Govcom.org, 2008.

'Google and the Politics of Tabs' is the first single-site history made that follows in Udell's footsteps, and tells a history of the web through the changes made to one page. It is the history of Google seen through its interface from 1998 until early 2008, and through seemingly tiny changes to the tabs above the search box it tells a larger story about the history of the web (Rogers and Govcom.org, 2008). It makes use of all the available, updated Google front pages in the Internet Archive, captured and played back, in the style of time-lapse photography (see Figure 4.5). 'Google and the Politics of Tabs' chronicles the subtle changes to the Google front-page real estate, showing the services that have risen to the interface, achieving tab status, and the others that have been relegated to the 'more' and 'even more' buttons. As its main theme, it tells the story of the demise of the directory (particularly Dmoz.org's), and how the back-end algorithm has taken over the organization of web information at the expense of the human editors and librarians.

Conclusions: The value of capturing website histories

Archived websites may be re-rendered for web, media and digital history. In terms of those to be told in the voiceover narrative of a webpage history, one could be of loss; something of value has been taken or replaced. In 'Google and the Politics of Tabs', which details a decade's worth of subtle changes to the google.com interface, ultimately the algorithm has taken over from the librarian on the web. Another is about transformation, or even continuity. Despite massive change around it, the object or subject has remained remarkably the same (or nearly so). In another variation, despite transformation, it has returned to its original form. As discussed above, the enthusiastic embrace of new media or its stubborn resistance is made the subject of the screencast by scrutinizing how a newspaper website has evolved. Has the old media form, so called, radically embraced cyberspace and new media features, only to settle back (largely) into a digitized form of its original self, as in the case of nytimes.com? How have newspapers domesticated the blog, or tamed the comment space where readers once could talk back to the institution referred to historically as gatekeepers? Here the story concerns incorporating new media into established practices. In each case one is considering the overall narrative of change, concentrating on a limited number of storylines, and leaving out the rest. A third strategy is to allow the history of an idea, individual, organization, institution or other entity to unfold in the changes to a website. The wedding as institution could be simple, or it can be industrialized, as a website, theknot.com, and the web is further monetized with the rise of e-commerce. One can thus build in the recipe of a great novel. Capture the times through the changes occurring in the life of an institution – on its leading website.

Table 4.1 Top issues at whitehouse.gov before and after the transition from President Obama to President Trump.

19 January 2017	20 January 2017
Civil Rights	America First Energy Plan
Climate Change	America First Foreign Policy
Economy	Bringing Back Jobs And Growth
Education	Making Our Military Strong Again

Foreign Policy	Standing Up For Our Law Enforcement Community
Health Care	Trade Deals That Work For All Americans
Immigration	
Iran Deal	

Source: Wayback Machine of the Internet Archive (archive.org).

On 20 January 2017, with the incoming presidential administration, whitehouse.gov changed dramatically. A story in the *New York Times* opened: 'Within moments of the inauguration of President Trump, the official White House website on Friday deleted nearly all mentions of climate change... The purge... came as part of the full digital turnover of whitehouse.gov, including taking down and archiving all the Obama administration's personal and policy pages' (Davenport, 2017). Capturing 'transitions' such as the Papal in 2005 by the Library of Congress is an event-based web historiography, pioneered in the websphere technique that curates a collection of thematically related and interlinked sites over a period of some months. One also may capture such transitions through website histories, where changed front pages are made into screenshots (or otherwise captured) and played back as a screencast documentary or even as an animated gif. Here the display of content removal tells the story of changes in political (and policy) priorities. One may also focus on additional sections or pages on the website, such as the changes under the 'issues' tab, where after 20 January 2017 whitehouse.gov had such issues as 'America First Energy Plan' and 'America First Foreign Policy', which are distinctive in (sloganeering) style and substance to those on 19 January 2017 prior to the administration turnover (see Table 4.1).

The Internet Archive (and web archives generally) are commonly thought of as sources for 'digital history', however much actual historian use of web archives appears to be limited (and is understudied). With such use digital source criticism becomes a focal point with concerns about how in the archiving a 'digitally reborn' source may be reconstituted in a form that never existed in the first place. Here is a particular case where digital history may draw from web history, and its study of different forms of ephemerality (Chun, 2013). Indeed, web archives have not necessarily been justified for the purposes of telling web history (or media history), however much active use may be made of them by researchers in that field. Above I reintroduced the notion of 'website history' and put forward a particular approach to it (screencast documentary) that allows one to pursue a variety of histories: web, media as well as digital history.

The screencast documentary approach derives from digital methods, or the use of tool-based methods for web data extraction and analysis. The research affordances of the Wayback Machine are the point of departure, for it provides a list of stored pages (and an indication of which ones have new content, aka the 'diffs') that can be captured and played back in the style of time-lapse photography. The website history, it is argued, could be seen in the web historiographical tradition of website biography, which is distinctive from event, national or autobiographical styles of collection and curation. Once captured, the website history may be narrated; in the examples given the stories revolved around loss, continuity and transformation. They concern how the history of a single website may encapsulate the history of the web, how so-called old media perpetuates itself in the new media, and how the transformation of an institution may be captured.

PROJECT

Produce a screencast documentary on the history of a website

RESEARCH GOAL To capture past versions of a website via the Wayback Machine of the Internet Archive and narrate website history in a screencast documentary.

1   Consider the type of website history to tell: web history, media history or digital history.

  a   Web history. The history of some websites may be seen as encapsulating a larger story of the history of the web. See 'Google and the Politics of Tabs', where it is put forward that with the demise of the Directory in Google, ultimately the algorithm took over from the librarian on the web (see below and Figure 4.6).

  b   Media history. The relationship between old and new media forms can be scrutinized by examining how a newspaper, a radio station or a television channel has 'webbified' itself over time. Has the old media form translated its features and ported them onto the web, or embraced 'new' media, transforming itself along the way? Has it experimented only to revert to its original self, with perhaps a smattering of online cultural forms retained? Newspapers are intriguing candidates for a study of the collision between the web and print, for the web promised to do away with gatekeeping through debate and comment spaces and introduce citizen journalists, with content sourced from the crowd.

  c   Digital history. A third strategy is to recount the history of an institution or other entity to which a website has been dedicated. A typical example would be the analysis of the issue lists of the US White House over time. One can view the changing times and priorities through the changes to a webpage. Counter-intuitive stories are of particular interest; one could find stability despite outward, massive change.

2   Choose a website to study and obtain the list of archived versions of its URL from the Internet Archive Wayback Machine.

3   Type the URL into the Internet Archive Wayback Machine Link Ripper. Choose to exclude duplicates and multiple page versions per day to show broad changes over time, and a longer arc of history. There are scenarios where one may be interested in multiple page versions per day. In a micro-temporal project, one could consider a 'developing' story over short periods of time, such as the changing headlines of a newspaper on election night.

4   Once the tool has completed its task, choose the tool's output menu and save the list of URLs of the archived versions as a text file.

5   Make a selection of the archived versions. Consider using a threshold technique (halving or zooming) in order to remove archived versions less relevant to your narrative. In your screenshot collection, select an image from the middle of the list, and compare it to an earlier and later screenshot; if the one in the middle is the same as the earlier screenshot, all in between are probably the same as well. Consider an 'even' history by choosing archived versions at stable intervals or an 'uneven' history by using only archived versions from key dates.

6   Use a screenshot generator to produce the snapshots of the archived versions.

    a   Insert URL list.

    b   Screenshot generator is set to 1024x768.

    c   Time to wait is 20 seconds between screenshots to allow Wayback Machine URLs to load. You may wish to conduct a test to determine whether the time to wait should be adjusted.

    d   Wait until all screenshots have been captured. This may take a couple of hours, depending on the number of archived pages in your selection.

    e   Check if all went well by looking at the screenshots. Sometimes the archive returns an error. Note the URLs of the erred screenshots in a new text file and use the screenshot generator to capture them anew.

7   Prepare your narration. Here are some considerations based on Jon Udell's 'Heavy Metal Umlaut' screencast on the evolution of the eponymous Wikipedia article. Below is also the narrative of the seminal screencast documentary, 'Google and the Politics of Tabs'.

    a   Jon Udell's narrative strategy provides an overview of the story at the beginning ('quick flight'), and then delves into a set number of sub-elements or aspects in detail, closing with a larger point. As in a presentation of a network visualization, first is the overview, then zoom in to a few clusters, and zoom back out so as to conclude.

    b   Consider the overall narrative of change. The story to be told may be one of loss; something of value has been lost or replaced. It may have returned but the environment has changed. Another is about transformation, or perhaps continuity. Despite massive change around it, the object or subject has remained remarkably the same. Despite transformation, it has returned to its original form.

    c   Concentrate on discrete storyline(s) and cut the less relevant. Resist exhaustiveness. Select a small number of key aspects to focus on rather than narrating every minute detail.

    d   Consider web attention span, and the YouTube style. Compile the images into a video with narration that is maximum ten minutes in length (an early YouTube cut-off), but preferably half that amount of time.

8   Load screenshots into an image viewer. Consider annotating the screenshots to highlight specific narrative elements.

9   Make project in a movie-maker. Sort by name, which keeps the pages in chronological order. Record narrative. Alternatively, there is a built-in screen-recording feature in QuickTime.

Screencast documentary example: 'Google and the Politics of Tabs'

Narrative voiceover. This is the history of Google as seen through its Interface. From the beginning, sometime in November 1998 all the way up until late 2007. These are screenshots of Google Interface taken from the Wayback Machine of the Internet Archive. The history of the Google is important. For some people, Google is the Internet. And for many, it's the first point of access. And

Google, as the face of the Internet, has remained virtually the same over the past ten years. But there have been some subtle changes to the Interface. So let's go back and look at this in a little bit more detail.

You see initially Google with a standard Web search button and its intriguing 'I'm feeling lucky' button have been your only options. Then the Directory gets introduced with some front-page fanfare. It's the Open Directory Project, Dmoz.org, that Google's built an engine on top of. Then come the Tabs on top of the Search box with the Web search being privileged at the far left, followed by Images, Groups (that's searching Usenet), and the Directory makes it to the front page. News, the Google news service, the news aggregator was next. Froogle is introduced; that was that cost comparison e-commerce service. And that stayed on the front page for a while, then was dropped. Followed by Local, which later became Google Maps. You can see that the services are becoming more and more present; there are now five or six at the top bar. Then they add a 'More' button. What we're interested in is which services remain on the front page and which get relegated to 'More' or 'Even More'. But let's look at this in some more detail.

Let's look at the fate of the Directory over time. It's a story of the demise of the librarian, of the demise of the human editors of the Web, and the rise of the back-end, of the algorithm taking over from the editors. Now you see that it's introduced with great fanfare in 2000. The Web is organized by human editors. It remains on the front page. It achieves the Tabs status that we talked about previously. Fourth Tab here. And keeps its place on the front page even as other services are introduced. However, in 2004 something happened: it got placed under the 'More' button. You had to click 'More' to find the Directory. And in 2006, if you clicked 'More', the Directory wasn't there; you had to click 'Even More' and there you would find the Directory. As it loses its standing, it also loses recognition. Lots of people don't really remember that there is a Directory just like other services that have left the front-page real estate. Also of interest are the services that climb from being 'Even More' to 'More' and all the way to the front page. But with the Directory, it's a sadder story. As the interface of Google moves upper left, and you click 'More', you see that there's no Directory any longer. And you also see that there is no 'Even More'. So nowadays you have to search Google for its Directory to find the Google Directory.

'Google and the Politics of Tabs' by R. Rogers and Govcom.org, Amsterdam, 2008.

Quicktime movie, 5'00', https://movies.digitalmethods.net/google.html (see also Figure 4.6).

Figure 4.6 Google's Directory on Google's front page in 2000 and receiving tab status in October of 2001 (left), before being relegated to under the 'more' (middle) and finally the 'even more' buttons (right). Excerpt from Digital Methods Initiative and Kim de Groot, 'The Demise of the Directory: Web librarian work removed in Google', Information Graphic, 2008, www.govcom.org/publications/drafts/GCO_directoryfall.pdf

Video tutorials

View these two tutorials on how to operate the Wayback Machine:

- 'Research with the Internet Archive's Wayback Machine' (7'02'), www.youtube.com/watch?v= mShvg718JN8sssss
- 'The Internet Archive Wayback Machine Link Ripper' (2'04'), www.youtube.com/watch?v= DVa2TBhp4a4

Tools

- Internet Archive Wayback Machine Link Ripper, https://tools.digitalmethods.net/beta/internet ArchiveWaybackMachineLinkRipper/
- Screenshot Generator, https://tools.digitalmethods.net/beta/screenshotGenerator/

FIVE

GOOGLE CRITIQUE
Auditing search engines

*Probing Google to identify privileging
mechanisms and bias*

Google, information politics and algorithmic auditing

What follows is search engine critique, concerning Google in particular, that leads to methods to audit or evaluate engine privileging mechanisms. It begins with a brief discussion of the seemingly innocuous Google Doodles, the colourful graphics occasionally festooning the Google logo on the search interface. Thereafter I focus on six types of critique: the objects and subjects brought into being by Google (such as 'spammy neighbourhoods'), Googlization (connoting globalization and hegemony), Google's information politics (including participating in state censorship), its licensing (or what one is agreeing to when searching), its materiality and environmental footprint as well as issues surrounding certain products such as Google Street View, as Google leaves the web, capturing more spaces to search. Finally, I turn more specifically to Google biases as they have been charted through 'algorithmic auditing', or studying the outputs of search, autocomplete and other results for discrimination.

Google's Doodles have been around since Google's inaugural year in 1998, when the founders made the first one of the Burning Man festival and have evolved from being static and sporadic cartoons to elaborate and routine animations and miniscule interactive games. There is a coterie of Google Doodlers on staff. In recent years, Google's Doodles have become an object of study and papers have emerged about them, discussing Google's 'fluid brand identity' as well as a gender and racial bias indicated by those chosen to appear on the front-page interface (Elali et al., 2012; Montaño and Slobe, 2014). Google's Doodles largely fall into two broad categories: that of great achievements of humankind (and their achievers), and national holidays, such as ones that have appeared on the Polish national day as well as on the Mexican Day of the Dead. These seemingly innocuous Doodle types represent two significant sides of Google's preferred image: the global and the local (or glocal). That is, they befit the two kinds of messages that Google would like to communicate about itself: Google web search as belonging in the lineage of the great creations, and

Google as a series of national machines (hewing to national legal jurisdictions) rather than merely a single, universalizing one that Americanizes or globalizes online cultures and search markets. There was once a trivia question concerning the few national online spaces Google search does not dominate, owing to still vibrant national engines or legacy partnerships: China (Baidu), Russia (Yandex), South Korea (Naver), Japan (Yahoo!) and the Czech Republic (Seznam). (Taiwan (Yahoo!) was often in the mix, too.) Nowadays that list is shrinking with perhaps only China and Russia having clearly dominant national engines, if one aggregates desktop and mobile search.

Figure 5.1   AIDS Google Doodle.

Source: Prada, 2007

Piotr Prada, the Polish artist, was one of the earliest to make a series of artworks using the form of Google's Doodles with his 'On Occasion' project that comprises a series of logo alterations that comment on what Google does not address (2007). Prada portrays what they might look like if there were ones for HIV/AIDS, the crisis in Darfur in South Sudan, or the Asian tsunami and its victims (see Figure 5.1). Google's demureness towards doodling the issue of HIV/AIDS on its international awareness day (1 December) has drawn attention almost every year since 2010 (Baughman, 2010; Anderson, 2012; Fratti, 2014). Doodles have been made for other days on the international issue calendar such as Universal Children's Day; the occasional ribbon will appear under the search bar on other meaningful days, such as International Women's Day. Thus, there is an issue day hierarchy – those with doodles, those with ribbons and those without acknowledgement. Whilst not a doodle per se, one major exception to the apolitical Google web search interface occurred in 2012 when the company, like a number of particularly US-based tech firms, protested the Stop Online Privacy Act or SOPA, the US legislative proposal, by blacking out its logo, in the style of redaction, thereby joining other organizations including Wikipedia that 'went black' entirely for a day.

When discussing how Google critique assumes cultural forms, I would like to venture further than its globalizing, de-politicizing interface, and touch upon quite specific treatments. There are four different types I identify. The first is what I call Google objects and subjects, which are things and people that Google brings into being, such as the deep web, flickering man, attention deficit and filter bubble. A further Google embodiment is the data body, one of the terms that refers to the collection of data on you that in itself 'acts'. The second category of critique is Googlization, a notion coined by tech journalists but which was taken up in particular by library scientists in the late 2000s, during which time well-known books were written called *Google and the Myth of Universal Knowledge* and *The Googlization of Everything* (Jeanneney, 2008; Vaidhyanathan, 2011). Googlization of course evokes monopolization (or at least hegemony) as well as globalization, referring to how Google takes over industry after industry (in country after country) with its particular 'free' business model, based on furnishing a service in exchange for user data (Anderson, 2009). The company then makes use of that data to earn revenue through advertising. The term 'Googlization', however, was proffered when Google entered the hallowed halls of the library with its Google Books Project, which it subsequently used as a blueprint of sorts for its Google Art Project by again partnering with major institutions and digitizing and putting online their holdings under the Google banner. For Googlization scholars, those projects – rather than 'just' trying to organize the world's information as its motto has read – crossed the line, and librarians, including the national librarian in France, began using this term to admonish against 'Googlizing' every industry and institution, prompting alternative European search engine projects (the infamous Quaero), non-partnering (the Louvre) as well as a new term of derision of French origin that speaks to American, digital cultural imperialism: GAFA, standing for Google, Apple, Facebook and Amazon (Chiber, 2014).

Google's information politics is the third type of critique, referring to a series of epistemological crises concerning censorship and results ordering, which Google has become embroiled in over the past couple of decades. I would like to highlight the case of Google China in particular, when Google was caught furnishing state-filtered results, in an evidentiary interface, created by the Citizen Lab at the University of Toronto, that placed google.com's and google.cn's respective engine outputs side by side. The other kind of information politics concerns more specifically how Google orders and ranks websites in its search results. Certain websites are privileged by Google and others are not, and work targets the issue of whether all websites receive equal treatment by Google. A handmade gif, 'Wikipedia is the new Google', captures the seemingly hard-coded appearance of Wikipedia at the top of substantive engine queries. In this context, the notion of 'spammy neighbourhoods', a characterization offered by Matt Cutts, the long-time in-house blogger, is also central in the privileging question, for it introduces parts of the web populated by content repeaters, illegitimate aggregators, pirates and other engine fodder makers that Google's frequent algorithmic updates address and, in fact, suppress (Cutts, 2006). In a sense, 'personalization' or what Eli Pariser (2011a) famously referred to as the 'filter bubble' extricates the engine from the debate surrounding universalizing engine results, in that they are now co-authored by engine and user. No longer are Google results the product and purveyor of the Matthew Effect (rich becoming richer), however much, even with personalization, the engine still regularly puts it on display. With personalization, the user also authors the results, shifting the blame away solely from the engine.

A fourth critique of Google, targeting the topic of licensing, concerns what one agrees to when typing something into Google's search bar and hitting return, clicking on search or the 'I'm Feeling Lucky' button, Google's intriguing, lesser used option that bypasses Google's ad-serving pages and main revenue source. Whichever form of activation is used, one enters into a contract with Google, and as such that deal has been worthy of exploration, including the futility of 'agreeing' to the contract, as well as the derivative works one could make of Google results, if they were not forbidden and if the contract one has entered into were broken.

Certain Google products have been the object of scrutiny, especially Google Maps and Street View, whose camera cars photograph houses, sidewalks and streets, and stich them together. Having lost the 'social space' to Facebook, Google's quest to dominate the locative space (maps) may be regarded as search in need of space, or an attempt to create or at least enclose new spaces for its search technology.

Finally, I take up Google as discriminatory machine and the family of techniques by which such claims are made. 'Algorithmic auditing', which derives from a rich social sciences history of documenting housing discrimination through fieldwork, is the practice of examining the outputs, in this case, of Google, be they search results, Google ads, autocompletion or related sites. These techniques are briefly reviewed and applied, where one can research such auditing critiques as preferred placement, credibility hierarchies, discrimination, personalization, political bias and (successful or less successful) content moderation. There is also a brief discussion of neo-colonial results, or the extent to which they may or may not be decolonized.

Figure 5.2 Rendition of uploading a file to the Icelandic cloud.

Source: Metahaven, 2013.

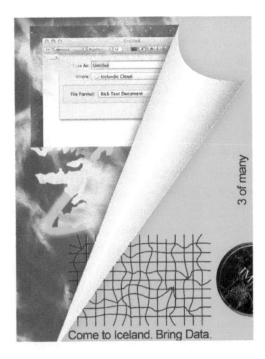

Google objects and subjects

The first example of an object that Google (and its early competitors such as Northern Lights, Excite, Alta Vista and Lycos) brought into being is the deep web. The term was coined around 2001, having emerged from studies in the 1990s of the heretofore 'invisible web', where researchers found that search engines index only a relatively small portion of the entire web (Lawrence and Giles, 1998, 1999). At the time, engine coverage, whilst varying by technique, was at most 16 per cent, meaning that there is this other web 'out there', beyond reach and ken. It turned out to be vast, and far greater in size than the World Wide Web (Bergman, 2001). This deep web is often depicted as the submerged core of an iceberg, with its tip being the small part of the 'surface web' that one can access through search engines skimming its top layer. Later, the unindexed web darkened and also became a kind of temporary autonomous zone. Initially one could still Google parts of it, locating BitTorrents and other ripped and remixed content, often under copyright, that had been uploaded for others to download. With the rise of illicit or dirty downloading – before the cloud would clean that up – came defences of remix culture and off-shore server farms, such as the Principality of Sealand, a disused British sea fortress in international waters, that drew interest from the Pirate Bay, the Swedish file sharing site and global social movement, and was the source of the Metahaven's Sealand Identity Project, and other critical identity work on data havens and alternative clouds (see Figure 5.2). Gradually, as national jurisdictions took on the pirates, bringing copyright infringement lawsuits, a still darker web emerged, which Google perhaps chooses not to index; apart from references to experiments in 2008, the official Google blog rarely mentions the deep, and never the dark web. The online underworld (notably the erstwhile Silk Road run by Dread Pirate Roberts) is made available not through Google but Tor browser search, where one reaches so-called 'onion land'.

A related object brought into being by Google is the orphan website. This is a sad site that through its lack of inlinks does not become indexed by Google, and thereupon does not receive attention. It resides in not so much a deep but a kind of pitiful web, which does not garner (engine) traffic, and does not have any comments on its blogs, any ratings on its sites and is never liked, even if the sitemaster has taken the trouble to implement social buttons (Lovink, 2008). In this web, sites are not returned in Google's search results and, hence, they are also neglected. Artworks have commented on how Google buries websites and disregards orphan websites. One is called Shmoogle, created by Tsila Hassine, joined later with a group called De Geuzen. When one types a query into Shmoogle and hits return, it randomizes Google's results (see Figure 5.3). Together with 'democratizing' sources, Shmoogle also seeks to intervene in the hierarchy of source credibility suggested by rankings. As the artist writes:

> [L]et's take 'art' for example. Google's first page consists of the Metropolitan museum, the National Gallery, MoMA, and some art portals on the web (not

much of a surprise). On Shmoogle, a (possible) first page features sites entitled 'we make money not art', 'Olga's gallery', and 'Art Passions', among others – did you know these sites exist? (Hassine, 2005).

As cultural critics have pointed out, a subject that Google brings into being is one with an attention deficit, also known as 'flickering man' (Carr, 2007). The expectant search engine user types a query into the search bar, and is returned results forthwith, as Google reinforces by advertising the speed with which they are returned, e.g., 'About 43,100 results (0.14 sec)'. This sense of being served immediate results is a development trajectory that continues with autosuggest (and what was called Google Instant) as well as with the voice activated search beginning with 'OK, Google'. Over the last 25 years, one of the subjects of related research has been how users interact with search engines, where some of the earliest studies, beginning in 1997, found that people were mostly only looking at the first few pages of results (Jansen and Spink, 2006; Jansen et al., 2009). Defaults of ten results per page remained set, meaning glancing at more than 30 results would be extraordinary. Over the years, however, people began browsing fewer pages still, and, ultimately and most recently, not even leaving the first results page or looking past the first result itself. Such a perfected Google, where there would only ever be one result, harks to the Google game, googlewhacking, which you win when your query returns only one result. Together with googlebombing and what was once known as ego-googling, these were considered the well-known alternative uses of Google, before Philipp Lenssen published *55 Ways to Have Fun with Google* that extended the list to include more (2006). But more poignantly, returning the sole, ultimate result per query is actually a company goal, as its CEO pointed out in 2015: 'When you use Google, do you get more than one answer? Of course, you do. Well, that's a bug' (Ferenstein, 2015).

Figure 5.3 Shmoogle.

Source: Hassine, 2005.

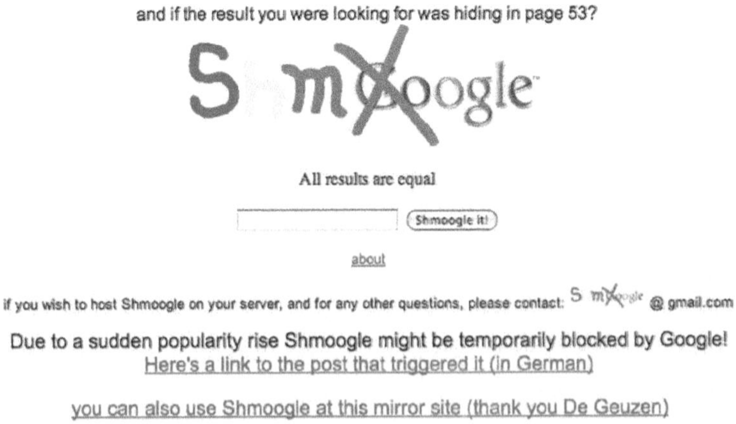

and if the result you were looking for was hiding in page 53?

All results are equal

(Shmoogle it!)

about

if you wish to host Shmoogle on your server, and for any other questions, please contact: S m∕oogle @ gmail.com

Due to a sudden popularity rise Shmoogle might be temporarily blocked by Google!
Here's a link to the post that triggered it (in German)

you can also use Shmoogle at this mirror site (thank you De Geuzen)

As fewer results pages and fewer results are perused, the greater the value of the front-page real estate, or the top of Google's search engine results page, known in the search engine optimization (SEO) literature as SERPs. Heat maps of user eye movements across these results produced the object called the 'Golden Triangle', the area at the top left where most eyes gravitate the longest (in left-to-right reading cultures) (Mediative, 2011). In a more recent study the same digital agency found that people are now looking further down the SERP. Instead of the 'Golden Triangle', the image outputted in the heat map work looks more like a scrolling finger, somewhat similar to the oft-remarked F-shape of user gazing. The noticeable change in behaviour may be the result of smartphone user scrolling together with a variation on 'banner ad blindness' and dissatisfaction with the results; one glazes over the Google properties at the top of the returns, such as the Google News or Google Images sets, until setting one's eyes on the top organic results, as they are called by industry.

Having appeared under a few names, the third Google subject is the data double, software self or the data body. Data double (put forth by Mark Poster, 1990) and, later, data body (by the Critical Art Ensemble, 1998), both describe the aggregated data points collected about an individual, kept by governments (turning one into a number, in the 1960s-style critique), or by corporations, making one a niche market to be behaviourally targeted. The various data points collected such as flight itinerary, credit card type, special meal and nationality of passport via the US Advanced Passenger Information system arrive to the authorities before the air traveler does, resulting in an advance profile or 'data derivative' that is acted upon by the security team, such as in an additional screening (Amoore, 2011). The data body as referred to in the case of Google (or search engines more generally) is considered to be a new one, brought into being on the basis of one's search history. An example is the case of the America Online search engine, when it released user search histories to scientists in 2006. The engine company released search queries from a period of six months for hundreds of thousands of users. Each individual's search history, or data body, was anonymized in the sense that each was given a number. One is AOL user 311045, who apparently owns a Scion car, is interested in the US Open, but also has queries such as [how to get revenge on an ex], [how to get revenge on an ex girlfriend], and [how to get revenge on a friend who f---ed you over]. In his search history, 311045 then reverts back to the less animated [replacement bumper for scion xb] (McCullagh, 2006a). In this particular sense, John Battelle (2003b) has remarked that the search engine houses a 'database of intentions', one that saves one's aims and plans prior to acting. Rather than new software selves as the life blog or quantified self, it was thought of as a private search self. At least no one would expect that one's search history would be made public, given the usual context of searching (others peeking over the shoulder?). Indeed, AOL search engine users who were de-anonymized in the research data release said the same, including an old lady from Georgia USA (4417749) who was located and interviewed by the *New York Times*. She explained that she was querying the medical conditions of her friends (Barbaro and Zeller, 2006). The artists and video-makers Lernert Engelberts and Sander Plug made a 13-part documentary (or set of mini-movies) about another AOL user, 711391 (2009). 'I love Alaska' (one of the queries) chronicles her 'heart-breaking' search history, providing a particularly intimate portrait; 711391 converses with the search engine, typing in statements and questions about a snoring husband, online romance, gay churches and God.

There are at least two modes of Google use: logged in or not. The data body that Google has formed has more agency when one is logged in, for there are more signals to work with. Even when not logged in, however, results are personalized (or pushed) and data extracted (or pulled) because of the cookies that Google sets, and information it gleans (one's location from the IP address, for example). Scroogle, in operation for about nine years before it was forced to discontinue in 2012, owing to changes Google made to its advanced query settings, sat on top of Google, and 'crumbled its cookies'. With the Dickensian Google logo (itself a kind of Doodle commentary), it invited one's queries, and outputted Google results, without the user being tracked or without any data being collected. It would serve no ads. There would be no Google properties in the results, such as YouTube videos, Google Images, Google News. It pinched pennies in the sense that no revenue was generated by Google when queries were made through Scroogle.

Another reaction to Google's collection of user data is the 'artware' Firefox add-on, Track Me Not. It is a play on words on the radio button in the browser's privacy panel, Do Not Track, which only 'asks' websites not to collect data, in the voluntary industry gesture. Track Me Not practices the art of obfuscation, for when installed, the extension sends random text to search engines every once in a while, not allowing a 'sensible' search history (and data body) to be built. After Scroogle ended, questions arose (e.g., in articles in the industry-standard *Search Engine Land*) concerning alternatives.[1] Continuing the wordplay (in a so-called domain hack), donttrack.us, makes the case for DuckDuckGo in its three-slide presentation: 'Google trackers are lurking on 75% of websites, Google uses your data for ads that follow you around, and your personal data remains in Google indefinitely' (2017). The alternative engine, in its 'herpes query' example, essentially argues that we share our problems with search engines, which save and profit from them as well as remind us of them, continually, for they follow us around, website to website, in the form of discomforting ads.

Relatedly, privacy enhancing technology (as it is often termed) also should allow the 'right to oblivion', or the capacity for forgetting, a concern that ultimately became Google regulation in the European Union. In the EU privacy directive, individuals may make requests for 'delinkings', that is, the removal of links from search engine returns that are personally damaging. The content remains online; it is only delisted from the SERP.

One final object that Google has brought into being is the 'filter bubble', a term for the confined cognitive space one finds oneself in, after Google 'filters' results based on one's data body. It was coined after Google 'flipped the switch' in December 2009 from universal results for all to personal results for each. Eli Pariser, developer of significant new media mobilization concepts – 'moveon.org' (for organizing people in 1998) and 'upworthy.com' (for virally circulating content in 2012) – speaks (in his Ted talk) of two friends who query 'Egypt', where one is presented with results about the Egyptian Revolution of 2011 and the other about holiday-making in the land of the pyramids. Incidentally, these results are both from google.com, rather than from google.com and google.com.eg, respectively. The larger point Pariser makes with the filter bubble argument is that we do not know whether there is a difference, given Google's 'invisible algorithmic editing of the web' (Pariser, 2011b). Users rarely compare one set of results with the previous set or with each other.

---

[1]The trade publications that follow the search engine industry include *Search Engine Land*, *Search Engine Watch* and *Search Engine Roundtable*.

Googlization

Googlization is critique of another nature than inclusion and exclusion or personal data collection and personalization, for it casts a much wider net about Google's impact across societally significant institutions. Coined by John Battelle in 2003, who referred to it as a 'creeping dominance of Google over nearly all forms of commerce on the web', Googlization spells the end of the innocence of the internet, and introduces a mass media critique of new media (Battelle, 2003a). When Wikipedia first asked its users in 2010 to donate, it promoted itself as one of the top five websites in the world with servers that need to be maintained and so forth. In contrast, 'Google might have a million servers', said Jimmy Wales, Wikipedia's founder (Wikimedia, 2011). When considering that a search engine has a million servers, geographically distributed, one is no longer in a start-up environment. Given this scale of infrastructure, the question is, should Google be reframed as mass media?

If mass media is constituted by barriers to entry contiguous with large-scale production and distribution, as well as striving to reach the largest possible audience, Google fits the description. New media were often distinctive from mass media, given the 'interactivity', but one cannot 'talk back' to Google. There is not a comment space below the search results, for example (as ridiculous as that may sound). Power is just as asymmetrical as when there is a strict separation between producers and distributors on the one hand, and receivers on the other, as with television. Another mass media critique is that relations between senders and receivers are commodified, impersonal, and anonymous. Google has sought to change the advertising model, from broadcast advertising (say, billboards) to what is called direct or personalized advertising (Turow, 2006). This is advertising that is increasingly based on a personal profile of attributes and desires. Whilst the growing relationship we have with our search engine may be described as commodified, it is certainly not anonymous, whether logged in or not. Finally, the tendency to standardize content (downwards) does not appear to apply to Google, given personalization, however much the actual amount of personalized content in engine returns seems empirically low (Feuz et al., 2011; Puschmann, 2017; Le et al., 2019).

In its early form, PageRank performed a kind of citation analysis, where websites rose in the rankings owing to inlinks from influential websites (Rieder, 2012). Some 500 or more so-called signals later (sometimes divided into 'content factors', 'user signals' and 'technical factors' by the SEO industry), Google Web Search, however, relies more heavily on user clicks rather than influential inlinks (web citations) (Smart Metrics, 2016). In other words, Google returns pages that have been 'voted up' by users, making it into a 'popular content' machine – rather than one based on web citations. Google, in outputting popularizing web search results, appeals to the masses.

Googlization could be said to have spread across front-ends and back-ends. Front-end Googlization would be the desire to implement (or emulate) Google aesthetics, including single input field, fast loading time, instant returns, anticipatory results, geo-detection, no settings or filters, hidden affordances (such as quotation marks for exact matches) and so forth. At the interface level, Google (especially when Doodle-free) is remarkably clean. It has decluttered itself over the years, shedding first the tabs in place since 2001 as well as the drop-down menu, upper left, that replaced the tabs in 2007 (as per the movie 'Google and the Politics of Tabs', mentioned above). There is just a single search bar, with two buttons, including I'm Feeling Lucky, a vestige said to be a cultural reference (from Clint Eastwood's *Dirty Harry* movie from 1971) referring to the 'confidence and swagger' of the start-up company betting it could produce the result the user wanted in one shot (Remaker, 2015). It also humanizes the machine (CHM Tech, 2017). The languages (spoken at one's geo-detected location) have been added beneath the search bar. The minimalism suggests algorithmic brilliance and belies not only the complexity of the engine's back-end, but also the messiness, summed up in the quip that 'Google doesn't know how its engine works, but only that it works' (Schwartz, 2016). Whilst there is no 'content moderation' (described as the 'soul-crushing' job at social media companies), results are checked by humans. During the Covid-19 pandemic, official sources were added as side bars, however, revealing the humans behind the machine once more.

The back-end of Google is complex in other ways, as the phrase 'multi-sided market' would suggest, which is used to describe a platform's business model. Google 'coordinates' multiple parties finding and doing business with each together, whilst being rewarded for their interactions. Back-end Googlization would be the uptake of such a market or 'platform logic' across the web (and app space), as practiced by Facebook, Uber, Airbnb and others (Schwarz, 2017). How Google makes its money was described in 2002, in some of the earliest ad word art, as 'semantic capitalism' (Bruno, 2002). Google sells words. 'Free', it turned out, was the most expensive word of all. Ads must be ads, related to the website to which the user is sent, rather than poetry; after the artist created short ditties and embedded them in ads, his account was disapproved. More recently, Pip Thornton (2017) demonstrated Google's 'monetization of language' by valuing entire books (like Orwell's 1984) by pricing the words as AdWords (1984 came in at £58,318.14).

One of the more well-known works to explore Google's back-end is by Ubermorgen, Ludovico and Cireo (2005; Dewey, 2014). They generated revenue from the ads, and the money was spent buying company shares in Google. 'Google Will Eat Itself' relied on bots visiting a network of so-called hidden websites, and clicking on banner ads, which prompted the company to revoke the account (click fraud). Google Will Eat Itself is one in a trilogy of projects (GAFA-related) that pulls back the curtains on the back-ends (and business models) of the erstwhile new media. Amazon Noir (Ubermorgen et al., 2006) glued together the previewed pages of a number of books sold on Amazon (hacking the 'search inside' feature), making them available in noir or black-market versions. The work describes Amazon's history (and business model) as 'hyper-contextualizing' every book with categories, tags, user reviews, ratings, author portraits, further recommendations, etc., until it finally introduced the sneak preview of the original text itself, whereupon book marketing became a tantalizing 'cultural peep show'. The other is Face to Facebook (Ubermorgen et al., 2011), which scraped a million profile photos from Facebook, placed them on lovely-faces.com, and used image recognition software to sort them into categories like 'easy going women' and 'climber men'. The artwork explores Facebook's appeal as the encouragement of 'comfortable voyeurism'.

Google information politics

A third cluster of critique that is generally made of Google is that of information politics. For example, in a project by the Citizen Lab of Toronto, queries for 'Tiananmen' were made in two versions of Google Image Search: google.com and google.cn (Google China at the time). The two sets of results appeared to be very different, with the one outputting pictures of the uprising in Tiananmen Square in 1989, including the iconic image of 'Tank Man' standing in front of a column of armoured vehicles. The Google China version excludes protest images, and instead replaces them, if you will, with the Tiananmen Square that is for tourists. (As mentioned above, that particular type of results discrepancy depending on the user (conflict vs. tourism), was also used by Eli Pariser in his filter bubble story for the query, 'Egypt'.) Google China arguably cleansed the historical record, neatly redacting or 'touching up' the Tiananmen photos, all the while following Chinese state censorship guidelines. Here, information politics refers to the removal of unpalatable information for ideological, political or other purposes (such as state-run business). The company was accused of being a 'functionary' of the Chinese government (and a 'sickening collaborator') by US congressmen in the legendary congressional human rights hearings in 2006 that also witnessed testimony by Yahoo!, Microsoft and Cisco (McCullagh, 2006b).

How to repopulate the Chinese Google results with unfiltered content? The artist, Linda Hilfing, discovered that misspellings such as 'tianamen', when queried in Google China, would return the Tank Man and other images from the 1989 events. That revelation led to the Misspelling Generator, which outputs related words to the search term (slightly misspelled) that likely would not be censored, and also could lead to the otherwise forbidden content (Hilfing, 2007). The tool is customizable: misspellings can be typographically or phonetically generated, with additional options to repeat or swap letters. Publishing misspelled words or coded language to dupe the censors is well known in China (and elsewhere), where in that context the meme, Grass Mud Horse, is often mentioned.

The second form of information politics is subtler and refers to Google's treatment of individual websites and whether it treats them equally. One would assume that if one were following a 'pure' PageRank algorithm on the web, all links would count the same; that is, the more links a website receives from websites that themselves have a large quantity of links to them, the higher that website would rise in the rankings. Over the years there arose 'link fodder' or 'link spam', which refers to websites created for the purposes of furnishing quantities of links to particular sites, thereby boosting them in the eyes of the algorithm. As a result, Google ceased equal link treatment, in at least two senses. Firstly, the 'No

Follow' tag was introduced to the comment space, as a directive to crawlers. Google pushed websites to implement the No Follow attribute in the comment space and ceased indexing comments and links that appeared there. Having earlier co-produced the 'deep web', Google thereupon relegated the comment space to what is referred to as the 'bottom of the web' (Reagle, 2015). Secondly, Google began to identify what it called 'spammy neighbourhoods'. These are the 'bad' areas of the web, where one might not want to visit, because of undesirable websites and their special activities. These are parts of the web with so-called backdoor pages and other black hat search engine optimization practices in evidence. Through some of the major algorithmic updates (such as 'Big Daddy' and later 'Panda'), Google no longer gave the links that came from spammy neighbourhoods much weight. Panda was described as 'improving the rankings for a large number of quality websites', when in fact it devalued web property. 'Spam' of course only seems to be a clear-cut product. 'Franchise' websites (such as 9/11 conspiracy websites with many local branches) would be affected for they often repeat content on every subsite, as did Indymedia, the alternative journalism space. Business models based on engine queries also may have been affected. Demand media, for example, is a kind of digital sweatshop labour, which pays people to make videos, cheaply, for popular search queries. 'How to pack for a trip to Rome' is such a query, and in the video a woman lays out clothes, and discusses the weather and fitting clothing choice into luggage sizes. Such rather web native content, too, appears to have been affected.

Licensing, and breaking the terms of service

There is a series of online software licenses, which one may or may not be aware of. The first one is called shrink wrap, a practice some consumer electronics still use. If one were to buy a CD or DVD, it would be wrapped in plastic or shrink wrap with a kind of holographic seal on it. The moment one breaks the plastic and seal, one agrees to a series of stipulations. A second tech license is called click wrap, and it refers to the 'Agree' buttons one checks or clicks online. Finally, a third one is called browse wrap, whereby one agrees to certain terms simply through the act of browsing. One does not explicitly agree, for that would be cumbersome. These licenses have been the source of a series of artworks, one of which is the 'Whatever button', a Firefox add-on that replaced 'Agree' with 'Whatever' (Stevenson, 2007). In a sense, it expresses the user behaviour of never reading the license ('whatever'), but perhaps more to the point it relates the futility of disagreement. Similarly, turning off cookies, for example, would become so infuriating to the website visitor, receiving prompt after prompt, that even the Safari browser issues the warning, 'Websites may not work if you do this'. 'Participatory surveillance' is the term often employed to describe the assurance of a seamless web experience. In order to participate online, one must allow cookies. The European legislation which by default only allows necessary cookies may seem like relief but every returning visit prompts the same request to accept marketing cookies until one relents and 'accepts all'.

When searching Google, the user agrees to at least three terms of service. The first is that you only search Google through the search bar, which may sound trivial but in certain contexts of work (running batch queries) it is not. The second point is that you agree not to save the results. Such would put paid to empirical work detecting the extent of personalization, for example, or studies of results like conflict versus tourism, discussed above. It also would prevent the algorithmic auditing techniques described by way of conclusion. The third one is you also agree not to create a derivative work from the results. There have been several art projects and other software projects that have broken these terms. The first one is Newsmap, which won an award at Ars Electronica in Linz in 2004 (Weskamp, 2004). Newsmap sat on top of Google News and outputted a tree map, showing which news stories were resonating the most across Google News in total as well as per region. It thus displayed a news attention economy and geography. Newsmap broke the three terms of service in that it likely does not search Google through the search bar, it loads the results in a database (however temporarily), and it creates a derivative work, the news attention visualization, from the results. Another project developed by the Dutch art group De Geuzen places the results of anxiety-related queries in local domain Google images side by side (2006). The results of the queries 'terrorism', 'conflict', 'financial crisis' and 'climate change' each shows different levels of societal concerns, as expressed in the top images. (The project was discontinued when Google changed its advanced search settings, which is the same issue that befell Scroogle.) 'Rights Types: The Nationalities of Issues' also shows the top results for the query 'rights' across some 30 local domain Googles, allowing one to compare cultural concerns (Rogers et al., 2009a). The 'right to roam' is particularly dear to Finns, for example. Finally, 'RFID: Wet and Dry' displays the top hundred (thumbnail) images from the query 'RFID' in Google Images and indicates whether the representation of RFID is wet (humans or animals in the picture) or dry (non-humans in the picture) (Digital Methods Initiative, 2007) (see Figure 5.4). Is RFID only about logistics and warehouse packaging, or are pets and humans, together with their collars and garments, tagged, too? Newsmap, the Anxiety Monitor, Rights Types and others are all are derivative works of engine results, and Google's forbearance would be required to display such politics of images and representation.

Finally, with respect to individual Google products such as Maps, Paolo Cirio utilized Google Street View to create the artwork called Street Ghosts (2012), which is a series of Google Street View images printed out and glued in the same spots on the streets where images of individuals were originally taken. It contributes to the debate concerning how Google takes unauthorized pictures in the sense that it does not request permission to photograph people or their abodes. Google make addresses and streets searchable and shows pictures of them for panning and zooming. It does have a so-called blacklist of properties and places which are not on Street View – or Google Earth, for that matter – raising the question of how one would have one's property removed from it, apart from having one's city or country ban the Google vehicles. Preventing a drive-by may be of interest, too, given that the company acknowledged, in its collection of WiFi data, that 'in some instances entire emails and URLs were captured, as well as passwords' (EPIC, 2017).

Figure 5.4   Top RFID results from Google Images, categorized as 'wet' or 'dry'. October 2007.

Source: Digital Methods Initiative, 2007.

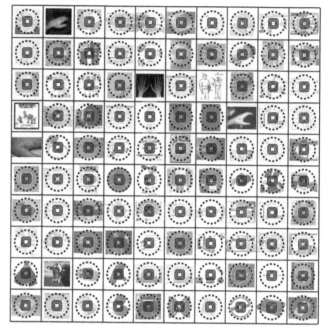

RFID Imagery: Wet and Dry Associations Compared

Research Question_How "wet" is the RFID imagery according to Google?
Findings_According to Google Images, the RFID imagery is dry insofar as associations to the biological are limited, e.g., human tagging, animal chip implants, etc. Associations with machines and machinic diagrams predominate.

RFID's 'wet' associations

Source_images.google.com
Method_Scrape top 100 results from Google Images and visualize as 'dry' and 'wet' assocations turned on or off.
Query_RFID
Tools_Google Image Scraper and Tag Cloud Generator
Date_20 October 2007

Product_of the Digital Methods Initiative, dmi.mediastudies.nl. Analysis_by Anne Helmond, Richard Rogers, Laura van der Vlies and Esther Weltevrede. Recalling RFID Icon_by Loes and Leon. RFID Icons_by Timo Arnal. Design_by Anne Helmond.

CC_BY.NC.SA

Rematerializing the cloud

The materiality of Google, once understudied, has become the subject of a variety of exposés, ranging from investigative reporting on negotiations between the company and city and state governments, artistic and ethnographic trips to data centres and works of art that show buildings scrubbed from Google Maps (Burrington, 2014). To be sure, there is a vast technological infrastructure in the service of delivering fast engine results and seeding 'the cloud'. The infrastructures in turn compete for natural resources with the local population, farmers and others in what are dubbed 'water wars', for they require cooling (Gallucci, 2017). The materiality of the cloud is captured in Timo Arnal's (2014) artwork, 'Internet Machine', as well as in Trevor Paglan's (2016) 'Deep Web Dive' where the artist swims to an undersea cable. Paglan's work is about surveillance, though it does point to the physicality of the cloud (and the lengths to which one must go to uncover it). In Arnal's work, the nondescript, often secret, data centre is actually entered (see Figure 5.5). After a series of security layers, the camera takes us down long corridors, laced with cables, and through doors to the server rooms that whirr with the sounds of fans. Apart from surprisingly high noise levels there are also temperature extremes; there are 'hot aisles' and cold ones (Levy, 2012). To keep the systems up there are massive diesel generators for back-up power, and steel containers of cooling water in case of calamity. It is remarkably emptied of people, with few signs of maintenance workers.

The cloud, the airy metaphor that deftly stands in for physical systems of cables, data centres, servers and electricity, is often illustrated with impressive numbers – the billions of searches served in milliseconds around the world and the number of bytes (zettabytes even) held 'up there', in what technology historians would call exemplary of the 'arithmetic sublime', whereby the reader stands in awe of its incomprehensible vastness, well beyond any human mathematical capacity. The term 'technological sublime' was coined to capture the statistical and other mind-numbing descriptions of great technological displays such as the illuminations of city streets in the nineteenth century, when electricity and public lighting were introduced (Nye, 1994). Such thinking is often followed by what these numbers (and the awe) obscure: a sprawling political economy of resource extraction, low-wage work and data centre user capture, fuelling growth, such as when Apple OS nudges its users to save files onto iCloud rather than their own hard drive (Merritt, 2013).

Figure 5.5 Facebook data centre signage. 'Other companies don't put their names on their data centers'.

Source and picture credit: Lardinois, 2016.

The clouds of the likes of Amazon, Google, Apple and Facebook have now been brought down to earth through the materialist and environmental critique, one that has found a starting point for research in the lists of data centre locations as well as their resource consumption provided by the companies themselves in displays of corporate social responsibility. That is, for some years now the companies have issued reports not only on 'transparency' (related to requests from governments around the world to block content or identify users) but also on 'environmental responsibility' where in one of Apple's documents, for example, it is stated that in 2016 the company used 630 million gallons of water (up 10 per cent from the previous year's consumption owing to the data centres) (Apple, 2017). On back-ups, it also burned 261,580 gallons of diesel. The listing of such figures is couched less in the prose of technological wonderment than in the incremental progress towards a more sustainable pace.

Conclusions: Looking for spaces to search

To summarize, I have discussed varieties of Google critique that have arisen over the past two decades, and how these have been conceptualized and rendered in art and cultural commentary: Google objects and subjects, Googlization, information politics, licensing and Google materiality.

From the beginning, Google has promoted a particular web epistemology that has evolved from universal results to personalized ones, making them befit the individual searcher and their (increasingly accurate) location. Engine use has evolved, too. Where one once consulted multiple pages, now only the top results matter. In fact, Google would like to provide the ultimate engine result – the perfect one – thereby transforming the web from a browsing and surfing space to a single Q&A. As a consequence of how users interact with Google, the very top of the results page, high above the fold, has become more and more valuable, as the eye-tracking study of the 'golden triangle' indicated. Google subsequently populated the expensive real estate with its own properties. Most recently Google has become a pre-mediation machine, suggesting or autocompleting results for what one is typing (and thinking). It thereby massifies and flattens the internet with everyone else's searches, as the art group, Studio Moniker, pointed out with its work, 'State of the Queries' (see Figure 5.6).

Figure 5.6 State of the Queries. Google art from autocompleted results.

Source: Studio Moniker, 2012.

There remains the question of which results remain privileged, even if results are personalized. It is an inquiry of lasting interest, formulated in 1998 as the 'preferred placement critique' (Rogers, 2000). At the time Alta Vista was accused of obscuring editorial content (or organic results) with advertising. One could buy the top engine results. Advertising in search engines has changed, as one also can purchase words (in what Bruno calls 'semantic capitalism' and Thornton the 'monetization of language'). These ad products, whilst marked as such, still remain prominently placed, above the fold and higher than the so-called organic results.

Though there is a new term (GAFA, standing for Google, Apple, Facebook and Amazon) that captures the take-over of industries by 'big tech', and digital cultural imperialism more generally, Googlization continues to capture the idea, formulated by tech writers and more forcefully still by librarians. Letting the company digitize holdings may have unintended consequences. In the debate in France, where the term GAFA originated, a particular expression was used to describe the decision whether to become Google bedfellows: 'What matters the jug, if drunkenness be within?' (Losh, 2009). The question, discussed above, concerns how Google derives commercial value from the digitized books and artwork that were once public property. As Ubermorgen pointed out in its critique of 'look inside' Amazon books as 'cultural peepshow', the 'preview' feature drives traffic to Google Books. Therein lies the eventual revenue, such as purchases of e-books for Android through the Google Play Store.

Google's information politics, the third critique, were revealed in the results from its China engine, where conflict was outputted in google.com and tourism in google.cn for the same 'Tiananmen' query. They are also at work in Google's suppressive treatment of websites in so-called spammy neighbourhoods as well as its demeaning of the comment space. Once heralded as the site of 'talking back' and the end of mass media gatekeeping, the comment space, where links no longer count for the engine, became the 'bottom of the web'. Both spammy neighbourhoods and the web's bottom came into being through their undervaluation and suppression by Google's algorithms.

Saving engine results may shed light on what may be missing in them, or the extent to which the user is enveloped in a filter bubble, but doing so would break the terms of service, as Google licensing critiques have bared. One may put up a notice, asking for forbearance, or invite company reaction and document it as part of the artwork, as was the case for both the semantic capitalism work as well as Google Will Eat Itself. The specific licensing, also known as browse wrap, discourages algorithmic observability, or the capacity to study missing results, privileging mechanisms as well as filter bubbles.

'Planetary-scale computing' (Bratton, 2016) is another way of phrasing 'the cloud'. Both, however, obscure Google's materiality, especially the natural resources required to operate and interlink data centres around the world. The scholarship on data centre impact emphasizes the chosen locations, often next to large waterways as well as their increasing size or 'hyperscale' (Carr et al., 2022). They also power the blockchain. Referred to in the scholarship as 'a new way to cause pollution' (Truby et al., 2022), cryptocurrencies and other blockchain products and services also have been held up to critical scrutiny as extraction industries.

Finally, 25 years since it went live the engine finds itself looking for spaces to search. As one writer put it, '"What" came first, conquered by Google's superior search algorithms. "Who" was next, and Facebook was the victor. But "where", arguably the biggest prize of all, has yet to be completely won' (Fisher, 2013). In the event, rather than digging deeper online, Google's product expansion lies in creating 'locative media' by capturing and digitizing physical places and spaces. With projects such as Google Places and Google Street View, it continues to envelope or enclose more spaces for search.

Algorithmic auditing

Algorithms, which Sandvig et al. (2016) describe as synonymous with 'recipes', have come under increased scrutiny as commercial mechanisms that operate in the interest of the social media and search engine companies that employ engineers to develop and tweak them. Here the classic critique is that they boost either the companies' own properties or those that have purchased a high ranking, as in the case of preferred or paid placement. They also encourage more engagement with the platform (or what was once termed 'stickiness'), keeping the user clicking and posting. In another approach dubbed 'hierarchies of credibility', the study of algorithmic outputs concerns which sources have the privilege of providing information and which others are buried. Algorithms used by websites, engines and platforms also have been the object of study for their harmful discrimination, be it for differentiated prices one receives on online shopping sites depending on one's geography or computer operating system (or even browser) or for the ads one receives (or does not receive) for particular keyword queries. There have been calls to audit algorithms to uncover not so much epistemological inequalities or advertising in disguise, but rather machine bias and discrimination, such as when African-American name searches trigger Google ads for background checks or when women receive ads for lower-paying jobs on Google's ad network (Sandvig et al., 2014; Datta et al., 2015). Relying on the study of Google ads and search keyword autocompletions, Noble calls them 'algorithms of oppression' (2018). In Sanchez-Querubin's work, engines have been found to deliver 'neo-colonial' result sets (Rogers, 2013b). Results from Spain appear at the top of engine results across Latin American Google regions. The 'filter bubble', the term that takes aim at the harmful effects of personalization and micro-targeting, also has been examined for its capacity not only to shrink horizons and exposure, but also to polarize or even radicalize (Pariser, 2011a; Spohr, 2017). Most recently, especially in the context of the Trump information ecology, 'big tech' or Silicon Valley is accused of political bias, that is, in not having 'balanced' results. In all of these critiques one is examining or 'auditing' algorithmic outputs, which is the aim of the project.

PROJECT

Produce an algorithmic audit

RESEARCH GOAL To capture Google results (or another engine's) and scrutinize them for privileging mechanisms, bias and authority. Consider the type of audit you would like to perform (see also CR+DS, 2022): preferred or paid placement, hierarchies of credibility or 'relevance' critique, discrimination, personalization, political bias or content moderation. Each is taken in turn.

1   Preferred or paid placement. Here one wishes to uncover the boosting of one's own properties or those who have paid for higher rankings. The question also has to do with whether such paid placements are legible or hidden.

Recipe: Formulate queries for products and enter them into a search engine. Are the search engine's own 'shopping' sites routinely returned at or towards the top? Consider comparing multiple search engines. Document the findings with screenshots.

2   Hierarchies of credibility or 'relevance' critique. How far from the top of engine returns are the experts versus internet celebrities for substantive queries? Are junk sources returned as prominently as quality ones?

Recipe: Formulate a series of substantive queries in web and/or social media search engines (such as Google, YouTube, Facebook, etc.). Inquire into the extent to which the engines return experts or online personalities. Document the findings with screenshots.

3   Discrimination. From autocompletion and micro-targeted ads to one-sided imagery for queries such as 'unwanted pregnancy', the outputs of search engines, in particular, have been investigated for offensive results.

Recipe: Formulate a series of queries that seek to expose discrimination or disprove its existence in engine returns. For examples of such queries, see Chonka et al. (2023), Noble (2018), Baker and Potts (2013) as well the work of the Guardian journalist, Carole Cadwalladr (2016). Focus on image searches and/or autocompletions in one or more engines. Consider making a list of queries that once returned problematic results and re-running those queries to explore the extent to which they have been remedied or patched, e.g., by producing diversified results (in image search) or suppressing any returns (in autocompletion). Document the findings with screenshots.

4   Personalization. The original filter bubble critique (by Eli Pariser) concerned the distinctive results sets for a query for 'Egypt', one touristic, the other revolutionary. Non-personalized results, created through research browsers or API calls, may not reflect actual engine results seen by users.

Recipe: Formulate a variety of queries (substantive, navigational and/or transactional). Compare search engine results with a research browser installed, and without one. Develop an understanding of the effects of personalization, describing it. For an example, see Puschmann (2017). Document the findings with screenshots.

5   Political bias. Keywords (or frames) may have inbuilt political proclivities and return politically charged results. But what of more neutral words? Especially in the run-up to elections, whose points of view are returned higher or more consistently? How may these be considered political or 'politicizable'?

Recipe: Make a list of election-related issues, candidates and/or parties (keywords). For the issue keywords choose framings of these issues from the left and the right of the political spectrum. Also choose a more neutral framing of each issue. In the US context, an example would be 'gun control', 'second amendment' and 'firearms'. Query these keywords in one or more search engines. Scrutinize up to the top 50 results (may be fewer), characterizing the sources or stories (hosts or webpages) politically. Note the quantities of progressive, conservative and neutral sources, as well as how far they are from the top. For an example, see Torres (2023). Also consider an analytical framework that looks into the extent of junk or misinformation sources. As an example, consider the junk news source classification scheme in Hagen and Jokubauskaitė (2020). For the US, one may consult the scheme employed in Rogers (2020). Document the findings with a spreadsheet where the results of queries are in columns.

6   Which content is moderated? Content moderation, or the practice of applying a set of rules to remove, retain, label or downrank content that is considered offensive or misinformation, may be interrogated through a kind of reverse engineering where one formulates offensive or misinformation queries in order to test the system's content moderation policies. One may also compare the same queries across a number of platforms, or the same queries in one or more platform's geo-located results.

Recipe: How effective is content moderation? Is it over- or under-moderating? In order to answer these questions, make a list of offensive or misinformation queries and search for them in one or more platforms, noting the extent to which one receives 'clean' results, or befouled ones, so to speak. Consider a cross-platform analysis or a cross-geo analysis. In the cross-platform analysis one queries the same terms across multiple platforms, comparing the results. In the cross-geo analysis one queries the same terms in the same platform but for different locations. For example, does Instagram remove content in the UK that is available in Hong Kong? One also may consider controversial queries (e.g., *Zwarte Piet* in the Netherlands), examining the results for blackface (see the interview with Sarah Roberts in Chotiner, 2019). Alternatively, consider studying how well platforms moderate 'algospeak', or code words used to circumvent content moderation. For example, 'unalive me', or #unaliveme, is employed to tag videos discussing suicide and other self-harm topics, because that category is usually heavily moderated. Document the findings with a spreadsheet where the results of queries are columns.

Tools

- Google Bookmarklets, two buttons to be added to the browser to extract in a few clicks a set of Google Search results as CSV, https://medialab.sciencespo.fr/en/tools/google-bookmarklets/
- Zoekplaatje, search engine results scraper, https://github.com/digitalmethodsinitiative/zoekplaatje.

SEARCH AS RESEARCH
Repurposing Google

Transforming the consumer information
appliance into a research machine

Search engine results for repurposing: Google studies and societal search

The chapter is dedicated to the question of search as research, and in particular how Google, the dominant web search engine, may be repurposed as a research machine both for medium as well as social research. After considering the extent to which one is only studying Google when perusing search engine results, ultimately, the goal is to consider how to perform social research with Google, or what, in short, may be termed 'societal search'. Here one would employ Google, in separate exercises elaborated below, for the study of local or national concerns as well as the study of partisanship.

Since the mid-2000s Google has offered so-called local domain Googles, where one performs searches at google.nl (in the Netherlands), google.fr (in France), google.de (in Germany) and so forth (see Figure 6.1); they are also called 'regions' and are accessible via the advanced settings if one is not located in the country corresponding to the local domain Google (Kao, 2017). In other words, the engine user is directed by default to the local domain Google on the basis of their location, read from the IP address or set location preference. After an engine query is made, the results are returned in the local language, as are the advertisements. Google's 'local' also serves its business model, and the results are delivered within national legal jurisdictions, such as European countries where users have the right to oblivion, or certain results removed (Floridi et al., 2015).

Visit Google's Site in Your Local Domain

www.google.ad
Andorra

www.google.ae
United Arab Emirates

www.google.com.af
افغانستان

www.google.com.ag
Antigua and Barbuda

www.google.com.ai
Anguilla

www.google.am
Armenia

www.google.co.ao
Angola

www.google.com.ar
Argentina

www.google.as
American Samoa

www.google.at
Österreich

www.google.com.au
Australia

www.google.az
Azerbaijan

www.google.ba
Bosna i Hercegovina

www.google.com.bd
Bangladesh

www.google.be
Belgium

www.google.bf
Burkina Faso

www.google.bg
България

www.google.com.bh
Bahrain

www.google.bi
Burundi

www.google.bj
Bénin

www.google.com.bn
Brunei

www.google.com.bo
Bolivia

www.google.com.br
Brasil

www.google.bs
The Bahamas

www.google.co.bw
Botswana

www.google.by
Belarus

www.google.com.bz
Belize

www.google.ca
Canada

www.google.cd
Rep. Dem. du Congo

www.google.cf
Centrafrique

www.google.cg
Rep. du Congo

www.google.ch
Switzerland

www.google.ci
Côte d'Ivoire

www.google.co.ck
Cook Islands

www.google.cl
Chile

www.google.cm
Cameroon

www.google.cn
China

www.google.com.co
Colombia

www.google.co.cr
Costa Rica

www.google.com.cu
Cuba

Figure 6.1 Local domain Googles, where one is sent by default when located within that country. The graphic shows how Google globalized, or glocalized, in the sense of making its global product local.

Source: Google language tools, https://web.archive.org/web/20111118022541/www.google.com/language_tools. See also 'See results for a different country', https://support.google.com/websearch/answer/873?hl=en.

Apart from returning advertisements and legal context, local domain Googles also return 'local' results, and the question concerns how the local is epistemologically constituted by Google. Which types of sources are returned (by default as well as by special advanced settings)? In what sense are they local sources, or how to describe Google's sense of local? Thus, prior to being able to conduct social research with Google ('societal search'), one must interrogate the engine's definition of the local, or conduct medium research ('Google studies').

We start thus by examining the utility of Google's sense of the local. Does it enable the study of local (or national) concern? May one ultimately read societal tendencies or trends through search engine returns? These questions are posed so as to develop a new form of search engine critique as well as usage, where search becomes research, or the engine becomes more than an information, advertising and legal machine. Put differently, may one perform social research with Google, or is one always only studying Google?

Google studies or societal search?

The very idea that one may use Google as social research machine is not unusual, when one considers that the science built into its algorithms (and entire apparatus) is in the first instance a variation on citation analysis, adapted to the web (Brin and Page, 1998; Rieder, 2012; Marres, 2017). The difference between the engine as it was and as it grows, however, lies largely in a change in the engine's definition of 'relevance' (Van Couvering, 2007). Where once results were deemed to be the best match between document (page) and subject matter (query) (and ranked by influential inlink counts), increasingly that match has been made less on the basis of content than on other variables, too, such as user clicks, page freshness and domain age. Where it once had little or nothing to do with it, now relevance is in some sense user-driven, or perhaps consumer-driven, if one prefers to emphasize the commercialization of Google's results. More conceptually, search results are a product of our 'living within [Google's] lab', meaning that we as users are all a part of Google's experiments and beta-testing that previously would have been performed in-house, with user groups or with students spot checking results against a list of what would constitute desirable outcomes (Davies, 2015: 377). Results now are adjusted according to how they are actually used rather than arriving preconceived from the beautiful mind alone or tested in-house.

The delivery of relevant pages based on user feedback could be thought of as one means of determining hierarchies of sources and societal concerns. Or such is the question. What sorts of source hierarchies are revealed when studying engine results? Is one able to study societal concern, or is one always only studying Google? In the following the answer lies somewhere in the middle, given that (on the one hand) engine effects are not to be eliminated, but (on the other) may be identified as well as mitigated.

Medium research as Google studies

Below I begin by using the engine for medium research ('Google studies'), before determining how (and whether) it may be used for social research ('societal search'). The Google studies projects ultimately seek to pave the way for societal search.

The first ones concern the types of sites returned in local domain Googles (google.nl, google.be, google.de, google.fr and so forth, now accessible as 'regions' in the advanced settings) and invite questions concerning Google's definition or sense of the 'local'. What is local to Google? Here one is able to critique Google's capacity as research machine for cross-country analysis by showing the extent to which Google returns transnational, regional or some (other) combination of results in its local domain engines. One compares the results of the same query across multiple local domain Googles (see Figure 6.2).

Figure 6.2 Visualization of google.com and google.cn results as technique for comparison.

Source: Langreiter, 2017.

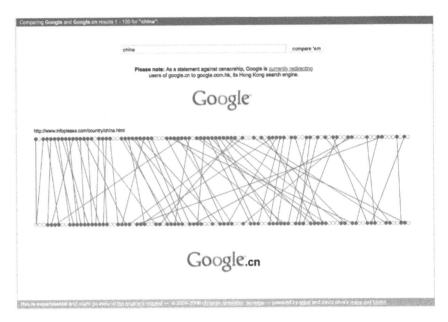

This project is medium research in the sense that the analysis seeks to tease out a Google notion of the local. In this project one queries one ambiguous or underspecified term of relevance in multiple locations or local domains (Rogers, 2013b). The analysis in question queries [diversidad] (or diversity) first in three pertinent local domain Googles (Colombia, Peru and Venezuela, all in the Amazon River basin) and subsequently across Spanish-speaking domains, finding that the vast majority of the results are sources in Spain, rather than from Latin America (see Figure 6.3). Spanish sources are identified not only by the country domain (.es), but also from the 'about us' information as well as the specificity of the Spanish language used on the pages.

In another exercise of this sort [Amazonia] (Amazon) is queried in Spanish-language local domain Googles, and the URLs returned per domain are compared. For Spain (google.es) the results originate largely in Spain. For all the other countries Google provides in each sources from Spain, and the remainder are Latin American results, nearly uniform for each country. It is as if there is a result set for Spain and another one for all of Latin America (see Figure 6.4). Google's local is national for Spain but transnational (and rather colonial) for Latin America, where Spanish sources retain authority. Here one may pursue search engine returns as one expression of the coloniality of knowledge (Grosfoguel, 2004).

Google studies with social research implications

In a comparative source origin project, ['human rights'] is queried in various local domain Googles (in the respective local languages), asking whether the results return local or non-local pages. This undertaking is medium research, or Google studies, but the implications

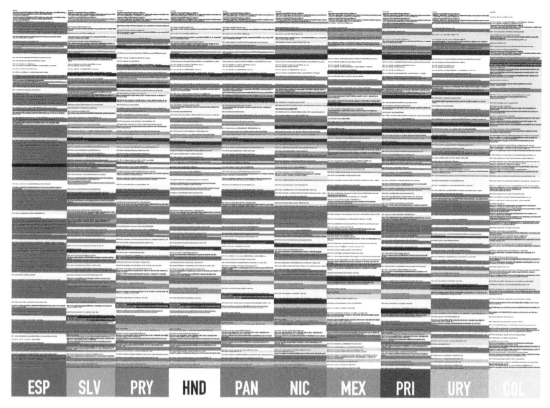

Figure 6.3 Locations of sources compared in local domain Googles in Spanish-speaking countries, where the majority are from Spain. Analysis by Natalia Sanchez Querubin and the Digital Methods Initiative, 2011.

Source: Rogers, 2013b.

begin to fall into the realm of social research or societal search. That is, taking the query into account, one also may ask which countries have well-developed content providers for human rights issues, and which rely on non-local, perhaps even establishment sources. The case study explores the distinctiveness of local results across local domain Googles, with the additional consideration of the type of query made, human rights, which to some is a universal as opposed to local or regional issue, as in the first sample project.

Where are the returned information sources based? The aim is to retrieve the location of the information sources outputted per local domain Google engine. The location of a website may be thought of in a number of ways, including country code top-level domain (ccTLD), registration (site owner's geographical location) and/or host (geographical location where a website is stored) (Sottimano, 2013). In this project location is gleaned from the address of the website's registrant (through the contact address on the website and/or its 'whois' information, when available). 'Local' sources are defined as those registered in the country of the local domain Google (e.g., for the results provided by google.com.eg, the source, anhri.net, is considered 'local' because it is registered in Cairo, Egypt).

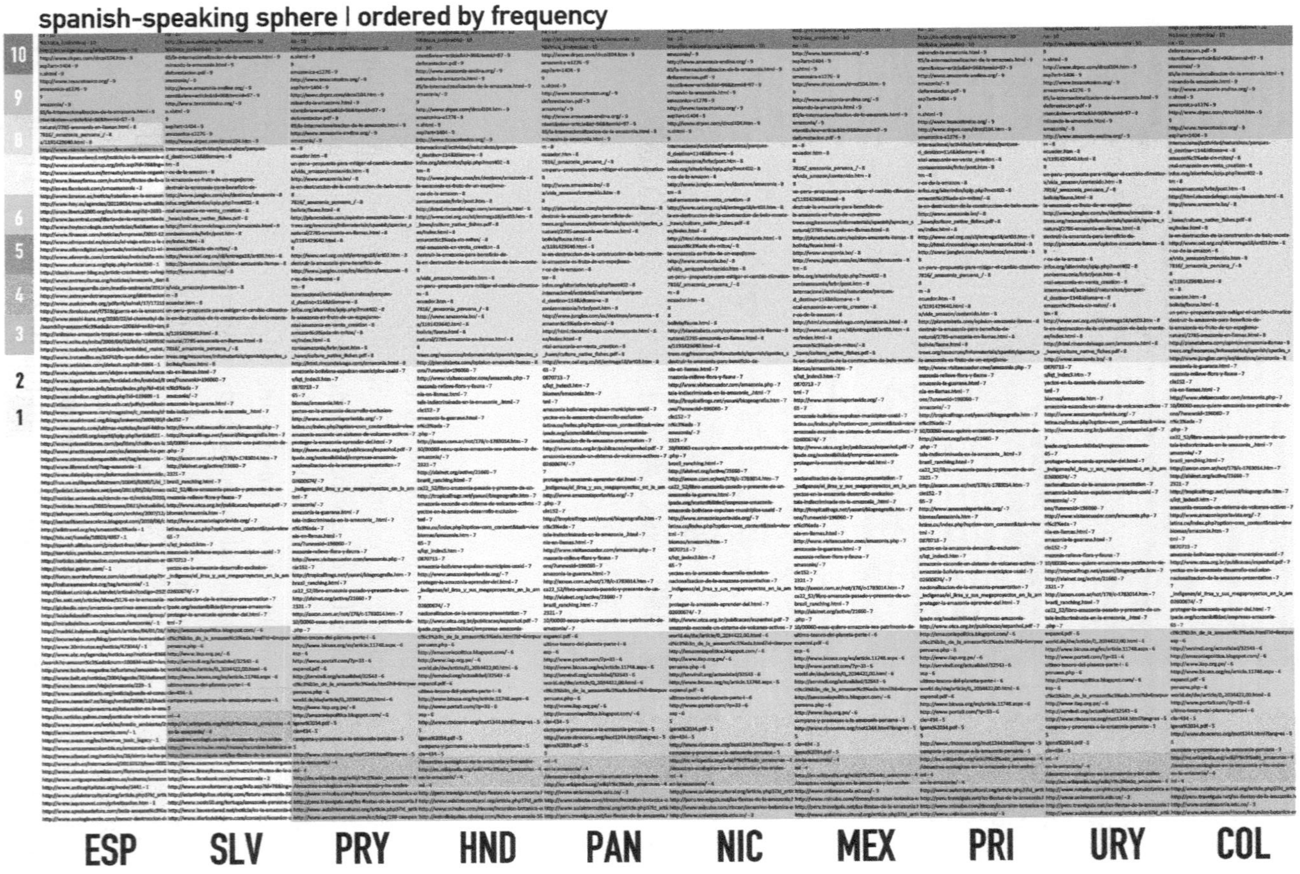
spanish-speaking sphere | ordered by frequency
10
9
8
6
5
4
3
2
1
ESP
SLV
PRY
HND
PAN
NIC
MEX
PRI
URY
COL

Figure 6.4 URLs compared across local domain Googles in Spanish-speaking countries; colours indicate the number of local domain Googles in which a set of results appear. Analysis by Natalia Sánchez Querubín, Diana Mesa and the Digital Methods Initiative, 2011.

Source: Rogers, 2013b.

After the term ['human rights'] is queried in the local language, the top ten information sources are captured and geolocated, and the results visualized on a geographical map (see Figure 6.5). Remarkably, nearly half of the local domain Googles have no local results in the top ten sources returned. When comparing the number of local sources, the uneven distribution across national webs becomes apparent. The countries with the most local

Map generated from the issuegeographer by the Digital Methods Initiative, Amsterdam

Local and International Information Sources
Human Rights Sources According to Local Domain Googles

About this map | Digitalmethods.net

Findings

(**Default to Global**) (Regional Hubs)

The issue of human rights is articulated differently depending on where, and in what language, one searches. The map displays the sources returned for the query 'Human Rights' in over 50 languages and in 135 national and regional Google search engines.

Analysis_ Erik borra, Chris Castiglione, Martin Fuez, Carolyn Gerlitz, Michael Stevenson, Marijn de Vries Hoogerwerf and Esther Weltevrede. Design_Marieke van Dijk. Digital Methods Summer'09

121 Google-language combi

Select a url from the Google countries it was in the top 10

www.un.org (80)
www.ohchr.org (53)
www.hrw.org (43)
en.wikipedia.org (31)
www.hrweb.org (30)
es.wikipedia.org (19)
www.monografias.com (19)
www.derechos.net (17)
www.asil.org (12)
anhri.net (11)
www.unhchr.ch (11)
plato.stanford.edu (11)

Currently seeing all countries their top 10 human rights res

Mouseovers and clicks in the click Deselect All to enable th

Figure 6.5 Bordered sources: local and international information sources. Graphic by Esther Weltevrede and Erik Borra, Digital Methods Initiative, Amsterdam, 2009.

sources are European, some North American, South American and Asian countries. Most countries in the top ranks have location-specific languages. African and Middle Eastern countries are found towards the bottom of the list.

The most prominent information source across 121 national Googles, queried in 43 languages, is un.org, with 80 of the local domain Googles returning un.org as one of the top ten results (see Figure 6.5). In the Arab-speaking Middle East and northern Africa (MENA), local sources (with the exception of anhri.net) are virtually absent (see Figure 6.6). The shared sources are primarily USA-based, and also include the Brazilian NGO, huquqalinsan. com. Half of the sources returned in the Arab-speaking countries are identical; in the 11 national Googles, un.org, arabhumanrights.org, hrw.org, ar.wikipedia.org and anhri.net appear at the top. On a number of the MENA Googles, we found local results on the second page.

Figure 6.6 Bordered *sources*: where are the human rights information sources from Arab-speaking countries based? Graphic by Esther Weltevrede, Digital Methods Initiative, Amsterdam, 2009.

Societal search with Google studies artefacts

This project is principally societal research as we are looking to Google to provide a ranked list of societal concerns per local domain Google. Are there distinctive or similar rights that reach the top in Finland, the Netherlands, France, Italy, Switzerland, Germany, Austria, Sweden, Russia, Japan, Canada, the UK, Australia, the Philippines, the Ivory Coast and other countries?

The first step is to query the term [rights] in the local languages in the local domain Googles, e.g., [õigused] in google.ee, [direitos] in google.pt, etc. One may use a VPN to be located in the country or use the region setting in advance search. The second step is to read and interpret the results and make lists of the top ten distinctive rights types, leaving them in the order that Google provided.

SWEDEN	FINLAND	ESTONIA	LATVIA	UNITED KINGDOM	NETHERLANDS	BELGIUM (Flemish)	BELGIUM (French)
human rights	children's rights	citizen's rights	animal rights	human rights	works council rights	human rights	human rights
patients' rights	everyman's right (freedom to roam)	children's rights	human rights	author's rights	air passengers' rights	disability rights	internet rights
children's rights	animal rights	environmental rights	air passengers' rights	digital rights	children's rights	cyclists' rights	youth rights
air passengers' rights	consumer rights	air passengers' rights	pension rights for non-citizens	minorities' rights	human rights	volunteers' rights	citizen's rights
creator's rights	women's rights	author's rights	immigrants' rights	citizen's rights	minorities' rights	air passengers' rights	intellectual property rights
equal rights	air passengers' rights	patients' rights	copyright	employment rights	prostitutes' rights	works council rights	patients' rights
citizen's rights	renter's rights	property rights	children's rights	publicity rights	taxpayers' rights	children's rights	women's rights
women's rights	patients' rights	landowners' rights	social rights	abortion rights	youth rights	job applicant's rights	children's rights
right of collective bargaining	youth rights	workers' rights	teachers' rights	photographers' rights	islam and women's rights	immigrants' rights	workers' rights
food rights	right to education in native sign language	sexual and health rights	consumer rights	children's rights	author's rights	patients' rights	the right to defend yourself in court

Figure 6.7 The nationality of issues: rights types (excerpt). Digital Methods Initiative, Amsterdam, 2009.

Source: Rogers et al., 2009a.

As noted above, the query design takes advantage of Google as research machine, and particularly its strength in dealing with ambiguous queries such as [rights] rather than its other strength of massive (fresh) site indexing, which is behind a second set of societal search projects below. With respect to its original strength, as Brin and Page (1998: 9) phrase it, 'the benefits of PageRank are the greatest for underspecified queries'. Discrete or less ambiguous keywords would decrease the salubrious algorithmic effects.

When reading and interpreting the results, there are editorial decisions to be taken with respect to Google artefacts. Since the effort is to mitigate them (for societal search) rather than to highlight them (for Google studies), artefacts, however fascinating, may be removed.

For example, Wikipedia is a top result or nearly so for most Google region queries. Another Google artefact is the result R.I.G.H.T.S. (rightsforartists.com) in google.com. It is a Google artefact in the sense that it highlights how Google relies on certain 'signals' to boost websites in the rankings (Dean, 2016). Among other indicators of how Google boosts sites, the word 'rights' is part of the URL, and R.I.G.H.T.S. is in the page header.

In the findings, rendered as labelled icons, countries could be said to have diverging hierarchies of concerns per (Google) country (see Figure 6.7). For example, everyman's rights in Finland, prostitutes' rights in the Netherlands, computer programmers' rights in Japan and the right to oblivion in Italy (the right to have personal data deleted) are unique to the respective countries. The order of appearance per country invariably differs.

Given the focus on cultural distinctiveness, it should be noted that the specific issue language per country is retained, rather than grouped as equivalents. Thus, LGBT rights in the United States and homosexual rights in Hong Kong are not considered the same. Indeed, one could make a small sub-study of the terms (and thus inclusiveness) across the local domain Googles for these particular rights as well as others.

In all, the short case study starting with the underspecified query, [rights], has found distinctiveness between rights types and rights hierarchies across the local domain Googles. One could consider techniques to harden these findings, such as making these queries in other search engines as well as other means of grounding the findings online. It is also a thought piece for discussing rights types cross-culturally.

Google studies and societal search combined: Source distance and partisanship detection

Google, as related above, creates hierarchies of credibility through returning ranked sources for a query. When the query is substantive, such as ['climate change'], sources at the top are given the privilege of providing information on the matter of concern, while others lower down are less likely to be read. Here the question concerns the distance from the top that partisan sites appear, giving voice to a particular side or position. The case in question is the climate change issue. Partisanship concerns giving voice, or a platform on its website, to climate change sceptics. Which sites mention the sceptics, and quote and represent their viewpoints? Are they close to the top of the engine returns for the query ['climate change']? Source distance is medium research, as it asks whether the web via Google (or Google in particular) gives the sceptics top-ranked space.

Indeed, in the first instance, it could be said that we are studying Google. Query Google and consider whether the engine's ranking procedures place sceptic-friendly websites towards the top of the climate change space.

It is a two-step query design (see sample project below). First, query ['climate change'] and save the results. Subsequently, keeping the results in the order they appeared, query each individual result for names of climate change sceptics, through [site:] queries, or the use of the advanced setting 'search one site'. Visualize where the sceptics appear in the top results (see Figure 6.8). (Such work also may be performed with the Lippmannian Device, also discussed below.) The sceptics are represented in a few sites returned (in the first 50 or so) but not at the very top. Put differently, in the journalistic convention both sides of the story are represented, but in the climate change space provided by Google the sceptics' presence is relatively scant, it was found.

When considering the results anew, however, it also could be said that we are undertaking social research as we are considering the presence of sceptics in the climate change source space more generally, and we are identifying specific sources where they are present. Without considering positive or negative mentions, one is studying the 'impact' of the sceptics – whether their overall presence is felt. One is also able to evaluate sources according to sceptic mentions. After closer reading, one notes there are sceptic-friendly 'science' websites as well as sceptic-funders. Another website type where sceptics appear is a watchdog site, with critical mentions of the sceptics. There are also those that do not name sceptics, providing no mentions. Through sceptic presence and absence source evaluation and characterization are performed.

Figure 6.8 Top climate change sources on the web, according to Google Web Search, resized according to the quantity of mentions of a climate change sceptic. Output of the Lippmannian Device and Tag Cloud Generator, Digital Methods Initiative, Amsterdam.

Source: Rogers, 2013b.

Conclusions: Repurposing Google results

Above the question was posed concerning the capacity of Google to serve as a research machine, despite becoming a consumer information appliance (as well as a national advertising and legal machine) over the past two decades. Google is still a research machine in how it allows for foraging through online information as its creators envisioned in their seminal paper (Brin and Page, 1998). In the search engine critique that has since arisen, related in the previous chapter, it also has evolved into a hegemon (market-wise), 'Googlizing' industries and public resources (such as libraries and art institutions). It has purportedly had cognitive impacts (as illustrated by the coinage of 'flickering man'). Rather than an equalizer, it boosts, both through its original algorithmic innovations as well as its subsequent tweaks, the rich and now the popular. As an advertising company, Google also has been described as a front-page real estate hog, populating search engine results pages with its own properties, as well as a surveillance machine, inviting privacy-enhancing technologies that mask and obfuscate users as well as competitors such as DuckDuckGo that trades on privacy. Google also captures users, nudging one to stay logged in, so disentangling oneself from the device is burdensome.

But because Google recursively collects a user's data and recommends URLs on the basis of its 'knowledge' of the user, a researcher could consider avoiding obfuscation techniques such as 'track me not' or others (Howe et al., 2011; Kurt, 2016), as they would potentially sully the engine results (garbage in, garbage out). Another approach would be having few traces available in the first place.

By installing a separate instance of a browser (such as Firefox) as a 'research browser', the researcher prepares a clean slate, free of cookies and other engine entanglements such as history and preferences. If one has a Google account, disable customized results, an option in one's web history. ('Do not track' could be enabled.) If one does not have a Google account, the Google cookies should be removed and not allowed to be set. The slate is cleaner (rather than completely refreshed) because Google by default serves localized results zoomed in to a city or similar. In the advanced settings, change the setting to a region (where there is a country drop-down list to choose from). Now results should be rather depersonalized.

Once a browser is so prepared, the work to undertake medium and social research commences. As indicated, medium research concerns engine effects on sources (including their placement in returns), whereas social research is conceived of as source evaluation with the aid of the engine.

To be clear, here we are turning the tables on Google, seeking to use it as a research machine – making social studies via or on top of engines – rather than being used by it as a subject of surveillance and targeted advertising. As you work, be aware that researching with Google requires vigilance, for the engine is continually striving to know you, and customize the results.

PROJECTS

Determine the impact of climate change sceptics using search engine results

RESEARCH GOAL To show the impact of climate change sceptics through their quantity of hits and their distance from the top of search engine results in a set of sources on climate change (e.g., the top 100 Google returns for the query ['climate change']).

1 Make a list of climate change sceptics. There is a variety of sources that provide lists of the names of climate change sceptics, as well as the organizations that sponsor them. One may triangulate expert lists or make a list based on an associative query snowballing, as explained in the query design chapter. One may also make a list on the basis of the keynote speakers and/or attendees of climate change sceptics conferences.

2 Set Google preferences to return 100 results. Query ['climate change'] in google.com.

3 Retain as a list the top 100 Google results. Use the Google Bookmarklets, https://medialab. sciencespo.fr/en/tools/google-bookmarklets/.

4 Extract hosts. Paste that text into the Harvester, a separate tool at http://tools.digitalmethods. net/beta/harvestUrls/. Choose as output 'exclude URLs from Google and YouTube', 'only return hosts' and 'only return uniques', meaning unique hosts will be returned and later queried (e.g., www.epa.gov, rather than www3.epa.gov/climatechange//kids/index.html).

5 Select and copy the list of hosts into the top box of the Google Scraper.

6 In the bottom box of the Google Scraper, enter the keywords (i.e., a list of climate change sceptics), one per line. Place the names in quotation marks.

7 Select the number of desired results (1–100). Use a smaller number for presence/absence analysis per source and a larger number of results if there is an expectation that most sources mention the keyword. Name the output file and press Scrape Google (or Scrape Search Results on the Search Engine Scraper, with Google selected; if Google does not allow the scrape, try Bing or another search engine).

8 Keep the Google Scraper window open, and wait until the scrape is completed (i.e., until the output file is available). If a pop-up window appears, type in the captcha and close the pop-up window, and the Scraper will resume.

9 View the results as a source cloud. View multiple sources and single issue for a source cloud of each sceptic. View multiple sources and multiple issues for a source cloud of all sceptics.

10 View visualization for source distance or partisanship (see Figure 6.8).

Choose 'order of input in Google Scraper' to view how close to the top of the Google results the sceptic or sceptics resonate (source distance). Choose cloud output 'ordered by size' for a hierarchy of sources mentioning one or more sceptics, with those sources mentioning one or more sceptics the most at the top (impact and partisanship research).

In the sample project, it was found that there is distance between the sceptics and the top of the search engine returns (see Figure 6.8). Note that few sceptics appear on the websites of the top ten results in Google. When they do appear, their resonance is not particularly resounding.

One may evaluate sources according to the frequency with which each mentions the sceptics. There are sceptic-friendly sites, and less sceptic-friendly sites. From the visualization one is able to see the sceptic-friendly sources, such as realclimate.org and, to a lesser extent, climatescience.gov. Sourcewatch also is prominent, albeit as a progressive watchdog group 'exposing' the sceptics.

Remarkably, news sites, generally speaking, do not mention the climate change sceptics by name. While news watchers and listeners may have the impression that 'uncertainty' in the climate change 'debate' continues in a general sense (as opposed to, say, in more specific, scientific sub-discussions), 'uncertainty' appears to be discussed without resort to the well-known, or identified, sceptics.

With respect to the implications of the findings, one question concerns the extent to which the web stages climate change as a controversy *vis-à-vis* other media spaces, such as the news. Here the web is understood as a search-based medium, and controversy as the relative penetration of the sceptics in the climate change search results space. A comparison between the sceptics' resonance on the web and in the news could be a next step.

Video tutorial

For the project on source distance, watch the video on how to operate the Google Scraper.

* The Search Engine Scraper and Lippmannian Device (13'28'), www.youtube.com/watch?v= hIPTrTM53ho

Tools

* 'Google Scraper', digitalmethods.net. Available at https://wiki.digitalmethods.net/Dmi/Tool GoogleScraper
* Zoekplaatje, search engine results scraper, https://github.com/digitalmethodsinitiative/zoekplaatje

Google studies with the Google Scraper and societal search with the Lippmannian Device

There is a series of further assignment options, where we are researching how (and for whom) Google works, or societal trends with Google. One option (set out in considerable detail below) compares the results pages of local domain Googles, so as to provide an understanding of Google's sense of the local and discuss the implications of that understanding. In the second option, one employs the engine to output hierarchies of societal (or organizational) concern, following one of the Lippmannian Device research protocols below.

Before choosing one of the options, consider whether you wish to study the medium, some combination of the medium and societal trends, or societal trends. Generally, medium research here is considered to be diagnosing how Google works. Techniques are described for studying Google's sense of the local, comparative source origin and societal search (with Google artefacts considered). Doing medium studies of Google would be teasing out Google's sense of the local. A combination of medium studies and social research would be to diagnose how Google works and consider the societal implications such as which types of sources are privileged, and which ones are buried. Finally, studying societal trends refers to relying on Google's rankings either through substantive, underspecified queries such as [rights] or by working with the Lippmannian Device to identify how close to the top are the sceptics in the climate change space, or the global human rights agenda (to name two specific examples).

PROJECTS

Investigate Google's sense of 'the local'

RESEARCH GOAL To ascertain Google's sense of the local by comparing the results of pages of local domain Googles (otherwise known as Google 'regions').

1   Query design. With respect to choice of term, choose a discrete term, and substantiate your choice (e.g., an unambiguous or underspecified query term). Use an unambiguous term such as [Amazonia] for the question of which sources dominate the results across Latin American countries (i.e., Google regions). Use an underspecified term such as [rights] for the question of which rights are dear per country (i.e., Google region).

2   Language. Apart from dictionaries, there are at least three options to translate a term between languages. Use languages that are available to you or your group, use Google Translate, or use 'languages' in the left-side column of Wikipedia articles.

3   Selection of Google regions to be queried. For the [Amazonia] query, the Google regions may be countries that are in the Amazon River basin, or Latin American countries more broadly. For the [rights] query, the sources may be varied and numerous. Consider building in comparison or contrast into your Google region selection, such as all former Soviet countries (where some are now in the European Union). Unless you use a research browser, and specific (re)search settings, Google will auto-detect your location, and privilege city-level results.

4   Query the term in local language(s) per Google region. Use Google advanced search, setting language and region.

5   Saving results. Set your preferences to the number of returns you wish to save. In your browser, choose File > Save as > html, and name your file using a naming convention such as BE_rechten_50_1DEC2019, where BE is the Belgian Google region, [rechten] the query,

50 the results count and finally the date of the query, with the month indicated in letters in order to avoid confusion between US and Western European date formatting conventions.

6   Analysing search engine results pages: source origin and categorization.

a   There are multiple techniques for locating the 'origin' of a source: country domain (ccTLD), 'whois' information of the site registrant, and the contact information located on the websites. For the [Amazonia] query, the origins of the sources constitute the analytical question concerning Google's sense of the local.

b   Categorization – keyword specificity and A/B schemes. For the [rights] query, the specific rights privileged per country are of interest, such as the 'right to roam' in Finland. Here it is important to retain specificity and resist the urge to group similar rights under umbrella terms. For the [Amazonia] query, one could consider employing an A/B scheme (presence or absence; programme or anti-programme), such as the presence of extractive industries in the top ten results per country.

c   Categorization – source types in the results. For the [Amazonia] query, one may be interested in the presence of non-governmental or more specifically environmental sources in the results per country, or of non-Latin American results. One may glean source types from the top-level and second-level domains. See Wikipedia's articles on 'Top-level domain' and 'Second-level domain' for country-specific ones. For a finer-grained sense of the source type, peruse the 'about' page. One may pose critical questions of the dominance of one source type over another, inquiring into which sites have the privilege of being top sources, and providing information. For example, a ['climate change'] query may be dominated by intergovernmental sites, governmental agencies, NGOs and news outlets, while academic sources may be largely absent.

For finer-grained categorizations, consider using the 'other' category for items that do not fit the scheme, rather than 'neutral' which itself could be efforts made by actors (see the query design chapter).

7   Visualizing the findings. For the [Amazonia] query, a spreadsheet has Latin American countries as columns and source origin countries as rows. The 'visualization' is a colour-coded spreadsheet. For the [rights] query, per country (i.e., Google region), there is a list of rights types that have been artfully rendered as icons. One may consider using the triangulation tool, which takes lists of items as inputs and outputs commonalities and unique items.

The tag cloud generator at tools.digitalmethods.net provides a means to visualize hierarchies. If using an online tag cloud generator, consider outputting all words horizontally and ordering them by frequency.

One also may consider populating a world map.

8   Drawing conclusions. Note that there are generally three discussions: medium research, some combination of medium and societal research, and societal research only, so to speak. For

medium research, one is critiquing Google's sense of the local. If one chooses the combination of medium and societal research, the discussion could concern the extent to which Google is a globalizing or localizing machine, and the related issue of whether it may be used as a research machine, under what conditions and to what ends. If one is undertaking societal research, the capacity of Google to render countries' significant rights types becomes meaningful.

Video tutorials

There is a series of videos on how to transform Google into a research machine, set up a query, localize the outputs of a query and compare multiple results.

* 'The Research Browser' (1'35'), www.youtube.com/watch?v=bj65Xr9GkJM
* 'Google Research Settings' (3'48'), www.youtube.com/watch?v=Zk5Q_3g86qM
* 'Comparing Lists with the Triangulation Tool' (2'54'), www.youtube.com/watch?v=jg9UzKcuuOE
* 'Localizing Web Sources' (4'08'), www.youtube.com/watch?v=lyNMDUSBd9s

Consider watching a more general tutorial on analysing engine results in three ways:

* 'Analysing Engine Results: Organization Types, Hierarchies of Concern, Political Leanings' (3'50'), www.youtube.com/watch?v=MsnSJPXpFno

Tools

* Search Engine Scraper (and Google Scraper), digitalmethods.net. Available at https://wiki.digitalmethods.net/Dmi/ToolGoogleScraper
* Harvester, digitalmethods.net. Available at https://tools.digitalmethods.net/beta/harvestUrls/
* Triangulation, digitalmethods.net. Available at https://tools.digitalmethods.net/beta/triangulate/
* Google Bookmarklets, medialab.sciencespo.fr, two buttons to be added to the browser to extract in a few clicks a set of Google Search results as CSV. Available at https://medialab.sciencespo.fr/en/tools/google-bookmarklets/
* Zoekplaatje, search engine results scraper, https://github.com/digitalmethodsinitiative/zoekplaatje

Resources

* Google Translate, google.com. Available at http://translate.google.com/
* 'Top 50 Sites on the Web by Country', similarweb.com. Available at www.similarweb.com/top-websites/

PROJECTS

Map and interpret bias with the Lippmannian Device

RESEARCH GOAL Determine source partisanship (side-taking) as well as its distribution of concern.

The Google Scraper, when used principally for societal search, is also referred to as the Lippmannian Device. There are two overall use cases for the Lippmannian Device: source partisanship and source distribution of concern. For source partisanship, the question concerns the detection of side-taking by a particular source through its mentioning or failure to mention specific issue language. Above it was noted that particular organizations mentioned the climate change sceptics while others averred. For research on the distribution of concern one is often given a list of issues that a particular organization engages in, advocates for, or otherwise 'does'. The question is whether certain organizations show attention to particular issues (over other issues) through frequency of mentions on their websites. Here one relies on Google's second strength (massive, presentist site indexing) and renders a distribution of attention to a set of issues.

Lippmannian Device?

As a term the Lippmannian Device refers to a piece of equipment for mapping and interpreting bias, or, as indicated, it may be employed to gain a rough sense of a source's partisanship and distribution of concerns. It is named after Walter Lippmann, the American journalism scholar who in his *Public Opinion* book of 1922, and particularly in his sequel to it of 1927, *The Phantom Public*, called for a coarse means of showing actor partisanship:

> The problem is to locate by clear and coarse objective tests the actor in a controversy who is most worthy of public support. (Lippmann, 1927: 120)

> The signs are relevant when they reveal by coarse, simple and objective tests which side in a controversy upholds a workable social rule, or which is attacking an unworkable rule, or which proposes a promising new rule. By following such signs the public might know where to align itself. In such an alignment it does not... pass judgment on the intrinsic merits. (Lippmann, 1927: 120)

The device does not answer all of Lippmann's calls, though it seeks to begin with them by addressing a seminal Lippmannian sense (partisanship) as well as an extended one (distribution of partisanship). It also advances the calls by Lippmann, in an attempt to enrich the partisanship notion with the idea of distribution of concern on the part of actors. They may have a list of campaigns or issues they are working on, but which garner more returns? The Lippmannian device queries Google, in a two-step process, and makes the results available in issue or source clouds (as well as in a spreadsheet).

Lippmannian Device project: Source clouds for the display of partisanship

The Lippmannian Device may be used to create source clouds that reveal partisanship towards a particular issue. With the tool, one may query a list of sources for one particular issue, or for a set of issues (keywords). Which source mentions 'security fence', which 'apartheid wall' and which neither (for the barrier between Israel and the Palestinian territories)? Source clouds display sources, each resized according to the number of mentions of a particular issue, according to Google.

Here is an example of employing the Lippmannian Device to study the 'synthetic biology' issue. Craig Venter has been considered a somewhat polarizing figure in the issue space, given that the science in his work often serves commercial interests and the (best-known) work itself is often construed as 'patenting life' (Glasner and Rothman, 2017). Thus we will ask which actors appear sympathetic to Craig Venter in the synthetic biology space.

Automated method

1   Set Google preferences to return 100 results. Query ['synthetic biology'] in Google.
2   Select and copy the top 100 Google results. That is, on the Google results page, select all results (avoid the sponsored results), right-click and use 'view selection source' (in Firefox) and then copy the highlighted text.
3   Paste that text into the Harvester, a separate tool. Choose as output 'exclude URLs from Google and YouTube', 'only return hosts' and 'only return uniques' – meaning unique hosts will be returned and later queried.
4   Select and copy the results into the top box of the Lippmannian Device.
5   In the bottom box of the Lippmannian Device, enter the keyword [Venter] or, for greater specificity, ['Craig Venter'].
6   Select the number of desired results (1–1000). Use a larger number of results if there is an expectation that most sources mention the keyword. Name the output file and press Scrape Google.
7   Keep the Scraper browser window open and wait until the scrape is completed (i.e., until the output file is available). If a pop-up window appears, type in the captcha and close the pop-up window, and the Scraper will resume.
8   View the source cloud results – multiple sources and single issue.
9   View different orderings. Choose cloud output 'ordered by size' for a hierarchy of sources mentioning Venter, with those sources mentioning Venter the most at the top (see Figure 6.9).

Manual method

1   Query Google for ['synthetic biology']. Save results. Commit each host in the results to a row in a spreadsheet.

2   Query each individual result in the top 100 for 'Craig Venter'. Use 'site' queries: [site:www.synbioproject.tech 'Craig Venter']. For each host queried, place actual and optionally estimated result count in spreadsheet.

3   Show the quantity of mentions of Craig Venter in top sources on synthetic biology with a source cloud. Resize sources (e.g., synbioproject.tech) according to the number of mentions.

You may wish to consider normalizing the findings on the basis of the overall sizes of the websites.

Figure 6.9 Craig Venter's presence in the Synthetic Biology issue space, March 2008. Top sources on 'synthetic biology' according to a Google query, with number of mentions of Venter per source. Source cloud ordered by frequency of mentions. Output by the Lippmannian Device, Digital Methods Initiative, Amsterdam.

nature.com (200) ncbi.nlm.nih.gov (200) nytimes.com (200) sciencemag.org (200) genome.org (200) biomedcentral.com (200) jcvi.org (191) berkeley.edu (191) etcgroup.org (126) connotea.org (104) physorg.com (80) lbl.gov (67) lse.ac.uk (63) rachel.org (53) sciencedaily.com (45) springer.com (38) boingboing.net (34) sciam.com (33) innovationwatch.com (28) economist.com (21) embl.org (14) sciencefriday.com (12) parliament.uk (11) bio.davidson.edu (10) bbsrc.ac.uk (9) foresight.org (8) springerlink.com (7) commondreams.org (7) paraschopra.com (7) eetimes.com (6) labtechnologist.com (5) selectbiosciences.com (4) lewrockwell.com (3) nestconference.com (1) esf.org (1) eecs.mit.edu (0) jbioleng.org (0) qb3.org (0) ietdl.org (0)

Lippmannian Device project: Issue clouds for concern distribution

The Lippmannian Device can also be used to create issue clouds that can reveal varying levels of concern by one or more sources. With the tool, one may query one or multiple sources for a set of issues or keywords. For example, Greenpeace International lists several issues for which it campaigns. Are there particular ones that are granted more attention (and perhaps resources)? Issue clouds display the campaign issues, each resized according to the number of mentions on the website (according to Google).

Another case in question are the issues listed by an NGO, Public Knowledge, dedicated to digital rights. Having copied and pasted their issues into the Lippmannian Device, and querying via Google publicknowledge.org for each issue separately, one may gain a sense of a distribution of concern. Here the next step may be to ground the findings with the actor itself and/or compare them to a larger agenda of the (digital rights) field.

1   Extract issues for the NGO by finding and copying its issue list. Public Knowledge's issue list is at www.publicknowledge.org.

Copy and paste the issue list to the bottom box of the Lippmannian Device, one issue per line, placing quotation marks around multiple-worded issues. An issue such as 'Digital Millennium Copyright Act (DMCA)' could be inputted as follows:

'Digital Millennium Copyright Act' OR DMCA

'700 MHz Spectrum Auction' OR 'Spectrum Auction'

'Anti-Counterfeiting Trade Agreement'

'Broadband'

'Broadband Stimulus'

'Broadcast Flag'

'Comcast Complaint'

'Copyright'

'National Broadband Plan'

'Network Neutrality'

'Open Access to Research'

'Opening the White Space'

'Orphan Works'

'Patent Reform'

'Selectable Output Control'

'Text Message Petition'

'Trademark'

'WiFi Municipal Services'

'WIPO Broadcasters Treaty'

2   Place Public Knowledge's URL in the top box of the Lippmannian Device, www.
    publicknowledge.org.
3   Select the number of desired results (1–1000). Use a larger number of results if there is an
    expectation that the source mentions the issues in great quantity. For the public knowledge
    case, the setting 1000 results is entered. Name the output file (e.g., publicknowledge_
    issues_1DEC2019), and press Scrape Google.
4   Keep the Scraper browser window open, and wait until the scrape is completed (i.e., until the
    output file is available). If a pop-up window appears, type in the captcha and close the pop-up
    window, and the Scraper will resume.
5   View the issue cloud results. View issues per source. Choose cloud output 'ordered by size' for
    Public Knowledge's issue hierarchy (see Figure 6.10).

Video tutorials

There are videos on how to extract URLs from a web page and how to operate the Lippmannian
Device.

* 'Extracting URLs from a Web Page via the URL Harvester' (1'25'), www.youtube.com/watch?v=
  kzaq9DXfO_g
* The Search Engine Scraper and Lippmannian Device (13'28'), www.youtube.com/watch?v=
  hIPTrTM53ho

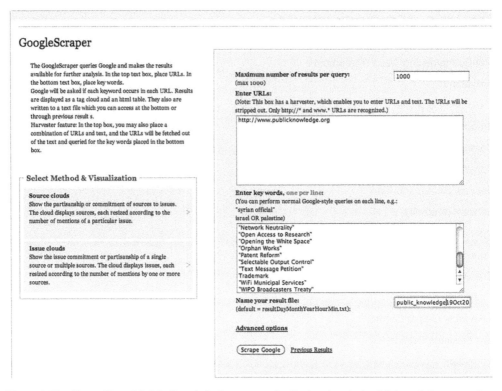

Figure 6.10   The making of Public Knowledge's concern distribution. Input of publicknowledge.org and its issues into Lippmannian Device. Output rendered as word cloud, showing the lower six issues on Public Knowledge's issue list, ranked according to number of mentions of its website according to Google site search, 2 October 2009. Output by the Lippmannian Device, Digital Methods Initiative, Amsterdam.

Tools

- Lippmannian Device, digitalmethods.net. Available at https://tools.digitalmethods.net/beta /lippmannianDevice/

SEVEN

CULTURAL POINTS OF VIEW
Comparing Wikipedia language versions

The counter-intuitive consideration of Wikipedia
as source for cultural particularism

Wikipedia as cultural reference

The chapter is dedicated to the study of Wikipedia as cultural reference. On the face of it, such an approach to Wikipedia appears counter-intuitive, or even a category mistake, as Wikipedia is meant to be an online equivalent to and extension of an encyclopedia, with principles and standards that would prevent articles from being particularistic or parochial. One is not meant to read an encyclopedia, even one with distinctive language versions, for cultural points of view. Wikipedia articles follow core principles that would remove any perspectives or points of view that are not construed as neutral. The articles also are meant to be universal, or 'global', in their outlook. For example, the instructive 'globalize' template, similar to the scores of other banners placed on articles that are deemed to require editing work, points up the kind of view that Wikipedia articles should attain, and would err when they do not: 'The examples and perspectives in this article may not represent a worldwide view' (see Figure 7.1). In other words, articles should be drained of (national) cultural perspective, and arguably over time would have any perspective contained therein smoothed over, whereupon the template would be removed.

Figure 7.1 'Template:Globalize', Wikipedia, https://en.wikipedia.org/wiki/Template:Globalize.

Moreover, articles should season, even mellow, eventually becoming emblematic 'featured articles' that, apart from being 'well-written', 'comprehensive', 'well-researched' and 'neutral', are also 'stable', meaning that they are not subject to edit wars or dispute (Wikipedia Contributors, 2018b). As Jimmy Wales, the founder, put it during a fundraising drive: 'one person writes something, somebody improves it a little, and it keeps getting better, over time' (Wikimedia, 2010).

Generally, Wikipedia articles follow principles that seek to prevent specific viewpoints and bias and stabilize. They should have a neutral point of view, 'representing fairly, proportionately, and as far as possible without bias, all significant views that have been published by reliable sources' (Wikipedia Contributors, 2018c). They should be verifiable, with references made in the articles to reliable sources, often with outlinks. The verifiability principle means that articles are anchored by recognized knowledge. Wikipedia's third core principle is that the articles should contain no original research, however much it may be factual. One should be able to look up, outside of Wikipedia, the subject matter and contents of articles.

Counter-intuitively, then, this chapter discusses the specificity of Wikipedia language versions, such as quantities of unique articles, distinctive editing cultures as well as software projects that identify and highlight incompatibilities (so to speak) between them. The differences between the Bosnian, Serbian and Dutch language versions of articles on Srebrenica serve as a case study for the study of Wikipedia as 'cultural reference'; mention is also made of the differences between the German and Polish Auschwitz articles. The overall purpose of comparative Wikipedia language article analysis is to tease out cultural difference (both manually and with comparison tools), and ultimately account for it.

Wikipedia as reference work

In order to contextualize the very idea of Wikipedia as cultural reference, it is of interest to discuss the online encyclopedia as reference more generally, and how it has been the subject of empirical study of its contents. It should be mentioned at the outset that Wikipedians have set up a project on the encyclopedia's so-called systemic bias, which is described as Western in terms of both the distribution of quality and sheer volume of articles (Livingstone, 2010; Graham, 2011; Hargittai and Shaw, 2015; Wikipedia Contributors, 2018d). The main empirical work (and to an extent the critique of Wikipedia) follows from certain qualities of the online encyclopedia, all of which capture the improbability of the project *in toto* upon first inspection.

One is that Wikipedia is authored by 'amateurs' (or volunteers), who 'work' gratis, pointing up the significance of the empowerment of everyday web users as 'editors', who previously were shut out of content contribution by so-called old media gatekeepers (Baker, 2008; Reagle, 2008). While the work could be considered volunteering, it also makes Wikipedia more and more valuable (e.g., for attracting donations and building an endowment), thereby opening up the online encyclopedia to critique as accruing value from free labour (Terranova, 2003). The value 'gifted' to users, however, could be said to be much greater than that gained by Wikipedia or its foundation.

ERRORS IDENTIFIED: ENCYCLOPAEDIA BRITANNICA

Agent Orange

1. A very minor error is that Agent Orange is considered by the Vietnamese to be the cause of the diseases listed in the second paragraph from the 1970s to the present, not just from the 1970s to the '90s.
2. The entry should include the statement that other mixtures containing dioxin were also sprayed, including Agents Purple, Pink and Green, albeit in lesser amounts.

Aldol

1. The aldol REACTION is not the same as the aldol CONDENSATION.
2. Sodium hydroxide is by no means the only base to be used in the aldol and acid catalysed aldol reactions also occur (usually with concomitant loss of water).
3. The reaction steps in the second reaction sequence should be equilibria up to the dehydration step.
4. In particular, there is no mention of the acid catalysed process and scant mention of related reactions

Archimedes Principle

Reviewer: Prof. Timothy J. Pedley, G. I. Taylor Professor of Fluid Dynamics, University of Cambridge, UK.

1. In the fourth sentence the word 'floating' is used to mean 'at rest' and does not necessarily mean that in common parlance.
2. The very last sentence is true only for an object at rest; when a body is moving there are pressure forces, as well as viscous stresses, associated with the motion.

Australopithecus africanus

1. Dart did not find the fossil. It was brought to him by others.

Bethe, Hans

1. It should say that Bethe was dismissed from his post in Germany in 1933 because his mother was Jewish.

Cambrian Explosion

1. "Numerically dominant" [and in passing note this is not defined: species? individuals?] forms in the Cambrian are arthropods and sponges; neither phylum "became extinct".

ERRORS IDENTIFIED: WIKIPEDIA

Agent Orange

1. This entry implies that it was the herbicides that are problematic, which is not the case. It was dioxin, a byproduct of manufacture of 2,4,5-T that is of concern. Dioxin is persistent in the environment and in the human body, whereas the herbicides are not. In addition, there was a significant amount of dioxin in Agents Purple, Pink and Green, all of which contained 2, 4, 5 - T as well. However, we have less information on these compounds and they were used in lesser quantities.
2. The entry is on the verge of bias, at least. By use of the word "disputedly" in the second sentence there is at least an implication that the evidence of harm to exposed persons is in question. That is not the case, and the World Health Organization has identified dioxin as a "known human carcinogen", and other organizations such as the US National Academy of Sciences has documented harmful effects to US Air Force personnel.

Aldol

1. The mechanisms of base and acid catalysed aldol reactions should have every step as an equilibrium process
2. The acid catalysed process should include the dehydration step, which occurs spontaneously under acid conditions and, being effectively irreversible, pulls the equilibrium through to product.
3. The statement that LDA is avoided at all possible as it is difficult to handle is rubbish. Organic chemists routinely use this reagent – which they either make as required or use commercially available material.

Archimedes Principle

Reviewer: Prof. Timothy J. Pedley, G. I. Taylor Professor of Fluid Dynamics, University of Cambridge, UK.

1. In the section on acceleration and energy, which discusses how a body moves when it is not neutrally buoyant, it is rightly stated that the acceleration of a body experiencing a non-zero net force is not the same as in a vacuum, because some of the surrounding fluid has to be accelerated as well. However, it is implied that the mass of fluid that has to be added to that of the body, in using Newton's Law to calculate the acceleration, is equal to the mass of fluid displaced. This is not in general true - for example, the added mass for an immersed sphere is half the mass of fluid displaced.
2. The entry is rather imprecise. In line 3, for example, the object is said to "float" if the buoyancy exceeds the weight, so here "float" must mean "rise" and not "stay at the same level", which is probably not what was intended because the word has the other meaning in the second paragraph of the section on "Density".

Figure 7.2 Errors identified in the same entries in Wikipedia and *Encyclopaedia Britannica*, 2005.

Source: Giles, 2005.

While edited by volunteers, Wikipedia is surprisingly encyclopedia-like, not only in form but also in accuracy (see Figure 7.2). The major debate concerning the quality of Wikipedia compared to *Encyclopaedia Britannica* (and other reference works) has been the source of repeated scrutiny, not only in the famous article published in the journal, *Nature*, where it was found (and trumpeted in headlines) that Wikipedia is nearly as accurate as *Britannica* (Giles, 2005). It also has been the subject of subsequent analysis and follow-up work by information and library scientists, where most found that Wikipedia was less accurate (and far more prone to glaring errors) than *Britannica*, *Encarta*, the *Dictionary of American History* and the *American National Biography Online*, to name certain of the sources for the comparative analysis (Rosenzweig, 2006; Rector, 2008).

Figure 7.4   The publishing project, The Iraq War: A Historiography of Wikipedia Changelogs, 2006–2009.

Source: Bridle, 2010.

Figure 7.3   Featured articles in English-language Wikipedia collected, laid out, printed and bound.

Source: Matthews, 2009.

Of course, Wikipedia is much larger in scope than the other reference works, and uneven in quality, with certain subject matters (such as contemporary events) enjoying far greater coverage and editor attention than others, additionally leading to thoughts of Wikipedia, instead of the newspapers, as authors of the proverbial first draft of history (Halavais and Lackaff, 2008). Moreover, articles in Wikipedia are always only versions, making the encyclopedia alone among its kind in its unfinished state. It also allows for pulling back the curtains to view the occasionally unruly discussions and debate on talk pages per article. Its unfinished state and rough-hewn origins did not stop Bertelsmann from publishing selections (featured articles) from the German Wikipedia as an encyclopedia in print (Bertelsmann Lexikon Institut, 2008)! There also have been art projects that have done the same, for example, printing out all the edits that have been made to a particular article, on the Iraq war, in an effort to introduce materials for history-writing (see Figures 7.3 and 7.4), or striving (on multiple occasions) to print out the entire English-language Wikipedia, whose size at 7500 volumes proved insurmountable (Mandiberg, 2015). An ever-evolving and debated store of knowledge online is perhaps resistant to print culture.

The quality of Wikipedia

Print by reputable publisher may be one imprimatur of quality, but what is the source of Wikipedia's? Mention was made above of the core principles: neutral point of view, verifiability and no original research. On top of the principles, scholars are studying the relationship between the bureaucracy that is Wikipedia's consensus-building process, and the quality of articles, normally taking 'featured articles' as examples of such (Mesgari et al., 2015). Quality articles edited by power editors may be more likely to become featured articles, and thus quality may be attributed to a particular type of editor work (Butler et al., 2008).

Quality is additionally the outcome of Wikipedia's other editors – the bots. Without them the online encyclopedia could fall prey to spam, like certain comment spaces without moderators that finally were closed down. For quality control, there is also collaboration between the human editors and other non-human tenders such as alert software (Niederer and van Dijck, 2010). Indeed, in the 'Heavy Metal Umlaut' screencast documentary by Jon Udell (discussed in the Website History chapter), he appears astonished by the agility of Wikipedians, catching (and correcting) vandalism just minutes after the defacement of an article has taken place (2005). One could argue that the bots and alert software keep not just the vandals, but also the experimenters, at bay, those researchers as well as Wikipedia nay-sayers making changes to a Wikipedia article, or creating a new fictional one, and subsequently waiting for something to happen (Chesney, 2006; Magnus, 2008). This other strand of work that seeks to understand the quality of Wikipedia, together with the so-called vigilance of the crowd, has been performed through article tampering that was 'caught' by the bots or by individual editors (Halavais, 2004; Read, 2006). In the experiments that also took into account the automated monitoring of reverts and other signs of flame wars and malicious editing (choosing to insert errors more randomly than in a pattern), it was found that some but not all of the errors were corrected. Often errors are the product of non-scholarly 'sneaky vandalism' (Tran et al., 2015), and the question concerns whether to rely on vigilant Wikipedians (with bots and software assistants) or develop more stringent thresholds to editing. Higher thresholds to entry, however, may remove the charm of volunteer work, especially when Wikipedia editing activity faces decline.

Research has been undertaken in reaction to findings that there is only a tiny ratio of editors to users in crowdsourced, substantive platforms, which became known as the myth of user-generated content (Swartz, 2006). As mentioned above, there is also work on the decline in the number of editors in Wikipedia, where the debate concerns the question of natural maturation versus overzealous regulation by Wikipedians, often summarized by the term 'deletionism' (Silverman, 2013). In this decline narrative faced by Wikipedia, heavy-handed editorial culture (and the busy work of writing edit summaries after editing) is exacerbated by the algorithmic toolbase (Halfaker et al., 2013). The boldness (without recklessness) Wikipedia recommends for its editors is met with automated pushback. Increasing mobile access to Wikipedia has been pointed out as adding to the decline, for mobile users edit much less than those on desktop (Brown, 2015). Wikipedia co-founder Jimmy Wales often remarked (in the early days) that the dedicated community is relatively small, at just over 500 members. Beyond the small community there are also editors who do not register with the system. The anonymous editors and the edits they make were the subjects of the Wikiscanner tool, developed by Virgil Griffith at the California Institute of Technology. Anonymous editors may be 'outed', leading to scandals, as collected by Griffith himself. Among the better known (at least in the Netherlands) is the 'royal edit', where a computer in the Dutch royal household apparently was found to have made an edit to Princess Mabel's entry, whereby the information she gave about her past relations with a drug kingpin (Klaas Bruinsma) to the Dutch vetting authorities was changed from 'incomplete and false' to 'incomplete', thus excising the word 'false'. It is indicative of what Udell called the 'abnormally vigilant' Wikipedia community that the edit was reverted quickly after it was made, never since to reappear. That part of the story is rarely told.

Perhaps the most infamous edit was not anonymous. In his own article, Jimmy Wales edited out Larry Sanger as co-founder of Wikipedia. The editing of a Wikipedia article by its subject or by a representative of its subject matter has been critiqued as publicity management rather than encyclopedic editorial care, however much the subject may be closer to the material and thus both more informed as well as passionate about it (Aula, 2010). Thus quality (rather unexpectedly) may be gained, at least occasionally, from what is otherwise known as publicity management, though tools such as the Wikiscanner would remain a check against boosterism.

Wikipedia's relationship to Google

Quality also lies in how articles are sourced, and continuing traffic to Wikipedia articles where the 'many eyes' may spot errors and indeed become editors themselves. How is the knowledge sourced that appears in Wikipedia, including the outlinks? Wikipedians often refer to Google as a source to check for a subject's prior art. So, if it is not returned in Google results, it may not be considered as published. Wikipedia thus could be said to ground knowledge claims in the online, or at least routinely seek evidence for them there. That Wikipedians look up subject matters in Google (to confirm their existence) is one of the relationships between the search engine and the online encyclopedia.

Wikipedia is the new google.

Even if you google something, the first hit will be a wikipedia page anyway.

Figure 7.5 The relationship between Wikipedia and Google by leftintherain, home-made picture thumbnail, rendering gunkglumb's Urban Dictionary definition of Wikipedia from 2005, www.urbandictionary.com/define.php?term=wikipedia&page=6

Source: Leftintherain, 2011.

The other, more prominent interrelation concerns the regular appearance of Wikipedia articles (their links and description text) at the top of Google results pages for substantive (or information) queries (see Figure 7.5) (Vaidhyanathan, 2011). The placement of Wikipedia at the top of Google results pages prompted the president of *Encyclopaedia Britannica*, Jorge Cauz, to call Google and Wikipedia's relationship 'symbiotic' (Carr, 2009). At the time of writing, the query for [encyclopedia] returns Encyclopedia.com as the top result at google.com, with Wikipedia second and Britannica third. Encyclopedia.com appears to be a Google artefact (discussed in the search as research chapter) in the sense of the proper name matching the query as opposed to being more renowned than Wikipedia and Britannica.

For years Wikipedia has hovered around fifth in the top global website rankings, according to Alexa. One may attribute widespread usage of Wikipedia in part to the top position regularly achieved in Google results, however much one may desire to peruse Wikipedia's hit logs to confirm such a supposition (Zachte, 2015). To Alexa (2018), Wikipedia receives a disproportionate amount of traffic from search, compared to others at the top (nearly 60%, compared to 13% for YouTube and 7% for Facebook). Wikipedia ranks highly in Google results pages (perhaps better than any other website) for informational queries, rather than for transactional or navigational ones, as a number of industry studies have found. Search engine optimization (SEO) and online marketing researchers have regularly lamented that Wikipedia does not appear to optimize its webpages for search, yet still comes out on top. Responding to an early study that found that over 95% of Wikipedia (English-language) articles are in Google's top ten search results (for a query related to the title of the article; Googlecache, 2007), one SEO developer wrote a Firefox search plug-in that removes Wikipedia from Google results pages (Critchlow, 2007). It is a form of critical commentary concerning the 'symbiotic relationship' between Wikipedia and Google, but also perhaps of interest for actual use to those who monitor search engine results (and tire of Wikipedia's steady appearance). It also could be employed to remove a Google artefact.

The roles reversed in the relationship between Wikipedia and Google, however, with the introduction of Google's knowledge graph in 2014–2015, and its outputs on search engine results pages. The text boxes or 'knowledge panels' appearing alongside so-called organic results (from substantive queries such as 'Leonardo da Vinci') contain short descriptions taken from Wikipedia articles as well as other scraped sources. The use of Wikipedia material for Google's purposes has had its side effects – for Wikipedia. A Google user looking for a capsule summary of the medieval Italian polymath may be satisfied enough with the Google knowledge panel so as to not click through to the Wikipedia page. Wikipedia's traffic is thus affected by having had its content cherry-picked, at least according to an observation made in 2015, which appeared to point to a traffic decline on Wikipedia since the introduction of the knowledge panels (see Figure 7.6).

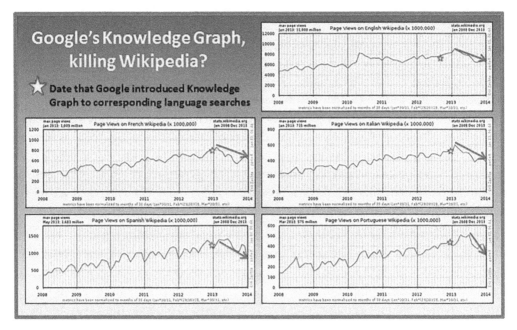

Figure 7.6   The apparent impact of Google info boxes (knowledge graph panels) on Wikipedia traffic.
Source: Kohs, 2014.

Studying culture with Wikipedia

National Wikipedias

At the time of writing the English Wikipedia has nearly 7000 disputed articles. These are neutral point of view (NPOV) disagreements (often having resulted in edit wars) about wide-ranging topics. That there are so many *ongoing* disputed articles is an indication of the difficulty of attaining a 'stable' state so that disputed articles might eventually become 'featured'. Wikipedia administrative culture – including the manner in which disputes are resolved – is an object of study in itself as is how Wikipedians stigmergicly and routinely achieve decent quality (Loveland and Reagle, 2013; Jemielniak, 2014; Elliott, 2016). Here the culture of Wikipedia, including the distinctive social manner in which Finnish Wikipedians may resolve disputes and other issues compared to the Japanese, is one means of considering cross-cultural study with Wikipedia. In the event, the Finnish have no NPOV disputes (as a study reported), and the Japanese tend to make little use of the talk pages to resolve disputes (Nemoto and Gloor, 2011). As another case in point, featured article approval processes differ between Arabic and English Wikipedia communities, with the former far less formal than the latter (Stvilia et al., 2009).

Wikipedia as socio-cultural data

Another approach to studying societal and cultural specificity with (and on) Wikipedia is to consider its articles as sources of data, especially the hit logs and editing history. Taking the presuppositions of Trends (discussed in the query design chapter) as their points of departure, Wikipedia data-driven monitoring devices for seasonal flu fluctuations have been demoed (Generous et al., 2014; McIver and Brownstein, 2014; Bardak and Tan, 2015). To chart the incidence of flu, studies use Wikipedia flu article hit logs (rather than, for example, page editing history or talk page activity). Other researchers expanded the log data of articles under scrutiny to include gastroenteritis, bronchiolitis, chickenpox and asthma, finding a significant relationship between page views and emergency department visits (Vilain et al., 2017). Other Wikipedia data show cultural priorities, such as the geolocations of the editors of particular articles, where the question may be which countries edit which articles with great fervour. Here the study concerns less Wikipedian platform culture (as above) than national and regional cultures. Why do certain African Wikipedians tend to edit the English-language Wikipedia far more than other specific language versions closer to home (Graham et al., 2014)? Why does the Japanese Wikipedia have far more anonymous editors than other Wikipedia language versions (Lih, 2009)?

Apart from article activity as an indicator of cultural specificity, the meta-substance of Wikipedia articles (such as article titles per language) is also a source of data. Wikipedia article titles have served as keywords for censorship research in China (the Weibo study) and have been queried in Google to check Wikipedia page rankings, as mentioned above. In both instances Wikipedia's breadth of topics is made use of. Indeed, researchers have described Wikipedia as 'a giant multilingual database of concepts' (Milne and Witten, 2013).

Wikipedia and cultural difference

In a fourth approach to studying culture with Wikipedia one considers substantive differences across Wikipedia language versions (Gallagher and Savage, 2013). The basis for studying cultural differences and their implications has been well laid. As has been found, certain Wikipedias (e.g., the Arabic and the Korean) have substantial quantities of articles unique to themselves (Stvilia et al., 2009). Thus, it should not be expected that there is universality, however much certain Wikipedia language versions may have their specificity 'suffer' from translation from the English or another dominant language (Warncke-Wang et al., 2012). The Korean has a higher percentage of articles translated from English than the Arabic. Cross-cultural comparison is best served through organically written articles, whereupon the contents are of interest, rather than Wikipedia's administration, article activity or keyword availability. Across Wikipedia language versions, the accounts of historical events may differ. In another set of studies, the particular cuisines covered per Wikipedia show certain cross-cultural appreciations and lacks thereof (Laufer et al., 2015; Gieck et al., 2016).

Studying societal controversies with Wikipedia

In a fifth approach, treated briefly, the question of controversial articles is less a prompt for ethnographic Wikipedia work (why the Finnish do not appear to have NPOV disputes) but rather concerns which subject matters (and specific claims or findings) are disputed societally. A variety of projects take up the question of detecting and following controversiality in single articles, in the 'same' article across Wikipedia language versions as well as in ecologies of related articles, where, for example, a controversy in one piece migrates (or forks) to another article. Contropedia, as the software project is called, places a layer on an article showing which wikilinked passages have been most controversial over time (Weltevrede and Borra, 2016). Another project, 'the most controversial topics in Wikipedia', the interactive tool once featured in *Wired* magazine, ranks controversies per country, and also aggregates them by categories where, for example, the most controversial category on the Spanish site is sports which elicits no controversy on the Arabic site (see Table 7.1).

Wikipedia language version comparison projects

The approach taken here for the comparative study of Wikipedia language versions is relatively straightforward. The comparisons are based on a form of content analysis which focuses on basic elements that comprise an article: its title, authors (or editors), table of contents, images and references (McMillan, 2000). Added are two further elements that are more medium-specific: the location of the anonymous editors (based on IP address), and a reading of the discussion pages that are behind the articles. Left out (but not forgotten) are other similarly specific elements of interest in the study of Wikipedia articles, such as the activity of software robots (bots), which are often highly active editors both across an entire language version of Wikipedia and within a single article (Geiger, 2011). Another medium-specific object is not emphasized but remains on offer. The special study of templates such as the 'globalize' one discussed at the outset may be undertaken when making comparative study of articles; these templates also appear when comparing the images from a series of the 'same' articles across language versions, as discussed below. Thus, the opportunity for template study is built into a tool for cross-article image comparison.

Table 7.1 Most controversial articles in select Wikipedia language versions. Italicized titles are translated for the sake of comparison. Source: Yasseri et al., 2014.

en	de	fr	es	cs
George W. Bush	Croatia	Ségolène Royal	Chile	Homosexuality
Anarchism	Scientology	Unidentified flying object	Club América	Psychotronics
Muhammad	9/11 conspiracy theories	Jehovah's Witnesses	Opus Dei	Telepathy
LWWEe	*Fraternities*	Jesus	Athletic Bilbao	Communism
Global warming	Homeopathy	Sigmund Freud	Andrés Manuel López Obrador	Homophobia
Circumcision	Adolf Hitler	September 11 attacks	Newell's Old Boys	Jesus
United States	Jesus	Muhammad al-Durrah incident	FC Barcelona	Moravia
Jesus	Hugo Chávez	Islamophobia	Homeopathy	Sexual orientation change efforts
Race and intelligence	Minimum wage	God in Christianity	Augusto Pinochet	Ross Hedvíček
Christianity	Rudolf Steiner	Nuclear power debate	Alianza Lima	Israel
hu	**ro**	**ar**	**fa**	**he**
Gypsy Crime	FC Universitatea Craiova	Ash'ari	Báb	Chabad
Atheism	Mircea Badea	*Ali bin Talal al Jahani*	Fatimah	Chabad messianism
Hungarian radical right	Disney Channel (Romania)	Muhammad	Mahmoud Ahmadinejad	2006 Lebanon War
Viktor Orbán	Legionnaires' rebellion and Bucharest pogrom	Ali	People's Mujahedin of Iran	B'Tselem
Hungarian Guard Movement	Lugoj	Egypt	Criticism of the Quran	Benjamin Netanyahu
Ferenc Gyurcsány's speech in May 2006	Vladimir Tismăneanu	Syria	Tabriz	*Jewish settlement in Hebron*
The Mortimer case	Craiova	Sunni Islam	Ali Khamenei	Daphni Leef
Hungarian far right	Romania	Wahhabi	Ruhollah Khomeini	Gaza War
Jobbik	Traian Băsescu	Yasser Al-Habib	Massoud Rajavi	Beitar Jerusalem FC
Polgár Tamás	Romanian Orthodox Church	Arab people	Muhammad	Ariel Sharon

Srebrenica in the Serbian, Bosnian and Dutch Wikipedias

In a comparative study of Wikipedia language versions, one goal is to extract and place side by side significant differences. The first case in question concerns the Serbian, Bosnian and Dutch Wikipedia articles about the events of July 1995 in Srebrenica, so as to learn about the specific cultural points of view (if any) of each (Rogers and Sendijarevic, 2012; Rogers, 2013b). Thousands of Bosniaks were killed by Bosnian-Serb forces in the 'safe haven' of Srebrenica where Dutchbat, the Dutch UN battalion, was stationed.

The three language versions, in other words, are chosen for the significance of the countries during what is known as the Srebrenica massacre, Srebrenica genocide or the fall of Srebrenica, as the Serbian, Bosnian and Dutch Wikipedia versions respectively refer to it in the title of the articles. As a starting point, not only the titles of the article but a particularly salient fact appearing in each are compared (see Table 7.2). Through the comparison of the victim counts, it is observed that the Serbian and Dutch versions tend to round down, and the Bosnian lists the higher figure only. There are also differences in the articles not only substantively but also in terms of illustration and reference, where the images and sources are often unique. The most significant unique image, included in the Bosnian article, is the gravestone of a 13-year-old boy. It provides support for the genocide designation in the article title, for he is not of fighting age. The Dutch and Bosnian versions contain neither that term in the title nor the image. Moreover, the only reference shared (from a comparison of the links at the base of the articles) is un.org; the sources otherwise tend to be national, which should not be a surprise, given the distinctive languages. One could argue (or at least consider) that the article differences may stem from the distinctive sources anchoring the articles, and sourcing cultures deciding which ones to choose. To that end the talk pages ('behind' the Wikipedia articles) are open for browsing, for there are discussions about how to handle new information that has come to light and choose sources to reference. When studying sourcing decisions, one may pinpoint specific moments in the timeline of an event, or annual commemorations of events. Every year in July Srebrenica article editing activity has increased.

Table 7.2   Wikipedia articles on same subject compared across Wikipedia language versions, 20 December 2010. Comparison of article titles and victim counts.

Wikipedia language version	Name of Srebrenica article	Number of Bosniak victims
Dutch (Nederlands)	Fall of Srebrenica	7000–8000
Bosnian (Bosanski)	Srebrenica Genocide	8000
Serbian (Srpski)	Srebrenica Massacre	6000–8000

Through a comparison of the Wikipedia language versions, one may discover the extent to which Wikipedia articles express not so much a neutral as a cultural or national point of view. Alternatively, one may seek to view the neutral and the national points of view as mutually reconcilable by asking, neutral for whom? The specificity of one Wikipedia language version's account over another may be framed as divergent collective memories, where two sets of editors arrive at accounts of events that are neutral to them, so to speak. One also could argue that the debates in the talk pages together with the discussions about the choice of sources, images and other information provide the scholar with material to describe the 'circumstances under which counter-memory becomes collective memory' (Whitlinger, 2011).

Auschwitz in the Polish and German Wikipedias

A second case study takes up how Auschwitz is described in Wikipedia (Bielka et al., 2017). In particular, it inquires into the unique aspects of the German, Polish and Portuguese articles on Auschwitz. There is occasion to make such a comparison. US President Obama (in 2012) and others have referred to Auschwitz as the 'Polish death camp', presumably using a possessive adjective referring to place rather than complicity. Associating them with the Polish rather than with the Nazis was not only offensive to the Poles (and others) but also prompted observers (including the Polish foreign minister) to call Obama ill-informed and incompetent and his statement as anathema to the struggle against denialism (Dharapak, 2012). In the event, there is extensive discussion of the notion of 'Polish death camps' in the Polish version of the article, whereas no such discussion exists in the German or Portuguese. It is the most significant finding by far in the overall comparison, but another smaller observation concerns how Auschwitz has become so synonymous with the concentration camp that the article names in both the Portuguese and even the Polish (where the city is located) are just Auschwitz or Auschwitz-Birkenau rather than having camp in the title. The German article bears concentration camp (or KZ in German) in its title, and also redirects from Auschwitz.

Conclusions: Cross-cultural article comparison

Wikipedia articles, whether they have achieved some measure of quality through feature article status or maturity, may be considered neutral, yet have a national or cultural point of view, teased out through comparison with other articles of the same subject matter, as exemplified in the cases of Srebrenica (comparing Dutch, Bosnian and Serbian versions) and Auschwitz (comparing Polish, German and Portuguese). Omnipedia (from Northwestern University) as well as Manypedia (from the University of Trento) are computer science projects (and computational achievements) that derive compatibility or similarity scores between articles (see Figure 7.7; see also Hecht and Gergle, 2010; Massa and Scrinzi, 2011; Bao et al., 2012). They are useful for spotting differences from which one may subsequently make an account (e.g., on 'Polish death camps') which presumably would be flagged by the software, should it be able to handle the language translation.

There are also relatively simple digital methods tools that may be used to compare the articles, including the Wikipedia TOC Scraper, Wikipedia Cross-Lingual Image Analysis and Wikipedia Edits Scraper and IP Localizer. The TOC Scraper extracts the tables of contents from the inputted articles for comparison at a glance, where one may note (for example) if the articles contain a controversy or criticism section in one language version, but not in another. The brevity of TOC Scraper is advantageous when relying on online translation tools.

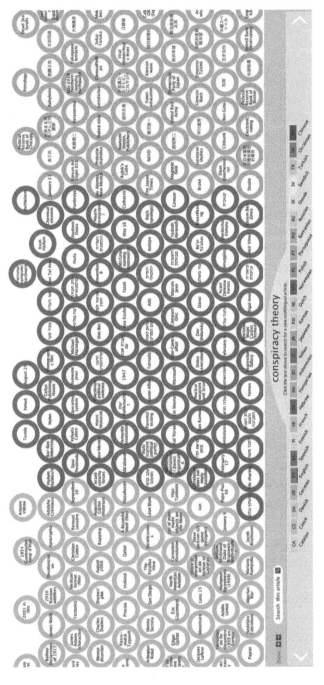

Figure 7.7 Omnipedia, the project of CollabLab, Northwestern University, compares Wikipedia articles across language versions, http://omnipedia.northwestern.edu.

The Wikipedia Cross-Lingual Image Analysis extracts and places in a grid the images of the respective articles for comparison. The tool enabled the ready discovery of the image of the 13-year-old boy's gravestone in the Bosnian version of the Srebrenica article, and its absence in the Dutch and Serbian ones. The Wikipedia Edits Scraper and IP Localizer extracts the anonymous edits and geolocates the place from where the edits were made, allowing findings such as whether the Serbian Wikipedia article on Srebrenica is largely edited from within Serbia only, and the Dutch one within the Netherlands.[1] (Only anonymous edits are geolocated; it would be telling to know the location of the non-anonymous edits, too, but that information, even if logged, is not available.) One other piece of software, the Triangulation tool, allows for the comparison of the references in the articles, where it was found (as mentioned above) that the Dutch, Bosnian and Serbian articles share hardly any sources. Taken together these techniques enable the identification of discrepancy and specificity among the articles in question that enable more in-depth study and close reading.

---

[1] At the time of writing Wikipedia is considering no longer supplying the IP address of anonymous edits.

PROJECT

Compare the 'same' article across Wikipedia language versions

RESEARCH GOAL To undertake comparative analysis of the 'same' Wikipedia article across different language versions.

Wikipedia, as a top website both in terms of traffic and placement atop Google results, is deserving of study, however much it may be considered counter-intuitive to study it as a cultural reference rather than as a reference work like an encyclopedia, where questions revolve around accuracy and quality. Here we consider the difference between the same article across Wikipedia language versions, including how the Wikipedia articles have evolved over time, inquiring into whether they converge (one point of view across all Wikipedia language versions) or diverge (cultural particularism).

1 Choice of article and language versions. Choose a subject matter that is shared across two or more Wikipedia language versions. Note that the same articles in other languages are often linked from one Wikipedia version to another in the sidebar on the left-hand side of the article, under languages. You need not be restricted to the other language version linked from the article, as there may be similar articles.

    a Consider choosing an article where the two or more language Wikipedia versions share its subject matter significantly, as in the Auschwitz case related above, or are likely to have varying views on the same subject matter, such as gay (or LGBT) rights. To begin, note the distinctive titles of what may be considered the same article.

    b Consider choosing languages which are associated with a particular country or culture, as opposed to many countries and cultures. English, for example, is spoken in many countries and may thus not be a good indication of a cultural point of view, however much there is a discussion about its particular 'American' biases (and Wikipedia articles about that). Consider that different language Wikipedias may have particular user and information cultures too (e.g., that there are relatively few disputes on the Finnish). Shared language versions, however, can be places where different cultural perspectives are in evidence in the edit history and talk pages, such as in the English-language article on the 'Srebrenica Massacre', where, for example, both Serbian and Bosnian editors have been active (and certain ones banned).

    c Articles may have been translated from one language to another, often originating in the English-language Wikipedia. These are less organic (or *sui generis*), and perhaps should be avoided, unless one wishes to compare the original English-language version with the current reworked article, demonstrating those differences. Additionally, analysing the most recent English-language version compared to the most recent translated language version may show distinctive variation worthy of analytical treatment.

2   Comparative analysis. There are generally two approaches to comparative Wikipedia analysis, both resulting from the online encyclopedia's affordances (or 'research affordances'): networked content analysis and medium-specific features analysis. The one is concerned more with the substance of the articles, and the other with the bureaucracy or apparatus behind the articles.

　a   Networked content, generally, refers to how the content in Wikipedia is both interlinked or tethered to other content and held together by the network of humans and non-humans (bots) that keep the content in good shape. Without them spam build-up and other deleterious effects would turn Wikipedia into gobbledygook. More specifically, it concerns the content fields in the Wikipedia database, so to speak, such as title, table of contents, images, references and info-boxes.

　b   Medium-specific features refer to (among other elements) the editing history and the talk pages behind articles. They also include the 'templates' or those banners indicating that the article is featured, disputed, locked, up for deletion, etc.

3   Networked content analysis. Compare the title, tables of contents, images, references and info-boxes. What is shared and what is unique? Develop an account of the specificity of a Wikipedia language version.

To compare tables of contents, there is the Wikipedia TOC Scraper. For comparative image analysis, there is the Wikipedia Cross-lingual Image Analysis tool. Lay out tables of contents and images in side-by-side pages or columns, so as to enable comparison. Organize the items to show presence/absence. For comparative reference analysis, consider employing the link ripper as well as the triangulation tools. Note that not all references are always hyperlinked. Truncate URLs of references to hosts to enable source-level comparison; retain long URLs for article-level scrutiny.

4   Medium-specific features analysis. Consider an analysis of (power) editors, anonymous editors as well as templates regarding the style of editing or bureaucratic culture of a Wikipedia language version *vis-à-vis* another. More specifically, take note of how Wikipedia's core policies and guidelines are deployed. NPOV does not mean that there cannot be different perspectives in a page, but that the perspectives should be written from a third person standpoint (balanced, neutral and verifiable). Apart from NPOV, other policies may be referenced. Consult the talk pages to analyse how editors back up their claims.

Each Wikipedia article has a revision history page. On that page, note the external tools which can come in helpful: revision history statistics, contributors, etc. One may make a comparative analysis of the editors using the history stats of each of the articles under study.

For anonymous editor analysis, consider using the tool, Wikipedia Edits Scraper and IP Localizer. It can be used to extract all edits from a particular Wikipedia page and to geolocate the anonymous edits. Here one may begin to perform an analysis of the 'places of edits', inquiring into the amount and specific type of content anonymous editors edit together with their locations.

5   Interpretation. Refrain from cultural clichés, and instead describe, in a comparative framework, the substantive viewpoints (for networked content analysis) or styles (for medium-specific features analysis).

6   Citing Wikipedia. When citing a Wikipedia page, use the permanent link pointing to the exact revision of the page, available in the sidebar of the Wikipedia article.

Video tutorials

For the project, watch 'Analysing Wikipedia Articles through the Front-End' for an overall introduction to comparing the 'same' article across different Wikipedia language versions. For more specific techniques, watch the 'Cross-lingual Image Analysis' video to learn how to extract and compare images across two or more Wikipedia articles, and the 'Triangulation Tool' video to compare the references listed on two or more Wikipedia articles. For those undertaking talk page and revision history analysis, see the Wikipedia 'Back-End' tutorial.

- 'Analysing Wikipedia Articles through the Front-End' (14'21'), www.youtube.com/watch?v=w-c1GdGpv5QE
- 'Wikipedia Cross-lingual Image Analysis Tool' (2'16'), www.youtube.com/watch?v=L49fFd_O8ZA
- 'Wikipedia2geo Tool (Wikipedia Edits and Scraper and IP Localizer)' (1'37'), www.youtube.com/watch?v=Pd51MaRUhzM
- 'Comparing Lists (Triangulation Tool)' (2'54'), www.youtube.com/watch?v=jg9UzKcuuOE
- 'Analysing Wikipedia Articles through the Back-End' (10'37'), www.youtube.com/watch?v=-tY7E8sXCAWw

Tools

- Wikipedia cross-lingual category analysis, digitalmethods.net. Available at https://tools.digital-methods.net/beta/wikipediaCategoryAnalysis/
- Wikipedia cross-lingual image analysis, digitalmethods.net. Available at https://tools.digitalmeth-ods.net/beta/wikipediaCrosslingualImageAnalysis/
- Wiki TOC scraper, digitalmethods.net. Available at https://tools.digitalmethods.net/beta/wikitoc/

EIGHT

YOUTUBE TEARDOWN
Deconstructing recommendations

Deconstructing (and reconstructing) YouTube related videos, engine results and channel subscriptions

From the people's content to the vlogger's permanent updates

Once considered a platform for you to 'broadcast yourself', as its original motto phrased it, over the years YouTube gradually transformed itself from an amateur content hub to a hosting site for music videos (and other more specific video genres), pirated content and, finally, for 'YouTubers' – online personalities and microcelebrities whose work is described as 'permanent updating' (Jerslev, 2016) (see Figure 8.1). These videographers are known as vloggers, or bloggers with video recorders, and are characterized as those who regularly post videos to their own YouTube 'channel'. Popular channel genres include video gamers (such as PewDiePie) who walk through and comment on games and gameplay, a culture that also has its 'own' platform in Twitch and a live spectator sport called 'e-sports', which has been described as the 'phenomenon of competitively playing video games' (Smith et al., 2013). 'Unboxing' videos are also well watched (Marsh, 2016), including those falling into the 'ElsaGate' category, which are videos that appear to be made for children but have inappropriate content (Maheshwari, 2017; Walczer, 2021). Originating in the consumer electronics tech press (unboxing mobile phones) and extending to children's toys, the genre shares its

Figure 8.1 YouTube logo evolution, away from user-generated content, 2005 and 2018. The tagline, 'broadcast yourself', was removed in 2011.

Source: YouTube.com

lineage with 'product tear downs'. These are recordings of the dissembling of a gadget to lay bare its components. Teardown efforts pertain to the politics of knowledge. In reaction to undertakings by electronics companies to keep repair knowledge (and manuals) out of the public domain, iFixit, perhaps the most well-known teardown artists, routinely take apart products and posts YouTube videos on how to fix them. They race to be the first to do so, thereby piling up views.

YouTube is thus also a (competitive) 'how-to' site, with videos dedicated to fixing and making things, but also to preparedness. For example, in 'how to pack for Rome in September', clothes and travel items are laid out and discussed. The arrangement of garments and accessories has elements in common with 'what's in your bag?', a genre popularized by *The Verge* magazine, where the contents of one's bag are either unfurled (as in 'haul' videos showing one's purchases) or meticulously arrayed and photographed, not so unlike the haul of a drug or arms bust or even the reconstructed aftermath of a plane crash, where the retrieved parts are arrayed in a hangar. Like the video and computer game walkthroughs as well as unboxing videos, the unfurling and the arraying videos are forms of deconstruction and reconstruction.

How to begin to deconstruct YouTube? (I return to reconstruction below when discussing an approach to studying YouTube's video removals or 'purges'.) More recently, the deconstruction approach has been applied to platforms more generally, as in the 'Spotify Teardown' project (Johansson et al., 2019). Broadly speaking, deconstruction is a manner of reading or reinterpreting, whereby the text or object becomes more or different than it appears to be or functions as, through an examination of the assumptions behind it, or built into it. Platform scholars in the teardown mode have taken apart Spotify, the music streaming service, producing an alternative history and challenging the assumptions about its origins, controversially as a system that originally contained pirated music files. They also 'looked inside' it by experimenting with its front-end and back-end through scraping, network sniffing and starting a music label and uploading homespun songs. Each technical intervention both breaks down how the system works as well as for whom (with how much labour). For example, how do songs become 'discoverable' in the system, and what kind of toil is required for new artists to have their songs aired and liked? Notions such as 'relational labour' capture the work done to build and maintain an audience or fan base (Baym, 2018).

Figure 8.2   Youtube.com's (brief) origins as a dating site, 28 April 2005.

Source: Wayback Machine of the Internet Archive, https://web.archive.org/web/20050428014715/www.youtube.com:80/

For YouTube, to begin a deep deconstruction, histories such as by Jean Burgess and Joshua Green (2018) aid researchers in contrasting how 'new media' were promoted to the public by the company and discussed in internal emails. Owing to the copyright infringement lawsuit brought by Viacom against YouTube in 2006, the founders' early pitches to venture capitalists as well as other internal documents have been made public. In them it becomes clear that the social side of YouTube was emphasized over the content, or its contribution to 'participatory culture', or that the *new* in new media meant that one-time consumers would become producers of content in their own right (Jenkins et al., 2005). Contrariwise, YouTube was originally something of a dating site (see Figures 8.2 and 8.3); 'broadcasting yourself' was a means to attract attention from potential partners. Sharing content (or creating a content community) would build a user base, who would consume advertising and eventually might subscribe to (ad-free) 'premium content' (which YouTube now offers). Rather than idealistic, YouTube as a business model was a form of platform capitalism, whereby the 'intermediary' or 'aggregator' would fill its platform databases with any and all content (with the exception of violence and pornography) so long as it quickly grew ('scaled') its user base.

Figure 8.3   'Me at the zoo' by Jawed Karim. First YouTube video upload, 23 April 2005.

Source: https://en.wikipedia.org/wiki/Me_at_the_zoo

In an essay in the *YouTube Reader*, Burgess and Green (2009) discuss the users and the evolving relationships between the commercial and non-commercial, and the professional and the amateur. In arguing that the commercial and non-commercial should not be seen in opposition to one another, the authors point out that YouTube grew its user base through both types of content and users. Professionally made content could be uploaded, and erstwhile amateurs or non-professionals may become professionals in their own right, raising themselves to the level of YouTubers, or influencers and micro-celebrities well known in the medium. The relationship between amateur and professional may be further complicated. Empirical studies at the time showed a shift in uploads from 'self-generated' content to videos of 'amalgamated' content that was originally professionally produced (Kruitbosch and Nack, 2008). On YouTube, remix joins prosumption, or consumer-produced content (Bruns, 2009).

Studying YouTube commercialization

Commercialization, symbolically at least, may have begun with the first YouTube commercials. Actual ten-second spots were aired initially in 2007, though the commercialization of YouTube has a variety of starting points for its study. Marketing data companies that track user statistics on social media have metrics for YouTube based on the two most basic statistics: channel subscriptions and video view counts. YouTube also measures total video 'watch time'. Those who run channels seek subscribers, views and watch time. To earn money on YouTube, at the time of writing, a channel owner with 1,000 subscribers and 4000 hours of watch time may join the YouTube Partner Program and sign up for Google AdSense, whereupon the owner can earn ad revenue from their videos (55% accrues to the channel owner, and 45% is retained by YouTube). Those with larger numbers are rewarded by YouTube with business tools that allow the tracking of copyright infringement or video reuse. When reaching the threshold of 100,000 subscribers (at the time of writing), the channel owner has access to 'content match' systems, which show whether one's own videos have been re-uploaded by another, and whether revenue has been earned by another through this 'freebooting'. (Snippets of 29 seconds or less and remixed content appear to be fair use for they are not currently 'matched'.) As mentioned, prior to this 'native' commercialization and copyright hunting toolkit, YouTube was the site of a copyright struggle over 'migrated' commercial content, when in 2006 and again in 2013, Viacom sued YouTube for copyright infringement of SpongeBob SquarePants and other video that appeared on the platform on a mass scale. The 'content matching' tools were originally developed as a result of those cases. Subsequently, they have been rolled out for premium, native users who also earn money for the platform.

In reaction to YouTube's decision to provide business tools to only large channels, the YouTubers Union was founded, with demands including 'equal treatment for all' content

The Spark

Welcome to the official homepage of the YouTubers Union!

We are a community based movement that fights for the rights of YouTube Creators and Users. Our core demands are:

- *Monetize everyone - Bring back monetization for smaller channels.*
- *Disable the bots - At least verified partners have the right to speak to a real person if you plan to remove their channel.*
- *Transparent content decisions - Open up direct communication between the censors ("content department") and the Creators.*
- *Pay for the views - Stop using demonetized channels as "bait" to advertise monetized videos.*
- *Stop demonetization as a whole - If a video is in line with your rules, allow ads on an even scale.*
- *Equal treatment for all partners - Stop preferring some creators over others. No more "YouTube Preferred".*
- *Pay according to delivered value - Spread out the ad money over all YouTubers based on audience retention, not on ads next to the content.*
- *Clarify the rules - Bring out clear rules with clear examples about what is OK and what is a No-No.*

Everyone is welcome to join - we need you! No matter if you are PewDiePie or just a user.
You don't have to pay any money and you have zero obligations.
You can join us simply be becoming a member of our Facebook group and/or by joining our forum.

United We Stand!

Figure 8.4   Demands by the YouTubers Union.

Source: https://youtubersunion.org, 2018.

creators (see Figure 8.4). For an understanding of how the system works (and for whom), it is instructive to read the claims and demands. There is a YouTube 'content department' that takes 'censoring' decisions. Bots do some of the dirty work. Small creators are under-appreciated in the sense that they cannot receive ad revenue; also, they do not have access to the content matching tools.

Another form of commercialization, rather webbier than platform-native, concerned YouTube video ideation. Which videos should one make in the first place? Which would attract viewers? Should they be to broadcast oneself (and one's pets), as the founders had it, and as vloggers would later perfect, achieving robust subscriber bases and annual incomes? Are there other ways to seed the platform and monetize content? Apart from the genres discussed above (and others such as alternative influencers engaged in 'blood sports' mentioned below), video creation and monetization schemes include those made to match popular search engine queries. In what is termed 'demand media' or 'automated media', videos would be made to match popular search queries, and then optimized so that they would be found on top of the search engine query results (Roth, 2009; Napoli, 2014). A micro-industry (and so-called digital sweatshops) was born to create cheap videos for searchers, such as 'how to pack for Rome in September', as mentioned above. When coupled with advertising, videos optimized for search engines could result in high view counts and micro-payments adding up.

YouTube as user-generated, commercial and propaganda platform

Judging from its 'top videos' as well as the scholarship that has taken YouTube as its object of inquiry, the study of YouTube could be roughly characterized as beginning with the 'user-generated content' period (2005–2011), where questions revolved around both the deleterious 'cult of the amateur' and the mass consumption of poor taste and, conversely, the amateur's quasi-professionalization through the producerly use of professional grade equipment (Bird, 2011). *Time Magazine*'s 'You' as person of the year placed YouTube at the centre of the story of the rise of people's content: 'It's about the cosmic compendium of knowledge Wikipedia and the million-channel people's network YouTube and the online metropolis MySpace' (2006). These were the new halcyon days of the web, having recovered from the dot.com crash just a few years earlier, and buoyed by the coinage of the new term, Web 2.0, or the web as platform. 'Participatory culture', the notion coined by Henry Jenkins and colleagues in 2005, described how software and online infrastructure (platforms) would enable creative expression and its sharing with others so it could be valued (2005). This is the rise of media creation and prod usage as an alternative to consumer culture, or mere spectatorship. Having dropped the tagline 'broadcast yourself' from its logo, from at least 2012 YouTube as a platform commercialized further, in the sense that the 'top' videos had become less amateur, as in 'Charlie bit my finger', and more polished, as in 'Gangnam Style' (see Figure 8.5). Scholarship indeed confirmed such a shift, while pointing out the great trove of amateur content (and produser material) still uploaded to the 'digital wunderkam-mer' (Gehl, 2009), and the complications of maintaining a dichotomy between commercial and non-commercial content, given the advent of the YouTuber, who builds subscribers, or a 'fan base', and generates advertising revenue, as discussed above.

Figure 8.5 Illustrated rendition of 'Charlie bit my finger' video and 'Gangnam Style' by Psy.

Sources: Unknown and Wikipedia, https://en.wikipedia.org/wiki/File:Gangnam_Style_Official_Cover.png

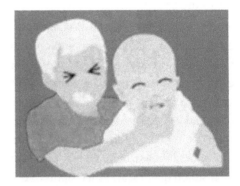

In the most recent period, starting roughly around the US presidential elections of 2016 (but with deeper historical roots), YouTube has become a site known not only for its genres and rising commercialization (challenging or overtaking MTV as a premier music video site), but also for darker communities that consume YouTube content. ISIS propaganda videos, and exhortations by one of its founders, Abu Musab al-Zarqawi, have long been found on YouTube, and remained for years. Indeed, YouTube videos are a part of the media infrastructure of recruitment, which open intelligence and other researchers have docu-mented (see Figure 8.6). While the platform made efforts to address the issue in the past, 2016 proved to be a turning point, as YouTube took steps (see also Figure 8.7). Among the initiatives, YouTube (with Facebook and Twitter) began sharing 'fingerprints' of extremist content in a joint effort to combat it. At YouTube, advertising controls, warning labels, 'trusted flaggers' as well as the 'redirect method' for users searching for extremist content (to counter-narratives) were introduced in 2017, as the platform engaged in curbing not only violence (as in the past) but also extremism (Counter-extremism Project, 2018).

Figure 8.6 Four stills from the YouTube video, 'You have made me cry, Oh Osama bin Laden. Paradise is yours, God willing'. Osama bin Laden speaks about the 9/11 martyrs. Posted 2 May, 2011.

Source: Memri, 2012.

Figure 8.7 YouTube take down page (with empty related video template) for the Osama bin Laden video in Figure 8.6.

Source: www.YouTube.com/watch?v=8TLHtE-za1Y

Reconstructing YouTube's video removal

In an effort to describe the extent of YouTube's removal or 'purging' of extreme content after a YouTube content removal policy was announced, researchers culled a list of extreme videos from 4chan in a thread, the 'most extreme one they could find', dedicated to 'National Socialism general' (OILab, 2019). They loaded them in YouTube on the day the policy change was announced and then on the day after. The result, depicted in 'before-and-after' image walls, shows the extent of the video deletion of videos 'promoting or glorifying racism and discrimination' as well as the remains (OILab, 2019). Methodologically, it is an example of studying one platform (YouTube) with the aid of another (4chan), also known as 'platform perspectivism'. More conceptually, it is also a reconstruction of removal as well as an investigation into what remains, or what is not considered extreme enough to be removed. In reconstructing removal (so to speak) the researchers used the few clues available to them (YouTube error messages and the timing of the removals) to conclude that the removals were likely automated, for they were largely of entire channels (rather than single videos) performed in a single sweep and included the channel of an official Dutch archive with WWII footage.

YouTube deconstruction techniques

While not as extensive as the Spotify teardown methods of scraping, sniffing network data, and becoming an artist and populating the service with one's own songs, the experimental deconstruction of YouTube could entail the use of some digital methods described below, which aid gaining an insight into YouTube's workings. These approaches to studying YouTube as media (e.g., platform recommendations) are complemented by ones that employ YouTube data for insights into societal and cultural conditions. That is, one may also repurpose YouTube to undertake research into not just how but for whom the platform works (e.g., political operatives or platform performers, more generally). The approaches relate to three modes of accessing YouTube: *watching* videos (and receiving recommendations for what's 'up next'), *querying* the search engine (and receiving ranked returns) and *subscribing* to channels (and receiving recommendations for 'related channels').

When watching YouTube, and studying it as a media platform, one may ask, which videos arrive next in the carousel? Do they remain on-topic, or even ever come to an end? Do they tend to be more popular (higher view counts), newer (fresher), more niched (thus privileging discoverability) or some combination?

In the second mode, querying, one can inquire not only into how the platform ranks, but the consequences of such rankings or source hierarchies per subject matter returned. Which videos have the privilege to arrive at the top for viewers of videos concerning the Syrian War? Are there news channels or perhaps micro-celebrities returned as 'authorities'? Here one captures the top results of multiple queries (on one date) or those of a single query (over time). Are these results relatively consistent over time (Rieder et al., 2018)? Do particular sources persist at the top? Are there voices or points of view that dominate (at certain times)?

The third mode of watching (and eventually tearing down the system) is through channel subscriptions and their linkages. Channels may subscribe to other channels, thereby linking them to each other. They also may feature each other (see Figure 8.8). These linkages may be made into an object of study for relational, substantive mapping, locating pockets of thematic distinctiveness and their proximity to others. How far away are game walkthroughs from gamergate, and how far is that from the alt-right? Do they overlap?

Rather than a network approach, one also may retrieve the data from an individual channel, inquiring into the 'permanent updating' culture, and the regularity or rapidity in which one posts content. For health vloggers or others with a particular condition, one may follow the changes in vlogging patterns together with view counts as well as comments (Sanchez-Querubin et al., 2018).

With the above related techniques, larger questions and concerns may be addressed not only about the effects of recommender systems but the reach of 'algorithmic governmentality' (Rouvroy and Berns, 2013), which are platform exercises of power and order. Such a point of departure could be combined with the study of the platform as 'potential memory' (Bowker, 2005) or 'active memory' (Chun, 2008). That is, at one time it picks out of its video storage particular items, but at another time could assemble a fresh set, refreshing memory of events and changing the order of things.

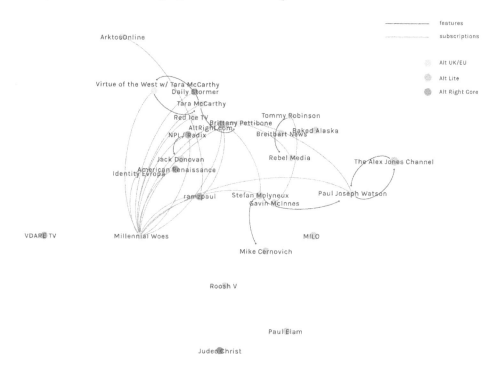

Figure 8.8 Alt-right subscription and feature networks.

Source: Alt-Right Open Intelligence Initiative, 2017.

PROJECT

'Tear down' YouTube's related videos, ranking culture, or channel and feature networks

RESEARCH GOAL To map and interpret YouTube's recommendations (related videos, ranked engine results and channel networks).

1   A network mapping of YouTube's related videos based on co-commenting.

    a   Query design. First, choose one or more discrete terms. These may be unambiguous (or specified) queri/es, or alternatively, underspecified ones. Unambiguous queries (e.g., Donald Trump) would return video content associated with the former president, whereas underspecified queries (e.g., firearms) would return video content related to guns, but not a position on them (gun control or second amendment, in the US context). Alternatively, choose a single video to show what's related, or pair of videos for a comparison of the sets of videos related to them. One also may make a list of videos as starting points, or a pair of lists for comparison.

    b   Analytical procedure. Using the YouTube data tools, video network module, either enter the term or terms for which one is querying, outputting results ranked according to 'relevance' (default), or enter one or more YouTube video IDs, which is the alphanumeric set of characters in the YouTube URL, where for www.youtube.com/watch?v=XMzygllSH9s, the ID is XMzygllSH9s.

    c   Visual output. Visualize results using Gephi.

    d   Interpretation of results. Identify and describe clusters using the visual network analysis approach (see Table 8.1), where one concentrates in the first instance on an analysis of the whole network (or panorama), identifying and labelling clusters (the camps) and holes, together with their sizes and densities.

Table 8.1   Network story-telling routines (often utilized for Gephi-related work)

1	Entire network – panorama
(a)	the groups or themes (clusters and holes)
(b)	their (im)balance (size and density)
2	Single nodes (with specific positioning)
(a)	authorities and hubs (centrality)
(b)	bridges and brokers (betweenness)
3	Routes (linked node chains)
(a)	grand tour (diameter/perimeter) – 'Eulerian walk'
(b)	short cuts (shortest paths)

Source: Adapted from Venturini et al., 2017.

2 An analysis of YouTube's ranking culture through the study of its search engine results.

   a Query design. First, choose one or more discrete terms. These may be unambiguous (or specified) queries, or alternatively, underspecified ones. Unambiguous queries (e.g., Donald Trump) would return video content associated with the former president, whereas underspecified queries (e.g., firearms) would return video content related to guns, but not a position on them (gun control or second amendment, in the US context).

   b Analytical procedure. Using the YouTube data tools, video co-commenting network module, query the term or terms, outputting results ranked according to 'relevance'. For the over-time analysis (as in Rieder et al., 2018), choose a timeframe and output ranked video list for each day in the timeframe. It will enable a comparison of top videos over time. Optionally, consider an exercise in cultural comparison by comparing outputs of multiple Google region searches. One enters region codes for each search of the same keywords (or translated keywords). (One may choose a timeframe, but not the videos published each day, so it is a comparison of top videos per country rather than top videos per day.)

   c Visualize results using the Rankflow tool (see Figure 8.9).

   d Interpretation of results. Identify and describe changes or differences in the top results either over time or at one time across queries (and/or, optionally, Google regions).

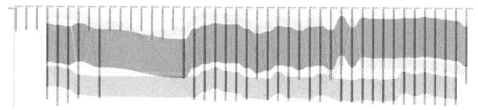

Figure 8.9 Rankflow visualization.

Source: Rieder et al., 2018.

3 An analysis of channel and/or feature networks on YouTube.

   a Query design. Choose one or more channels. These may be micro-celebrities, influencers, political operatives or actors in a social movement, among other types. Alternatively, you may search for a channel.

   b Analytical procedure. Using the YouTube data tools' channel network module, enter one or more channel IDs. If searching, output results ranked according to 'relevance'.

   c Interpretation of results. Identify and describe clusters using the visual network analysis approach (see Table 8.1), where one concentrates in the first instance an analysis of the whole network (or panorama), identifying clusters and holes (the camps), together with their sizes and densities.

Resources

- YouTube Data Tools, https://tools.digitalmethods.net/netvizz/youtube/
- YouTube Data Tools worksheet, https://bit.ly/youtube-data-tools-how-to

- Gephi, https://gephi.org/
- Rankflow, http://labs.polsys.net/tools/rankflow/
- Raw graphs, https://rawgraphs.io/
- Video tutorials on the use of YouTube Data Tools, www.youtube.com/watch?v=sbErTW2MzCY (original) and www.youtube.com/watch?v=TmF4mWZYnbk (updated)

NINE

PLATFORM AND FACEBOOK STUDIES
Identifying engaging content

*When fake news becomes the most engaged-
with content on Facebook*

The 'platform'

'Platform studies' could be said to inquire into the (research) uses of a certain class of online software, exemplified by X/Twitter, Facebook, Instagram, YouTube and others. Platforms, roughly, are online services that host and deliver user-created content, or, in Tarleton Gillespie's (2010: 350) terms, are 'content-hosting intermediaries'. In introducing platform studies, Gillespie relates why it is worthwhile to study the evolution of the usage of the term 'platform', together with its understanding, by both social media companies and users. Initially, the platform could be understood as a software code base that roots an ecosystem of products, such as Apple's OS, Microsoft Windows and Google Android. The 'computing platform' article in Wikipedia defines it as 'simply… a place to launch software' (Wikipedia Contributors, 2014). The term's deployment by social media companies also may be attributed to its other meanings and connotations. A platform is a raised plateau or surface where people may stand or things may be placed; the political platform derives from this first dictionary meaning – a stage where politicians would stand – and is also a manifesto or set of positions of a political party, known, too, as a plank, which refers to the wooden boards from which the stage is built. Platforms, then, provide an opportunity to launch one's ideas, and dress up and present oneself. Especially in his follow-up blog posting on the same theme, Gillespie (2017) notes that the definition that emphasizes software is no longer *au courant*. The platform has become a space where users can have their say, build fan bases, and settle into niches of interest to advertisers. Even more importantly for the business side, the term also connotes a mere channel, like a telephone line, where people speak freely without editorial interference. '"Platform" suggests an impartial between-ness' (Gillespie, 2017). If they are only conduits rather than publishers, platforms are not considered (mass) media companies, and thus their content would not be regulated under laws that protect the public interest, such as striving for diversity of viewpoint and preventing concentration of power in single sources, situations enjoyed by such market leaders as Google (for search), Facebook (for social) and Instagram (photo-sharing). Following Latour (2005b), platforms could be called 'mediators' (rather than intermediaries), for they transform the material the user enters rather than merely transmitting it (Grusin, 2015).

Walled garden and platformization critiques

For both enclosed content spaces and proprietary software environments, however, platform connotes 'walled garden', where access, publishing and content rights are limited (Dekker and Wolfsberger, 2009). Critiques of walled gardens follow from the constraints put on users, developers as well as researchers. Facebook's content is described as 'trapped' behind password (and privacy) protections and unable to be directly linked to, crawled, archived or indexed (McCown and Nelson, 2009). Log in to continue, or create an account, as Facebook's interface reads, when a user is unregistered or logged out, and wishes to browse the content. Until recently, users tired of Facebook could only deactivate rather than delete their accounts, which led Dutch artists to create the so-called 'Web 2.0 Suicide Machine' that provided an automated means to witness the slow deletion of one's Facebook-led social life (Langelaar, 2012). (Facebook threatened legal action until the artists removed the little Facebook Connect 'f', or social button, from the Machine's interface.) Since then Facebook has made account deletion and the capacity 'to be forgotten' more manageable.

It has been argued that Facebook not only encircles or walls in its users, their friends and the content they produce. In a double logic, Facebook also makes the open web 'platform-ready' (Helmond, 2016). Logging into a website via Facebook places web users into Facebook's database. In doing so it allows the social media company to track users and ultimately categorize them for advertisers (see Figure 9.1). In all, 'platformization' is a data capturing ploy that strives to integrate the web into Facebook and vice versa. Much like Googlization was once used, platformization also could be applied to how the web is being transformed by social media (Vaidhyanathan, 2011; Thielmann et al., 2012).

Unlike mere channels or conduits, platforms are involved in decisions about publishing, and there are human editors taking decisions about content fitness. Facebook has (outsourced) low-wage content moderators and volunteer fact-checkers (Riesewieck and Block, 2018). Overexposure to online vitriol and indecent content led a Berlin-based company that cleans Facebook content to issue a statement that it has appropriate mental health services in place for its employees to turn to (Krause and Grassegger, 2016). Google once had students look over search engine results, via http://eval.google.com, to see whether they seem to make sense (Van Ess, 2005). X/Twitter has a 'trust and safety' team, looking out for abusive trolls.

Figure 9.1 'Taxonomy of humans according to Twitter'.

Source: Lavigne, 2017.

Other platforms control content, too. Apps made by developers to be sold in the App Store are vetted by Apple. Politically and socially charged apps may be kept from the store; an app game where the user could throw a shoe at the then US President George W. Bush was banned, as was one to bounce President Obama up and down in the Oval Office so as to pop balloons on the ceiling. 'Me so holy', where one may paste a selfie onto a Jesus-like figure (or other holy men), was pulled. A drug-peddling game (selling heroin and other substances across New York City) was kept from reaching users. Perhaps most famously, 'I am rich', which sold for a day for the maximum iTunes store price of US $999.99, was also banned. An artwork, it was described as having the sole purpose of demonstrating one's wealth by holding up the phone and showing onlookers a shimmering bauble (see Figure 9.2). They are intended to be humorous. But the theme that runs through the withdrawal decisions is presumed offensiveness, where Apple decides the fitness of the app for public consumption. (The 'I am rich' work by a German artist was seemingly construed as a scam.)

The 'walled garden' was originally put forward as a term for hardware, where without a common standard one would be locked into using only one company's products (Arthur, 1989; Pon et al., 2014). It also applies to interlocking hardware and software ecologies. As a case in point, iPhones need 'jail-breaking' to run unapproved apps, including a series of operating system 'tweaks' that allow custom modding, such as removing bloatware (unneeded software that comes pre-installed with phones) or installing home screens with enhanced functionality such as weather tracking.

Figure 9.2   'I am rich', $999.99 iPhone app by Armin Heinrich, August 2008.

Platforms and research restrictions

More to the point here is critique of walled gardens with respect to researcher use of platform data (Lomborg and Bechmann, 2014). Over the past decade or so, platforms have 'updated' their terms of service to disallow more and more data on them being scraped, stored, redistributed or repurposed. Since a brief attempt at a web search API (or data access point in 2010), Google has not allowed its search engine to be queried outside of its search bar, its search engine results stored or derivative works made of them. Facebook's terms of service (and its API) were once more open, too. It allowed one to study one's own friends, and their friends, making the social networking platform a site for 'tastes and ties' research; a researcher could delve into whether friends have similar profile preferences, for example, making them into cliques, a question sometimes put by social network analysis. Access to such data was shut down with Facebook's 2.0 version of its API (in 2015), whereupon only pages (and groups) could be studied, not friends and profile information, or their actions such as likes, shares, comments, shared comments and later reactions (Hogan, 2014; Rieder, 2015a).

Instagram shuttered its data interface for researchers (in 2016) and had those who had built tools upon it 'reapply' for access, often without success (Rieder, 2016). The ability to query for hashtags as well as geo-coordinates (for 'selfie city' research, for example, or hashtag publics) was thereby thwarted (Bruns and Burgess, 2015; Tifentale and Manovich, 2015). Unauthorized workarounds or enlisting the services of a media monitoring company would be some means to regain researcher access, as discussed below.

In the wake of the Cambridge Analytica scandal, where university researchers harvested Facebook profile data for the purposes of performing a psyops campaign, Facebook also had researchers reapply for access to its Pages API (Bruns et al., 2018; Rogers, 2018c). Access was not granted, leaving users of the data extraction software applications (such as Netvizz and Netlytic) in limbo (Rieder, 2018).

'Fake news' on Facebook

Facebook, with its mass user base of 2 billion monthly users (including 200 million in the USA), has been implicated in ideologically polarizing its users, abetting the preparation and circulation of so-called fake news (especially right-wing content), and allowing a Russian influence campaign to take place on its platform in the run-up to the US presidential elections (Broderick, 2016; Statistica, 2017). It also has been found to boost content that stirs emotion, such as posts that receive 'angry' reactions.

Where polarization is concerned, the creation and amplification of filter bubbles has had the effect of drawing users towards the increased consumption of (ideologically) similar content, some of which is of questionable provenance (Pariser, 2011a). In its 'Blue feed, red feed', the *Wall Street Journal* famously demonstrates the types of sources one would likely encounter on Facebook, given a particular political persuasion (Keegan, 2016). One's bent is gleaned from one's profile and other activity, and also offered to advertisers.

Figure 9.3   Meme (image macro) by Right Wing News. Highly ranked photo, with counter-jihadist sentiment.

Source: Right Wing News, September 2017.

Figure 9.4   Freedom Daily's news item, construed as misleading and false in Buzzfeed analysis (Silverman, 2016).

Source: Freedom Daily, 23 September 2016.

Where fake news circulation is concerned, the top sites in the feeds (by fan count) are often partisan rather than mainstream news, and many could be construed as 'hyperpartisan' sources, a term referring to 'openly ideological web operations' (Herrman, 2016) (see Figure 9.3). The initial 'fake news' crisis (Silverman, 2016) had to do with fly-by-night, imposter, conspiracy as well as hyperpartisan news sources outperforming mainstream news on Facebook in the run up to the 2016 US presidential elections. In a sense it was both a critique of Facebook as 'hyperpartisan political-media machine' (Herrman, 2016) but also that of the quality of a media landscape witnessing a precipitous rise in the consumption and sharing of 'alternative right' news and cultural commentary (Benkler et al., 2017; Holt et al., 2019). As a case in point, Freedom Daily, the most inaccurate according to the analysis, garnered the greatest engagement (sum of reactions, shares and comments), with stories such as the then President Obama calling for a world government during his final speech at the UN (see Figure 9.4). The greater the user engagement, the higher these stories are positioned on the news feed (Silverman, 2016). Accordingly, engagement-driven news feeds, together with their use, have pushed the most misleading stories to the top.

The events of the first crisis have been overtaken by a second one where politicians such as President Trump in the US and elsewhere employ the same term for certain media organizations in order to undermine their credibility. Against the backdrop of that politicization as well as rhetorical tactic, scholars have demurred using the term 'fake news' and instead offered 'junk news', 'problematic information', 'false news' and others (Vosoughi et al., 2018). Some definitions are roomier, and others stricter in their source classification schemes. Subsumed under the original 'fake news' definition are imposter news, conspiracy sources and hyperpartisan (or 'overly ideological web operations') (Herrman, 2016), and the newer term 'junk news' covers the same types of sources but adds the connotation of attractively packaged junk food that when consumed could be considered unhealthy (Howard, 2020; Venturini, 2019). It also includes two web-native source types. 'Clickbait' captures how the manner in which it is packaged or formatted lures one into consumption, and 'computational propaganda' refers to dubious news circulation by bot and troll-like means, artificially amplifying its symbolic power. Problematic information is even roomier, as it expands its field of vision beyond news to cultural commentary and satire (Jack, 2017). Stricter definitions such as 'false news' would encompass imposter and conspiracy but are less apt to include hyperpartisan news and cultural commentary, discussing those sources as 'misleading' rather than as 'fake' or 'junk' (Kist and Zantingh, 2017). Rather than an either/or proposition, 'fake news' could be understood as a Venn diagram or matryoshka dolls with problematic information encompassing junk news, junk news fake news, and fake news false news (Wardle, 2017).

Depending on the definition, the scale of the problem changes as does the range of means to address it. With 'false news', it grows smaller, and fact-checking again would be a profession to which to turn for background research into the story and the source. Fact-checking has been critiqued in this context because of the enormity of the task and the speed with which the lean workforces must operate. Facebook for one employs the term 'false news' and has striven to work with fact-checking bodies, though its overall approach is multi-faceted and relies more on (outsourced) content reviewers (Roberts, 2016; Gillespie, 2018). Other qualitative approaches such as media literacy and bias labelling are also manual undertakings, with adjudicators sifting through stories and sources one by one. When the problem is scaled down, these too become viable.

Roomier definitions make the problem larger and result in findings such as the most well-known 'fake news' story of 2016. 'Pope Francis shocks world, endorses Donald Trump for President' began as satire and was later circulated on a hyperpartisan, fly-by-night site (Ending the Fed). It garnered higher engagement rates on Facebook than more serious articles in the mainstream news. When such stories are counted as 'fake', 'junk' or 'problematic', and the scale increases, industrial-style custodial action may be preferred such as mass contention moderation as well as crowd-sourced and automated flagging, followed by platform escalation procedures and outcomes such as suspending or deplatforming stories, videos and sources.

As more content is taken down as a result of roomy source classification schemes, debates about freedom of choice may become more vociferous rather than less. It recalls the junk food debate, and in this regard, Zygmunt Bauman (2013) stressed how we as *homo eligens* or 'choosing animals' are wont to resist such restrictions, be it in opting for 'hyperprocessed' food or hyperpartisan news and cultural commentary. Labelling hyperpartisan news as 'fake' or 'junk', moreover, may lead to greater political backlash, as witnessed in the Netherlands where the publication of such a determination drew the ire of the leader of a conservative political party, who has targeted the mainstream news with the neologism, 'junk fake news' (Rogers and Niederer, 2020; Van Den Berg, 2019).

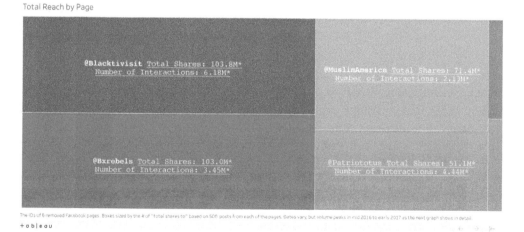

Figure 9.5   Shares and interactions scores of select Russian propaganda pages on Facebook.

Source: Albright, 2017.

The 'influence campaign' and 'meme war'

Around the same time, Facebook unwittingly facilitated a Russian influence campaign, which made use of analytics to hone the message. The campaigning was effective. According to the data journalism work by Albright (Timberg and Dwoskin, 2016), the then known Russian IRA disinformation Facebook Pages were 'shared 340 million times' (see Figure 9.5), although Facebook-furnished data reduced this figure (Howard et al., 2019). These Facebook pages, impersonating activist groups with such names as Blacktivists, United Muslims of America, Being Patriotic, Heart of Texas, Secured Borders and LGBT United, specialized in memes (see Figure 9.6).

Figure 9.6   Meme by Secured Borders, an activist organization with a Facebook page run by a Russian 'troll army'.

Source: Kovalev, 2017.

There are at least four official reconstructions of the Russian IRA influence operation in social media during the campaigning prior to the US presidential elections of 2016 (DiResta et al., 2019; Howard et al., 2019; Mueller, 2019; US Senate, 2020). Having received data from the social media companies (that otherwise is not publicly available), each details the computational propaganda campaigning, including the strategy of fomenting divisiveness, together with criticizing Hillary Clinton and supporting Donald Trump as well as Bernie Sanders, all presidential candidates at the time (Mueller, 2019). They also have long lists of tactics to meet their strategic goals such as organizing both 'sides' of a protest in Houston, Texas in May 2016, where people unwittingly supporting the 'United Muslims of America' fictitious group showed up at the same time as those from another, the 'Heart of Texas'.

The campaign is described as employing dozens of 'specialists', working out of an office building in St. Petersburg, Russia, meeting content quotas, specializing in particular topics, copy and pasting from media stories, and posting in acceptable English (Chen, 2015). Much of it was manufactured from found content online (photos, news, ads, artwork), memeified on generators (with two-liners) and branded with a logo often in the form of a slogan (e.g., Stop All Invaders, which was the second-best performing 'activist group' after Being Patriotic). Logos also evolved over time, keeping campaigns fresh.

Operating like a digital marketing agency or analytics-driven newsroom (Tandoc, 2019), they also monitored the success or resonance of their social media activity and acted upon that knowledge. Those posts that performed well according to the analytics would be reused. The same can be said for certain images as well as slogans. The analytics-driven approach, akin to early Buzzfeed's or Upworthy's philosophy of spreadability, seeks to find what 'stirs virality' and tailors content accordingly. The operatives amplified the content organically and through bots or other means.

To gain a sense of the quantity of memes deployed in the campaign, from 2015 until deactivated in mid-2017, on Facebook its 81 pages posted 67,502 times, and on Instagram there were 116,205 posts from 133 accounts (Howard et al., 2019). According to one report, there were over 100,000 pieces of visual content deployed (DiResta et al., 2019). Certain of the research reports use the term 'memetic warfare' to describe the campaign (DiResta et al., 2019). Another term that captures how ordinary users amplify the tactical memeing is 'memetic participation' (Miltner, 2018). Here the memes are evaluated for their effectiveness in a variety of senses. From the 'memetic warfare' standpoint, effectiveness lies in their 'propagation, persistence, and impact' (DiResta et al., 2019). Reach, retention and engagement, in the language of marketing, would be a similar way of phrasing it. 'Memetic participation' emphasizes the collaborative nature of meme-making, for memes are not only broadcasted, they are added to by the creators but also by their users.

When examining the examples of visual content across the reports, most of it would be considered memes, or more specifically image macros, mostly two-liners, some one-liners, and even longer blog-like posts next to an image macro. Moreover, memes were the most engaged-with content overall and per 'activist group' (Facebook page / Instagram account), at least as far as the reports show. These memes are datafied with analytics behind them. They are made to engage, endure and propagate ('memetic warfare'), but also for others to join in, be it in meme-making, the causes they espouse or the protests they organize ('memetic participation').

Therefore, the study of memes as analytics-driven campaign media emphasizes their performance, rather than their aesthetic fit as native internet phenomena or their standardization as image macros, though they benefit from the latter. It also does not foreground memeing as pranking for the lulz, as on 4chan, but it could be seen somewhat analogously as 'cultural hacking' (Confessore and Wakabayashi, 2017).

Advertising on Facebook and preferential content

Part of the influence campaign took place through advertising on Facebook. When one wishes to advertise on Facebook, one types a keyword (e.g., immigration) and receives an audience size (about 34 million for that particular term at the time of writing), upon which one decides to make a buy for that audience. Facebook has tens of thousands of interest or demographic categories for advertisers to search through; when choosing a category there are suggestions of adding other related ones, increasing audience size. An investigation by reporters in ProPublica's 'machine bias' series describes how Facebook advertising may be used to target particular groups in the culture war:

> [W]e logged into Facebook's automated ad system to see if 'Jew hater' was really an ad category. We found it but discovered that the category – with only 2,274 people in it – was too small for Facebook to allow us to buy an ad pegged only to Jew haters. Facebook's automated system suggested 'Second Amendment' as an additional category that would boost our audience size to 119,000 people, presumably because its system had correlated gun enthusiasts with anti-Semites. (Angwin et al., 2017)

Another analyst argues that the influence campaign not only supported a particular candidate (Trump) by using Facebook pages with wedge issue memes and targeted ad buys, but also by supplying US media with compromising materials on Hillary Clinton (the leaked emails), thereby successfully exporting Russian-style *kompromat*. Facebook (not to mention the web) allowed an opening into the US media system, once 'separate' from Russia's and its narratives, it is argued (Oates, 2017). Regarding the separation of media systems, in the 1990s 'cyberspace' once was thought to collapse them, but since the routine implementation of geolocation in the 2000s by web and platform services there are also geographical and linguistic lines drawn online. Even though it has country subdomains, Facebook, among other social media sites, arguably reglobalizes the web, or at least enables multiple languages and geographies in one space.

Among the revelations in the internal Facebook documents furnished by the Facebook whistleblower, Frances Haugen, is how Facebook calculates preferential content (Hagey and Horwitz, 2021). It applies a scoring system to posts and boosts those with higher scores in its news feed. In the Facebook parlance, it is called 'downstream MSI', or meaningful social interaction that will drive more interaction. In the calculation, 'likes' receive 1 point, 'shares' and other reactions receive 5 points, comments and reshares 15 points and significant comments or reshares 30 points. ('Significant' ones have longer threads.) The Facebook files, a series of articles by *The Wall Street Journal*, reported that Facebook would boost content that provokes vexation or has users arguing. Such content is also referred to as 'angertainment'. (A student of mine called the Facebook feed an 'angerithm'.) It was effective, downstream, in that overall engagement on the platform increased. Haugen, in testimony, said Facebook would turn off downstream MSI prior to elections and turn it on again thereafter.

Studying 'memeification'

In the examination of meme campaigning, discussed above, researchers employed analytical software to cluster visually similar images to understand 'memetic tactics' (DiResta et al., 2019). They made at least two kinds of findings. Having grouped the images by visual similarity, they noticed that the same image was reused across platforms, indicating, in their analytics approach, that since it performed well on one platform, it was subsequently introduced onto another. They also found that the same image was reused on multiple occasions, albeit with different two- and one-liners, suggesting that the image was effective, but various messaging strategies were tested.

Visual similarity analysis will group the same images as well as what Steyerl (2009) has called their 'poor image' counterparts, meaning those that have been cropped or otherwise downsampled as well as those which have been given another caption. The most successful memes (out of a large meme collection such as the Russian IRA influence campaign) are those quantities with the same image and text, followed by those with the same image and different text. Thus, meme impact analysis becomes a matter of visual cluster inspection.

One may also locate the extent to which one or more memes are among the dominant visual content in sets of images and at the same time seek out the 'failed images', or those memes that do not meet the standards of what is expected (Van Alphen, 2018). While having multiple analytical features, PicArrange (as well as ImageSorter and others) group images by formal property, where those with the same or similar hues are clustered.

Computer vision software (such as Google Vision) takes advantage of various web or text entities (such as alt text or alt image tags) and labels and groups them more substantively rather than by image similarity only. That is, while the visual similarity analysis favours the image, the web entity approach privileges associated text. Here, with a large collection of images queried for keywords, one would investigate which themes are well memeified, and which less so. Are the memeified issues expressed in a particular tone, such as jokey and/or divisive?

For the techniques that favour the image, visually similar arrangements enable the study of the 'intactness' of memes as they are remixed and circulated (Knobel and Lankshear, 2007). Indeed, it is the modification of the original that is of interest when studying how new contributions add to the meme. Here visual analysis makes perhaps its finest contribution to meme research for it can identify 'additive content' as visually similar collections.

There are also meme-inspectors (Chao, 2021), or analytical software applications that identify image macros among a set of images. After inspecting the extent to which a visual media space is or is not populated by memes ('memeified'), the researcher can extract all the memes and then group them anew to study the most successful memes as well as intactness at the same time.

With vision techniques, memes become collections of single pieces of image content that have been reused and/or recaptioned. They tend to be image macros, for meme inspection software is usually trained to locate those.

Facebook engagement studies

How is Facebook engagement conventionally measured and studied? Whether on CrowdTangle, Meta's social media monitoring dashboard, BuzzSumo, the content marketing platform, or another data access point, engagement is the sum of reactions, shares and comments. One can query Facebook data dashboards for keywords, e.g., Covid-19, the global pandemic. CrowdTangle, for one, returns posts containing the keywords, while BuzzSumo returns web URLs. Both are ranked by interactions, or engagement. With the results from the query, researchers can study the extent to which the posts or the web URLs (on Facebook posts) are suffused with conspiracy theory or other misinformation, thereby studying the so-called 'infodemic' and at the same time the efficacy of the platform's content moderation efforts.

One can also build a list of Facebook Pages (e.g., the Somali diaspora) and study the engagement of posts per page as well as across all pages. It is a technique that allows one to study what animates groups, such as in the Somali diaspora case homeland or host land matters (Kok and Rogers, 2017). One can consider giving greater weight to certain types of interaction, with (at least according to Facebook) comments being the most significant, followed by shares and reactions other than likes. Here one can note which posts anger a community, for example.

Engagement studies are analytics-driven. They ask to which extent certain content and content formats (as memes) 'work' well in digital culture, compared (for example) to iconic images that have worked well in print and other media. They ask at the same time which content and formats are most engaged with on the platform and across platforms by certain groups of users? Does the same content work as well on Facebook as on Instagram? Do the same formats stir groups of users, or communities, on a particular platform and across multiple ones?

Engagement studies also show which content and formats have been amplified by the platform, though the disentanglement of user-driven and platform-driven engagement is not often studied. Rather, the difficulty in measuring 'platform effects' is employed as a critique of the reliance on engagement when considering group animation. Social media metrics are not measuring user behaviour in the wild. Rather, they could be said to show analytics-driven user behaviour, where content is optimized by producers as well as the platform for engagement.

As discussed above, there is a format, the meme, that has been found to drive engagement, and thus could be construed as analytics-driven. Limor Shifman, author of an essential guide to memes in digital culture, has written, 'almost every major public event sprouts a stream of memes' (2013: 4). She also argues that memes and digital culture appear to be a 'marriage made in heaven' (2013: 5). Do memes tend to 'work' in digital culture better than other media (content) formats? Can Facebook be explored as meme machine, where memes work so well that they collectively dominate an account of the event? Have they supplanted the 'iconic' image of mass media as a dominant media format of an event? Could iconicity on new media, or on platforms, be thought of in terms of the extent to which users contribute to a meme and build a meme collection?

Shifman also has empirically examined memetic content (in her case, YouTube videos), and found common features: ordinary people, flawed masculinity, humour, simplicity, repetitiveness and whimsical content. On Facebook memes are often image macros, from meme generators, which are images with overlaid text, typically a two-liner above and below the image, opening and closing a thought. They contribute to the ongoing story of an event, campaign, movement or another content cloud in the making. Memes, as 'contributive content', also may provide ongoing 'additive comprehension'. How would one describe the unfolding of a meme as a collection of content building over time? How would one describe how memes fill in or add to a specific or competing comprehensions of events, campaigns, movements, etc.?

The idea of Facebook as meme machine rests on the spreadability of image macros and other meme formats on the platform. As has been found, memes are the most engaged-with content on particular pages, such as Breitbart News (see Figure 9.7). Hyperpartisan pages regularly deploy memes, too, as a format of communication of standpoints. Media organizations memefy the news by placing captions on news images.

Figure 9.7 Most shared content from Breitbart Facebook page, 2016.

Source: Renner, 2017.

One may capture most engaged-with content on one or more Facebook pages, and study the extent to which they are memes, thereby testing the claim of their (analytics-driven) dominance. CrowdTangle also has a 'meme search', which through a keyword query enables one to build a collection of images overlaid with text. The search function allows for searching post text or image text. Searching for post text allows one to build a topical collection; image text searches are useful for phrasal meme research, e.g., Make America Great Again, the slogan employed by Trump supporters.

PROJECTS

Analyse the 'most engaged-with content' of a set of Facebook pages

RESEARCH GOAL To determine the content that most animates a movement, group or community.

One may examine networks, movements, followers, sympathizers, supporters and other loosely organized collections of publics in Facebook, and inquire into the content that engages them. The study of engagement (or interactions) concerns a combination of rating (like), reading (comment) and circulating (share). In that sense, it is a rather comprehensive measure, though it is driven by a combination of platform and producer content optimization together with user preference.

Specifically, what type of content (and which types of formats) is most engaged with (or 'interacted with')? Is it predominantly 'angry' content? Are the formats predominantly memes? To what extent is Facebook an 'angertainment' machine?

The assignment is to examine related Facebook pages, inquire into the content and formats that engage, together with their significance for the study of the platform as well as the group.

Alternatively, one may create two sets of Facebook pages (e.g., supporters of competing candidates) and discuss the differences between what animates each.

The procedure for curating a list of thematically related pages and determining 'most engaged-with content' is as follows:

1   Consider the theme to study before curating a list of Facebook pages related to it (e.g., right-wing groups in Europe or European migration crisis).
2   Query Google for site:facebook.com and theme. Make list of Facebook Pages on a spreadsheet.
3   Query Facebook's graph search for the names found through Google (e.g., individual right-wing groups or individual migrant aid groups) or theme (e.g., European migration crisis), and place on spreadsheet.
4   Triangulate or concatenate lists (use a threshold, e.g., top ten pages by like count).
5   Using CrowdTangle, on the dashboard create a list of Facebook pages by searching for their names.
6   Obtain 'most engaged-with content' scores (total interactions) of all the posts on the Facebook Pages. Is it predominantly 'angertainment' or memes?
7   Consider visualizing the outcome as a tree map (see Figure 11.14).

Studying 'fake news'

RESEARCH GOAL To determine the extent of 'fake news' in a Facebook issue space, where issue space is a set of results for substantive queries, such as Covid-19 or election-related issues.

The goal is to evaluate the quality and show the political leaning of the top sources returned. In other words, to what extent is 'fake news' (as defined in the seminal news article) present in the most engaged-with content in political spaces on Facebook? Is there more engagement with hyperpartisan conservative or progressive sources in political spaces on Facebook? How would such engagement imply a politicization of the 'fake news' problem?

1　First curate a list of social issues. For election-related issues, consult issue lists at voting aid sources. Note that the issue language should not be politically charged. As an example, use 'abortion' rather than 'pro-life' or 'pro-choice'.

2　Query Buzzsumo, the content marketing platform, for each issue keyword. Buzzsumo returns a list of web URLs, ranked by interactions, which is the sum of likes, shares and comments, and for every issue, examine at least the top ten stories returned.

3　Each of the source names, headlines and any description text are read, and the sources are roughly labelled either by how the sources self-identify and/or by using pre-existing source classification schemes. For example, in the US context there are media bias labelling sites including AllSides, Media Bias/Fact Check, 'The Chart' and NewsGuard. These labelling sites indicate whether the source is problematic or questionable as well as its political leaning.

4　Using a spreadsheet (where issues are columns and ranked sources rows), colour code in each cell the political leaning. Using another sheet colour code whether each is problematic.

Video tutorials

- 'Social Media Research with Digital Methods', www.youtube.com/watch?v=PtSNZfYKRnk
- 'Studying Fake News', www.youtube.com/watch?v=phOVLrzlj8c (31'06')
- 'How to make a Treemap', www.rawgraphs.io/learning/how-to-make-a-treemap (1' 37')

Data sources

- Crowdtangle, www.crowdtangle.com
- Buzzsumo, www.buzzsumo.com

X/TWITTER AS STORY-TELLING MACHINE
Following events

Debanalizing tweets (three ways),
rather than debunking
Twitter's role in the revolution

Twitter, renamed X, has been perhaps the most approachable social media platform for analytical research and as such the most used, even overused. In the following I discuss the evolution of Twitter as an object of study, beginning with its discovery of the value of its data (when the company went to the stock exchange) and its impact on academic research. I also treat questions concerning the ethics of storing and analysing Twitter data. Thereafter I detail how Twitter has been researched – from an ambient, friend-following medium, over one in which to follow events and monitor issues such as #blacklivesmatter to finally a medium known for its toxicity. I refer to the historical platform as Twitter until it changed its name to X, whereupon I call it X/Twitter.

Twitter goes to market

Twitter, which once was called the last of the Web 2.0 applications (for its openness to external, live data collection to make 'mashups'), changed its terms of service as it became a publicly traded company (in 2011), making the exporting of tweets and shared tweet collections a violation (Burgess, 2016). It was one of those moments when one's work is scuppered by a new version of software. A researcher at Harvard's Berkmann Center noted that Twitter is not 'considering the myriad number of PhD students who basically just lost their work, or the researchers that were close to saying something meaningful and now have no way to do it' (Watters, 2011). In the event, one is able to share a set of tweet ID numbers (rather than the tweets themselves), which then allows another researcher to recompile a tweet collection from them, effectuating sharing. (The term for such recompiling is 'rehydration'.) Among other effects, rehydrating a tweet collection filters out deleted, suspended and withheld tweets – three potentially interesting categories for analysis – of any newly reconstructed collection, in keeping with Twitter's rules.

Collections of such tweets exist for research purposes, however. Politicians' deleted tweets are captured by the Politwoops project by the Dutch Open State Foundation (and the Sunlight Foundation in the USA and later ProPublica), where one may study scandals prompted by impetuous and salacious tweeting. Twitter once cut its access to these foundations' data-collecting, before agreeing that politicians' tweets are matters of public record rather than violations of 'Twitter Rules' on users' expectation of privacy. The 2023 X/Twitter API outage also stopped the collection-keeping.

Twitter's 'transparency reporting', in part a product of that debate, provides facts and figures concerning withheld tweets, where for example in one year Turkey and France had the most tweets withheld, 2232 and 1334 respectively, though the actual number of blocked tweets appears to be much higher, at least for Turkey, raising questions about the transparency reporting practices (Tanash et al., 2015). As researchers did for Turkey, one could conceivably take stock of tweets withheld from one country by doing the capturing in another country. Suspended accounts (such as the wave of them that hit the 'alt-right' in the USA) are emptied of previous tweets, making them inaccessible to researchers. One such case, @nero, Milo Yiannopoulos's Twitter account, has no trace left on Twitter.com. Independent archiving services (such as tweetsave.com) may have the tweets, where one could study what constitutes behaviour worthy of suspension, to whom it applies and how the standards may have changed over time.

Twitter's reinstatement of accounts under the stewardship of CEO Elon Musk is also worthy of examination, not to mention the perceived deterioration of the platform's content moderation and the impact on academic research of the new monetization strategies. Perhaps the most well-known reinstatement is Donald Trump's account, 'permanently suspended' or deplatformed after the Capitol riots of January, 2021. He was relieved of his ability to tweet 'due to the risk of further incitement of violence' (Twitter, 2021). It is back online, reactivated since the change at the top of the company, though the account is frozen in time, with one of the last tweets from January 8th, 2021, reading: 'To all of those who have asked, I will not be going to the Inauguration on January 20th'. (He also tweeted his Georgia mug shot in August 2023, taken on the occasion of his indictment and booking for election interference.) After his suspension from Twitter and despite his reinstatement, he mainly has migrated to his own platform, Truth Social, where he posts in the same tweeting style, albeit to a fraction of the 87.5 million followers he had garnered on Twitter.

Many extreme internet celebrities have been reinstated in keeping with Musk's self-declared 'free speech absolutism' (Thornhill, 2022). At the time of writing X/Twitter's rules and more so their 'capricious' application concerning the moderation of content are the subject of scrutiny (Siddiqui, 2022; de Keulenaar et al., 2023). Empirical research additionally has found a rise in extremist and anti-Semitic content (Finkelstein et al., 2023).

The major changes also are in Twitter's monetization strategies, encompassed in the sale of blue account checkmarks once reserved for 'active, notable, and authentic accounts of public interest' until the roll out of the 'Twitter Blue subscription service' (Twitter, n.d.).

Another is the end of Twitter's gratis academic API, taken offline in early 2023. As with the previous API closures (by Facebook, in particular), multiple data-collecting tools broke and research projects stalled (Bruns, 2019).

Twitter as stored object, and its research ethics

Twitter was once particularly open to researcher access. In the halcyon days of Web 2.0, data mashups were common, such as placing Twitter's trending topics on a Google Map. Such a spirit of 2.0 openness, together with the significance of Twitter as data set, are expressed in the announcement, around the same time, of its donation of almost every tweet ever tweeted to the Library of Congress for scholarly usage (Raymond, 2010a). Twitter provided a 'historical record of communication, news reporting, and social trends', as well as a prism to study events such as the 'US presidential elections in 2008 and the green revolution in Iran in 2009' (Raymond, 2010b). Therein lies the presumed scholarly value: news, trends and event analysis together with communication studies.

Twitter described its agreement with the Library in another blog post, together with the limits placed on studying the most recent tweets: 'It should be noted that there are some specifics regarding this arrangement. Only after a six-month delay can the Tweets be used for internal library use, for non-commercial research, public display by the library itself, and preservation' (Stone, 2010).

As the Library described it, 'bona fide researchers' would have access, and deleted tweets are not included, thereby respecting user intent (Raymond, 2010a, 2010b). (Old tweets deleted from Twitter but already archived in the Library presumably would live on, however.)

Some years on, however, the Library has not been able to provide access, even after fielding hundreds of written requests from researchers (Osterberg, 2013; McGill, 2016). The Twitter archive has become data too big for the Library to handle beyond sheer preservation, though it remains to be seen how it will be accessed in future (Zimmer, 2015). By January 2018 the Library announced it would no longer preserve Twitter's entire volume but would curate selective events and themes, 'similar to our collections of web sites', which could mark a return, in the web archiving tradition, to disasters, (presidential) transitions and elections (Osterberg, 2017), as discussed in the Internet Archive chapter. The Library has the first 12 years of tweets (the text) stored.

What are some of the concerns about working with stored tweets? In an analysis of the discussions around the Twitter archive, Michael Zimmer argues that the Library is not taking into account users' expectations of privacy, raising the larger question of whether it is ethical to store tweets (not to mention mine and analyse them) without user consent. Are they publications (to be cited)? Michael Beurskens (2014) has argued that since the users do not hold copyright on their tweets there is no legal case to cite tweets or attribute them to an author, though there may be a normative and scholarly case to be made. Or are tweets utterances in a larger sea of clamour not intended to be captured, stored (and analysed)? If it is too unwieldy to ask users to grant permission, could they at least be given the means to opt out (as is the case with websites in the Internet Archive)? In a spirited debate in the comment space of a Zimmer blog posting, Zimmer (2010b) writes: '[J]ust because they are public doesn't mean the intent was to allow them to be automatically archived [and] processed. That's the issue regarding whether additional consent is necessary'.

In another article, Zimmer found that the vast majority of researchers using Twitter data do not consider the ethics of user data collection and analysis (Zimmer and Proferes, 2014). There appears to be an overriding assumption that the 'data are already public' and that users have agreed to Twitter's terms of service, granting researchers licence: 'The fact that users grant Twitter a license to use their tweets (which is necessary for the service to work) means nothing in terms of whether it is ethical for researchers to systematically follow and harvest public tweet streams' (Zimmer, 2010b).

Interpreting Twitter's terms of service for researchers

Should users expect that their tweets are analysed by researchers? Like other social media companies, Twitter generally seeks to follow a 'transparency and choice approach' to privacy, where the user is told how the tweets are disseminated and (re)used and is offered forms of protection in software settings (Nissenbaum, 2011). The approach is laid out in its policies. Twitter has terms of service, a privacy policy, more general policies on use and abuse as well as developer terms that include sections on 'user protection' and privacy expectations. Emphasizing the publicness and extensive reach of the service, each provides descriptions (sometimes graphic ones) about what users should expect when they tweet.

In the terms of service, one grants Twitter the licence 'to make your content available to the rest of the world and to let others do the same' (Twitter, 2017a). Here there is an emphasis on wide-ranging reach as well as reuse. In the privacy policy, the emphasis on reuse is expressed as an admonition that one's data is being mined:

> Twitter broadly and instantly disseminates your public information to a wide range of users, customers, and services, including search engines, developers, and publishers that integrate Twitter content into their services, and organizations such as universities, public health agencies, and market research firms that analyze the information for trends and insights. When you share information or content like photos, videos, and links via the Services, you should think carefully about what you are making public. (Twitter, 2017b)

Twitter thus explicitly states that university researchers are to make use of one's tweets. Once the warnings have been given, the more general policies put the onus on users to protect their privacy by protecting tweets (as well as modifying and deleting them). One also may create a 'verified' account to guard against impersonation, though the cachet implied by a verified account (and exploited by political actors on the far right, for example) later gave Twitter pause, and in early 2018 that service was suspended.

Developers, finally, are asked to respect user intentions and 'partner' with Twitter by not retaining deleted, withheld, suspended as well as modified tweets (where, for example, the geo-coordinates have been removed). Twitter also is explicit about disallowing certain types of mining and analysis, especially those that aim 'to target, segment, or profile individuals based on health (including pregnancy), negative financial status or condition, political affiliation or beliefs, racial or ethnic origin, religious or philosophical affiliation or beliefs, sex life or sexual orientation, trade union membership...' (Twitter, 2017c). Twitter is targeting work (presumably including research) that segments and profiles groups. I discuss one approach to audience segmentation below.

There is another section in the developer terms of service that relates to remote event-following (which is discussed as an analytical strategy below) that is addressed to governmental researchers. Twitter should not be used by states to surveil or monitor protesters, demonstrators and such, it reads. Twitter thereby provides some legal cover for (university and other) researchers to mine and analyse data, at the same time restricting some types of use. Indeed, the most specific scenarios of data use are contained in the developer documentation, including the suggestion that one can be 'grouped' among protesters at a demonstration, and sorted into a category such as climate change sceptics (Pearce, 2018). Such a label may be difficult to shed; users also may not know that they have been profiled.

An additional issue for ethics and privacy researchers is that people do not read the terms of service, as evidenced by their online behaviour. When Twitter users do not modify their behaviour, but rather just post away, it appears they have not read the terms of service, have no reasonable expectation of being mined and analysed, or think it is futile. 'If people expect to be monitored, if they anticipate that their recorded views will be shared with particular third parties for money or favors, they are likely to be more watchful, circumspect, or uncooperative' (Nissenbaum, 2011: 45).

Whenever users expect to be surveilled or monitored, they presumably will change their behaviour, as was the case during the Iran election crisis when it was rumoured that repressive state authorities were checking user locations; all people employing the #iranelection hashtag were subsequently asked to change their Twitter location to Tehran. Here one may study not just chilling effects (and self-censorship) but also media tactics. How are users affected by surveillance? Does surveillance kill content and info-sharing?

Before moving on to strategies of tweet collection-making and analysis, it is worth pointing out the first comment made by a web user to the Library of Congress's FAQs that questions the research value of Twitter generally and historical tweets particularly. He wrote: 'It's critical that future generations know what flavor burrito I had for lunch' (Raymond,

2010b). Thus summarizes the idea of the banality of Twitter (Farhi, 2009). It also has been the object of sampling analysis, one of which found that 40% of tweets are 'pointless babble' (Pear Analytics, 2009). The marketing research described pointless babble as the '"I am eating a sandwich now" tweets' (Pear Analytics, 2009: 3). The question to be posed of its study, then, is how to debanalize Twitter (Rogers, 2013a). Or, more specifically, what kinds of techniques and heuristics may be put to use to make sense of Twitter data, and to what scholarly ends? Previously, the presumed scholarly value (of the Twitter archive) was said to lie in the analysis of news, trends and events, together with communication studies.

To those ends, the research undertakings below follow from taking the digital objects given by the device (hashtags, @mentions, retweets, shortened URLs), and thinking how to repurpose them for social research, which could be seen as the digital methods approach. It asks how to make a tweet collection, and how to analyse the tweets so as to debanalize X/Twitter. It thereby takes advantage of X/Twitter as news or event-following medium rather than its earlier moniker as the what-I-had-for-lunch device. It also turns X/Twitter into an issue space, where publics organize and compete to establish what is at stake.

Twitter as urban lifestyle tool for ambient friend-following

Created by Jack Dorsey and partners in San Francisco in 2006, Twitter arguably began as an American urban youth lifestyle tool, meant as a means to provide status updates on friends' whereabouts (see Figure 10.1). The Twitter user would answer the question, 'What are you doing?' It is a tool for people out and about, adding what is sometimes referred to as 'ambient intimacy', and what Dorsey described as 'the physical sensation that you're buzzing your friend's pocket' (O'Reilly and Milstein, 2009; Sarno, 2009a). In 2006 and 2007 Dorsey maintained a Flickr account, where he posted photographs of his urbanite life and times, including his 'twttr sketch', which he annotated with an origins story, including his work at a start-up dispatch company in Oakland for courier, taxi and emergency services (Dorsey, 2006). In the two-part interview Dorsey gave for the *Los Angeles Times*, he notes how he borrowed the short messaging service (SMS) format, which has the constraint of 160 characters, before the message is split in two parts (Sarno, 2009a). The original 140 characters allowed in a tweet (later doubled) left 20 characters for username and other metadata needs. The URL stat.us (in Dorsey's original sketch) comes from the period when ccTLD name hacks like del.icio.us were *en vogue*, and twttr (a five-character code in keeping with messaging protocol) is also notably a Web 2.0-like name like flickr, thereby dating the application.

Often also originally associated with (and used at) events, Twitter outputs the real-time, and it is fleeting. In a sense, it makes new media more ephemeral than the web. Dorsey said:

> I don't go back in time. You're kind of as good as your last update. That's what you're currently thinking or doing, or your current approach towards life. If that

really interests me, I go to that person's profile page and read back a little bit. But in terms of my timeline, I'm just not obsessive about going all the way back in time and catching every single message that people have updated about. It's only relevant in the now, unless I'm fascinated by it. (Sarno, 2009b)

In 2009 Twitter changed the question it posed to its users from 'What are you doing?' to 'What's happening?', perhaps parlaying and translating Twitter's success at events, but also thereby creating a market for Twitter data from the once banal to the newsworthy. Indeed, why tweet? Is it to make news, gain followers, be retweeted or 'liked'? Is it to pad one's metrics? And who is one tweeting for? Is one treating one's audience as a fan base (Marwick and boyd, 2011b)? Populist politicians such as Geert Wilders in the Netherlands and Donald Trump in the USA (before he was deplatformed) have followed nearly no one, but rather have treated Twitter as a broadcast medium for large throngs of fans and supporters (or supporters as fans). Trump does the same on Truth Social, an alternative to Twitter.

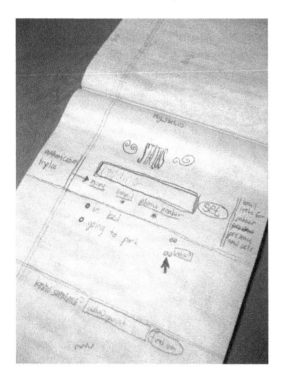

Figure 10.1 Original 'twttr sketch' by Jack Dorsey.

Source: Dorsey, 2006.

The research affordances of Twitter's natively digital objects

Apart from studies of phatic communication and 'remote intimacy' of Dorsey's Twitter (2006), researchers have approached it as more than a real-time personal status update machine (for young urbanites) (Miller, 2008; Marwick and boyd, 2011a; Papacharissi, 2012). Many of Twitter's research affordances are owed to their natively digital objects, which are in part user innovations (Bruns, 2012; see Figure 10.2). The hashtag groups tweets by topic, the retweet indicates pass-along value and the @reply and @mention are threads and references. Thus, through analyses of hashtags, Twitter is said to organize urgency and information flows such as around disasters and other events. One may study hashtag publics and explore the claim that they are 'fleeting' rather than stable (Rambukkana, 2015; Bruns et al., 2016). Concentrating on RTs (a button for which is built into the Twitter interface), they can be made to give an account of the unfolding of events, as discussed below (Rogers et al., 2009b). Here the question is the extent to which it may be employed for 'remote event analysis', and how these accounts would hold up to other first drafts of history, such as in newspapers and in Wikipedia articles (Bruns and Weller, 2016). By focusing on the @replies, Twitter may be analysed as a conversation-maker, where one may explore the extent to which there is dialogue, or broadcasting, on Twitter (Honeycutt and Herring, 2009; boyd et al., 2010). In considering @mentions, one also may pinpoint (and critique) dominant voice, as in who is being mentioned the most in a tweet collection, compiled to capture a certain issue space such as global health and development, where for example the Gates Foundation may be the actor most mentioned. Here the question may revolve around the extent to which these voices are driving the agenda and organizing urgency and symbolic power for some issues (and care strategies) rather than others (Couldry, 2001, 2012; Chouliaraki, 2013).

Figure 10.2 Chris Messina, Twitter user and Twitter hashtag inventor.

Source: Parker, 2011. Photo credit: Kris Cheng.

Tweet collection studies and critical analytics

Tweet collection-making generally follows from hashtag and keyword queries, though one can also query a user's account (Geert Wilders' or Donald Trump's historical tweets), or one or more @mentions (who mentions the alt-right?).

For the sake of robustness, it may be advisable to undertake a two-step query design. Having explored the (hashtag and keyword) language in an issue or event space (through Google or in X/Twitter itself), make an initial tweet collection through a search, and perform hashtag frequency or co-hashtag analysis with the results, which in the latter case is a list ranked by frequency of those hashtags that occur together in the tweets in your collection. Add newly discovered, significant hashtags to the query, and launch the search again. This second query, in the two-step process, is the one that results in the tweet collection under study.

With such tools as DMI-TCAT and 4CAT, there is often a battery of analytical modules to be explored (Borra and Rieder, 2014; Peeters and Hagen, 2022). The critical analytics strategy put forward here is only one means to study a tweet collection, and it is especially geared towards the critical study of social issues and their publics through relatively simple techniques (Rogers, 2018a). A second analytical strategy, for event-following or 'remote event analysis', follows below.

Among the critical analytics to study an issue space are dominant voice, concern, commitment, positioning as well as alignment. Dominant voice, as mentioned, is a list of those @mentions that appear in an issue space. Ranked by frequency (and by frequent co-occurrence) it provides a sense of whose voice resonates (or is referenced) the most. (Vocality, contrariwise, is a measure of who tweets with the greatest frequency in an issue space.) Hashtags are often embedded issues (as well as campaigns and events), so concern, as an analytic measure, is a list of hashtags most used. Co-hashtag lists may be employed to study the twinning of concerns, and issue hybridization, for example, #rivers and #humanrights (see Figure 10.3). Commitment is the persistent appearance of users and issues in a space and is measured over time. The technique could be employed for users as well as for users together with hashtags and/or keywords. Do particular NGOs move in and out of issue spaces depending on their newsworthiness, or do they remain engaged? Positioning is the use of specific keywords rather than others. Do I choose to use the term 'blood diamonds' (thereby taking a stand with activists) or 'conflict diamonds' (lining up with industry)? Alignment, finally, means those actors using the same issue language. Who else uses #apartheidwall (the official Palestinian term), and who else #securityfence (the official Israeli term for the barrier between Israel and the Palestinian territories)?

Twitter revolutions and other claims to be debunked (and empirically tested)

X/Twitter has often been dubbed a micro-blogging platform, but it may be characterized as a medium in a variety of ways. On Twitter users may follow other users, meaning that, like other social media platforms, one could view and study X/Twitter as a social network (Java et al., 2007; Huberman et al., 2009). If one studies the trending topics (a front-page interface item and metric on X/Twitter), one finds that they often concern news items, thus making X/Twitter a rebroadcaster (Kwak et al., 2010). As mentioned above, one may also study how populist politicians and others (with many followers, but who follow few to none) use the medium primarily for broadcasting. Do these together constitute an echo chamber, filter bubble or even culture war, or are there distinctive anomalies that would force those concepts to be stretched or rendered less usable? A larger question (for media research) concerns how to characterize the medium for specific user groups deemed worthy of research, despite Twitter's terms of use. How to describe the distinctive concerns of the new (populist) right? Who do they @mention, which hashtags do they use, and which sources do they reference? How to characterize their media tactics and communication strategy?

Figure 10.3   Issue hybridization of rivers and human rights. Tweet containing multiple, issue-oriented hashtags, a reference, as well as authoritative @mentions.

GEAG @GEAG_India · Jun 24

#Rivers get #HumanRights :They can sue to protect themselves bit.ly/2rFps0j
@indiawater @guardian @intlrivers @Indian_Rivers

There is another strand of research which may be called X/Twitter impact studies. For example, one undertakes analysis of how tweets organize awareness, and measure, or enunciate, word on the street and word of mouth (Jansen et al., 2009). Possibly the best-known ideas about Twitter impacts came into existence around the Iran elections of June 2009, where the term 'Twitter revolution' was coined (Berman, 2009). In its disambiguation page, Wikipedia notes that the term may be used in connection with a series of 'spring' and 'colour' uprisings: the Moldovan civil disturbances of 2009 as well as the Tunisian and Egyptian revolutions of 2011, otherwise known as part of the Arab Spring (Wikipedia Contributors, 2018a). It also could refer to Euromaidan, the Ukrainian uprising of 2013. Here one often strives to research the 'role' of Twitter (and other social media) in such events (Zuckerman, 2011; Srinivasan, 2014). Such a study of the role or part played by

Twitter often begins by challenging the idea of technology as revolutionary or central to social change. In one such undertaking, the researchers debunked the claim of Twitter as vital in the Iran election crisis (Burns and Eltham, 2009). In a turn of events similar to those described by Evgeny Morozov in *The Net Delusion* (2011), Burns and Eltham (2009: 306) write: 'Iranian Twitter users did not take counter-deception measures to deal with the Basij, who then used Twitter to identify, locate and in some cases kill Iranian protestors'. Rather than revolutionary, Twitter becomes the inverse. It is the authoritarian regime's tool to quell the disturbance.

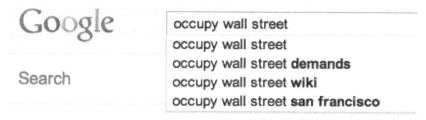

Figure 10.4 Occupy Wall Street, Google suggested searches, google.com, 2 December 2011.

The subject of Iran government-sponsored infiltrators was discussed (retweeted) in the #iranelection Twitter subsphere in June 2009, where users were asked to change their location to Tehran, so that everyone appeared to be there physically, as mentioned above. The introduction of noise became a media tactic. These manoeuvrings and their implications are some of the means by which a movement or network, and especially resistance, may be studied through hashtag analysis (Lindgren and Lundström, 2011; Poell and Borra, 2012). To what extent is the hashtag issue space tactical as well as substantively distinctive? What kind of an account of events does it provide? One may evaluate hashtag accounts of what is transpiring on the ground by contrasting them with the story told of the same events in the news or on Wikipedia, thereby inquiring into the features of the various first drafts of history, as mentioned above.

In the Occupy Wall Street protests in major Western cities in the autumn of 2011 and beyond, a variety of media accounts claimed that the protestors had no demands, until one list was made, and became the subject of debate among the OccupyWallSt.org collective (OccupyWallStreet, 2011). Occupy Wall Street demands also have been a top suggested search in Google (see Figure 10.4). Media accounts often serve as starting points for exercises that both critique the typical news frames (protest prompts violence) and provide alternative accounts (protest is substantive). The research question concerns the kind of account of Occupy Wall Street organized by its hashtags as well as its related hashtags *vis-à-vis* that in the news. Does it compete with or provide a corrective to dominant media accounts? Does it tell a compelling story of what is happening in the parks and on the grounds where tents have been raised (and torn down)? These are at least a few ways in which one may employ X/Twitter as a research tool, and at the same time debanalize it.

Debanalizing the medium, or X/Twitter as story-telling machine

In work completed in 2009, when Twitter emerged as a medium for remote event analysis (and debunking revolutions), the question concerned how to repurpose the output of Twitter to create a compelling account of what was happening on the streets and in social media (Rogers et al., 2009b). Entitled 'For the ppl of Iran: #iranelection RT', the piece followed the methods of the medium in so far as hashtags organize subject matters, and RTs (retweets) point to significant content. The top three retweeted tweets per day (for some 20 days) were captured, and placed in chronological order, inverting the reverse chronological order of Twitter (and blogging software more generally). As mentioned, Twitter's reverse chronological order (though later combined with algorithmic hierarchy) is one reason to call it a blogging platform, with the term 'micro-blogging' referring to the meagre amount of characters per post. With the remote event analysis technique, the overall story of the 20 days of the Iran election crisis is recounted (see Figure 10.5):

> The crisis unfolds on Twitter with the discovery of the value of the #iranelection hashtag, and tweeters both in and outside Iran begin using the tag to mark all tweets about the events there. Mousavi holds an emergency press conference. The voter turn-out is 80%. SMS is down; Mousavi's website and Facebook are blocked. Police are using pepper spray. Mousavi is under house arrest, and declares he is prepared for martyrdom. Neda is dead. There is a riot in Baharestan Square. First aid info is here. Bon Jovi sings 'Stand by Me' in support. Ahmadinejad is confirmed the winner. Light a candle for the ppl of Iran. (Digital Methods Initiative, 2009)

Employing the same technique (with the addition of manual filtering by theme), sub-stories also were created around censorship, Neda, arrests, internet, and violence. For example, the censorship sub-story concerns internet filtering by the state, and efforts (and tips) to circumvent it. Note that the well-known blocking of the networks by the Iranian government unfolded in that event space, and Twitter's famous announcement to postpone scheduled system maintenance resonated, too.

The great Twitter revolution debate revisited

How did the great Twitter revolution debate unfold, and how may it be studied? Contemporaneous bloggers and writers in the intellectual press (*Dissent*, *Foreign Policy*, *New Yorker*, *Prospect* and others) deliberated over the extent to which a 'Twitter Revolution' took place in Iran in 2009 and elsewhere, especially the protests in Moldova that transpired just weeks prior to the events in Iran and provided the revolution theme with momentum. Put

Figure 10.5 For the ppl of Iran – #iranelection RT.

Source: Digital Methods Initiative, 2009.

into circulation by the American blogger, Andrew Sullivan (2009), the notion elicited rounds of debunking, where the platform's role was repeatedly cut down to size. Among the seemingly most damning critiques of the revolution thesis is that the Iranian regime blocked access to the internet and the mobile phone network (mentioned above), thus rendering Twitter locally useless, despite the urging of the US State Department to Twitter to postpone its maintenance so that it could be used by Iranians (Ostrow, 2009). Another critical point made (and often repeated across the articles) is that only 19,235 people in Iran were registered Twitter users at the time, a mere 0.027% of the national population (Sysomos, 2009). Thus, Twitter certainly would not have been used *en masse*, however much 20,000 users also could be construed as a considerable number compared to the handful of Moldovan Twitter users during its own Twitter revolution (Bennett, 2009). Iran's uprising, rather than organized on Twitter, was coordinated by word of mouth, and was not principally technology-driven, it is said. As Golnaz Esfandiari (2010) writes in *Foreign Policy*: 'Twitter was definitely not a major communications tool for activists on the ground in Iran'. More poignantly, using Twitter and other social media would make Iranians targets of the authoritarian regime.

The value of the internet for the authoritarian regime and/or for activists proved to be a point of contention in the debate. On that subject, Clay Shirky (2010) writes, '[T]he net value of social media has shifted the balance of power in the direction of Iran's citizens', while Evgeny Morozov (2010) rejoindered, '[D]espite all the political mobilization facilitated by social media, the Iranian government has not only survived, but has, in fact, become even more authoritarian'.

There are also many stories worth considering that have aided in the debunking of a Twitter revolution in Iran, questioning the platform's veracity and 'ground-truthing' capacity. Mousavi, the green opposition candidate, was said on Twitter to be under house arrest, a claim later disputed, making Twitter into a rumour mill and unreliable source (Mostaghim and Daragahi, 2009; Esfandiari, 2010). Indeed, Evgeny Morozov (2009: 11) likened Twitter to child's play: '[T]his new media eco-system is very much like the old game of "Telephone", in which errors steadily accumulate in the transmission process, and the final message has nothing in common with the original'. Here one may compare contemporaneous accounts with more settled ones that have stood the test of time.

Another larger point worthy of investigation is that there were few Twitter users on the ground in Tehran at the time (tweeting in Farsi), making Twitter into something other than an eyewitness medium. Indeed, one of the more significant users tweeting about events on the ground was @oxfordgirl, residing in a village in the UK (Weaver, 2009; Esfandiari, 2010). How may one characterize the 'groundedness' of the users of the #iranelection hashtag? Here one may look at platforms used and inquire into desktop versus mobile use. Would a lack of groundedness damn the accounts of events? Does Twitter become an event commentary medium (another way of filling in 'event-following'), rather than one for witnessing?

Conclusions: From ambient friend-following to remote event analysis

Twitter's 'about' pages highlight the changing purposes of the platform. In 2006, Twitter was 'for staying in touch and keeping up with friends no matter where you are or what you're doing'; by 2017, Twitter was 'what's happening in the world and what people are talking about right now'. Twitter thereby has evolved from a local urban lifestyle tool (conceived for young San Francisco users) to an international news and event-following medium, at least in the renderings of the medium mission statements.

The research agenda has followed this transformation of Twitter from a banal 'what-I-had-for-lunch' medium to one purportedly and controversially having a hand in contemporary revolutions. As such, research also 'debanalized' Twitter. The techniques devised include taking advantage of the user-led research affordances of the platform, including the threading of topics by hashtag and the identification of significant content by retweet. Remaking Twitter into an analytical story-telling machine, with the capacity to chronicle events on the ground and in social media, is one digital method described above. Another concerns techniques to monitor and analyse substantive spaces of particular user groups, be they activists, NGOs or new social movements and formations, such as Black Lives Matter and the alt-right. The critical analytics put forward are means to evaluate the substance of these spaces, inquiring into who dominates the discussion. Is the matter of concern fleeting? That is the critical point made of 'hashtag publics' who appear like a flash mob and dissipate just as quickly. Their commitment, or longevity of concern, is another critical analytic. The competition between hashtags, and hashtag publics, may be studied in the programme/anti-programme approach put forward in the query design chapter. The idea of Twitter as a platform primarily for 'status updates' of users 'in bed' or 'going to the beach' (as in the original twttr sketch) has receded, and its vibrancy (and techniques to capture it) are put to the fore.

PROJECTS

Debunk the Twitter revolution (again)

RESEARCH GOAL To peruse the literature surrounding the great Twitter revolution debate of 2009–2010 (and beyond) and confirm, refute, modify or otherwise productively engage with the claims put forward.

To start, one would compile a catalogue of claims, and examine their robustness by analysing a tweet collection of the Iran election crisis, 10–30 June 2009, which includes some 650,000 tweets using the hashtag #iranelection. The hashtag is significant, for not only was it among Twitter's highest trending topics for the year, but it also was the object of scorn by analysts questioning users' blind faith in it: 'Western journalists who couldn't reach – or didn't bother reaching? – people on the ground in Iran simply scrolled through the English-language tweets post with tag #iranelection' (Esfandiari, 2010).

Data set

Tweets with hashtag #iranelection, 10–30 June 2009, http://rettiwt.digitalmethods.net/ (request login)

Data analyses available

Languages used (overall)

Platforms used (overall)

Platforms used per language

Tweets per user

Tweets per green_normal avatar

Tweets per day

Ranked list of retweets

Retweeted users (ranked @mentions)

Other hashtags used with #iranelection (co-hashtags)

URLs found in combination with #iranelection

Rumours (tweets containing the word)

Confirmed (tweets containing the word)

Sample project outcome

'For the ppl of Iran – #iranelection RT' (10'00'), www.youtube.com/watch?v=_h2B2CA-btY

PROJECTS

Debanalize X/Twitter by analysing a tweet collection for its substantive value

RESEARCH GOAL To debanalize X/Twitter by studying a tweet collection, constructed by queries for hashtags and keywords (issue spaces and/or events), user captures (populist politicians or other public figures and organizations), or social movements (networks as movements).

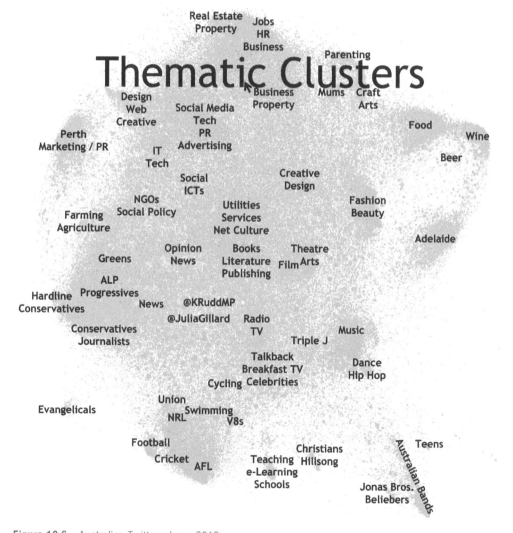

Figure 10.6 Australian Twittersphere, 2012.

Source: Sun, 2012.

X/Twitter data

X/Twitter users send 140–280-character posts, or tweets, either from the web or through dedicated applications on computers, smartphones and tablets. Each tweet is linked to a user account, the source of the tweet, publishing date and contents, including markers with potential analytical value such as hashtags (#hashtag), @username, RT (identical tweet, or modified tweet), a (shortened) URL and/or a geotag. While only a small (but growing) percentage of tweets are geotagged with a latitude/longitude marker, location, if the focus of the research, could also be derived from a user's account information, the date of account creation, a profile image, the specific language they post in, the message text or the time zone. The demarcation of the Australian twitterverse, for example, benefited from the time zone (see Figure 10.6).

Hashtags are used to thread or tag communication around specific events, topics, issues, locales and so on. They also may organize a subculture or a political persuasion. Mention markers (@username) allow users to directly address or refer to another user. Retweet markers in early tweet collections (RT @username) or identical (and quoted) retweets in tweet collections since 2015 indicate that a message from another user is forwarded, presumably because it has 'pass-along value'. URLs, shortened with t.co or other services, point to sources. All these elements can be employed for 'remote event analysis', that is, to understand events on the ground, and their interplay with social media – including the effects of the platform (the practices it supports), its users and of course the content, however succinct. They also may be used to study issue (or subcultural) spaces with critical analytics, inquiring into dominant voice, concern, alignment and commitment. Consider a comparative approach, #blacklivesmatter (and related hashtags) together with #alllivesmatter, as these may be considered antagonistic hashtag publics, with a respective programme and anti-programme (as discussed in the query design chapter).

Issue space analysis with X/Twitter

The research considerations below follow from the kinds of X/Twitter studies discussed above: (1) social issues and trends, (2) news and events, (3) politicians' (and other individuals' or organizations') historical tweets and (4) social movements (networks as movements).

Social issues and trends

Data collection: Make a tweet collection of an issue space or use an existing one

Historical and contemporary data sets of tweets may be created on 4CAT, which sat atop the Twitter academic API; other software also can be used such as Zeeschuimer, the browser extension. To create a data set, query one or more hashtags. (When querying hashtags, the results also may contain those including the keyword of the hashtag.) One manner to demarcate an issue space is to perform a two-step query design.

1   First spend time with the issue by reading tweets in that space. One may search X/Twitter and/or Google for hashtags concerning the issue(s) in question. Note the hashtags and keywords used. Alternatively, compile a list of hashtags using the associative query snowball technique, discussed earlier.

2   In 4CAT or another tweet capture software application, query the list of hashtags and/or keywords, and build a tweet collection over the period of a few days (or, if time allows, a week or two).

3   Perform hashtag and/or co-hashtag analysis, and list most frequently occurring or co-occurring hashtags by frequency.

4   Add newly discovered hashtags to original list and launch the query anew in 4CAT or another tweet capture software application.

5   The results of the second query constitute the tweet collection. Unless useful, one may dispose of the results of the original query.

For existing data sets (e.g., on an instance of 4CAT or DMI-TCAT), query inside them by date range, hashtags, keywords and/or @usernames.

Issue space analysis: Critical analytics procedures

1   Concern – hashtag analysis – social issues as embedded in hashtags. Make a list of hashtags as well as co-hashtags ranked by frequency, in order to show hierarchies of concern.

2   Dominant voice – @mention analysis – who speaks and whose speech is referenced? For who speaks, one may count the @usernames tweeting most often in the issue space, introducing a metric concerning 'vocalism', or the exercise of voice. Dominant voice concerns which @ usernames are mentioned the most. Interpreted differently, it also allows the identification of expertise. Make a list of @usernames mentioned, ranked by frequency. Note whether the dominant voices propagate the top concerns, thereby dominating the agenda.

3   Commitment – over-time analysis of persistence (repeated co-occurrence) of hashtags, users, or hashtags and users. Note which hashtags (and which co-hashtags) persist over time. Note whether there are certain users that persevere along with them. In DMI-TCAT, the 'associational profiler' performs a form of commitment analysis (Marres, 2015).

4   Positioning – competing keyword and hashtag deployment. #blacklivesmatter and #alllivesmatter (or #bluelivesmatter) may be considered programmes and anti-programmes in the overall issue space of (police) violence in America and elsewhere. Identify the hashtag competition, and consider scoping, substantive and media tactics analyses. Scoping refers to size and composition, substantive analysis to related hashtags as well as URL references, and media tactics to the tactical use of the space, such as by twinning issues, reverse hashtag use and hashtag hijacking. Consider how one group frames another, thereby creating an outgroup.

5   Alignment – co-occurrence of users and hashtags. What other company does a hashtag keep? Which other hashtags does a user employ? Here one may analyse alliances and unlikely bedfellows.

Remote event analysis and news

Data collection: Make a tweet collection of an event space.

1   Collect tweets as the event unfolds. As you learn about the event (spanning time with it), consider making multiple queries, and concatenating (or merging) tweet collections of the event.
2   An event space is often demarcated by sets of hashtags and keywords and competing hashtags (and their publics) may emerge. Consider making a collection that encompasses the competition to allow for an analysis of the different accounts of the 'same' event.

Which publics do competing hashtags organize, do they 'dialogue', and how 'fleeting' or part of a larger history of action are they? Here one could engage with the literature on hashtag publics (Rambukkana, 2015; Bruns et al., 2016).

Event space: Remote event analysis

1   Story-telling – retweet analysis – most retweeted tweets per day tells story of an event as it unfolds.
2   Source-mentioning – URL analysis – shows content that is most referenced. Note the 'missing references', or what one may expect to be present but is absent. How mainstream or fringe is the collection of sources? Compare the sources referenced by two camps, or programmes and anti-programmes, showing commonalities and differences (see Figure 10.7).
3   Competing accounts of events. With the help of a timeline, compare the account of the event given by the hashtag to an account provided by dominant media sources. Demarcate dominant media sources by date range and characterization of type of news (e.g., top quality newspapers or top tabloids).

Politician broadcasting: Issue and 'target' analysis

Data collection: Capture one or more politicians' tweets.

One may capture public figures' tweets or those of an organization or institution. Optionally, one may capture all leading politicians' tweets prior to an upcoming election, perhaps together with the political parties' tweets. Consider capturing tweets from verified accounts. Note that X/Twitter has a limit to the amount of tweets that may be captured in total per account (going back in time).

Politicians and other public figures as well as organizations often envisage the audience they are tweeting to (supporters and/or fan bases) rather than engaging in (direct) conversation and dialogue with other X/Twitter users. Whom do they target, and about which issues? Which sources do they reference (see also Figure 10.7)?

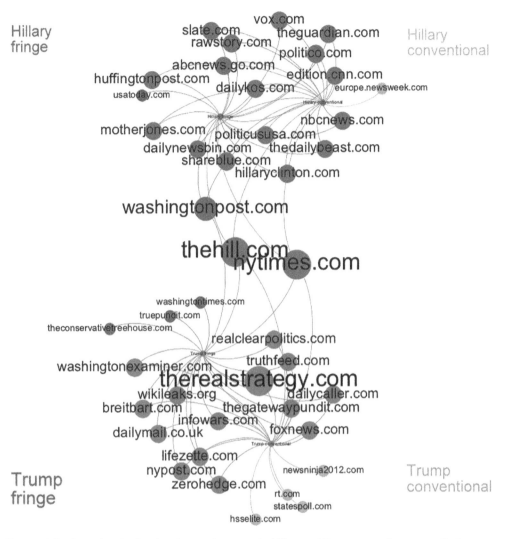

Figure 10.7 Shared and uniquely referenced sources by Hillary and Trump supporters, respectively, on Twitter, 2016.

Source: Bouma et al., 2017.

Here one may wish to explore a claim and fill it in substantively. For example, it has been claimed that Geert Wilders, the Dutch politician, is a leading figure in the 'new right'. How to characterize the 'new right's' issues? Are they primarily Islamophobic (or counter-jihadist), anti-establishment or another orientation? Here one would categorize (a subset of) Wilders' tweets.

Network as movement (audience segmentation)

On X/Twitter (and on other platforms) social movements are active such as Black Lives Matter and the alt-right. In order to chart the movement's concerns and tactics, one could first make a list of its leading figures, by reading contemporary news accounts, magazine and Wikipedia articles as well as otherwise spending time in the movement space online. Having made a list of the names of the leading figures (and looking up their X/Twitter accounts), one may query their @mentions. Who mentions these names? One charts the inner and outer rings of the movement (as network) by determining which users mention them all, mention all but one, mention all but two and so forth. Mentions of leading figures become links, and one can make a network diagram of the movement in ring form, from inner to outer. Such a technique is also sometimes called audience segmentation. Analytical pathways include those discussed above, from critical analytics to issue as well as target analysis.

Tools

- Zeeschuimer browser extension. Available via https://4cat.nl.
- 4CAT: Capture and Analysis Toolkit. Available at https://4cat.digitalmethods.net. Self-installation available via https://github.com/digitalmethodsinitiative. See also https://4cat.nl.
- DMI Twitter Capture and Analysis Toolset (DMI-TCAT). Available at https://github.com/digital-methodsinitiative. The DMI-TCAT tool should be installed on a server.
- Gephi. Available at https://gephi.org.

Video tutorials

- 'Social Media Research with Digital Methods' (57'06'), www.youtube.com/watch?v=PtSNZ-fYKRnk
- '4CAT: Capture and Analytis Toolkit' (1h 21'47'), www.youtube.com/watch?v=VRMWuJYOKHQ
- 'DMI-TCAT: Overview of Analytical Modules' (25'39'), www.youtube.com/watch?v=ex97eoorUeo
- 'Gephi Tutorial for Working with Twitter Mention Networks' (50'10'), www.youtube.com/watch?v=snPR8CwPld0
- 'Combine and Analyse Co-Hashtag Networks (Instagram, Twitter, etc.) with Gephi' (17'39'), www.youtube.com/watch?v=ngqWjgZudeE

VISUAL MEDIA ANALYSIS FOR INSTAGRAM AND OTHER ONLINE PLATFORMS
Metapicturing

Digital methods for arranging groups
of images for critical reflection

Analysing 'visual media online'

Instagram is currently the social media platform most associated with online images (and their analysis), but images from other platforms also can be collected and grouped, arrayed by similarity, stacked, matched, stained, labelled, depicted as network, placed side by side and otherwise analytically displayed. In the following, the initial focus is on Instagram, together with certain schools of thought such as Instagramism and Instagrammatics for its aesthetic and visual cultural study. Building on those two approaches, it subsequently focuses on other web and social media platforms, such as Google Image Search, X/Twitter, Facebook and 4chan. It provides demonstrations of how querying techniques create online image collections, and how these sets are analytically grouped through arrangements collectively referred to as metapictures.

As indicated by the title, the analysis is of 'visual media online', a term that could be more specific such as 'visual social media' (Leaver et al., 2020), 'digital visual media' (Dean, 2019), 'digital visual artefacts' (Leszczynski, 2018) or even 'digital images, digitally analysed' (Rose, 2016). An even more straightforward designation could be 'social media images' (Pearce et al., 2020). Each narrows the purview in a distinctive manner. The first concerns social media platforms driven by images (as Instagram, Tumblr, 4chan and perhaps even Flickr), the second emphasizes image formats as memes, the third the inclusion of visual objects as emojis and gifs and the fourth digital images, which covers the digitized together with the internet-native. Social media images, the last category, would widen the platforms under study beyond 'visual social media' to any with images. In the following, the online visual media discussed includes all the above categories or emphases and is restricted to images online, rather than video, though YouTube's thumbnails are addressed.

But the point of departure is not just the objects of study and their key terminological specificities. It is also the outputs of their study, i.e., their analytical and interpretive arrangement. Akin to the manner in which digital research methods often fuse the tool and the method, in what has been referred to as 'programmed method' (Borra and Rieder, 2014), here analysis and arrangement are melded, the outcome of which could be referred to as a metapicture, in Mitchell's terminology. The collections of images are framed in a manner of display that enables critical reflection on them (Grønstad and Vågnes, 2006; Mitchell, 1994).

This metapicturing, then, seeks to nestle itself between qualitative visual analysis and interpretation (from, say, art history) (Fernie, 1995) and quantitative knowledge visualization where one deftly chooses the visualization type to fit the data set (Börner and Polley, 2014). That is, rather than an emphasis on individual images, the metapicturing applies the analytical reading to images as groups or sets (Colombo, 2018). It also retains the images in the metapicture rather than rendering them as data points and visualizing them as abstractions.

What follows are approaches and techniques for deriving and arranging groups of images as metapictures that reflect upon them. The grouping arrangements (with built-in critical reflection) are further specified as image reuse, image trends, image vernaculars, dominant image, image presence, image quality, image staining (or tarnishing), image circulation, image engagement, image associations, image removal and feed competition. Each is taken in turn, together with how they meet the needs of critical questions concerning online reputation, style spaces, societal discourse, cultural conflict, versions of events, content moderation, polarization and alignment as well as others.

Finally, by way of conclusion, there is also an emphasis on making the metapicture active in the research undertaking. By making it active, I mean the consideration of software outputs and visual arrangements as starting points rather than culminations of investigations (though one may arrive at a metapicture strategy anytime throughout a project). Envisaging the output or metapicture with the built-in critical reflection thereby becomes a part of project formulation. But it also takes it a step further by inviting the formulation of questions that include the reflective arrangement of image groups, a theme to which I return in the conclusion.

Studying Instagram

Instagram launched in 2010 with the retro Polaroid icon, square picture format and well-named filters such as Lark (good for nature shots). As an object of study, it has evolved over the years, with its association with selfies (Rettberg, 2014), a staging aesthetic (Manovich,

2016) as well as a new kind of traveller outside of the tourist and traveller, the digital nomad (Bozzi, 2020). It is also connected with micro-celebrities and lifestyle influencers (Senft, 2013), who engage in 'visibility labour' (Abidin, 2016) through regularly posting, at once potentially earning themselves revenue as well as engaging in what one scholar has called the 'war of eyeballs' (Abidin, 2014).

These internet celebrities (large and small) build followings, or fan bases (Marwick and Boyd, 2011b) through active engagement on the platform by following others and liking and commenting on their posts. Some of this 'relational labour' (Baym, 2015) may be automated; among the tools deployed by heavy users to build relationships in the form of followings are software apps that automatically like posts of others who follow them, in a form of interactivity once referred to as 'interpassivity', where the machine acts on your behalf (Zizek, 1998). It also outsources a type of 'affective labour' (Hardt and Negri, 2000), the pleasant-seeming, outward display of a job one would rather not do.

The authenticity of the follower and like counts is an issue for especially Instagram (and to a lesser extent other platforms), given how follower factories (a term in the same family as click farm) offer 'fame for sale' (Crescia et al., 2016), where one can purchase followers, likes as well as comments (Lindquist, 2018). These can be of varying quality (and duration), given how some are detected by the platform itself and purged, resulting in infamous cases of sudden, telling drops in the follower counts of celebrities, athletes and politicians but also so-called pseudo-influencers (Confessore et al., 2018; Castro, 2021) (Figure 11.1). In keeping with the question of whether (and when) one can trust social media data and engagement analysis (Paquet-Clouston et al., 2017), such findings have been discussed in terms of 'manipulated reputation' (Aggarwal, 2016) and the 'engineered self' (Van Den Hoogen, 2019).

Figure 11.1 'Quick fix: Machine selling likes and followers', interactive installation by Dries Depoorter.

Source: Depoorter, 2019.

The detection of 'fake followers' is itself an academic (and marketing industry) under-taking, with online tools employing 'signals' (e.g., lack of profile picture; multiple followers with same creation date) and ratios (low like-to-follower ratio) to aid in the hunt (HypeAuditor, 2021), along with more elaborate techniques in the computational literature (Sen et al., 2018) (see Figure 11.2). It is often said that there is a percentage of inauthentic accounts that one has in one's follower count anyhow, especially influ-encers, who are 'bombarded with fake followers' (Purba et al., 2020: 2763) and also are used (as well as recommended) as seed accounts for new users building a nascent profile.

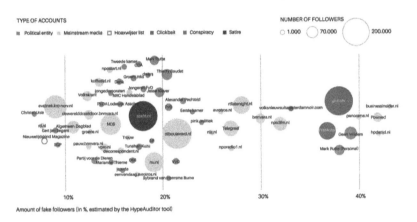

Figure 11.2 Comparison of percentages of fake followers on Instagram accounts held by political figures, media organizations and others, according to percentages of 'mass' and 'suspicious' followers, 2019.

Source: Colombo and De Gaetano, 2020.

Most recently, in the study of the platform, Instagram, like other social media, has been found to have a misinformation problem, first in its artful usage by Russian disinforma-tion operatives and their unknowing co-conspirators during and especially after the 2016 US presidential election campaigning (Howard et al., 2019), and also by purveyors of dubious content about Covid-19, vaccines and other contemporary topics (Cinelli et al., 2020; Colombo and De Gaetano, 2020; Massey et al., 2020). Whilst more attention in this regard has been paid to Facebook and X/Twitter, Instagram also has renewed promises of vigilance in their content review and moderation, an issue that came before them some years earlier with images associated with pro-eating disorder as well as other content removal controversies (Chancellor et al., 2016; Gerrard, 2020). Faced with content mod-eration, adherents in these communities would circumvent platform curbing through complex lexical and other manoeuvring (e.g., a hashtag switch from #thighgap to #thy-ghgapp). Other work has focused on users whose accounts were unexpectedly or illegitimately suspended. They have described inflexible account policies and clunky review pathways (Myers West, 2018). If cut off by the platform, account reinstatement has proven arduous.

Instagramism and style spaces

As it is an image-driven platform, Instagram (but also 4chan, which is treated briefly below), is often associated with image analysis, particularly selfies; however, many scholars remind us that those pictures comprise a relatively miniscule percentage of the images uploaded to the platform (Caliandro and Graham, 2020). It is said to have its own aesthetic, or evolving aesthetics (Leaver et al., 2020), and as such can be approached as a 'style space' (Manovich, 2011a).

With the notion of Instagramism, Lev Manovich (2016) seeks to capture the movement to create and record beautiful forms and appearances in a way that enables building (and maintaining) a following, evidenced by overall follower count and likes per post. He describes Instagram styling as design photography. It could be similar in composition to that in Kinfolk, the international 'slow lifestyle' magazine (Manovich, 2017) (see Figure 11.3). Many Instagram users are said to expect staging. Indeed, the practice of sharing a photo after meticulously setting the scene contrasts with the pointing, shooting and sharing performed on other platforms, including messaging apps, where the aim is the maintenance of 'ambient intimacy' (Burgess and Baym, 2020).

Figure 11.3 Instagramism. Design photography by Instagram users.
Source: Manovich, 2017.

Both selfie culture as well as Instagramism also could be said to be another instance of the internet hitting the streets, in at least two senses. The one concerns 'place-making' (Pink, 2008), that is, how shops, restaurants, museums and other locales are Insta-styled. They may create a space where Instagram-type photos can be taken, but they also may create a *mise en scène* that could be termed Insta-photogenic (Budge, 2020a).

Platform-place-making is a form of 'gathering power' (Casey, 1996) that privileges streets, buildings, bridges and squares by becoming Insta-destinations at once heavily hashtagged and geotagged (Boy and Uitermark, 2017). A second sense is what is sometimes termed participatory or 'social photography' (Budge, 2020b). Instagram-ready picture booths or styled settings are constructed for events, in order for platform users to have their pictures taken, eager to be remembered as a part of it (in front of the backdrop and associated with a hashtag). They also can snap their own selfies, individual or group ones, and subsequently post them with event hashtags, and other individuals tagged, to not just belong but also to be viewed and 'liked', thereby building platform capital.

Image similarity: Reuniting reused images

Studying style spaces could be performed by image grouping by similarity, or by using software that compares and groups similar images. As in other projects that employ it, such as network analyses, the grouping is a step in a more elaborate analytical procedure, rather than the endpoint. For example, ImagePlot (Software Studies Initiative, 2011) and ImageSorter (Visual Computing, 2018) group images according to their formal properties. Ingesting a collection (or folder) of images, the software orders them most often by similarity, particularly hue or saturation (see Figure 11.4). One use of such image grouping is to study the reuse of the same or similar images. The analysis rests on how the software bunches together similarity and sameness rather than sameness only. In other words, the

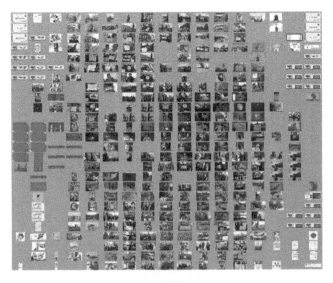

Figure 11.4   Image grouping. Originals, copies, original copies and poor images grouped together.

Source: Geboers et al., 2020.

cluster will amass both high-res as well as 'poor images' (Steyerl, 2009) of the same as well as visually similar ones. The poor image is one that is of lower quality than the original or the copy, because it is the product of copy and paste, reworking for meme production, downsizing for a thumbnail or a preview, or otherwise processed downward, so to speak.

Another image type of interest in this regard is the 'original copy', a term for digital imagery that blurs the distinction between the original and the copy (Fehrmann et al., 2010). It is described as secondary images, or off-shoots, that attain the status of the original. These, too, would be grouped together because their properties compare well with the original and any copies, however poor. Thus, software could be said to reunite the original with its reuses, such as the copy, the original copy as well as the poor images.

Image trends and vernaculars

The software output of arrayed images may be the starting point of an analysis into what the image groups communicate per subject matter or issue, or how the medium may shape the form the message assumes. As a case in point, the images associated with #climatechange on Instagram or X/Twitter, for instance, can provide a sense of how the framing of the issue is evolving (in a form of social or environmental communication research) (see also Figure 11.5). With the entrance of youthful activists and influencers such as Greta Thunberg and Extinction Rebellion, are we seeing more urgency expressed in the imagery (burning planet)?

We also may examine how platforms depict an issue in a particular manner (Niederer, 2018; Pearce et al., 2019b). Overall, when sorted by popular posts tagged with #climatechange, Instagram may portray more individual 'small actions' ('teens plant trees'), whereas X/Twitter may have more of the charts and figures of science, or the memes of politicians (French Premier Macron's 'Make our planet great again'). Depending on the platform used to access the issue, the question of who acts, and how it is visually displayed, is answered differently.

Studying how platforms, or communities within them, have a particular style of presentation and cultures 'native' to them is also known as platform vernacular research (Burgess, 2006; Gibbs et al., 2015). In a particular issue space such as climate change, the one will prefer a certain format (the landscape), whereas the other routinely deploys another (the chart). To visualize such image languages or vernaculars, there is the image stack technique, which falls under the larger category of composite images (Colombo, 2018). In this visualization practice, the order of the images is retained, and each image's opacity is lowered equally (e.g., with ten images, each is dimmed by 10%). The retention of the order of the layers grants more visibility to the higher ranked images (see Figure 11.6). Ranking here also can be by engagement score.

Figure 11.5   'Climate change' query results from Google Image Search, over time, 2008–2019.

Source: Pearce et al., 2019a.

Platform vernacular composite images

Composite images of the top 10 most engaged with images of climate change per platform

Facebook   Google   Instagram   Twitter   Tumblr   Reddit

Figure 11.6   Image composites comparing top ten most engaged-with climate change images across platforms, and technique.

Source: Colombo, 2018 and Pearce et al., 2019b.

Platform vernacular research, it should be pointed out, ought not ignore the absence of a typical user of a social media platform (Gerlitz and Rieder, 2013), let alone one with over one billion registered users such as Instagram. There are myriad uses of platform, be they documenting everyday life, styling like an influencer, campaigning or posting pictures of kittens (Caliandro and Graham, 2020); diversity of use lies within countries and cultures (Leaver et al., 2020). But, as discussed below, when one queries Instagram, demarcates a substantive space and compares it to the same space on another platform, meaningful distinctions for media and social research may emerge. For example, one platform may perform content moderation particularly well or poorly, in one language space versus another, when the topic explored is the relationship between 5G and Covid-19, a subject of popular conspiracy theory (EU DisinfoLab, 2020). One may have more divisive content, others healthier dialogue (Niederer and Colombo, 2023).

The dominant image

Whether for social or media research, there are basic approaches to studying sets of images with software. When one orders images by formal property and outputs an array of them in the form of an image wall or cluster map (for example), initially one will note one or more dominant images (see Figure 11.7). The dominant image may be studied in terms of a format (such as meme) or as a message (slogan or counter-slogan). It should be noted that the technique also shows the opposite of the dominant. It yields marginal and orphan images. One may also place arrayed image collections from competing hashtags side by side – #blacklivesmatter and #bluelivesmatter or #protectthevote and #stealthevote – so as to enable comparative dominant and marginal image analysis.

There is an additional application, exemplified in work performed on the use of the climate-related hashtag, #parisagreement, before and after US President Trump's announcement in June 2017 that the US would withdraw from it (see Figure 11.7). Here, the software allows one to compare the quantities of images, and thus activity, one month before and after in a form of 'direct visualization' of all the images (compared to translating the images to data points and visualizing as a data representation, as in Figure 11.2) (Manovich, 2011b; Niederer and Colombo, 2019). It allows for both a distant reading (Moretti, 2013) in the quantity comparison as well as a close reading as one can zoom in and take note of the dominance of 'Make Our Planet Great Again', the placard-like image (and cut-out hashtag) that launched the campaign by French President Emmanuel Macron on 1 June 2017, in reaction to the Trump announcement. With the US abdication, it calls on France (and Europe) to lead the way. Here, close reading refers both to the method as well as the account one can make from it (Schur, 1998).

But the software also can order the images chronologically. If, in a cultural analytics approach (Manovich, 2020), one studies the digitized covers of a magazine over time, or the works of an artist, one can pinpoint instances of change in order to enable a fledgling periodization (Manovich, 2016). A large collection of Instagram images, chronologically visualized, could point to larger style trends, such as the rise (and potentially fall) of a particular aesthetic associated with the platform. Is Kinfolk waning in favour of cottage core, the internet aesthetic associated with an idealized rural life? Or are particular formats becoming dominant (e.g., sudden memeification of an issue space)? In both examples of image analysis with software – grouping by formal property and ordering by date – the metapicture is the prompt for interpretation. The interpretative work is often practically undertaken through forms of annotation: labelling the clusters and the transition points and periods, respectively.

#parisagreement　　　　one month after 1/6/17 - 20:36

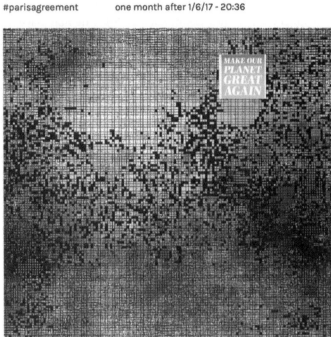

one month before
1/6/17 20:36

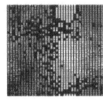

1.203 images　　　　　14.395 images

Figure 11.7　Dominant image analysis with ImageSorter. French President Macron's meme, 'Make our planet great again' as dominant image on Instagram, both one month before and one month after US President's Trump announcement that the US would withdraw from the Paris climate agreement.

Source: Niederer and Colombo, 2019.

Instagrammatics: Querying for image sets

Whereas Instagramism could be construed as media style and trend research, Instagrammatics is closer to internet as well as social research (Highfield and Leaver, 2016). It utilizes queries of the Instagram API (when it was accessible), Instagram scrapers, CrowdTangle or other social listening software, making collections of posts for further interpretive study. Queries can be made of hashtags, user accounts and geo-coordinates, including combinations thereof. Hashtag-based queries include influential single hashtags (#blacklivesmatter, #metoo, #stealthevote), sets of related hashtags or competing hashtags (either single or sets of related ones such as #lovewins and #jesuswins – see Figure 11.8). One may create co-hashtag maps and label the clusters, showing the subcultures or discourses in a particular movement or issue space, such as 'settler superiority' in Canada's indigenous territories (Karsgaard and MacDonald, 2020). Here, Instagram becomes a platform to study the size of publics and counter-publics, together with their discursive imagery and hashtags.

The queries also can be user accounts, e.g., influencers. When queried together with hashtags, the research could concern the extent to which influencers use responsibly their symbolic power and voice, both generally and in a particular hashtag space (Niederer and Colombo, 2023). The queries could be geo-coordinates. The sourcing of a set of geotagged posts, together with a date range, may result in a collection of images of an event, such as the storming of the US Capitol building. Geotagged posts from Washington, DC on 6 January 2021 (the day of the storming) would be a collection of significant historical interest. Making such a collection close to the event, and subsequently making another one with the same query design sometime later, would enable the study of content moderation, the cleaning up of the platform and of evidence. Combining geo-coordinates with hashtags, such as in the well-known #selfiecity project, opens further avenues of analysis, for it allows one to geo-locate particular moods and sentiments (Tifentale and Manovich, 2015). Where is #stealthevote most prominently located? Is it just as urban as rural?

Figure 11.8   Geo-locating posts tagged #lovewins or #celebratepride (program) and #loveloses or #jesuswins (anti-program) after the US Supreme Court ruling on same-sex marriage, 2015.

Source: Rogers, 2018a.

Metapictures as visual media analysis

I would like to turn to a set of metapictures that, like Instagrammatics, result from visual media analysis with digital research methods but make image sets from other platforms, including Wikipedia, Google Image and Web Search, X/Twitter, Facebook as well as YouTube. One is a technique that creates an image grid that compares the presence or absence of images in articles about the same subject matter but written up in different languages on Wikipedia. How to interpret 'missing' images? Another examines the top images for a Google Image Search of the Gezi Park (Istanbul) protests, extracting the embedded metadata in the pictures taken, in order to determine the price of the cameras that took them and the presence of citizen journalists in the so-called 'pop-up news ecology'. A third employs a 'staining' technique that shades (and, in a sense, tarnishes) search engine results that are construed as preferred placement or misinformation. The others concern the posts (with images) that most animate a movement or group on Facebook, the emojis that are used in tandem with particular war images, the videos (expressed as thumbnail images) referenced by 4chan users that have been removed by YouTube and the contrasting feeds of US-based conservative and progressive Facebook users.

Image presence

In the study of cultural (and national) points of view on Wikipedia, Emina Sendijarevic and I deployed cross-cultural (or cross-lingual) image analysis to compare the 'same' articles in different Wikipedia language versions (2012). Certain images are dear to one article to make a cultural case, whilst conspicuously absent in another (see Figure 11.9). The absence may explain or provide context to emphasis, such as the image of a gravestone of a 13-year-old boy, prominent in the Bosnian article on the 'Srebrenica genocide', and for years absent in the Serbian one entitled 'Srebrenica massacre'. (At the time of writing it is a part of a 'picture gallery' on the bottom of the Serbian article, rather than incorporated into the article itself.) The image analysis, outputting a grid, or rows of images from each article next to one another, shows either their order (and thus prominence) or their matches (and thus distinctiveness). It can include the templates, too, such as if an article has an issue with its 'neutral point of view' (in this case the Serbian) or has attained the status of 'featured article' (as has the Bosnian).

The cross-cultural image analysis may be paired with other analytical techniques such as comparing references from two or more articles or placing side by side (translated or original-language) tables of contents, where one notes for example that the Bosnian article on the Srebrenica genocide closes with a section on revisionism and the Serbian-language Srebrenica massacre piece with the controversy of calling the events a genocide. The cultural specificity of the differing accounts of the events continues decades later, seemingly hardening in stance rather than dovetailing. Stance solidification over time may also be depicted by highlighting the lack of change. For example, one accentuates (through shading) telling section headers or sentences that have long endured.

Image quality and camera grade recognition

In data journalism research, a technique in the open source intelligence tradition may be utilized for a form of 'source criticism', where one is interested in the origins of the source, in our case whether a picture was taken by a professional grade camera (and thereby presumably by a professional photojournalist). With EXIF data one can discern the camera type, date the pictures and examine the extent to which it has been edited or 'touched up'. One can look up the prices of the cameras, too.

Content Warning

Content Warning: Please note that this example contains content relating to genocide which you may find distressing.

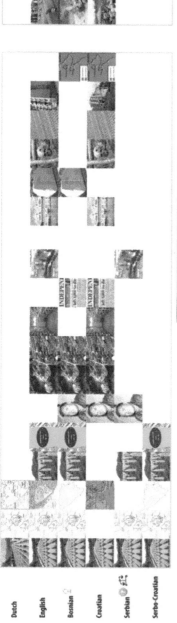

Dutch

English

Bosnian

Croatian

Serbian

Serbo-Croatian

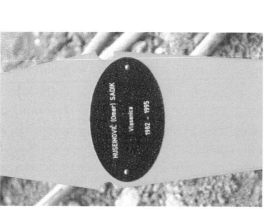

HUSEINOVIĆ (Omer) SADIK
Vlasenica
1982 – 1995

Figure 11.9 Image grid analysis comparing images in the 'same' Wikipedia article on the Srebrenica massacre/genocide across different language Wikipedias. Image insert is of the grave of a 13-year-old boy, present in the Bosnian and not present in the Serbian article.

Source: Rogers and Sendijarevic, 2012 and Rogers, 2013b.

This form of visual media analysis may be applied in the examination of the apparent significance of citizen journalism and the 'pop-up news ecology' (Wall and el Zahed, 2015) at Gezi Park in Istanbul as demonstrators gathered in 2013 to protest the planned construction of a shopping mall in the urban green space (Ozduzen and McGarry, 2020). The environmental concerns evolved into multi-issue, political demonstrations, met with water cannons and other security apparatus, where many images were taken by the protesters themselves and subsequently circulated. It often has been argued that amateur or citizen documentation of events is significant for how they are reported on and ultimately remembered (Robinson, 2009). They may challenge dominant and official accounts (Robinson and DeShano, 2011); they may supply alternative (evidentiary) material (Bruns and Highfield, 2012).

In an analysis of Google Image results for the query 'Gezi Park', we found that particularly iconic images (particularly the 'lady in the red dress' pepper sprayed by a policeman) remained at the top for well over a month (see Figure 11.10). Thus, searching Google Images for events would not be a way to follow the goings-on, as they rather cement depictions rather than track them, at least at the time.

In the event, the iconic photograph of a lady in a red dress was taken by a professional photojournalist. Other top-ranked images were also shot by photojournalists or stringers.

Particularly poignant findings can be made on the basis of the metadata available in the images made iconic by Google in the sense of granting them their presence at the top of the results over time. Examining the data embedded in the top images, or EXIF data, we found that the photos with the most staying power were taken by professional grade cameras and edited by costly software, rather than from smartphones or cheap consumer devices without filters (De Amicis et al., 2013; Allan, 2015). We thereby relied on both 'mechanically captured metadata' (e.g., camera make, exposure) and that derived from user activity (software editing) (Rubinstein and Sluis, 2008; Hochman, 2014). Looking up the brands and models, we graphed the price tags of the cameras that took the top images, showing the continued significance of professional journalists and their documentation of the events rather than (mainly) upstart citizen journalists, at least in the event documentation returned by Google Image Search.

Image staining (or tarnishing)

A third example of visual media analysis is in the realm of search engine returns critique, otherwise known as algorithmic auditing (Sandvig et al., 2016). How to make an account to describe and expose the trouble with the top returns for an engine query? In the legal, commercial realm, accounts are often made of how search engines return their own properties (or those that bought space) at the top of the results, once known and scandalized as preferred or paid placement (Vaidhyanathan, 2011). Google notoriously returned its own e-commerce site over those of its competitors, landing itself in antitrust lawsuits (Scott,

Top 3 images of Gezi Park per day,
using cumulative query technique for [Gezi]

The cumulative query technique refers to associating with the start
date 26 May and adding a day every day to the end date until 3 July.

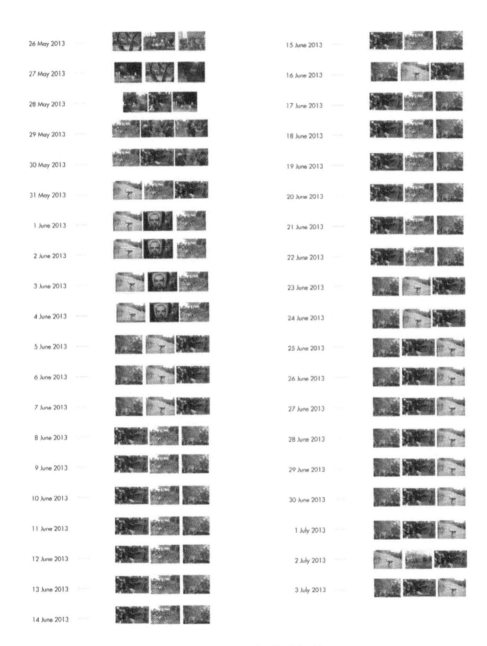

Figure 11.10 Top images in Google Image Search for 'Gezi Park',
26 May – 3 July 2013.

Source: De Amicis et al., 2013.

2017; Romm, 2020). It is also accused of populating search engine returns with its own services, YouTube videos as well as information (or knowledge graph) panel, prior to serving other 'organic' results, as they are known in industry parlance. For example, search for any place and one is returned 'Google places'. In the event, in 2019 Google reached a milestone in that more 50% of Google searches resulted in zero organic clicks (Fishkin, 2019).

As mentioned in the Google critique chapter, autocomplete (when the engine suggests a query) has been criticized for its ill-mannered suggestions (Baker and Potts, 2013). Autosuggested completions for Jews, for example, prompted the engine company to intervene, removing offensive outputs (Cadwalladr, 2016). Google ads have been found to be racist, raising the question of how algorithms work, and whether (and how) their training material should be reconsidered (Sweeney, 2013). Google images have been found to have issues of representation when comparing the outputs of professional versus unprofessional hairstyles for work as well as pregnancy versus unwanted pregnancy (Noble, 2018; Bogers et al., 2020). In both cases, the research strategy of employing 'counter-queries' (e.g., 'professional'/'unprofessional') serves to root out what is considered the ideal.

There are metapictures of preferred placement or rankings of one type of result compared to others that make use of annotating or 'staining' certain results and leaving others alone (see Figure 11.11). In one example, a journalistic piece emulates scrolling through engine results and by shading Google properties demonstrates that the first 35% (quite a long scroll) are Google's own (Jeffries and Yin, 2020). (The article is entitled: 'Google's top search result? Surprise! It's Google'.) The scrutiny of engine results by classifying them one way or another (through the lens of discrimination, misinformation, political leaning and other manners) can be visualized by colouring cells in a spreadsheet, as in misinformation is reddened, whilst other information is left blank (Torres and Rogers, 2020). One notes both the placement and amount at a glance. The ranking of a website for the same query over time may be graphed, for example in the Issue Dramaturg project that portrayed the 'drama' of search engine space as a website, routinely returned at the top of the results, one day vanishing from the first 1000 returns, likely because of an algorithmic 'update' (Rogers, 2013b). Changes over time to rankings are also visualized with RankFlow, where one compares how a number of websites or videos in YouTube, for example, wax and wane in the search engine returns (Rieder et al., 2018).

Image circulation

Apart from critiquing their occasional, discriminatory labelling practices, lack of ethnic diversity and the scraped origins of the training sets behind them (Crawford and Paglen, 2019; Sinders, 2020), computer vision, a catch-all term for the automated recognition and classification of images, may be repurposed for critical social and media research, mainly into image resonance and circulation (d'Andrea and Mintz, 2019) but also as exploratory work into the imagery associated with an event or issue (see Figure 11.12).

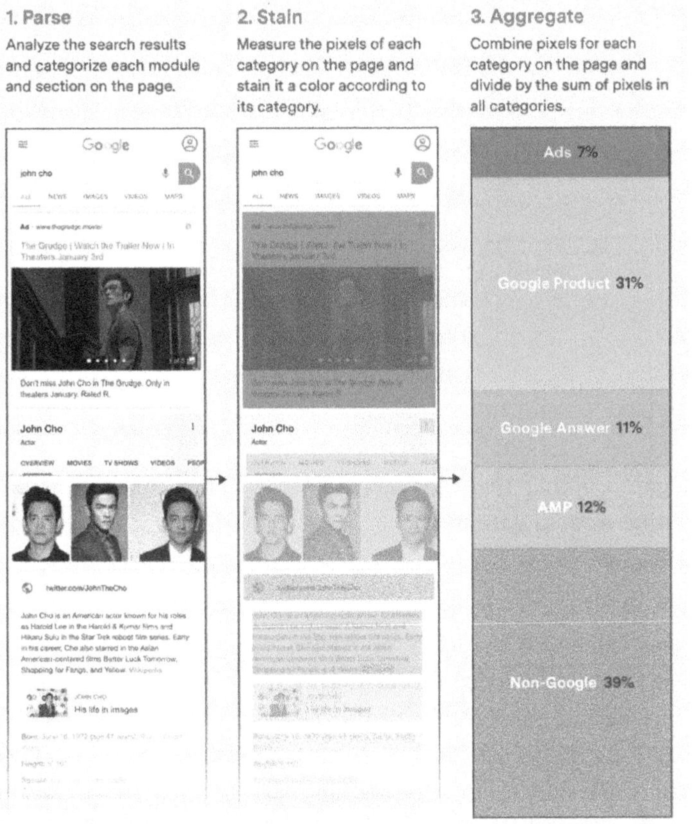

1. Parse
Analyze the search results and categorize each module and section on the page.
2. Stain
Measure the pixels of each category on the page and stain it a color according to its category.
3. Aggregate
Combine pixels for each category on the page and divide by the sum of pixels in all categories.
Ads 7%
Google Product 31%
Google Answer 11%
AMP 12%
Non-Google 39%
John Cho

Percentages in aggregate image are based on the entire page search results for a search of the term 'John Cho.'

Figure 11.11 Image staining technique. Percentage of an entire page of Google results that contain Google properties.

Source: Jeffries and Yin, 2020.

Youth
Community
Fun
Stage
Performance
Team
Green
Headgear
Selfie
Leisure
Child
Running
World
Costume
Spring
Crowd
Hand
Games
Human
Red
People
Physical fitness
T-shirt
Magenta
Summer
Graphics
Marching
Metal
Cloud
Botany
Recreation
Night

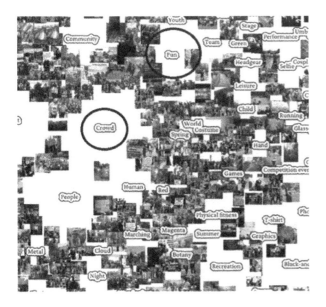

Figure 11.12 Cluster map of #georgefloyd images from Twitter and Google Vision API labels.

Source: Stepnik et al., 2020.

A project studying the adoption of the lean-in photo collection by Getty images is one example (Aiello and Parry, 2020). The stock photo set has been heralded as ground-breaking, for it portrays women in powerful ways rather than as soft, sexualized and motherly (Miller, 2014). But how are these empowering stock images actually put to use in the media? By employing reverse image search (either via a computer vision API or in an image search engine), the research may locate instances of image usage, and enquire into whether they indeed break new ground. The images may be empowering, but their actual usage was not as intended. It did not match the evolution of Getty women's image usage (from 2007 to 2017) as headlined in a *New York Times* article as 'from sex object to gritty woman' (Miller, 2017). Instead, the researchers found that their usage rather reinforced pre-lean-in collection themes. For example, it was found that portrayals of women in scientific or tech environments were found in stories about the challenges of breaking into the fields rather than ones simply about that work. Working women of colour were used mainly in publications with such a target group, rather than not. The most circulated image from the collection was of a young, white woman with long hair. Thus, the collection, at least in its actual usage, did not appear to meet its goals.

Computer vision techniques offer more than reverse image search for the study of resonance and circulation of particular imagery. They also label images, both in terms of content as well as format. When studying social media images, the labelling of image content has been critiqued for its inability to appreciate the 'social value of the picture', which includes the intention of the uploader, such as 'social capital, self-image and memory' (Bechmann, 2017). Researchers emphasize how the labelling should be accompanied by data enhancement, namely an additional data layer, such as hashtags (Geboers and Van De Wiele, 2020).

One image format type of interest is the meme, which CrowdTangle detects on Instagram and Facebook, Twitter as well as Reddit. One may search for memes with a keyword query, e.g., #stealthevote, one of the more significant hashtags implicated in the mobilization of those who rampaged the US Capitol. Given that CrowdTangle enables cross-platform comparison, one notes which platforms have tidied away posts containing the hashtag and which still has them in evidence. The effects of content moderation can be analysed per platform, including its sophistication, whereupon one notes that only those posts that rally people to the cause are now scarce, rather than those that report on it. In another such use case, AFP, the French news wire service, queries CrowdTangle's meme search for keywords related to misinformation (CrowdTangle, 2021). Misinformation may concern the Covid-19 pandemic or national elections, but also other issues they monitor. Those posts that are 'over-performing', a filter one can select, they consider worthy of further investigation and potentially deserving of fact-checking.

CrowdTangle's coverage, however, has been questioned, given that misinformation (that would constitute election interference) may be circulated in posts not indexed by the system such as by individual accounts and private groups (Tech Transparency Project, 2020).

Image engagement

Studying engagement on platforms, through CrowdTangle or other marketing tools such as BuzzSumo, should not be equated with popularity measures, at least according to Facebook's head of news feed, John Hegeman (Newton, 2020). In an exchange on Twitter with Kevin Roose, the *New York Times* tech journalist, he made the distinction between engagement (measured by interactions) and popularity or reach (impressions), which is a common marketing distinction. The latter data point, however, is available only internally at Facebook, indicating the value of the data. The context of the exchange concerns how far-right conservative sources dominate the content with the most engagement on Facebook (Roose, 2020). In fact, the journalist has been making a daily list, posting it from the Twitter account, @FacebooksTopTen. Facebook's internal list of most popular (measured by 'reach'), contrariwise, were far less politically charged, thereby downplaying the journalist's claim and Facebook's culpability (see Figure 11.13).

Figure 11.13 Facebook pages with most engagement (interaction counts, on left) and greatest reach (view counts, on right). List tweeted by Kevin Roose (New York Times), with response by John Hegeman (Facebook).

Showing engagement by ranked list is one method of enabling interpretation (of who's on top and who's on the list), and another is a tree map, where visual media posts are resized according to engagement score. It is a visual analysis technique whereby one curates a list of pages or accounts (such as alt-right or less extreme 'alt-lite' actors) and subsequently determines which posts have received the highest engagement scores, resizing them by score. In the example of research conducted with the UK Home Office, it was found that anti-Islam (or counter-jihadist) posts particularly animated the alt-lite, as visualized, though it should be remarked that other, even more extreme posts may well have been removed (through content moderation) prior to the analysis (see Figure 11.14) (Alt-Right Open Intelligence Initiative, 2017).

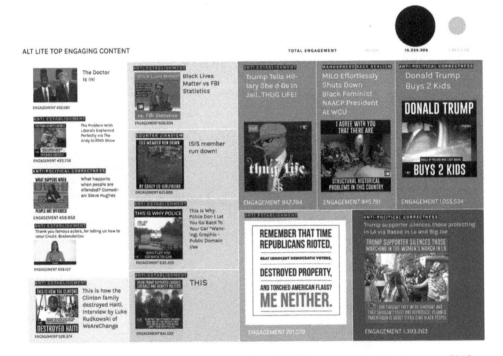

Figure 11.14　Most-engaged with Facebook posts of set of alt-lite pages, arrayed as tree map, 2016.

Image–emoji associations

The comparative study of image formats, more generally, is one operationalization of platform vernacular analysis. Others would be how hashtags, reactions or emojis are used together with images. On Facebook, for example, sad and angry reactions tend to be chosen together, as was found when analysing posts concerning the Syrian war (Geboers et al., 2020). In order to make findings such as these, one analytical technique is the production and interpretation of a co-occurrence network map, where images and another digital object or artefact (in this case, reactions) appear on the same map (see Figure 11.15).

Figure 11.15   Image-reaction (emoji) bipartite graph from posts on Facebook pages concerning the Syrian war, 2017.

Source: Scuttari et al., 2017.

Bunches of images together with hashtags, reactions or emojis come together in a graphing technique that seeks to optimize clustering. It relies on the 'networked-ness' of the images by virtue of being linked by the same hashtag and/or reaction (Niederer, 2018).

Typically, in Gephi, the network analysis software, a force atlas algorithm is chosen followed by community detection (Jacomy et al., 2014); such a combination encourages distinct clusters to appear. Once so rendered, the second step in the visual media network analysis is to label the clusters by inspecting their contents. For reactions and emojis, one would ask, which sentiments cluster with which images? For hashtag-image networks, the question concerns both how the images may be interpreted through their linkage to hashtags, and vice versa.

Apart from deriving and labelling clusters, visual network analysis has as part of its *instrumentarium* the study of centrality, brokerage and distance. Which reactions or emojis are central to a particular image space? How far apart are hashtag-image clusters? Which ones link or bridge the subspaces? Here, one annotates and tells stories with network maps.

Image removal

Scholarly attention to 4chan, the image board associated with extreme speech and visual content as well as snark, waxed considerably with the election of Donald Trump as US president in 2016, given the role of /pol/, the 'politically incorrect' board, in rallying Trump support through 'meme magic' (Tuters, 2019; Ling et al., 2021). 4chan is ephemeral, meaning that it must be routinely scraped or archived for its meaningful study. One can envisage an image grid timeline that is additive, showing in chronological order (per board) what is accruing on the platform. Arraying them in such a manner could show memeification or the hardening (or softening) of content, as also mentioned above in the discussion of the dominant image. Grouping through similarity in an image wall could show the extent to which memes dominate (and which memes).

In an approach where one platform is used to study another, discussed also in the YouTube chapter, researchers harvested YouTube URLs shared on 4chan/pol/and entered these into YouTube at two intervals in time, fetching the video preview image (and other data) (OILab, 2019) (see Figure 11.16). The before-and-after image walls display the widespread (and seemingly simultaneous) removal of videos, though with some still available for viewing. Here, one is able to visualize the scale and timing of content removal, using a presence/ absence technique. The videos that survived the sweep become of special interest to study where the platform draws the line, given that they are not quite extreme enough.

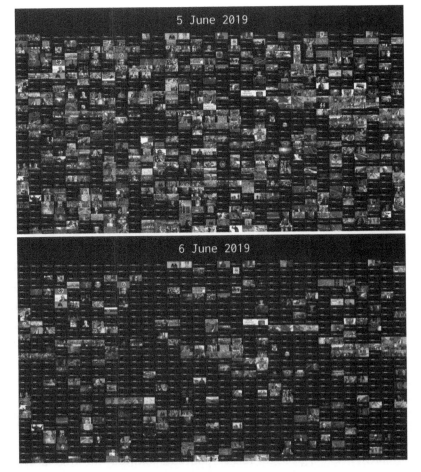

Figure 11.16 Content removal on YouTube. Comparison of extreme video availability before and after 'purge' on 6 June 2019.

Source: OILab, 2019.

Feed competition

The main purpose of putting source sets side by side is to consider alignment or agreement. Comparing Google Image search outputs in 2005 between 'apartheid wall' and 'security fence' show two distinctively different structures that had just been erected between Israel and the Palestinian Territories, the one concrete and graffitied, and the other lightweight and high-tech (Rogers, 2013b). There was next to no agreement between the two sets of visual outputs when comparing the preferred official Israeli terminology compared to the Palestinian.

The comparative display of political media feeds has become prevalent in the past few years, given concern with filter bubbles (Pariser, 2011a) (see Figure 11.17), or homophilic recommendation systems (Chun, 2018), especially Facebook's news feed. The 'Blue Feed, Red Feed' project by the Wall Street Journal (2016–2019) interactively displayed the stories published by conservative and progressive media sources on Facebook, refreshed hourly (Keegan, 2016).

Figure 11.17   Filter bubble as differing personalized Google results.

Source: Pariser, 2011b.

The side-by-side presentation afforded a good view of perspectival divides in media. It was a simulation of stories the users would be expected to receive. In the Citizen Browser project by the data journalist group, The Markup, the technique is taken a step farther, in that they seek not just to simulate the divide in media but rather to demonstrate it by showing the viewers' actual feeds, i.e., the 'content social media companies choose to amplify to their users' (Faife, 2021) (see Figure 11.18). Feed capture would be a step towards auditing the filter bubble, and the extent to which Facebook's feed narrows or broadens horizons. Relying on nationwide panels of internet users who donate their feeds to the project, it was found that after the Capitol rampage progressive Facebook users were routinely fed mainstream media such as CNN and NPR, whilst conservative users sources considered rather less reliable (The Daily Wire and Breitbart being the most salient) (Lecher and Keegan, 2021). Reliability measures of sources may be gleaned from NewsGuard, among other media labelling organizations.

Red rule indicates that a post contained misinformation. In the example here, The Washington Times later corrected the post. Source: Citizen Browser/The Markup. Complete data available on GitHub.

Figure 11.18   Feed competition. Side-by-side view of stories fed to feeds of liberal and conservative users of Facebook, showing competing accounts of events, January 2021.

Source: Lecher and Keegan, 2021.

Visual media analysis

Above I discussed image reuse, image trends and vernaculars, dominant image, image presence, image quality, image staining (or tarnishing), image circulation, image engagement, image associations, image removal and feed competition as approaches for visual media analysis. Having collections of images as inputs, these seek to output a kind of metapicture that retains and frames the images in a manner that invites critical reflection upon them. It enables close reading of images (through their retention) as well as more distant reading through their arrangement.

They also open lines of inquiry made implicit when the approach is combined with the metapicture technique. For example, do dominant images emerge when grouping sets of them that share the same issue hashtag? When does a new style appear in a set of chronologically arrayed covers of a magazine? When placed side by side, to what extent do sets of pictures or media feeds show agreement? These formulations would exemplify how the visual media analysis outlined above seeks to make the metapicturing active in the research.

The critical reflection of the images through their arrangement is born of digital research methods that curate or demarcate a set of them by making use of the affordances of the platforms (e.g., hashtags as substantive, grouping markers). While there are exceptions, such as adopting a user persona (in the case of the feed columns of progressive and conservative Facebook users) and extracting data from one platform to understand the workings of another (the YouTube deletion image walls made from URLs on 4chan), much of the demarcation work is undertaken through querying a platform, be it for hashtags or keywords (or both).

The queries of the platform result in sets that could be thought to organize substantive spaces. Subsequently, in the next step, those spaces' content engagement is measured, whether taken from the interface (front-end or user mode) or through the API or other means by which a developer would access the data (back-end or developer mode). Comparison of the two is occasionally of interest, given that a user's view (on Facebook, for example) could be considered less expansive than the API's, especially if one is interested in (politicized) news feed critique. In sum, the visual media analysis is the study of engagement and ordering in demarcated online spaces.

Finally, in striving to display the results of the work, the notion of a metapicture is invoked as a technique that retains and frames the images under study so as to enable critical reflection on them. As related in the introduction, it straddles the hermeneutic and the data-driven at once by de-datafying the images (in the sense that they remain images) as well as by arranging them as an analytical interpretation, such as the counter-meme as dominant image, stained engine results as tarnished or 'news' feeds as out of alignment or politically polarized.

PROJECTS

Perform a dominant image analysis using visual similarity software

RESEARCH GOAL Undertake a dominant image analysis using visual similarity (aka image grouping) software.

1   Decide upon the platform under study and create an image collection through querying it. For example, query climate change, Covid-19 or Ukraine war in Google Images and use a data scraper to collect a set of images, saved to a folder. Manual capture is also an option (for fewer images such as the top 100). Collections of thumbnails will suffice for the dominant image analysis.

    a   For Google Images, install a browser extension such as Instant Data Saver and save up to 1,000 images or fewer.

    b   For Instagram or Facebook, use CrowdTangle (if available), its alternative offered by Meta or employ a data scraper.

    c   For Twitter, use 4CAT or TCAT, if installed. For scraping X/Twitter, use Zeeschuimer. Alternatively, use another X/Twitter data collection device.

    d   For Reddit, Tumblr or 4chan, use 4CAT or alternatives.

2   Install ImageSorter, PicArrange or similar visual similarity software.

3   Open the folder and load into software. The images will be grouped by similarity (hue).

4   Once the tool has completed its task, choose the tool's output menu and save the list of URLs of the archived versions as a text file.

5   To enrich the analysis, consider making multiple image collections.

    a   One option is to search with date ranges, thereby allowing for an image trend analysis. In this case, choose time chunks, such as monthly, quarterly or yearly.

    b   Another option is to search multiple platforms and compare their image styles or vernaculars.

Tools

- For ImageSorter, PicArrange and other image grouping software, see Visual Computing at HTW Berlin – University of Applied Sciences: https://visual-computing.com/.
- 4CAT Capture and Analysis Toolkit: https://4cat.digitalmethods.net/.

Perform an over-time image analysis using Google Image Search outputs

RESEARCH GOAL Compare how the images outputted for an image search query have changed (or remained similar) over time.

1   Decide upon the image search engine under study (or choose multiple ones) and choose one or more queries to research. For example, query climate change, Covid-19 or Ukraine war in Google Images and use a spreadsheet to collect a set of images (see image grid instructions below).

2   Populate the spreadsheet with query results over time. Consider an annual comparison, querying the engine on the same data for ten years, for example. If comparing engines, repeat the population of the spreadsheet for each engine.

3   Note the extent to which the style, format and/or substance of the images change (or remain the same) over time.

Resource

•   For inserting images into a spreadsheet for over-time comparison, see the 'creating an image grid' recipe, with instructions, from the Public Data Lab: http://recipes.publicdatalab.org/image_grid_ranking.html.

TWELVE

CROSS-PLATFORM ANALYSIS
Co-linked, inter-liked and cross-hashtagged content

Overcoming single-platform studies

Single-platform studies

This chapter develops a critique of single-platform studies, as they have taken shape with the displacement of the 'info-web', or websites, by the 'social web', or social media platforms as a dominant focal point for digital methods. Single-platform studies have arisen together with the rise of the API, or Application Programming Interface, as the main source or gateway to social media data. Next to the API (for YouTube data, for example), there is also the marketing data dashboard, as CrowdTangle, where Facebook and Instagram data may be queried. While one has access to multiple platforms through the dashboard, queries are made for only one platform repository at a time, thereby reinforcing the single-platform studies outlook. Having discussed the transition to single-platform studies, I develop a case for multiple or cross-platform studies that seeks analytical commensurability across platforms while at the same time respecting platform vernaculars or cultures of use.

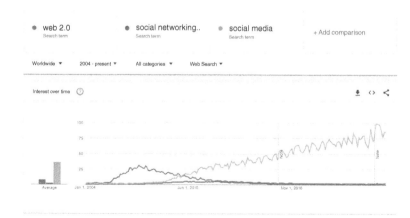

Figure 12.1 Comparison of search volume for [web 2.0], [social networking sites] and [social media], according to Google Trends, 23 September 2022.

Digital methods before social media

One of the earliest digital methods maps the hyperlinking patterns between websites involved in the same social issue area to study the politics of association of actors from the purposively made as well as the 'missing' links between them. The Issuecrawler, the software tool developed in the early 2000s for the info-web (as opposed to the social web), provides a method for studying associations in issue networks online, or clutches of NGOs, funders, think tanks, academics as well as databases, widgets and other online objects, working on or serving a particular issue (Bruns, 2007; Rogers, 2019. Once the links between actors have been found, one may begin to study association as well as the organization of networked publics (Latour, 2005b; Ito, 2008).

Subsequently, by calling for a move from 'so-called web 1.0 http or html approaches to 2.0 cross platform-based methods', Greg Elmer and Ganaele Langlois (2013: 45) have argued that to study the social web requires new methods that step past the hyperlink as the pre-eminent digital object tying it all together. They issue a much larger invitation to rethink the web more generally as an object of study, recognizing its increasing platformization, or the mass movement by web users to social media (Helmond, 2015). In the shift from an info-web to a social web, recommendations are made through the participation of platform users rather than only by site webmasters (to use a throwback term). That is, recommendations, especially in the news feeds of platforms, follow from 'friends'' activity, such as 'liking', 'sharing', 'retweeting' and 'commenting'. The content recommendations thereby distinguish themselves epistemologically from those derived from site owners or webmasters linking to another webpage for referencing or other purposes. Following Tim O'Reilly, the terms 'Web 1.0' and 'Web 2.0' have been used (or overused) to periodize not only the transition from the info-web to the social web, but also from the open web to the closed web or the walled gardens of platforms, where data collection differs substantially from crawling and scraping (O'Reilly, 2005; Dekker and Wolfsberger, 2009).

On the web's 25th anniversary, Tim Berners-Lee, who 'slowly, but steadily' has come to be known as its inventor, called for its 're-decentralization', breaking down new media concentration and near monopolies online working as walled gardens without the heretofore open spirit (Berners-Lee, 2014; see also Agar, 2001: 371). The web's 'appification' is analogous. Next to increased government internet censorship, mass surveillance and punitive copyright laws, Berners-Lee (2014) lists 'corporate walled gardens' or social media platforms as grave concerns related to the very future of the web and its mobile counterpart.

Digital methods after social media

Langlois and Elmer's point, however, implies that one should not only periodize and critique the dominant phases of the web, but also do the same for its methods of study. There are those digital methods that rely on hyperlinks, and thereby are in a sense still committed to an info-web, and those that have taken on board 'likes', 'shares' and other forms of valuation and currency (such as 'comments' and 'liked comments') on online platforms. Indeed, this analytical periodization is reflected in the much broader study of value online, reflected in the rise of the 'like economy' over the 'link economy' which itself supplanted the 'hit economy' (Gerlitz and Helmond, 2013). As a case in point, Google's Web Search once valued links higher than other signals (Hindman, 2008; Rieder, 2012). Through the rise of user clicks as a source adjudication measure, one could argue that Google Web Search, too, is valuing the social web over the document or semantic matching of the info-web (van Couvering, 2007). Metrification online, which starts with like counts and follower numbers and progresses towards 'vanity metrics' scores, similarly considers and makes rankings social (Rogers, 2018a). Thus, the new analytics, both Google's updated ones as well as follower and like counts, are oriented to a web gone social.

The notion of Web 2.0 (and the related idea of the social web) brought with it as its apparent forerunner Web 1.0 (with a more informational set of metaphors), but beyond the versioning rhetoric, Web 2.0 itself has been supplanted first by 'social network(ing) sites' and 'platforms' and later just by 'social media' (boyd and Ellison, 2007; Beer, 2008; Scholz, 2008; Allen, 2013; see Figure 12.1). The early distinction between social networking sites and social network sites, ushered in by boyd and Ellison, was normative as well as analytical. Social media users ought to have an interest in connecting with others online other than for the purposes of 'networking', which would suggest a kind of neoliberal activity of making sure that even one's social life (online) is productive. In a sense, the authors also anticipated the nuancing of social media into platform types, such as the ones for business (LinkedIn), family (Facebook) and professional doings (X/Twitter), though social media user practices in each remain diverse. Whether for networking or to connect with one's existing network, the analytical call made by boyd and Ellison seemed to be directed to the study of profiles and friends (together with friending).

The purposive use of the term 'platform', as Tarleton Gillespie (2010) has pointed out, could be viewed as particularly enticing for users to populate an otherwise empty database, thereby generating value for the companies. Platforms connote voice-giving infrastructure, where one can express one's viewpoints (political or otherwise), rise up, and make an online project of oneself. Polishing the profile, friending, uploading videos and photos, and liking, sharing and commenting become not only newly dominant forms of sociality, but also a kind of labour for a platform owned by others (Scholz, 2016b). Cooperative, user-owned platforms would provide alternatives. Other critical calls for the analysis of Facebook have been made, certain of which have resulted in invitations to leave the platform, to liberate oneself or even to commit so-called Facebook suicide, which would allow you 'to meet your real neighbors', as suicidemachine.org's software project's slogan had it (Portwood-Stacer, 2013; Facebook Liberation Army, 2015; see Figure 12.2).

With the info-web giving way to the Web 2.0, social networking sites and, finally, social media, social media methods also have evolved. In particular, digital methods for social media analysis initially relied on social network analysis (the study of interlinked friends) as well as profiles and the presentation of self. For example, Netvizz, the Facebook data extraction software, originally was considered a tool to map one's own Facebook friend network (Rieder, 2013). The early digital methods work on social networking sites similarly studied friends and profiles. Dubbed 'postdemographics', this approach to studying profiles considered preferences and tastes as a starting point of analysis as opposed to gender, age, education and such (Rogers, 2009c). One study examined the interests of presidential candidates' MySpace 'friends'. Did Barack Obama's friends and John McCain's friends share the same favourite television shows, movies, heroes and books, or was there a distinctive politics to media taste and consumption? For the most part, they did not share tastes, and thus TV shows and the other preferences could be considered to have politics of consumption (Rogers, 2013b). In the case of friend-network mapping as well as postdemographics, these methods could be called digital methods for social media 1.0, for they concerned themselves with profiles, friends and networking.

More recently, attention on social media in digital methods work has been directed towards events, disasters, elections, revolutions and movements, first through the so-called 'Twitter revolution' surrounding the Iran election crisis (2009) and later the Arab Spring (2011–2012) and other social media (and on the ground) events. Instead of starting with user profiles, friend networks or networking, such studies collect tweets containing one or more hashtags such as #iranelection (perhaps together with queried keywords) and #jesuischarlie, or focus on one particular Facebook page, such as We Are All Khaled Said (Gaffney, 2010; Lotan et al., 2011; Rieder et al., 2015). Movements such as #blacklivesmatter and #metoo also invite tweet collection-making.

The API, the dashboard and the ethics turn

Many of the more recent methods to analyse platforms rest upon and also derive from the individual APIs or dashboards that YouTube, Instagram, Facebook and others have to offer. As data are offered and delivered by polling one API or querying a dashboard, and are no longer screen-scraped or crawled from multiple websites (as in the days of the info-web), most work is a study of a page or multiple pages (and groups) on Facebook, or posts containing one or more hashtags on Instagram. In social media analysis with digital methods, in other words, 'single-platform studies' have become the norm.

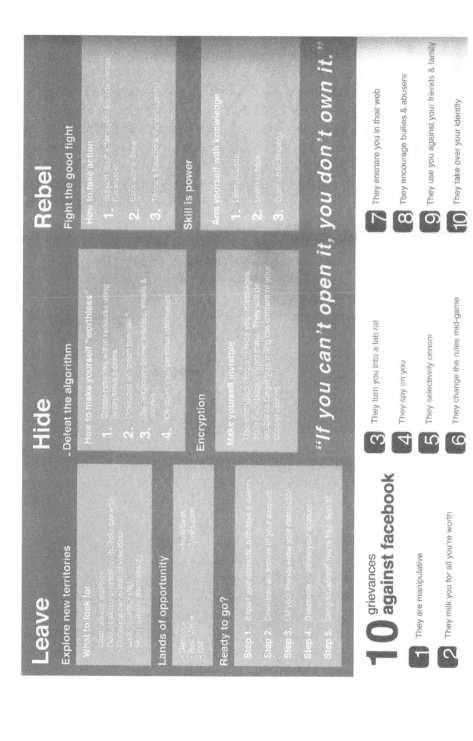

Figure 12.2 (a) Facebook Liberation Army flyer, initiated in 2015 by the Institute of Network Cultures and the Waag Society, Amsterdam, with franchiseable 'Facebook Farewell Party' as principal awareness-raising format of action. (b) Facebook Liberation Army flyer, with its so-called directives, instructions and grievances.

Source: fla.waag.org.

If there were a significant turning point towards single-platform studies steered by the API and, later, the dashboard (rather than by scraping), it may have been the critique of a social network analysis of tastes and ties that used college students' Facebook data (Lewis et al., 2008b; Zimmer, 2010a; Marres and Weltevrede, 2013). It concerned a set of presumably anonymized users from a so-called renowned university in the northeastern United States. Not so unlike the effects of the release of AOL user search histories in 2006, its publishing prompted detective work to uncover the identities of the users, who turned out to be Harvard College students from the graduating class of 2009 (Zimmer, 2008). Michael Zimmer, both in the detective work and in the reflection upon the way forward for social media methods, entitled his critique, 'But the data is already public', echoing one of the remarks of an author of the study. In giving rise to a sharper focus on ethics in web studies more generally, coinciding with a decline in scraping, Zimmer argued that in the Harvard study users' so-called contextual privacy was violated, for they not only did not give informed content, but also did not expect their publicly available data to be stored in a researcher's database and matched with their student housing data for even greater analytical scrutiny of their ties and tastes, the subject of the study (Nissenbaum, 2009). The actual data collection is described by the researchers as 'downloading' the profile and friend network data directly from Facebook, prior to the release of the Facebook API 1.0 in 2010. In other words, the data were obtained or scraped in some non-API manner, albeit with permission from Facebook as well as Harvard for the project funded by the National Science Foundation and approved by the university's ethics review board. Ultimately, in the evolution of its API to version 2.0 (in 2014), Facebook would remove permissions to access friends' data such as ties and tastes (i.e., friends and likes, together with profiles), thereby making (sociometric) social network analysis like that performed in the Harvard study improbable, including even those of one's own network with all friends' privacy settings adhered to, as one did with Netvizz (Facebook, 2016). 'Internal' studies may be performed, which Facebook data scientists also took advantage of with their 'emotional contagion' experiment (Kramer et al., 2014). The data science study (of some 700,000 users with a corpus of 3 million posts) analysed the risks associated with the Facebook news feed. Is user exposure to positive or negative posts psychologically risky (Meyer, 2015)? The study found that negative posts run the risk of 'emotional contagion'. In order to make the findings, Facebook selectively removed negative posts from users' news feeds. The ethics of the study were similarly questioned, for the users were unaware (and not informed) that their news feeds were being altered and their moods measured, however seemingly impractical and obtrusive it would be to gain such permission (Puschmann and Bozdag, 2014). Among the ethical issues raised, one concerned whether researchers can rely on the terms of service as cover for the otherwise lack of informed consent. Are users agreeing to being analysed for more than improvement of the site and services, as is usually stated?

It is worthwhile to recall from the AOL case that the 62-year-old search engine user told the *New York Times* that she never imagined that her search engine queries would be made public, or that she would have to explain to anyone that her information-seeking about medical conditions was undertaken for her friends (Barbaro and Zeller, 2006). In the event, highly personal and salacious query histories from unnamed individuals were published. One user's search engine query history was made into the mini-documentary, 'I love Alaska: The heartbreaking search history of AOL user #711391', by the Dutch artists and filmmakers Lernert Engelberts and Sander Plug (2009).

Neither the study of Harvard College's 2009 graduating class nor the emotional contagion study appears to have led to the subjects being identified and harmed through outing. It is also not straightforward to claim that informed consent would have been enough to preclude harm, given that the users may be unable to foresee the potential hazards of participation (van de Poel, 2009).

API-led hashtag and (liked) page studies

With the decline of scraping and the rise of issues surrounding human subject research in social media, the API-led studies (on events, disasters, elections, revolutions and social causes) rely increasingly on such content-organizing elements as the hashtag (for Instagram) and the (liked) post (for Facebook). Each is taken in turn, so as eventually to discuss with what limitations one may study them concurrently across platforms.

The original Twitter hashtag, put forward by the user Chris Messina (2007), was originally conceived as a means to set up 'channel tags', borrowing from similar practices in Internet Relay Chat. The proposal was to organize 'group-like activity' on Twitter that would be 'folksonomic', meaning user-generated rather than an editorial or taxonomic practice by the company or its syndicated partners. Messina also proposed to provide a ranked list of the channel tags by activity (i.e., most active ones in the past 24 hours), showing on the interface where the activity is. This feature is similar to trending topics which Jack Dorsey, co-founder of Twitter, described a year later as 'what the world considers important in this moment' (Dorsey, 2008). With hashtags and trending topics, Twitter not only gained new functionality but also became a rather novel object of study for what could be termed both on-the-ground and 'remote event analysis'. As such, it thus distinguishes itself from Dorsey's original Twitter, created to provide what he called 'personal immediacy – seeing what's happening in my world right now' (Dorsey, 2008). Dorsey himself, in the interviews he gave for the *Los Angeles Times* after his first stint as CEO, acknowledged the shift away from this more intimate Twitter, saying Twitter thrives on 'natural disasters, man-made disasters, events, conferences, presidential elections' (Sarno, 2009b). In the event, the study of Twitter as a space for ambient friend-following yielded, at least for a share of Twitter studies, to that of event-following (as well as disasters, elections, revolutions and movements), which is another way of distinguishing between digital methods for social media analysis 1.0 and 2.0 (Rogers, 2013a).

Not so unlike Google Trends that list the year's most sought keywords (with a geographical distribution), Twitter's initial cumulative list of the year's trending topics provides a rationale for the attention granted to the study of the single hashtag for events. In the announcement made by the Twitter data scientist Abdur Chowdhury (who incidentally was head of AOL Research when the search history data were released), one notes how serious content began to take a prominent place in a service once known primarily for its banality. In 2009 'Twitter users found the Iranian elections the most engaging topic of the year. The terms #iranelection, Iran and Tehran were all in the top 21 of Trending Topics, and #iranelection finished in a close second behind the regular weekly favourite #music-monday' (Chowdhury, 2009). Some years later the universal list of trending topics became personalized according to whom one follows and one's geographical coordinates, however much one may change one's location and personalize trending topics exclusively by new location. In some sense the change from universal to personalized results (like Google Web Search's similar move in December 2009, which Eli Pariser (2011a) relies upon for his notion of the 'filter bubble') made trends more unassailable, for no longer could one call into question why a particular hashtag (like #occupywallstreet) was not trending when it perhaps should have been (Gillespie, 2012). Trending topics (or trends on X) are in a sense now co-authored by the X/Twitter user, making them less compelling to study, at least as a cultural barometer. (The exception is trending topics that are location-based only.) They remain of interest to those who wish to make hashtags trend by gaming the system.

While the single hashtag, or more likely a combination of hashtags and keywords, remains a prominent starting point for making tweet collections to study events, disasters, elections, revolutions and social causes, as well as subcultures, stock prices, celebrity awards and cities, researchers have widely expanded their repertoire for assembling them, first through techniques of capturing follower, reply and mention networks, and subsequently using the 1% (and 10%) random sample(s) once made available by Twitter, geotagged tweets and the Twitter ID number space in combination with time zones to identify national Twitter spheres (Crampton et al., 2013; Gerlitz and Rieder, 2013; Bruns et al., 2014). Twitter would later remove certain fields (such as time zone), thereby subtracting a research affordance and at once providing a reminder that continual 'technical fieldwork' of platforms is a part of the research practice (Rieder et al., 2015; Omena, 2021).

Network analysis remains a preferred analytical technique in digital methods work, and as such it endures in the transition to method 2.0, but one somewhat novel strand of work worthy of mention here concerns Twitter content studies, discussed by way of a brief analytical tool description (Venturini et al., 2014a; Kennedy and Hill, 2016).

Twitter Analysis Tools and quanti-quali research

Both the Twitter Capture and Analysis Tool (TCAT) as well as the newer 4CAT can be installed on one's own server (with GitHub instructions) to analyse tweets (Borra and Rieder, 2014; Peeters and Hagen, 2022). The tools provide a battery of network analyses: social graph by mentions, social graph by in_reply to status_id, co-hashtag, bipartite hashtag-user, bipartite hashtag-mention, bipartite hashtag-URL and bipartite hashtag-host. There are also modules, however, that direct attention towards forms of content analysis that are 'quanti-quali' and referred to as 'networked content analysis' (Niederer, 2016). By 'quanti-quali' is meant that a quantitative, winnowing analysis (not so unlike sampling or curating a collection) is performed so as to enable not only a 'computational hermeneutics' but also a thicker description (Mohr et al., 2015). Quanti-quali is preferred over the more usual quali-quanti moniker, owing to the order of the methodological steps (Venturini et al., 2014b).

Departing from a collection of 600,000 tweets gathered through a single hashtag, an example of such an approach is the #iranelection RT project, which sought to turn Twitter into a story-telling machine of events on the ground and in social media by ordering the top three retweeted tweets per day, and placing them in chronological order, as opposed to the reverse chronological order of Twitter (Rogers et al., 2009b). #iranelection RT relied on manual retweeting (where the user types RT in the tweet), whereas the TCAT and 4CAT module outputs, chronologically, 'identical tweet frequency', or narrowly defined 'native' retweets.

Other forms of quanti-quali content analysis with a tweet collection are what I call 'critical analytics': hashtag as well as URL frequency list making to study hierarchies of concern and most referred-to content. It is the starting point for a form of content analysis that treats a hashtag as (for example) an embedded social cause or movement (#blacklivesmatter) and URLs as content for close reading. The (often fleeting) 'hashtag publics' mobilize around a social cause not only phatically (and affectively) but also with content (Bruns and Burgess, 2011, 2015; Papacharissi, 2015). Networked content analysis considers how and to what substantive ends the network filters stories, mobilizes particular media formats over others and circulates urgency (geographically), attracting bursty or sustained attention that may be measured. Techniques of studying social causes using hashtags in X/Twitter as well as Instagram are discussed below, including how to consider whether to downplay or embrace medium effects.

With the closure of Twitter's academic track with full archive search in 2023, tweet collection making for individual researchers became more challenging, given the high costs of subscribing to the company API and the issues that accompany scraping data (Woo, 2023). Via Zeeschuimer (the browser plug-in) or other software, one is able to extract on-screen data and save it for further analysis in 4CAT, the social media research tool. On the interface one queries hashtags, keywords, user accounts or @mentions, gradually building tweet collections for comparative or cross-platform analysis, where X/Twitter engagement is compared to that on Facebook, for example.

Positioning Facebook for cross-platform analysis

While, for more than a decade now, Facebook has included hashtags as proposed means of organizing 'public conversations', the straightforward 'cross-platform analysis' of X/Twitter and Facebook using the same hashtags is likely fraught. The study of Facebook 'content' relies far more on other activities, such as liking (or reacting), sharing and commenting, which is known as studying 'most engaged-with content'. For cross-platform work, the co-appearances of URLs (co-links), amplified perhaps by 'likes' (Facebook's as well as Twitter's) may yield far more material for comparative resonance analysis.

From the beginning Facebook (unlike Friendster and MySpace before it) positioned itself as a social network site that would reflect one's own proper circle of friends and acquaintances, thereby challenging the idea that online friends should be considered 'friends' with quotation marks and thereby a problematic category worthy of special 'virtual' study. In a sense, such a friend designation could be interpreted as another mid-2000 marker of the end of cyberspace. Together with the demise of serendipitous (and aimless) surfing, the rise of national jurisdictions legislating (and censoring) the internet and the reassertion of local language (and local advertising) as organizing principles of browsing, Facebook also reordered the web, doing away with cyberspace in at least two senses. As AOL once did with its portal, Facebook sought to attract and keep users by making the web 'safe', first as a US college website offering registration only to on-campus users with an .edu email address, and then later as it expanded beyond the colleges by ID-ing users or otherwise thwarting practices of anonymization (Stutzman et al., 2013). This was an effort to prevent so-called 'fakesters', and thus distinguish itself from online platforms like MySpace, which were purportedly rife with lurkers and stalkers as well as publicized cases of sex offenders masquerading as youngsters (boyd, 2013). Facebook's web was also clean, swept of visual clutter. In contrast to MySpace, it did not offer customization, skinning or 'pimping', so one's profile picture and the friend thumbnails would be set in a streamlined, blue interface without starry nights, unicorns and double rainbows surrounding the posts.

Facebook's safe and decluttered web brought a series of 'cyberspace' research practices down to earth as well, cleaning up or at least making seem uncouth such practices as scraping websites for data. For one, scraping social network sites for data became a (privacy and proprietary) concern and also a practice actively blocked by Facebook. Data would be served on Facebook's terms through its API (as mentioned above), and the politics and practices of APIs (more generally) would become objects of study (Bucher, 2013). In this case, terms-of-service-abiding, non-scraping data extraction tools would reside on Facebook itself as apps and require vetting and approval by the company. Be it through the developers' gateway or a tool on Facebook, one would log in, and the data available would respect one's own as well as the other users' privacy settings, eventually putting paid to the open-ended opportunities social network sites were thought to provide to social network research. With the API as point of access, Facebook as an object of study underwent a transition from the primacy of the profile and friends' networks (tastes and ties) to that of the page or group, and with it from the presentation of self to events and social causes (which I am now using as a shorthand for disasters, elections, revolutions, movements, and so forth). In a sense the company's acquisition, Instagram, could be said to have supplanted Facebook as the preferred object of study of the self through its ambassadorship of selfie culture (Senft and Baym, 2015). Its initiator once said he would like the company to take the route of X/Twitter, at once debanalizing and becoming a news and event-following medium, too (Goel, 2015), though at the time of writing Instagram has over 1 billion more registered users than X/Twitter. Instagram also has since become a platform of far more than selfies and influencers, as related, given its use by Russian disinformation operatives and the interest by research into the infodemic, elections and other events, making it not so dissimilar to Twitter's subjects of study.

Figure 12.3 One rendition of the Facebook like button depicting a man's hand, thumbs up, with a single-button barrel cuff. Originally the like button was to be called the 'awesome' button. See Bosworth (2009).

Image source: Wikipedia, 2015, https://upload.wikimedia.org/wikipedia/commons/1/13/Facebook_like_thumb.png.

If Facebook analysis is steered towards the pages of social causes, 'liking' is no longer considered as frivolous, and like-based engagement analyses gain more weight (see Figure 12.3). While it has been dismissed as a form of slacktivism (Christensen, 2011) (which requires little or no effort and has little or no effect), liking as a form of engagement has been studied more extensively, with scholars attributing to button clicking on Facebook distinctive forms of liking causes: '(1) socially responsible liking, (2) emotional liking, (3) informational liking, (3) social performative liking, (5) low-cost liking and 6) routine liking' (Brandtzaeg and Haugstveit, 2014: 258). In the event, low-cost liking would be especially slacktivist, though all forms of liking in the list also could be construed as a form of attention-granting with scant impact, as was once said of the 'CNN effect' when all the world's proverbial eyes are watching – but not acting (Robinson, 2002). The question of whether liking as a form of engagement substitutes for other forms, however, has been challenged, for social media activism, it may be argued, aids in accumulating action and action potential. It is also where the people are (online).

For some time now, reaction buttons would allow more nuanced engagement, where 'angry' and 'sad' would often be combined, for example in the case of the study of the Syrian war (Scuttari et al., 2017). The reaction buttons can provide analytical weights, as on CrowdTangle where one can select posts that received certain, such as angry. Facebook itself uses reactions (and other signals) to order content of its news feeds, where strong reactions (and longer threads) are boosted over merely liked content (Merrill and Oremus, 2021).

From single platform to cross-platform studies

Social movement, collective action and, more recently, 'connective action' researchers have long called for multiple-platform, and multi-media, analysis (to use an older term). In an extensive study based on interviews, Sasha Costanza-Chock (2014), for one, has deemed the immigrant rights movement in the United States a form of 'transmedia organizing'. The organizing approach is a deliberate strategy, and each platform is approached and utilized separately for its own qualities and opportunities. Here one may recall the distinction made by Henry Jenkins (2006) between cross-media (the same story for all platforms) and transmedia (the story unfolds differently across platforms). Thus, social media, when used as a 'collapsed category', masks significant differences in 'affordances' (Costanza-Chock, 2014: 61–66). (I return to a similar problem concerning collapsed digital objects such as hashtags or likes across platforms with different user cultures.) If we are to follow Jenkins, as well as Costanza-Chock, a discussion of cross-platform analysis would be more aptly described as trans-platform analysis.

Researchers studying social causes on platforms have also called for 'uncollapsing' social media. Lance Bennett and Alexandra Segerberg, who coined the notion of 'connective action' as a counterpoint to collective action, argue that to understand the forces behind social change one should study those multiple platforms that allow for 'personalized public engagement', instead of choosing one platform and its API in advance of the analysis (Bennett and Segerberg, 2012). It is, in other words, an implicit critique of the single-platform studies (as 'collapsed social media studies') that rely solely on X/Twitter for one issue (e.g., Fukushima in Japan) or Facebook for another (e.g., the rise of right-wing populism), when one could have ample cause to study them across media. It is not only the siloing effect of APIs and dashboards that prompts single-platform studies; as pointed out, the question of the comparability (and commensurability) of the 'same' objects across platforms (likes, hashtags) is also at issue.

The 'cross' in cross-platform, and platform vernaculars

For multiple-platform (and transmedia) analysis *à la* Bennett and Segerberg, the purpose of the exercise here is to develop cross-platform methods, or digital methods for cross-platform studies, where one learns from medium methods and repurposes them for social and cultural research. It begins with a sensitivity to distinctive user cultures and subcultures, whereby hashtags and likes, digital objects used to organize and boost content (among other reasons), should not necessarily be treated as if they are employed equivalently across all platforms, even when present. For example, Instagram has inflated hashtag use compared to X/Twitter's, allowing up to 30 tags (and far more characters per photo caption post – 2,200 – than X/Twitter grants for a tweet – 280). That is, users may copy and paste copious quantities of hashtags in Instagram posts (see Figure 12.4). X/Twitter recommends 'using no more than

2 hashtags per Tweet as best practice' (2022). While present, hashtags are under-utilized on Facebook. The culture of TikTok hashtag use often appears to be to drive traffic, rather than to categorize the contents of the video. A case in point is when a pro-Trump video contains both Trump as well as other candidate hashtags so that when searching for whichever candidate the video could appear. Such usage is distinct from so-called hashtag stuffing where one rides the wave of a popular event (such as the World Cup) in order for one's content to be found, discussed below.

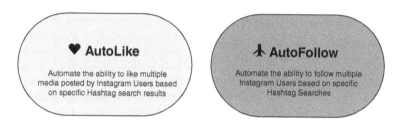

Figure 12.4   Sample of suggested tags to copy and paste as caption for an Instagram photo, in order to garner more likes and followers, as is claimed. Category of tags: 'most popular'.

Source: http://tagsforlikes.com, 25 May 2018.

Hashtags

A series of questions arises concerning the meaning of the term 'cross' in 'cross-platform analysis'. First, across which platforms are hashtags worthy of study (X/Twitter, Instagram, TikTok, Tumblr), which ones 'likes' (Facebook, Instagram, X/Twitter, Pinterest, TikTok, YouTube), which ones 'retweets' or 'repins' (X/Twitter, Pinterest), which ones '@mentions' (X/Twitter), and so forth (see Table 12.1)? The point is that platforms have similar affordances, such as like buttons and hashtags, but one should not necessarily collapse them by treating them equally across platforms. More specifically, if one were to perform cross-platform analysis of the same hashtags

Table 12.1   Elements of cross-platform analysis

	X/Twitter	Facebook	Instagram
Query design	Hashtag(s), keyword(s), URLs, location(s), user(s)	Keywords and URLs in group(s), page(s)	Keywords, hashtag(s), location(s)
Data capture	On demand (for over-time and recent data)	On demand (for over-time and recent data)	On demand (for over-time and recent data)
Platform user accounts (with primary actions)	user (follow)	user (friend, follow), group (join), page (reaction)	user (follow)
Content (media contents and digital objects)	tweet (text, photo, video, hashtag, @mention, URL, geotag)	post (text, photo, video, URL)	post (photo, video, caption, hashtag, geotag)
Activities (resonance measures)	like, retweet, mention, reply	like, reactions, comment, share	like, comment, share

Adapted from Rieder, 2015b.

across multiple platforms, how would one build into the method the difference in vernacular hashtag use in X/Twitter and Instagram? Because of hashtag proliferation on Instagram, does one devalue or otherwise correct for hashtag abundance on the one platform while valuing it steadily on another? One could strive to identify cases of copy-and-pasting hashtag strings, and downplay their value, certainly if posts are being 'stuffed' with hashtags.

Hijacking

Second, certain platforms (and, perhaps more so, certain topics such as large media events on almost any platform) may indeed have user cultures and automation activity that routinely befoul posts as well as activity measures. Hashtag hijacking is a case in point, especially when one is studying an event or a social issue and encounters unrelated hashtags purposively inserted to attract attention and traffic, such as when spammers monitor trending hashtags and use them tactically to promote their wares. Hashtag junk may distract at least the researcher.

Bots

Third, while a more complex topic, bots and the activity traces they leave behind are often similarly considered worth special consideration during the analysis (Marres, 2015; see Figure 12.5). From a digital forensics point of view, bots that like and follow may have specific (network) signatures; for example, they do not tend to be followed, or to be liked, meaning the bot often only has outlinks. For the purposes of this discussion, they may inflate activity in causes and such inflation may be considered artificial (though of course there are bots created for events and issues, too, and their activities are thereby purposive). Thus, manipulation as well as artificiality are additional (intriguing) complications in both single-platform and cross-platform analysis. Here bot detection becomes a sub-strand of study.

Most Popular

#love #TagsForLikes #TagsForLikesApp #TFLers #tweegram #photooftheday #20likes # amazing #smile #follow4follow #like4like #look #instalike #igers #picoftheday #food #instadaily #instafollow #followme #girl #iphoneonly #instagood #bestoftheday #instacool #instago #all_shots #follow #webstagram #colorful #style #swag

Figure 12.5   Features of iFollowandLike, the Instagram bot, that takes the work out of liking and following through automation.

Source: Screenshot from iFollowandLike.com, 4 December 2015.

Device or ranking culture

Fourth, platforms have 'device cultures' or 'ranking cultures' that affect how one interprets the data from the API or dashboard (Rieder et al., 2018). That is, all platforms rank and filter posts, optimizing and showing particular content and letting other posts slide downwards or off screen, so to speak (Eslami et al., 2015). Users thereby cannot react to all content equally, because it has not been evenly visible to those who would be able to like, share, comment, and so forth. That which is liked may tend to be liked more often, and thus there may be power-law and long-tail effects that differ per platform. But we may not know how preferred posting affects activity measures. APIs and data dashboards will return like and share counts (for example) per post, but they do not let us know how they have ranked and filtered the posts. And filtering styles and thus visibility effects differ per platform.

As mentioned, because of the Facebook whistleblower, we are now aware of how 'MSI downstream' (meaningful social interaction) is calculated. Content without reactions is least optimized, followed by liked posts and those that are reacted upon with strong emotions and commented upon with long threads. Given that knowledge, one could consider making a collection of posts (on a particular subject matter or within one or more pages) that have been most reacted to. One also can consider studying Facebook content amplification, as discussed in the projects below.

Engagement (rather than influence) as cross-platform approach

Above a series of questions has been posed concerning the limitations of comparing evaluations of content, recommended with the same type of button on different platforms, given that the platforms may have different user, spamming, bot and device or ranking cultures. How to nevertheless undertake cross-platform analysis? When studying recommendations and the content that rises, metrically, to the top of the platforms, it may be instructive to begin by examining briefly which digital objects are available in each of the platforms (as above and in Table 12.1) and subsequently inquire into how dominant devices (or in this case metrics such as engagement) handle these objects. Subsequently, it is asked, how to repurpose the metrics?

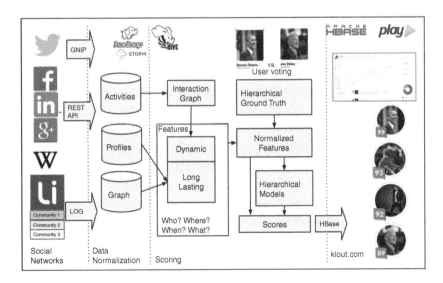

Figure 12.6 Klout scoring mechanism as flow chart.
Source: Rao et al., 2015.

There have been projects to calculate cross-platform performance. Klout, as the term indicates, was a measure of a user's 'clout', slang for influence, where the user is not only an individual but can be a magazine, institution, professional sports team, etc. Klout scores (from 1 to 100) were measured on the basis of activity on Twitter, Facebook, YouTube, Google+, LinkedIn, Instagram, and Foursquare (Rao et al., 2015). It is an influence measure that takes into account particular appearance signals across the seven platforms (e.g., mentions on Twitter), and those mentions by highly influential user accounts grant more influence or clout to the user in question. It also grounds (and augments) the online appearance measures with 'offline factors' that take into account a user's 'real world influence' from Wikipedia as well as resonance in news articles (Rao et al., 2015: 3). Job titles, years of experience and similar from LinkedIn are also factored in. It is also a computationally intensive, big data undertaking and an aggregated form of cross-platform analysis.

If one were to learn from Klout for social research, one manner would be to shift the focus from symbolic power (measures of increases or decreases in one's metrified online influence) to matters of concern (increases or decreases in attention, including that from significant others) – be these to events, disasters, elections, revolutions, social causes, and so forth (see Figure 12.6). The shift in focus would be in keeping with how social media is often currently studied, as discussed above. That is, one could apply Klout's general procedure for counting user appearances and ask which causes are collectively significant across social media platforms, and which (key) actors, organizations and other users are linked to them, thereby granting them attention. Just as importantly, the attention granted to a cause by key actors, organizations and users may be neither undivided nor sustained. Such an observation would invite inquiries into partial attention as well as attention span, which together could begin to form a means for the critical study of engagement across social media.

Co-linked, inter-liked and cross-hashtagged content

The purpose here is to develop techniques for multiple platform analysis that bear medium-sensitivity. First, stock is taken of the objects that platforms share (Table 12.1), whereupon cultures of use are also taken into consideration. For X/Twitter, Facebook and Instagram (the platforms under discussion here), all may be queried for keywords, and the posts can be ranked according to engagement. That approach is often favoured over querying hashtags (across platforms). While the hashtag is common to them, on the one no more than two are recommended (X/Twitter), on another it is rarely used (Facebook) and on the third it is used in overabundance (Instagram).

Having taken stock of the available digital objects as well as the platform vernaculars, the researcher can consider how content resonates across platforms. Co-linked content are URLs (often shortened on social media) that are linked by two or more users or platform pages. Inter-liked content is content liked by users and pages across platforms. Cross-hashtagged content is content referred to by hashtags across platforms. As they are often embedded social issues (as well as events and slogans), the hashtags themselves could be considered the content.

When discussing the kind of cross-platform research done with social media, even with the shift to the study of social causes over the self, it is worthwhile to point out that one may emphasize social research, medium research, or a combination of the two. For social research, the question concerns the impact of the story the content tells, despite the platform effects. For medium research, the question concerns how the platform affects the impact of the content, be it its presence or absence as well as its orderings. Additionally, specific cultures of use per platform, and (strategic) analytics-driven filtering and ranking, may inform the medium research, as discussed above. For a combination of medium and social research, the questions are combined: how does the platform affect the availability of content, and what stories do the content tell, given platform effects?

Conclusions: Digital methods for cross-platform analysis

In the call for methodological attention to the platformization of the web, Elmer and Langlois (2013) discuss how analyses based on the hyperlink do not embrace the analytical opportunities afforded by social media. Hyperlink analysis, and its tools such as the Issuecrawler, rely on an info-web, where webmasters make recommendations by linking to another website (or non-recommendations through not making links, thereby showing lack of interest or affiliation). Focusing on links only misses the novel objects of social networking sites, platforms and social media (as the social web has been called), such as the like, share and tweet. While Elmer and Langlois (2013) called for the analysis of the keyword over the hyperlink, but also perhaps over other social media objects, around the same time as their publication the API had arrived (Facebook's version 1.0 in 2010, Twitter's in 2006), and gradually became the preferred point of access to data over scraping, which the platforms actively sought to thwart. The API and subsequently the dashboard are of course controlled by the service in question, be it Facebook or others, and steers research in ways more readily palpable perhaps than scraping, for the data available on the interface (that could be scraped) and through the developer's entry point may differ considerably.

The ethics turn in web research, bound up with the rise of the social web and its publicly available, personal data, in turn has shaped the accessibility of certain data on the APIs such that Facebook no longer allows one to collect friends' 'tastes and ties', or likes, profile interests as well as friends. Such unavailability came on the heels of a critique of a study of the same name that collected (or scraped, albeit with permission) Facebook profiles and friends' data from Harvard students and enriched it with their student housing information, without their knowledge. The Cambridge Analytica scandal prompted Facebook as well as other social media companies to further winnow data availability. Concomitant with the decline in the study of the self in social media analysis with digital methods (given the increasing dearth of available data through API restrictions) has been the rise in attention to events, disasters, elections, revolutions and social causes. Not only is it in evidence in Facebook research on pages (and to an extent groups), but also in Twitter (events, revolutions), where Jack Dorsey, its co-founder, signalled the shift in interviews in the *Los Angeles Times*, mentioning that Twitter did 'well' during events such as disasters, elections as well as conferences. Instagram, according to its founder Kevin Systrom, expressed interest in following the same trajectory, becoming a platform of substance and thereby for the study of events (Goel, 2015).

The API and the dashboard, however, appear to have shaped social media studies beyond its selective availability of data. Rather, they serve as silos for what I call 'single-platform studies'. Unlike the Web 1.0 tools such as Issuecrawler, which find links between websites and between websites and platforms, the social web has not seen academic research tools developed for cross-platform analysis.

PROJECT 13

Develop a cross-platform analysis

RESEARCH GOAL To perform a cross-platform analysis on a chosen contemporary issue

1   Choose a contemporary issue (revolution, disaster, election, social cause, and so forth) for cross-platform analysis. You may choose to follow an active or unfolding issue (an issue in motion, so to speak), or one from recent history (an issue from the past, where over-time analysis is desirable). Here you should consider which platforms provide over-time data (Facebook, Instagram and X/Twitter).

2   Design a query strategy. For social issues and causes, consider querying for a programme and an anti-programme (see the query design chapter). For example, in the 2015 US Supreme Court ruling for same-sex marriage the competing Twitter and Instagram hashtags reflected hashtag publics forming around a programme and an anti-programme, #lovewins and #jesuswins, respectively (see Figures 12.7 and 12.8). If hashtags are preferred, for an election, consider querying a set of candidates or parties, such as #Trump and #Biden (perhaps together with additional hashtags as well as keywords). For a disaster (or tragedy), consider querying its name(s), for example, #MH17.

Figure 12.7   President Obama employs the #lovewins hashtag after US Supreme Court decision on same-sex marriage, Twitter, 26 June 2015.

3   Develop an analytical strategy. For social issues and causes, consider which programme or anti-programme is finding favour (including among whom). Does it have a set of networked publics? For an election, consider creating portrayals of the candidates via the associated issues, or comparing their relative resonance with current election polls. For a revolution, consider its momentum and durability (including the subjects that continue to matter and those that do not endure). For a disaster, consider how it is (continually) remembered or forgotten, and to what extent it has been and still is addressed and by whom.

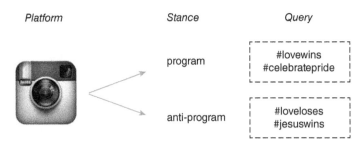

Figure 12.8   Instagram query design strategy for the study of the images (and its geographies) associated with the US Supreme Court ruling on same-sex marriage, 26 June 2015.

Source: Baccarne et al., 2015.

4   Cross-platform analysis. Undertake the platform analysis, according to the query design strategy as well as the analytical strategy discussed above, across two or more platforms. For each platform consider engagement measures, such as the sum of likes (or reactions), shares, comments (Facebook), likes and retweets (X/Twitter) and likes and comments (Instagram). Which (media) content resonates on which platforms? Consider which content is shared across the platforms (co-linked, inter-liked and cross-hashtagged), and which is distinctive, thereby enabling both networked platform content analysis as well as medium-specific (or platform-specific) effects.

5   Discuss your findings with respect to medium research, social research or a combination of the two. Does a particular platform tend to host as well as order content in ways distinctive from other platforms? Are the accounts of the events distinctively different per platform or utterly familiar no matter the platform?

Cross-platform practicalities

In practice certain platforms lend themselves to comparison more artfully than others, given both the availability of objects such as the hashtag or geotag as well as roughly similar cultures of use. Through the vehicle of the hashtag, X/Twitter and Instagram (as well as Tumblr) are often the subject of cross-platform analysis. One queries the APIs with such tools as 4CAT or scrapes with Zeeschuimer (for X/Twitter), CrowdTangle for Instagram and 4CAT for Tumblr, creating collections of tweets and posts for further quantitative and qualitative analysis. Take, for example, certain significant events in the so-called migration crisis in Europe, one concerning the death of refugee children (Aylan Kurdi and his brother) and another the sexual assaults and rapes on New Year's Eve in Cologne (Geboers et al., 2016). For each case X/Twitter and Instagram are queried for hashtags (e.g., #aylan), whereupon tweet and post collections are made. For X/Twitter, one 'recipe' to sort through the contents of the collections would include the following:

a   Co-hashtag frequency counts ascertain the other hashtags that appear in the issue space. For the Cologne rape cases, the hashtag #einearmlänge is present, which was a trending topic referring to the remarks by the Cologne mayor that (as a solution) women should remain an 'arm's length away' from so-called strangers.

b   Mention frequency lists the usernames of those who tweet and who are mentioned so one notes which users may dominate a space.

c   Retweet frequency provides a ranked list of retweeted tweets, showing popular or significant content.

d   URL frequency is a ranked URL list showing popular or significant media (such as images and video). The most referenced media, especially images, become a focal point for a cross-platform analysis with X/Twitter.

For Instagram, hashtag frequency is undertaken together with image and video frequency analysis. Ultimately, the means of comparison are hashtag as well as image and video use, where the former suffers somewhat from hashtag stuffing in Instagram.

The question of platform effects is treated in the qualitative analysis, where in both the Aylan and the Cologne New Year's Eve cases the incidence of news photos was much greater in Twitter than in Instagram, where there were more derivatives, meaning annotated, photoshopped, cartoon-like or other DIY materials with (implied or explicit) user commentary (see Figures 12.9 and 12.10). Twitter thereby becomes a professional medium (with effects) and Instagram more a user-generated content medium, becoming a particular, user-led form of news-following platform to which its founder has been aspiring, as mentioned above. The Aylan case, however, appears to reduce this medium-specificity, because there is a relatively greater quantity of images that have been edited so as to come to grips with the tragedy of the drowned toddler.

Tools

Instagram

CrowdTangle, www.crowdtangle.com

Zeeschuimer browser extension, via https://4cat.nl

X/Twitter

4CAT Capture and Analysis Toolkit, https://4cat.digitalmethods.net

Zeeschuimer browser extension, via https://4cat.nl

DMI-TCAT (Twitter Capture and Analysis Tool), https://github.com/digitalmethodsinitiative/dmi-tcat/wiki

Video tutorial for TCAT, 'Overview of Analytical Modules', www.youtube.com/watch?v=ex97eoorUeo

Video tutorial for 4CAT, www.youtube.com/watch?v=VRMWuJYOKHQ

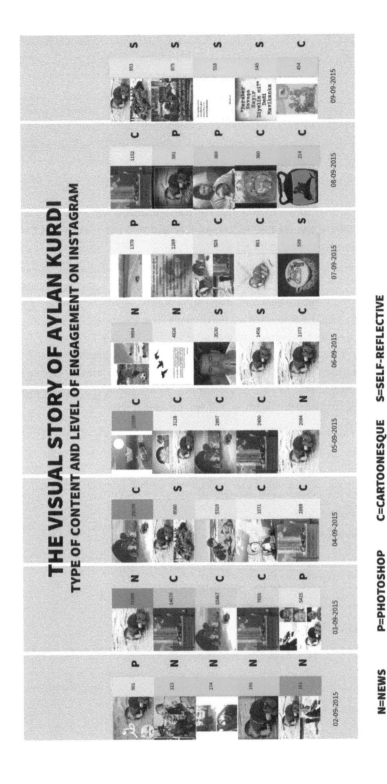

Figure 12.9 Categorized Instagram photos concerning the Aylan Kurdi case, which symbolized the European migration crisis, 2015.

Source: Heine et al., 2016.

N=NEWS   **P=PHOTOSHOP**   **C=CARTOONESQUE**   **S=SELF-REFLECTIVE**

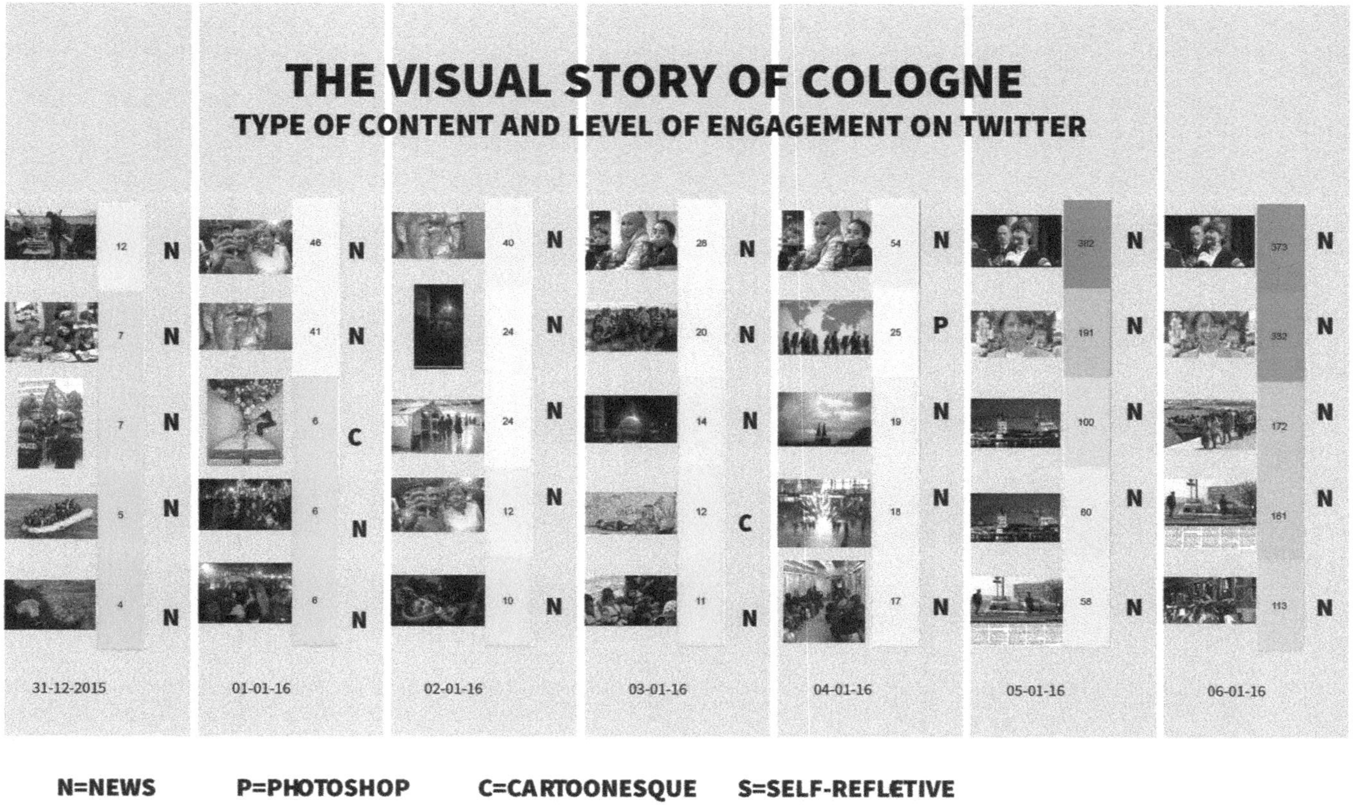

THE VISUAL STORY OF COLOGNE
TYPE OF CONTENT AND LEVEL OF ENGAGEMENT ON TWITTER

N=NEWS   P=PHOTOSHOP   C=CARTOONESQUE   S=SELF-REFLETIVE

Figure 12.10 Categorized Twitter photos concerning the Cologne New Year's Eve sexual assault issue, which symbolized the Europe migration crisis, 2015–2016.

Source: Heine et al., 2016.

Facebook

CrowdTangle, www.crowdtangle.com

Tumblr

4CAT Capture and Analysis Toolkit, https://4cat.digitalmethods.net

Video tutorial for 4CAT, www.youtube.com/watch?v=VRMWuJYOKHQ

Gephi-related

Gephi (The Open Graph Viz Software), https://gephi.org

'Gephi Tutorial for Working with Twitter Mention Networks', www.youtube.com/
watch?v=snPR8CwPld0

'Combine and Analyse Co-Hashtag Networks (Instagram, Twitter, etc.) with Gephi', www.youtube.
com/watch?v=ngqWjgZudeE

THIRTEEN

TIKTOK AS MEMETIC INFRASTRUCTURE
Studying imitation

And comparing TikTok to its Chinese counterpart, Douyin

Platform critique and repurposing

TikTok analyses with digital methods generally assume two forms. Treat it like another social media platform and probe it for its privileging mechanisms, interrogating the algorithms. Alternatively, consider its special affordances and repurpose them for research. Thus, when considering TikTok as an object of study, one may ask, how is it similar to other algorithmically driven platforms? One critiques the posts it boosts and moderates (or fails to). In the second type, repurposing, one asks, how may its specific features such as its linked sounds be productively put to scholarly use?

In the following, I outline each approach, considering TikTok in the realm of both media as well as social and cultural research. The chapter concludes with methods to study TikTok as a memetic infrastructure and as a space of imitation. Here, the question concerns the publics sounds mobilize, which is operationalized by plotting relationships between hashtags and sounds. It also puts forward means to compare TikTok with its Chinese counterpart, Douyin, enquiring into the presence and absence of content on each.

Figure 13.1 TikTok and Douyin use the same logo.

Source: Panda Buddy, 2020.

For the study of TikTok as media, the questions posed are especially related to algorithmic effects and the specificity of TikTok's vernacular style and affordances, such as its song and dance culture and features like 'duetting'. With respect to social and cultural research, one may study the quality of TikTok information (around the time of national elections, for example), and whether the TikTok feed narrows or broadens horizons in the style of filter bubble or echo chamber analysis.

I also briefly compare the outputs of the international TikTok with the Chinese version (Douyin), demonstrating stark differences, especially with respect to the social commentary that emerged around a controversial event in China (see Figure 13.1). Douyin's search results appear to be heavily filtered compared to TikTok's. Such comparative work is another social research approach, particularly in the realm of information politics, or how certain information is filtered from public consumption.

TikTok studies

Launched in 2016 (and in its contemporary form in 2018), TikTok, an app and website operated by the Chinese company, ByteDance, has exploded upon the scene, with over a billion registered users at the time of writing. It has prompted other major platforms to imitate its formats, such as YouTube's Shorts, described as a 'TikTok clone' (Nieva, 2022). It has stirred geopolitical concern, given the company's Chinese origins (Gray, 2021). With the vast US audience, not to mention other countries', it is thought that TikTok could provide user location information and other details to the state (Maheshwari and Holpuch, 2023). For national security reasons, TikTok has seen its app banned in India and in the US, Canada and the European Union on governmental devices.

TikTok posts are short videos or music clips. They are often made with sounds that can be selected from ones available on the platform (or added as original ones). Users can also apply effects, such as the addition of mouse ears or a green screen that detects and removes the background.

Among the video styles is lip-synching, which was the original genre of choice on Musical.ly, the service with which TikTok merged in 2018. Musical.ly, also of Chinese origin, lent some of its features and formats to TikTok such as the 15-second video (Rettberg, 2017). It also appeals to a similar user demographic as Musical.ly's, among them pre-teens and teens, arguably by positioning itself (for parents) as a fun space for creative performance rather than a social media platform to connect with others (Savic, 2021). In fact, researchers have found that pre-teens are heavier TikTok users than teens (Bossen and Kottasz, 2020). Another inheritance from Musical.ly is the feature, 'duetting'. To create one, users can 'react' to another video, whereby the new video sits astride the other on a split-screen. One also can 'stitch' a very short segment of another video into one's own.

Especially duetting allows for responses to 'challenges', part of the TikTok (and other social media) vernacular culture, where users answer the call to perform a dance or act out a scene (Kennedy, 2020). Another is the 'hack' which are videos showing a nifty trick or solution (Rauchberg, 2022); these are sometimes made in response to the problem (tangled hair) where a portion of a problem video is stitched into the hack (disentangling hair hack). There is also a special 'algospeak' or coded language, concocted to evade automated content moderation (Delkic, 2022).

TikTok's features and vernacular culture have been studied in a variety of contexts from politics to mourning. Embedding other videos into new ones invite a culture of retort and other linked commentary, where users engage in interactions about social issues, elections and events, particularly for a user base that has expanded beyond children. Indeed, researchers have described users as creating 'branches of responses' to the content created, particularly through making use of duetting (Medina Serrano et al., 2020). Among the political modes of engagement observed are 'playful political performance', where candidate support around elections is expressed in song and dance, and 'ambivalent critique', whereby users remix news clips with ironic and satirical commentary, where it is occasionally difficult to discern which side the user is on, unless one is in on the joke (Sanchez-Querubin et al., 2023). That there are TikTok vernaculars, or domain knowledge required to partake in the specific style of in-group dialogue, makes it similar to other platforms (Tuters and Hagen, 2020).

Another area where TikTok's features and vernacular culture have been studied relates to life's more sobering moments, such as grieving. Indeed, researchers have found that TikTok's affordances challenge 'mourning norms', finding that the seemingly ill-befitting style of singing and dancing appear to have salutary effects (Eriksson Krutrök, 2021). When coupled with the FYP's grouping of the user videos, or what is termed 'algorithmic closeness', the mourners found themselves in a safe space on the platform.

Both the duets as well as the stitches are specific to TikTok and could be thought of as inviting the study of how sets of videos are layered upon each other in a threaded discussion or even duel. Other linked objects on the platform are sounds. They are linked in the sense that one can navigate the platform by viewing other videos that make use of the same sound. TikTok users are also invited to 'use this sound', making them 'trend' and resulting in audio memes (Abidin, 2021). Like image macros, these sounds may be thought of as templates on top of which one may place content.

Other available digital objects are effects as well as hashtags. Combinations of these objects (linked sounds, effects and hashtags) may lead to productive use in research projects, which I come to. One example is a sound-hashtag network analysis. Do sounds trend across subject matters, as users imitate each other, or do some become affixed to particular subcultures, movements, or candidates?

TikTok's stickiness

Inherited from Douyin, TikTok is especially known for its recommendation system, the default 'For You Page' (FYP), which delivers personalized, suggested videos. It is often described as the source of TikTok's stickiness, or capacity for enduring time-on-app and user retention or return. Stickiness has a variety of determinants, such as habitual use and the fostering of parasocial relationships with social media influencers, which also can be two-way (Hu et al., 2020; Hund, 2023).

Compared to other platforms with personalized feeds, such as Facebook, X/Twitter, Instagram and YouTube, the primacy of TikTok's feed has been a source of study (Bhandari and Bimo, 2022). It takes up the entirety of the front page, relegating other elements of the platform experience (such as connections to other users) to the margins. It is also the source of 'algorithmic imaginaries', or ideas about how the algorithm works for the users (and for the company) (Bucher, 2017). It is regarded as particularly attuned to the user's wishes. Writing about content creators grasp of another platform, Bishop (2018: 69) previously described how 'algorithmic processes are learned and embodied within their own practices, influencing modes of self-presentation, tone of voice, choice of content covered…'.

Content creators on TikTok try to 'trick and please' the algorithms so that their videos trend and appear on the FYP of others (Klug et al., 2021). Among the assumptions is that engagement and posting time are important, together with populating videos with a pre-ponderance of hashtags. In examining these assumptions, the researchers found certain affirmations (engagement is important) but employing #fyp or #foryou hashtags did not appear to affect how well the videos ranked or trended.

The FYP does not work for everyone, however, or at least not all of the time. When discussing the experiences of the LGBTQ+ community (through a qualitative study based on interviews), researchers found mixed experiences. Asking the question, 'for you or for 'you'?', they found that TikTok constructs 'contradictory identity spaces' that occasionally affirm but also violate vulnerable and marginalized users (Simpson and Semaan, 2021). They couch their findings in the notion of 'algorithmic exclusion'.

When probing or auditing its recommended outputs, the researcher may pose questions typical of other platform or algorithmic critiques, such as whether the videos become more and more extreme, inviting one into a 'rabbit hole', as a well-known YouTube critique once had it. Does it tend to output misinformation when searching for social issues such as climate change? As some researchers have written, there are scientists and activists on the platform competing 'with mocking satirists, playful attention-seekers, and bored time-killers for visibility and clout' (Hautea et al., 2021). Here one could enquire into the visibility of credible professionals on the platform compared to that of other content creators (Basch et al., 2021).

If one makes other 'serious queries', do the results tend to boost TikTok's own content creators or performers over, say, news sources, non-governmental information or other experts who are also on the platform? Is TikTok's content moderation adequate, or when do we observe dubious or hateful content (Weimann and Masri, 2020)? One may also focus on concerns of the user demographic. How may one characterize the quality of the content, for example for self-help or the treatment of age-specific concerns such as acne (Zheng et al., 2021)? In one study, researchers characterized the majority of vaping or e-cigarette videos as 'comedy and joke' with a positive valence (Sun et al., 2023). In another study of top videos with the hashtag, #covidtesting, the youthful TikTokers more often viewed those that portrayed the testing experience as 'disgusting/unpleasant' rather than those (for example) happily showing a negative result (Basch et al., 2021).

Generally, these are privileging critiques, asking what comes out on top and considering the consequences, for example in the realm public health, but they also portray platform culture. As said, these questions may be posed for other platforms, too, such as YouTube (when enquiring into the prevalence of YouTubers or certain types of videos) and on Instagram (and the boosting of its influencers). If returned at the top, are these influencers demonstrating social responsibility? Is the platform demonstrating the same?

TikTok's special affordances

TikTok, however, has its idiosyncrasies. First, it is a platform with an attention economy said to be driven by individual posts rather than by platform personalities (though they do exist) (Abidin, 2021). In order to participate in this economy, inserted into posts poised for attention are the latest trends in sounds and effects. As mentioned above, some users also tend to place particular hashtags, such as #foryou or #fyp, with the hope that they will aid in the videos' coming virality.

Second, TikTok has linked sounds that arguably transform it into a memetic infrastructure, with users taking up songs like those who go on to whistle a tune overheard on the street, as the originator of the term, Richard Dawkins, once described it. Internet memes, in another influential rendering, are 'units of popular culture that are circulated, imitated, and transformed by individual internet users, creating a shared cultural experience' (Shifman, 2013: 367). Audio memes, a subcategory, have been associated with the platform, because each TikTok post offers a button that leads to the original video that deployed the sound and a list of other videos that have done so since. So, not only videos but also sounds trend, or rise in usage, collecting associated videos, so to speak. Abidin characterizes audio memes as foundational to the platform, not only in how they are linked and form a navigational pathway, but in how they are routinely employed to express 'tonality' (2021). For example, a sound is introduced to express sarcasm about the content of a news clip. She also writes that particularly successful uses of sounds, together with edits or transitions from one tone to another, can themselves become trends. There may be an accompanying how-to video, showing how to make such a transition, which itself earns an audience.

As the sounds trend, users seeking engagement, or view counts and other metrics of success, may imitate their usage. As such these sounds also invite the study of audio memes together with what scholars have called their 'imitation publics' (Zulli and Zulli, 2022). In this reading, TikTok content creators are typically engaged in remixing and restyling content and themes they already have viewed on the platform. But they also furnish their videos with their own signature touches. Some may become particularly well-known for adopting and adapting sounds and styles, while developing an authentic online personality, prompting one scholar to characterize their music as 'imitation pop' (Rauchberg, 2022). While 'imitation pop star', celebrity or personality is not appended, it could well be, for the view counts and other metric achievements may be signs of online celebrity.

TikTok and Douyin compared

TikTok, is the international version of Douyin, both of which are owned by ByteDance. The company is not in the ecosystem of the big platform players in the US and China, respectively known (amongst other acronyms) as GAMA (Google, Amazon, Meta and Apple) and BATX (Baidu, Alibaba, Tencent, and Xiaomi). Rather, it has followed its own trajectory, distinctive from some other Chinese apps which have strived to go global, as WeChat, which sought to merge geolocalized Chinese and non-Chinese user bases. Respecting the separate Chinese ecology, it decoupled Douyin from TikTok, developing a separate app that with some exceptions (as a 'beautify whitening' filter) 'minimises Chinese culture in it' (Chen, 2019). Contents and users are separate; the one app is available in the Google Play and Apple App store, the other in Chinese app stores. Douyin and TikTok are considered 'two separate, short video parallel universes' (Kaye et al., 2021).

While there are algorithmic and other similarities, Douyin differs in some features (as in-app shopping and the lack of a web version) but also in a separate tab, next to the 'discover' feature on both apps. Only available on Douyin, it opens to 'positive energy' posts, exhibiting 'playful patriotism', in line with Chinese state ideology (Chen et al., 2020). Given that another short video platform (Duanzi) was shut down by the state for its 'vulgar' content, the 'positive energy' section has been described more as ByteDance's 'survival tactic' rather than a platform affinity (Chen et al., 2020). It nevertheless deserves further scrutiny.

Along those lines, one may study the portrayals of the same events on the two platforms, gaining a sense of the extent of such 'playful patriotism' as dominant or perhaps receiving less engagement than one may expect on Douyin. While in a separate realm, does the sentiment travel to TikTok? When comparing top videos (or samples) in TikTok and Douyin of the same event, issue, politician or another subject, which accounts hold sway per platform?

Figure 13.2   #Chinaprotest, Douyin and TikTok search results compared, 28 November 2022.
Source: Screenshots from the University of Amsterdam.

As a case in point, in November 2022 a fire broke out in an apartment high-rise in Urumqi, the capital of the Xinjiang Uyghur Autonomous Region, killing a number of inhabitants. Protests immediately ensued; it was felt that official enforcement of stringent Covid-19 lockdown policies prevented escape as well as access by the firefighters. The protests reverberated on social media, including TikTok and Douyin, where researchers were able to capture significant posts per platform containing the hashtag, #chinaprotest (see Figure 13.2). On Douyin the protests are absent, supplanted by talking heads defending Covid-19 policies. On TikTok, the protests are visible; there is also a still image in one of the circulating videos of authorities removing a street sign of a road in Shanghai, whose name translates to Urumqi and which witnessed demonstrations and vigils (see Figure 13.3).

Figure 13.3   Still image from TikTok video, found through #chinaprotest hashtag search, of the removal of the street sign of a road in Shanghai, whose name translates to Urumqi, 28 November 2022.

Source: Screenshot from the University of Amsterdam.

Whilst a study in parallel, arguably such an approach continues to place US platforms in the centre, rather than de-centring them, as has been suggested (Steinberg and Li, 2017). Indeed, other scholars, taking up the notion of platformization, have shown how TikTok and Douyin accomplish it distinctively, pointing to diverging strategies (Kaye et al., 2021). Thus, the symmetrical study of western and Chinese platforms may follow another path.

TikTok as Chinese social media

TikTok, when seen through the purview of Chinese social media, is the international version of a popular format, the short-form video platform with clips of a maximum of 15 or 60 seconds. Its Chinese counterpart, Douyin, while existing in a 'parallel universe', competes in China with other popular platforms of a similar variety such as Kuaishou. When it merged with Musical.ly and relaunched as TikTok, it was taking over another short-form video company originating in Shanghai, with features quite distinctive from its US short-form video service predecessors like Vine. Indeed, duetting, stitching, linked sounds and the 'for you' algorithm are rather specific to TikTok, serving as the starting points for research projects that repurpose its affordances or treat it as another platform whose algorithmic privileging requires scrutiny.

That TikTok has in Douyin a mirror image platform (albeit with subtle differences) operating in China provides opportunities for comparative research. In one example, touched upon above one may inquire into the presence and absence of certain content such as the #Chinaprotest about the fire in Urumqi in November, 2022, that also sparked anti-lockdown demonstrations related to the strict governmental measures in place to thwart the spread of the Covid-19 pandemic. Where the one platform teemed with protest pictures, the other contained news and spokesperson videos extolling and explaining the measures. Other comparative work could take up the invitation, touched upon above, of treating the platforms symmetrically, at once decentring the US-based starting points.

PROJECTS

Perform a comparative analysis of TikTok and Douyin content

RESEARCH GOAL To compare and contrast the outputs for searches of the same keywords and hashtags (in English and Mandarin), perusing the top platform posts per event, issue, politician or another subject.

The procedure for comparing and contrasting platform content is as follows:

1   Select one or more keywords or hashtags that capture an event, such as Russian-Ukraine War or #Chinaprotest. Search and output the content.
2   Note, in the top posts, the presence and absence of particular content or themes.
3   Consider a co-hashtag analysis of each platform's top content.
4   Consider a hashtag-thumbnail image analysis of each platform's top content.

Perform a relational hashtag-sound analysis of TikTok (and/or Douyin) data

RESEARCH GOAL To explore the clustering of platform publics by their use of hashtags and sounds.

In a relational (bi-partite network) analysis of hashtags and sounds, the question is the extent to which TikTok (or Douyin) users can be characterized as 'imitation publics' or for some subject matters as sound or 'hashtag publics', which is how users concentrate on other social media platforms (such as X/Twitter). Do they use sounds and hashtags principally because they are trending or to organize around a cause (or both)?

The procedure for studying imitation vs. hashtag publics is as follows:

1   Select one or more keywords or hashtags that capture a platform phenomenon (#fyp) or an issue or event, such as Russian-Ukraine War, #Chinaprotest or elections.
2   Select one or more keywords or hashtags that capture a platform phenomenon (#fyp) or an issue or event, such as Russian-Ukraine War, #Chinaprotest or elections.
3   Scrape (or manually collect) the output of a search for the keywords and/or hashtags, where the scrape contains the top videos together with their associated hashtags and sounds. This step may be performed for TikTok, Douyin or both platforms.
4   Optional: Consider a co-hashtag analysis of one or both platforms' top content. Here one can note the specificity or generality of the contents of hashtag clusters.
5   Perform a sound-hashtag analysis of one or both platforms' top content.

6　Note how there do not appear to be significant clustering of hashtags and sounds around substantive issues ('imitation publics') or the presence of discrete clusters (hashtag publics which also could be called hashtag-sound publics).

Resources

- 'Capturing TikTok data with Zeeschuimer and 4CAT', https://tinyurl.com/nmrw-zeeschuimer-tiktok
- 'Zeeschuimer browser extension for Firefox', https://github.com/digitalmethodsinitiative/zeeschuimer
- 'Auto-scrolling browser extension for Firefox', via https://github.com/digitalmethodsinitiative/zeeschuimer

FOURTEEN

TRACKER ANALYSIS
Detection techniques for
data journalism research

Digital investigations and the study of
'telling data'

Digital forensics: Repurposing Google Analytics IDs

When an investigative journalist uncovered a covert network of Russian websites furnishing disinformation about Ukraine, it popularized a network discovery technique for data journalists and social researchers (Alexander, 2015). Which websites share the same Google Analytics ID (see Figure 14.1)? If the websites share the same ID, it follows that they are operated by the same registrant, be it an individual, organization or media group. The journalist, Lawrence Alexander, was prompted in his work by the lack of a source behind emaidan.com.ua, a website that appears to give information about the Euromaidan protests in 2013–2014 in Ukraine that ultimately forced out the pro-Russian Ukrainian president in favour of a pro-Western one and ushered in tensions between the two countries, ultimately culminating in a war. In search of the source, and 'intrigued by its anonymity', Alexander dug into the website code.

Viewing the source code of the webpage, he found a Google Analytics ID (see Figure 14.2), which he inserted into reverse look-up software that furnishes a list of other websites using the same ID. He found a (star-shaped) network of a single Google Analytics ID linked to eight other websites (in Figure 14.1 at the top), sharing a similar anti-Ukraine narrative. One of those websites also used an additional Google Analytics ID, which led to another cluster of related websites (in Figure 14.1 at the bottom to the right), also of similar political persuasion. Examining the whois records of several of these domains, he found an associated email address, and subsequently a person's profile and photo on VKontakte, the Russian social networking site. The name of this person he then found on a leaked list of employees from the Internet Research Agency in St Petersburg, known as the workplace of the Russian government-sponsored 'troll army' (Chen, 2015; Toler, 2015). Drawing links between data points, Alexander put a name and face on a so-called Russian troll. He also humanized the troll somewhat, by pointing to his Pinterest hobby page, where there is posted a picture of Russian space achievements. The troll is a Cosmonaut space fan, too.

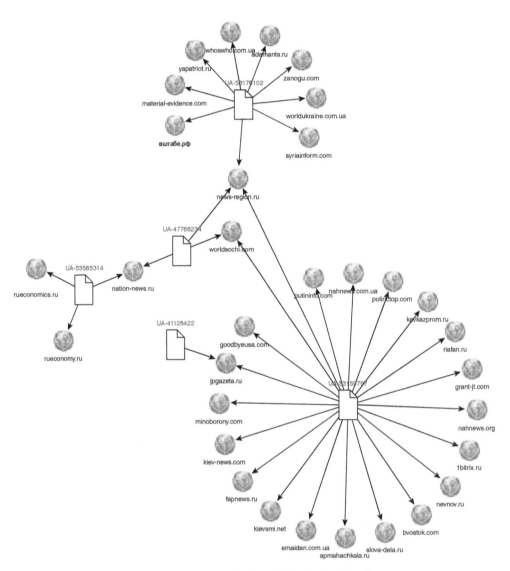

Figure 14.1   Website network discovered through (shared) Google Analytics IDs.

Source: Alexander, 2015.

The Google Analytics ID

The prefix stands for Urchin Analytics. the web analytics service bought by Google in 2005

This autoincremented number is your Google Analytics account ID. Add or subtract one to see who signed up before and after you.

Your website profile number, incremented from 1

Figure 14.2 Google Analytics ID, annotated.

Source: Baio, 2011.

Employing so-called 'open source intelligence' tools as discovery techniques (and also digital methods in the sense of repurposing Google Analytics and reverse look-up software), Alexander and other journalists make and follow links in code, public records, databases, and leaks, piecing it all together for an account of 'who's behind' particular operations (Bazzell, 2016). 'Discovery' is an investigative or even digital forensics approach for journalistic mining and exposure, where one would identify and subsequently strive to contact the individual, organization or media group to interview them, and grant them an opportunity to account for their work. The dual accountings – the journalist's discovery and the discovered's explanation – constitute the story to be told. The purpose is to make things public, to wring out of the hairy code of websites the covert political work being undertaken, and to have this particular proof acknowledged (Latour, 2005a).

Google Analytics ID detective work has a lineage in the practice of unmasking anonymous online actors through exploits, or entry points to personally identifiable data that had not been foreseen by its creators. Mining Google Analytics IDs for network discovery and mapping is also a repurposing exercise, using the software in an unintended fashion for social research. One originator of the technique, Andy Baio, a journalist at *Wired* magazine, tells the story of an anonymous blogger posting highly offensive material, who had covered his tracks in the 'usual ways': 'hiding personal info in the domain record, using a different IP address from his other sites, and scrubbing any shared resources from his WordPress install' (Baio, 2011). Baio identified him because the blogger shared a Google Analytics ID with other websites he operated in full view. The cautionary tale about this discovery and unmasking technique concludes with Baio providing a safety guide for other anonymous bloggers *with a just cause*, such as those monitoring Mexican drug cartels, whose discovery could lead to danger or even loss of life. Here one also could test the robustness of the anonymity and inform the journalists working undercover online of any vulnerabilities or potential exploits.

Discovering 'telling data' as research practice

Digital discovery concerns itself with code that leads to 'telling data'. On the websites represented in the Russian network diagram in Figure 14.1 there are digital objects, linked to data, concerning the websites' provenance. For example, on these websites a preponderance of Russian tracker and other objects is present: Yandex metrics, Yandex verification

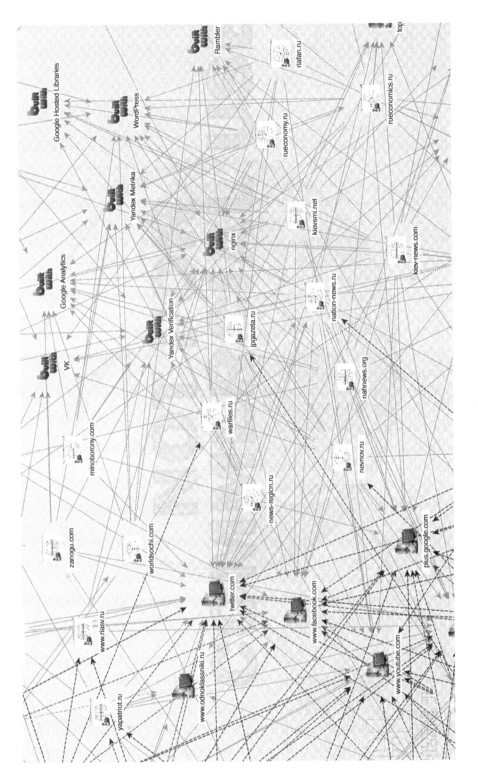

Figure 14.3 Embedded digital objects on websites, depicted as network diagram.

Source: Alexander, 2015.

software, Nginx servers as well as traces of components from Rambler and VKontakte (see Figure 14.3). Each may have registrants' information or clues that would lead one to the owner, and perhaps to his other properties, so that a more elaborate and telling network map can be fashioned, not so unlike those plotted by law enforcement agents tracing tax evasion or money laundering.

Metadata forensics

Apart from these components on the websites, there are other digital objects that are telling, including images. One may comb through the metadata of the websites' images by uploading them to forensic photo software; it outputs the name of the image editing software (such as Photoshop) that created and modified each image, together with the precise version. In the event, a variety of the websites in the Russian network has images modified with the same version of the same software, indicating a single hand behind the editing.

Photo forensics also can furnish the name of the camera model and make that took a picture, together with the date and other so-called EXIF data, such as geolocation, or where the photo was taken, especially if snapped from a smartphone. Not all data is available per image. Indeed, it may have not been completely stored (as is often the case with .png files), but it also may have been purposively wiped.

Cloaking

Apart from discovery, a forensic research practice could begin to understand the extent to which the user has been cloaking himself. Active cloaking could be a strong indicator of covert activity. How many of these websites in the network have been wiped of production (image editing software traces), distribution (tracker code) and ownership traces (domain records)? Are they consistently cleansed of the same traces? Does the website owner cover up more traces than in the 'usual ways', for example, the default options of known, standard services available for making account information 'private'? Here one would notice the difference between professional covert activity and, say, a consumer who takes great care in shopping discreetly. As the web is securitized, more and more account information may be private by default or routinely made so.

One other website in the Russian network is worth mentioning, material-evidence.com, for it too was the source of investigative journalism a year earlier, as it bore signs of influence campaigning and anti-Ukrainian propaganda (Cush, 2014). It is the website that accompanies the photo exhibition 'Material Evidence – Chaos, Civil War, World Terror in the 21st Century', which has toured internationally in such cities as Berlin and New York. A journalist digging into the exhibition (and its website) found a cloaking practice in the physical media on display, too. The photos have no credits, and there are otherwise no names of photographers in sight. Moreover, on the website, the only contact information is the generic email address, truth@material-evidence.com. Here purposive anonymity lies in plain view on the exhibition walls as well as on the website interface.

The covert and the discreet

As touched upon above, it is worthwhile to put forward the distinction between studying and uncovering covert versus discreet, protective or preventive activity (Whitford and Prunckun, 2017). They all refer to having activities remain undisclosed, but each implies different motives, and draws from distinctive vocabularies – one more from intelligence, military or policing, and the others from activism, awareness-raising and consumer protection. Rather than covert activity, discretion could be behind trace-covering. Activists and some NGOs may wish to leave no footprint as a matter of standard working practice, given routine surveillance regimes and the prospects for data error, misuse, cross-use, leakage and breach. Something similar may be said for wary consumers actively opting out of behavioural targeting online. Having a 'do not track' option activated in one's browser and signing up one's telephone number on 'do not call' registries are measures designed for consumer protection against a range of practices from ads following users around the web to robocall intrusion and predatory lending. Another form of consumer media literacy would be to leave no traces so as to prevent being bullied, harassed, stalked, trolled or otherwise made to feel uncomfortable online. These behaviours may be contrasted with those in the Russian influence campaigning case (both online and in the exhibition), where the investigative journalists were not identifying acts of discretion, awareness-raising or consumer protection, but uncovering covert 'ops', and in making them public, seeking disclosure and accounting by those behind the activities.

Figure 14.4　Pepper-spraying cops of California (2011) and Istanbul (2013), memeified and rendered as multi-coloured, stencilled graffiti. Banksy-style stencil, 'Casually Butterfly Everything' posted on Reddit, *source*: GeneralLudd, 2011, and 'The more you press, the bigger it gets', *source*: Gruber, 2013.

From digital forensics to media theory critique

Studying covert and discreet activity online are of interest when seeking to make a discovery and have one's own account as well as the discovered one's made public. It also has the purpose of showing (and explaining) exposure, and the potential risks appertaining. Training courses and lists of pointers follow, as do larger studies undertaken to contribute to societal awareness-raising of exposure and media literacy.

Digital forensics, often deployed in the evidential arena and investigative reporting, may also be used for scholarly purposes. How to make use of 'forensic' camera data for social and media research? What can cookies and third-party elements make visible that challenges contemporary claims and enables research findings?

To begin with photo forensics, one may examine the data embedded in pictures found online, including significant ones made at major protest events, determine the cameras that took them, the software that edited them, and critique claims about the pervasiveness and impact of user-generated content and citizen journalism, including the distinctive narratives of events they make *vis-à-vis* those of more established news (Van Dijck, 2009; Wall, 2015). One also may make accounts of the 'editorial' (or co-authorial) practices of engines. Are crowds taking the significant pictures, and do engines and platforms serve predominantly crowd content? While social media and crowd platform users may be gatewatching (actively filtering mainstream media), might the engines be filtering out crowd content (Bruns and Highfield, 2015)?

The lady in red and other Gezi Park picture data

As a case in point, demonstrators gathered in 2013 in Gezi Park, Istanbul, to protest the planned construction of a shopping mall in the urban green space (Ozduzen and McGarry, 2020). The environmental concerns evolved into multi-issue, political demonstrations, met with water cannons and other security apparatus, where many images were taken by the protesters themselves and subsequently circulated. Early in the protests, a woman in a red dress, carrying a tote bag, was pepper-sprayed by a policeman, and the image became both iconic and memeified, expanding on the theme (and meme) of the 'pepper spraying cop' from a Californian college protest two years earlier (Testa, 2013; see Figure 14.4). 'The lady in red' image spread in the (Western) news and online, reaching and maintaining the top of Google Image search results for ['Gezi'] for weeks. Variations on the image, both on hand-held banners and street graffiti as well as on websites and social media posts, captured the message of an increasingly authoritarian government (under the then Prime Minister, later President, Erdoğan) and bottom-up resistance (Toor, 2013). In an accompanying media crackdown, Turkish authorities chilled and fined the press (for reporting, among other things, the size of the protests), and delegitimized and eventually censored Twitter for the crowdsourced stories and accounts available in the platform via such hashtags as #ayfagakalk ('stand up') (Tunc, 2013). The story of Gezi Park ('Twitter and Tear Gas') has been written through hybrid eyewitness and remote event analysis (Yaman, 2014; Tufekci, 2017), but one question remains concerning how the engines and platforms handled the content. Rather than discuss Twitter (Karkın et al., 2015; Varnali and Gorgulu, 2015), here the inquiry is about how Google Images portrayed the protest events of May to July 2013. Which images flowed to the top of the engine results for ['Gezi'], and whose were they? Do crowdsourced images dominate engine results? Whose story of the events of Gezi Park do they tell?

Crowdsourced and professional pictures in Google images

The question has to do with the crowd as source, and the engines' capacity to capture and portray it. The research weighs into accounts of the power of user-generated content and citizen journalism, and especially the relationship between top engine content and the pictures taken by the smartphone-carrying legion. It concerns the work of engines ranking and serving it over the duration of the protests. How to determine whether the significant accounts of the protests were from citizen media and 'of the crowd'? To what extent can camera data shed light on the origins of top engine content over time?

In Google Images one may capture the most highly ranked images, day by day, using the date range in advanced settings, and note which images persist (and which fall from the ranks). One may also load the captured images into software that reads their (EXIF) meta-data, showing the camera brands and the editing software (if any). Has it been taken with a Canon EOS and edited in Canon's Digital Photo Professional? Or has it been taken on an iPhone, and left unedited? The grade of camera and the use of editing software provide indications of professional photojournalist, citizen journalist and/or crowd contributions.

Having arrayed the top images outputted day to day on a timeline, to begin with, one could inquire into the engine's style of output. Is it raw, newsy, or more editorially curated? That is, are the top images fresh content, day to day, or do the same 'select' images abide? The analysis could draw upon Vilém Flusser's (2000) documentarist or visualist distinction of photographic work: the images may document events (stationary outlook) or stylize perspectives (distinct angle). Secondly, there is also the question of the provenance of those images that make it to the top. The highly returned images may be the product of professional journalism, prosumer citizen journalists or the crowd (however much that distinction may be productively blurred).

In the event, from the image data, it is found that the iconic image (of 'the lady in red') remains at the top as time goes by – not surpassed by the graffitied additions to its meme collection (see Figure 14.5). Thus Google Images would not deserve the moniker of meme machine, but rather of editorial engine. But the ascendant content is also not of the day, in an event-following, news sense; it is rather iconic, a one-time, special visual angle. Here the

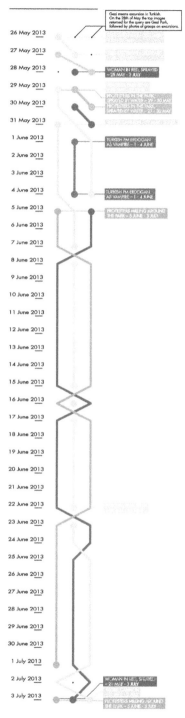

Figure 14.5 Timeline of top images on Google Image Search for the query, [Gezi], 26 May to 2 July 2013, with 'the lady in red' image moving in and out of the top slot, followed by 'the water cannon', both police reaction images (protest and violence).

Source: De Amicis et al., 2013.

image search engine appears to play the role of a magazine and of broadcast media, turning a particular image (or a small set of them) into iconic ones that then are repeated over time across the media landscape. The images also derive from the early days of the protests, and are thus also sticky, as if 'pinned' to the top, granting pride of place to the scoops, or early originality rewarded.

Camera brands and models that took the top pictures

What else is of interest from the camera data for our research purposes? With respect to the picture-takers, the top images that endure are from particular camera brands and models, such as a Canon EOS or Nikon D series (both professional grade, the latter retailing at €5000). At the top are not cheap pictures, so to speak; however, much lower down in the ranks (and by overall quantity) more economical, pocket-sized devices are well represented. Relating the price of the cameras that take the most visible pictures at crowded events to their placement in engines is a practice enabled by the availability of EXIF data as well as online price catalogues. More conventionally, one also can find, manually, the picture credits of the top three images: photographers at Reuters (lady in red) and the Associated Press (water cannon and green, peaceful sit-in) took the pictures. The overall point, though, concerns the dominance of types of coverage, and the extent to which the so-called 'flood of citizen content' and 'pop-up news ecologies' of protest camps and social media events are able to ascend, both in rankings as well as narrative (Aday et al., 2013; Wall and el Zahed, 2015). Ultimately, the more iconic but also violent protest images (police heavy-handedness covered in more established news) rise to the top and maintain their place, but the peaceful protest in the green park (an early crowd narrative) also endures, albeit lower down.

Tracker research and the politics of disclosure

When considering capturing and analysing cookies and other trackers embedded in websites, one may take on an investigative outlook as well as an academic one, examining conceptual claims, as above. To begin with, the journalistic story-driven exercises described here take advantage of the discoveries (to be made public) of trackers on certain websites: Jihadi websites that publish heinous acts and recruit extremists house Western ad-revenue software. In another discovery exercise, third-party trackers, serving data to corporate interests, reside on government websites. Extensions of such discovery work differentiate between tracker types on mainstream as well as junk or so-called fake news websites. As trackers proliferate, there is also the larger question of where on the web – a space increasingly undergoing platformization – the user is not watched. How to identify the trackerless web? Is it dying, or is there a particular vibrancy that may serve as an alternative space online?

Jihadi banner ads

With respect to the investigative outlook, a *Financial Times* headline read: 'Jihadi website with beheadings profited from Google ad platform' (Cookson, 2016). The strongly worded newspaper article pointed out that a jihadi recruitment site (with extremist content) had an AdSense account, serving clickable banners from other major Western firms (such as Citigroup, IBM and Microsoft), earning income for the website and the cause. The multi-nationals also received traffic and visibility in the jihadi online environment. Upon learning of the discovery and asked for an accounting of it, Google cancelled the AdSense account, and discussed how it violated its terms of service. The multinational advertisers, moreover, were unaware of their poignant placement and pledged vigilance going forward, lest their brands be damaged.

In the above case, one takes note of a jihadi website running an ad banner, discovers its use of Google AdSense and other off-the-shelf Western tracking and ad-generating software, and confronts Google (and the advertisers) with those facts. Such an undertaking could be less observational (the approach of noticing a single banner) and more forensic and sys-tematic in a multiple-site inquiry; in a data journalism exercise, one could curate a longer list of jihadi or other extreme websites, ranked perhaps by traffic and expertly categorized by well-known-ness and extremism. To determine whether the highest trafficked, best-known and most extreme jihadi websites are using Google Analytics (for example), one would pass the sites' code through software to extract trackers and other digital objects (see Figure 14.6). Expanding upon the above theme of jihadi use of Western software to gener-ate revenue (and damage reputations), the outputs possibly could introduce the story of a more widespread use of Western software by nefarious actors, and even (known) negligence after earlier promises of policy change or vigilance. Financial news may couch the story in legality, corporate social responsibility and/or brand sensitivity, though allowing the use to persist presumably enables the monitoring of visitors to jihadi websites, too. One could perform a similar undertaking for porn websites, where in asking for an accounting the question of public image and taste may weigh more upon the firms than unbroken terms of service. In the event, it was found that specific trackers are behind that genre of website (such as DoublePimp), though Google, DoubleClick and Facebook Connect all make healthy appearances, too (Helmond et al., 2016).

Governmental cookies

One last example of the investigative outlook concerns institutional websites which would not be expected to place cookies and third-party trackers. What is a government website putting in my cookies folder? Indeed, over a decade ago students and I discovered that an EU website was setting a cookie, without any privacy policy listed on the site, or indication how the data would be used. When we notified the EU webmaster, we were thanked, with the addendum that they would look into the matter (and presumably stop setting a cookie

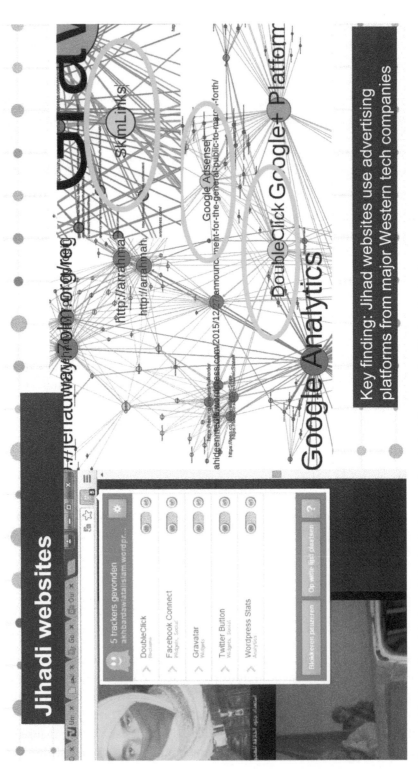

Figure 14.6 Depiction of findings of jihadi website use of Google Analytics and other Western firm trackers.

Source: Helmond et al., 2016.

until there was a policy, though we did not pursue the matter further). Some years later, cookies were no longer primarily considered aids for remembering user preferences and the lubricant for frictionless surfing (Elmer, 2003). They had become part of an ecosystem, together with so-called 'third-party elements', that enable the tracking of behaviour across the web (pulling data from users) as well as the customization of content and ads delivered (pushing content to users) (Gerlitz and Helmond, 2013).

Indeed, when the great cookie debate was under way in Europe that ultimately resulted in user consent notices popping up in one's browser, surveillance researcher Lonneke van der Velden took up the question of Dutch governmental cookie placement and especially the presence of third-party elements on government websites. She inquired not just into isolated incidents (like the single EU site we encountered without a privacy policy), but across the entire national governmental web landscape, some 1100 sites as listed in the registry (van der Velden, 2012). Over half of the active sites she found contained third-party elements, especially Google Analytics but also Facebook Connect and other ad and content delivery networks (see Figure 14.6). In all, the conclusion was that the governmental sites were not only playing their 'visible role as the main public service providers, but also contributing to the information economy by sharing (personal) data with major corporations' (van der Velden, 2014: 196). The participation of the government in the tracking infrastructure was made visible.

Tracking over time

Exposing (unknown or under-researched) entanglements of Western firms with repressive, extremist or otherwise dubious actors and milieux, and making them account for that consumption of corporate product, are examples of making things public with tracker forensics. In the other example, public sector websites are serving commercial interests with site visitor data, a practice that ought to be worthy of exposure and accounting. Van der Velden (2012) kept a running account of the exposure research in the form of a 'third-party diary', making public her findings through research blog entries.

Beyond those cases deserving of investigation and public exposure, there are research use cases, too, that seek to make new claims or examine existing ones about the prevalence and implications of tracking online, over time. Has tracking increased over time, both in scope as well as in depth? Is more data being shared increasingly with third parties? One could examine the kinds of trackers and third-party elements in use on everyday news websites and compare that usage over time. What kind of trackers have been present on the *New York Times* from 1996 onwards, when the website was first archived (see Figure 14.7)? Have they become more invasive (extracting more and more data) and permissive (sharing more and more data with third parties)? Could one characterize the newspaper as comparatively more invasive and permissive than others, whether they are quality, tabloid or even 'fake news' sources? More poignantly for the newspaper perhaps, is the *New York Times* similar

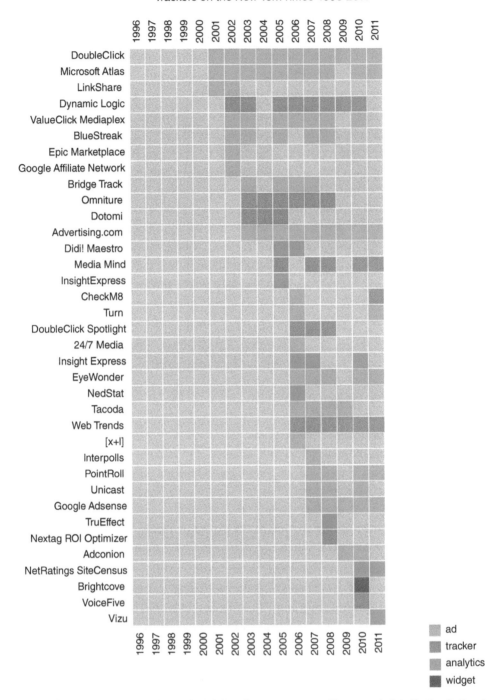

Figure 14.7   Tracker names and types found on nytimes.com over a 15-year period, indicating both a rise in overall tracking as well as specialized data sharing. Data from DMI's Tracker Tracker tool, Ghostery and the Wayback Machine of the Internet Archive.

Source: Helmond et al., 2012; see also Helmond, 2017.

to a tabloid and to 'fake news' websites in its tracking? In order to undertake such work, one would extract the trackers and third-party elements from the archived versions of the newspaper at the Wayback Machine of the Internet Archive and use Ghostery's database (or another) to begin to gain an understanding of the trackers' characteristics that have been operating, and how they have changed over time. One would do the same for other newspapers.

Such techniques have been put into practice in the study of the 'techno-infrastructure' of fake news websites (Bounegru et al., 2017). It has been found that mainstream news sites are quite distinctive in their deployment of trackers compared to 'fake news' sites, where the former have engaged in more behavioural and customized tracking, and the latter in cheaper, off-the-shelf product (see Figure 14.8). In making such findings, one can begin to shed light on the user strategies of fake news websites *vis-à-vis* the mainstream. The one is for all takers, so to speak, and the other appears to be more personalized, following in the footsteps of online services that increasingly customize content (and behaviourally targeted advertising) to fit history and preferences.

The platformization of the web

A larger question concerns the rise of social media and engines, and the decline of the open (content) web through its platformization, most palpably in the spread of Facebook's login and tracking mechanisms, across website types from commercial to non-governmental and so forth (Roosendaal, 2012). Is the open web disappearing or under dire threat, as its inventor, Tim Berners-Lee, claimed on the anniversary of its twenty-fifth year? Even more broadly, along the same lines one could inquire into the normalization of tracking, where one's remit would be to seek the ever-shrinking web that remains tracker-free. Where to find websites not participating in the turn to monitoring? Are they in particular sectors, or in certain countries? Are they mainly lifeless websites, or do some still thrive without user data? Should they be curated and showcased in a critical art exhibition?

Anne Helmond (2015) has discussed platformization as the double logic of 'extending' platforms across the web and making websites 'platform-ready'. For a platformization project, it may be of interest to chart across websites the use of Facebook as login mechanism as well as the Facebook social buttons (as trackers) and map the larger ecosystem, examining at the same time that which is independent of it. One may consider a snapshot or a more longitudinal approach, checking for the creep of Facebook across the web, as Googlization scholars once spoke of Google's 'free' model, taking over such hallowed institutions as the library as well as highly competitive areas such as comparative shopping websites (Vaidhyanathan, 2011). The latter ultimately resulted in an investigation by the European Union, and a multi-billion-dollar fine being levied.

DO MAINSTREAM MEDIA AND FAKE NEWS WEBSITES SHARE THE SAME TRACKER ECOLOGIES?

Scatterplot representing tracker usage on a series of fake news and mainstream media sites. While fake news sites and mainstream media sites share popular tracker services such as Google Adsense, DoubleClick and Google Analytics, mainstream media sites appears more mature and sophisticated in its use of trackers in terms of the number and diversity of trackers that it uses.

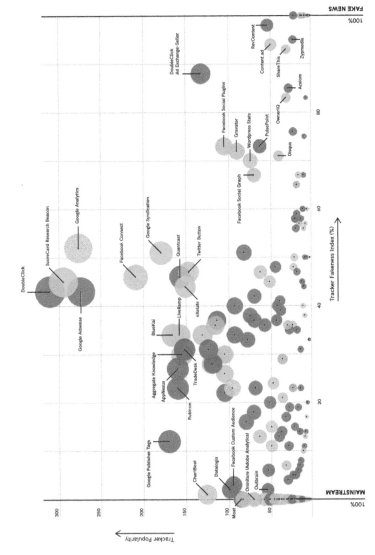

Figure 14.8 Comparison of trackers employed on mainstream and fake news websites.

Source: Bounegru et al., 2017.

To study platformization one may use the Internet Archive's Wayback Machine, and capture segments of the web (or representative sets of parts of the web), using top-level and second-level domains, such as.com,.org and.gov, as well as particular countries and their second levels. Once some nominal (small-scale) commercial, non-governmental, governmental and national webs are curated, the URLs may be passed through the Tracker Tracker tool, and thus Ghostery's database, to gain a sense of the similarities and differences in tracking cultures. Thereupon the historical work may begin, collecting URLs from years past, and fetching them through Tracker Tracker. It should be noted that it appears that Ghostery's database is cumulative, and thus not unlike a virus collector's, which would maintain 'old' viruses as they likely still 'survive' on machines with outdated software. In Ghostery's case, historical trackers remain, and their signatures can be found on older webpages.

Where the network discovery stops (and starts again)

As indicated, the purpose of network discovery and other digital forensics techniques, often developed in the evidentiary arena, is to make visible and public certain sources that would rather remain undisclosed, as in the case of the Russian influence campaign mentioned at the outset. Embedded digital object mapping, such as with trackers and third-party elements, may be utilized for exposing ethically dubious commercial practices (use of Western advertising software by jihadi websites) as well as ill-advised governmental undertakings (such as the use of analytics software that passes citizen online activity to advertising companies). The outcomes of these discovery and exposure exercises are shown (where possible) to the influence campaigners, commercial companies and governmental agencies so that the disclosure accounts may be acknowledged and responded to. The dual accountings – made public – constitute the story.

It is worthwhile to point out that exposure techniques are misused, such as when trolls dox, or spread personally identifiable information to harass and otherwise victimize. With widespread use of search engines and social media platforms, exposure techniques are also becoming routinized, well beyond the work of trolls. In putting forth the notion of 'lateral surveillance' and 'peer-to-peer monitoring', Mark Andrejevic (2005) writes of the rise of online prying practices 'associated with marketing and law enforcement to gain information about friends, family members' and others. Indeed, users of social media not only keep up with friends, but also look up and look at people (Joinson, 2008). Platforms cooperate. In the early days of social networking sites, one's profile information often was available by default to friends only; over the years, concomitant with the development of granular privacy settings, more and more of one's self and content have been made public by default (boyd and Hargittai, 2010; McKeon, 2010). The settings may be well used, especially by those on one side of the digital skills divide, but researchers nowadays still speak in terms of a 'privacy paradox', where there is great concern on the part of users but also vast self-exposure (Barnes, 2006; Kokolakis, 2017). Perhaps the more nuanced view of caring about privacy and still (over)sharing is the point made by Zeynep Tufekci (2008), who argued that youthful users are seeking to 'optimize' the relationship between 'disclosure and withdrawal'. There is also the idea that data may be public, but its (research) use would violate the 'contextual integrity' of the user, who does not consider the socializing space of the platform to be a site of surveillance or analysis (Nissenbaum, 2009; Werbin et al., 2017).

Conclusions: Digital investigations

Rather than being driven by the routinization of sniffing around online (if you will) or by the 'open source intelligence techniques' themselves, the starting points for the media and social research projects discussed above are often claims made about phenomena related to new media (the power of the crowd and the spread of online surveillance), the under-researched (the depiction of an ongoing event in Google Images), or the seemingly novel (fake news websites). The repurposed natively digital objects, together with the extraction and reverse look-up software, become less tools for 'intelligence' work and more the jumping-off point for 'inventive methods', in that they have a 'variety and variability of [research] purposes' (Lury and Wakeford, 2012: 5). The extracted EXIF camera and editing software data may be able to shed light on 'crowd sources' of the dominant pictures in 'pop-up news ecologies' at major events. Cookies and trackers, when extracted from websites and categorized in the collection database (such as Ghostery's), can be made to show the pervasiveness and permissiveness of surveillance and personal data extraction. When the presence of trackers on archived websites is added, an over-time dimension enriches the research outcomes. Analytics and third-party elements on websites can be mapped in order to put on display commercial data infrastructures, including those of fake news websites.

Finally, I made mention above to what could be called the applied hacker ethics of writing a safety guide for anonymous bloggers doing undercover work, scanning for vulnerabilities and potential exploits and exposure, and quietly communicating the results. These are also forms of digital investigation.

PROJECTS

Carry out the protocols for network discovery, crowdsourced content, tracker comparison, or tracker-free web

RESEARCH GOAL To follow one of the four research protocols concerning network discovery, camera picture data, and tracker analysis, either in the contemporary moment or over time.

1   A network discovery and thematic characterization using Google Analytics and/or AdSense IDs.

    a   Curate list of 'suspect' websites, by which is meant that they are anonymous, or their source is underspecified or not well attributed.

    b   Identify Google AdSense and/or Google Analytics IDs on the websites and create a spreadsheet with the websites in one column and the IDs in two subsequent columns.

    c   Use the Table 2 Net software to transform the spreadsheet into network data.

    d   Import the network data file into Gephi (or other network analysis software) and visualize.

    e   Annotate (and narrate) the network, discussing the commonalities in its clusters and nodes.

2   An analysis of the 'crowdsourced' content of a major event, and the consideration of the extent to which the significant content (and the narrative it tells) is 'of the crowd'.

    a   Curate a set of images from an event, and look up each image's EXIF data, using EXIF data viewing software.

    b   Note the camera that has taken each picture and make a spreadsheet with at least the camera make and the picture name. You may wish to add a column for the editing software and version.

    c   Characterize cameras as professional, prosumer or consumer grade.

    d   Consider looking up retail prices of the cameras.

    e   In the analysis, demonstrate the extent to which the image content of the major event is 'user-generated' or professional. Consider hybrid categorizations such as prosumer or produser.

3   An analysis of the trackers on a set of sectoral or national websites, including on mainstream versus fake news sites:

    a   Curate a list of websites in one of two ways. Either the list is sectoral, for example, governmental, non-governmental, commercial, and educational sites. (Other categories may be added.) Or the list is national, sourced from Alexa or through another approach.

    b   Run the list through the Tracker Tracker tool. It outputs a .csv file as well as a .gexf file for Gephi.

c   Examine the results with the.csv file. Here one may be interested in the amount as well as types of trackers per URL, or URL type (e.g., governmental and non-governmental). Visualize the results using Gephi. The relationships of interest are between the URLs and the trackers, and the extent to which certain clusters emerge that indicate (sectoral and/or national) patterns.

4   An over-time analysis of the trackers on one or more (sets of) websites, with the optional consideration of whether there is a part of the web that is (relatively) tracker-free.

a   Curate a list of websites as in 3 above.
b   Retrieve Wayback Machine URLs (from archive.org) for each website from regular intervals in the past. Optionally, using the digital methods tool, Internet Archive Wayback Machine Network Per Year, retrieve the URLs of past versions of the websites, annually.
c   Run the list of Wayback Machine URLs per website through the Tracker Tracker tool.
d   Consider visualizing the number of trackers per website over time. Also of interest is the type of trackers over time per website.

Resources

- uBlock Origin add-on (lists trackers on the websites visited).
- Ghostery add-on (provides information on the trackers on the websites visited).
- Tracker Tracker tool by the Digital Methods Initiative, https://wiki.digitalmethods.net/Dmi/ToolTrackerTracker.
- Video tutorial on the use of the Tracker Tracker tool, www.youtube.com/watch?v=UZpOrtjkyno
- Google Analytics reverse look-up, https://dnslytics.com/reverse-analytics/. The tool also provides reverse lookups for Google AdSense IDs.
- Gephi (the Open Graph Viz Software), https://gephi.org/.
- Table 2 Net software by Media Lab, Sciences-Po, http://tools.medialab.sciences-po.fr/table2net/

FIFTEEN

SUMMARIZING DIGITAL METHODS
An approach to the study of online data

And extending digital methods to the study of AI platforms

Increasingly employed as an umbrella term for tool-based methods used in the digital humanities and computational social sciences, digital methods have as their point of departure a series of heuristics with respect to how to study online media (Rogers, 2013b). The first historicizes the web as an object of study, one that has undergone a transformation from a (virtual) site for the study of online culture specifically to a source of data about broader societal and cultural trends. Second, to extract the data one not only employs crawlers, scrapers, API and dashboard logins as well as manual means, but also pays special attention to 'query design', based on keyword and source list building for creating (for example) tweet collections or sets of Facebook pages for social media analysis. To study those 'natively digital' source sets, digital methods learn from the methods of the medium (e.g., recommendation systems such as trending topics or news feeds). How may platform treatments of retweets and likes (for example) be repurposed for studying the unfolding of historical events (on X/Twitter), or the most engaged-with memes in a political campaign (on Facebook)? Digital methods, finally, consider the conditions of proof. When does it makes sense to ground the findings (e.g., about regional culinary preferences through geo-located engine queries and Instagram food photography)? When is 'online groundedness' less robust than mixed methods approaches?

This chapter summarizes digital methods by first briefly resituating them in the computational or data studies turn in intern`et-related research. It touches on areas that have yet to be covered, such as geotagged web data as well as generative AI based on large language models. It finally extracts some of the highlights of digital methods theory and concept development together with specific contributions made to such undertakings as single-site histories for web archive use, repurposing search engine usage, transforming Wikipedia into a cultural reference work, platform studies (particularly X/Twitter for remote event analysis and Facebook for most engaged-with content), YouTube recommendation deconstruction or 'teardown', the study of imitation in TikTok's memetic infrastructure and network discovery for data journalism and open source intelligence research. Upon conclusion, it extends digital methods to the critical study of AI platforms, including approaches to audit the platforms for offensive outputs.

Computational turn

Beginning around 2007, there occurred what has been referred to retrospectively as a turn in internet-related research – be it called the computational or data studies turn. It recognized that the web is no longer studied as a space apart ('cyberspace') or bringing into being an offline society. Though the digital divide remains, there was no longer a call to study the 'virtual' separately. The web, rather, came to be studied as societal and cultural data sets. Two key articles in this regard – 'A twenty-first century science' by Duncan Watts (2007) and 'Computational social science' by David Lazer et al. (2009) – discussed how one could study societal condition and cultural preference with web data. Put differently, in heralding the 'end of the virtual', as I argued, the web became the source for more than the study of online culture only (Rogers, 2009a). As an initial example, web data were called upon to glean American regional culinary preference. Published in the *New York Times* the day before Thanksgiving, the annual holiday feast, queries in the search engine of allrecipes.com allowed one to display, on a map, a geographical distribution of taste (Ericson and Cox, 2009). Queries for macaroni and cheese or corn casserole occurred with greater incidence in the old South and the corn belt, respectively, as cooks made their preparations for Thanksgiving. In a follow-up project, a similar technique was used to display not overall culinary trends, but the most specific recipe query for a particular geographical area, showing 'unusually popular' ones per state such as pumpkin whoopie pie for New Hampshire and Maine and funeral potatoes in Utah (Upshot Staff, 2014).

Geolocation data for studying events and diasporic cultures

There are generally three geolocated data types. Apart from engine queries, there are geotagged Instagram postings, as mentioned below. Another is the geolocated tweet. In a classic variation on the study of regional language differentiation, researchers explored *where* people tweeted 'pop', 'coke' and 'soda', the terms for soft drinks in the USA, and reaffirmed regional differentiation (soda in the Northeast and far Southwest, coke in the South and pop in the Midwest), albeit with some surprising term migrations.

There are two particular projects, and techniques, that I have referred to in the context of research using data that is linked to or derived with geolocation. Firstly, one is the study of an event in a place using Google Images, where in the project we asked the question: could we use the engine to follow the events, visually, or will we only be studying Google? The research conducted on the Gezi Park demonstrations in Istanbul in 2013 found that Google

Images, rather than an event-following media source (such as X/Twitter for 'remote event analysis'), is an iconic image producer. Indeed, the well-referenced (and memeified) image that emerged from the protests was that of 'the lady in red', capturing a woman being pepper-sprayed during the demonstrations. The analysis concerned the images of the demonstrations outputted by the engine across a 40-day period and found that the top ones were virtually the same, every day. Put differently, Google Images does not produce event chronology, but rather shows day after day the most iconic images in its search results. A second approach to the use of geolocation in research is with Facebook. To curate a list of Facebook pages, one may query Google, such as [site:facebook.com Somali diaspora], and subsequently follow up with a query in Facebook's graph search, merging the two results sets. For a geolocated set of pages, one would query Google regions, using the region setting in the advanced options, locating the diasporic pages in France, Belgium and other countries. We found that by using geolocated Facebook pages, one could compare diasporic activity per country, noting where they were more host land or homeland oriented, thus making findings about integration (Kok and Rogers, 2017).

In the remainder of this chapter, I would like to highlight both the concepts that have been developed together with methods and techniques for certain of the themes discussed above.

The website as archived object for screencast documentaries

The website is oftentimes considered to be the seminal object of study for the web; it is what the television show is to television studies or the movie to film studies. It is seminal especially from the point of view of its contents, as traditionally the website's content is privileged over other elements such as ads when archived. If one were to undertake the study of websites from an infrastructural point of view, contrariwise, one could well inquire into how a site is designed first and foremost to be crawled and indexed (and found) rather than read. Much of its traffic remains non-human (from non-readers).

Owing to the dominance of the view of the web as content, the website's body text (together with some images and other contents) has been considered valuable and worth saving. Recall that the Library of Congress also privileged the preserving of the text of tweets rather than other fields in Twitter's archive.

Over the years a few specific approaches to saving the web or archiving websites have been developed. One insight concerning web archiving is that each approach (biographical, event-based, national and autobiographical) has implications for the kind of historical work that can be done; if websites are selected for saving with a particular approach in mind (e.g., the national), this lends itself to a history that can be written, such as official and national heritage stories (Rogers, 2018b). As a case in point, many countries do not have a national web archiving institution, leading to the loss of 'their' historical webs and resources for history-writing and other archival uses (such as copyright infringement cases).

The preservation of the historical web began otherwise. The Internet Archive sought to 'save everything' through a 'webby' crowdsourcing technique, facilitated by the Alexa toolbar. Users would install the toolbar, and in exchange for information about the websites they visited, their surfing was logged, and the URLs, if not already archived, would be crawled by the Internet Archive. The proverbial crowd provided the URL lists and aided in the building of the archive. This was a cyberspace archive, borderless, though biased by the dominant users, their locations and the contents that interested them. The second type of web archiving tradition is called web sphere analysis, an approach for thematically related, time-bound events such as the national elections. While researchers were preparing to make an elections collection, 9/11 struck, and an agile redirection of attention yielded the 9/11 collection, now housed at the Library of Congress. It also ushered in the tradition of event-based archiving of 'disasters and elections'. A third approach, alluded to above, is undertaken by national libraries, whose archival mandates imply the saving of 'the national', be it the public record and/or national heritage. An influential definition of what constitutes a relevant national website was deployed in Denmark and includes those sites from that specific top-level country domain; websites in that particular national language; websites about Danish heritage ('Danica'); and content concerning that country but published in any foreign language. National history-writing is thereby enabled. The event-based tradition also lives on in the national web archiving institutions, as in Denmark (but also elsewhere), where approximately two events per year are archived. While they can be international, in the main they are domestic. A final approach is the recent autobiographical or selfie history, where one must save one's own content, since it is behind a login. Apart from combing through one's data dump, one approach that stands out is the recording of the evolution of a Facebook or Instagram account, enabled by webrecorder.io or Conifer, developed by Rhizome on the occasion of the art project and feminist social media critique, 'Amalia Ulman: Excellences & Perfections'. This project is a commentary on especially young girls' use of social media, and Instagram in particular, and how (and at what cost) micro-celebrity-seeking and follower-count build-up are achieved.

Many archived web collections are underutilized (in the sense of not well cited), and much of the digital methods work has concerned itself with undarkening the archive and opening it up to scholarly use, through repurposing. One technique stands out, for it seeks to follow the research affordances of the Wayback Machine of the Internet Archive. The screencast documentary approach plays back the history of the webpage in the style of time-lapse photography. Narrated with a voiceover, the recording invites web, media or organizational (or 'digital') histories by focusing on significant interface changes. In one example of a media history, the *New York Times* as seen through the changes to its front page reverted from a distinctive new media 'cybertimes' back to a remediated newspaper over a twenty-year period. One other approach is noteworthy, for it too recognizes that the archived website is not only content but also code. By loading archived websites into a browser that has installed the Ghostery add-on, one is able to capture the trackers, cookies and third-party elements contained in the site, over time, thereby enabling the retelling of a history of tracking or surveillance of one or more websites (or website types). Has government been setting cookies in the past without privacy policies? Has tracking only increased over time, across much of the web (including the non-governmental parts)?

Google critique and repurposing

Among the terms one agrees to when querying Google is that it is executed through the Google interface's search bar, the results are not to be saved, and no derivative works are fashioned. There is a particular award-winning work of media art (Newsmap) that did precisely that for Google News, capturing and resizing the stories by amount of coverage, thereby providing a news attention economy critique and a means to study it, too. It also built in geography. Which news articles and news sections are gaining the most attention and where are they receiving that attention? In a sense it is both a study of Google News and of news, where in the case of the former it shows geographical source distributions (and Google News's blind spots), and in the latter which stories the sources are (not) covering per place. The Google Scraper and its alter ego, the Lippmannian Device, have the similar dual function of performing engine and web critique, and facilitating source analysis. The Google Scraper's original research purpose and approach is 'source distance', whereby one is studying how far from the top are particular actors or points of view, as organized and outputted by Google. How close to the top of the climate change space are the sceptics? In other words, one is asking the extent to which Google gives prominent placement (and voice) to particular actors over others and grants them the privilege to provide 'information' that is more likely to be viewed. These are inquiries into engine epistemologies, together with their consequences. The other inquiry into engine proclivities is algorithmic probing or auditing, where one seeks to lay bare privileging mechanisms as well as bias. Does Google boost its own properties over what in the industry is called 'organic' search results, or information sources other than Google products? Does Google autocomplete shocking or offensive stereotypes? When one queries for social issues, do they return sources from that are considered rather neutral or toward the end of a political spectrum? These are some of the lenses through which one may examine search results.

In its other guise, rather than critiquing the engine and the web, the Google Scraper repurposes Google for 'societal search'. In this version, referred to as the Lippmannian Device to emphasize the other, distinctive use case, it seeks to provide a 'coarse means' – as Lippmann (1927) phrased it – to show bias or partisanship. Here one seeks to take advantage of Google's workings, including its proclivity to output fresh, user-clicked sites (making it presentist and *ad populum*) as well as its capacity to index individual sites. Here the use cases for individual site study include concern or distributions thereof for particular issues. Of all of Greenpeace's campaigns, which ones are returned with what frequency by a Google site search? One may expand the number of organizations of the site search to a curated list of human rights organizations, for example. Here the question concerns the current agenda. To gain a sense of it, one curates a list of human rights organizations (employing a list-building technique), visits each of the sites on the list, and extracts the issues on each webpage. At this point, one has a list of URLs and a list of keywords. One queries all the URLs for all the keywords, outputting an issue cloud, where each issue is resized according to how many human rights organizations list it as an issue. 'Estimated Google results' per issue provides a second indication of which issues are high on the agenda, and which are lower, where agenda in this case is a Google-assisted website collection search for human rights issue keywords.

Wikipedia as networked content for cross-cultural analysis

Wikipedia is oftentimes studied as a techno-knowledge project, placed in a lineage with P. Otlet's Mundaneum, H.G. Wells's World Brain, V. Bush's Memex, T. Nelson's Xanadu, M. Hart's Project Gutenberg and even T. Berners-Lee's World Wide Web, among others. As an encyclopedia, it has been compared to *Encyclopaedia Britannica* and others for its accuracy, initially faring well in the facticity checks, and also in the contrasts; Wikipedia has breadth and timeliness. It is also studied as a piece of wiki software for (remote) collaboration; wiki technology has been overshadowed by Google Wave, which is Google Docs or Drive. In Google's software, multiple people can edit and save the same document simultaneously, whereas even though a wiki enables multiple authorship, simultaneous editing results in edit conflicts. Wikipedia has also been considered a project of anonymous or collaborative authorship by 'Wikipedians', and one that reopens the debate surrounding the death of the author. With the rise of the author came a book that (with the help of critics) concentrates more on the author than on the contents (Barthes, 1967). Wikipedia also has been studied as an image burnishing or publicity management tool; many Wikipedia articles are authored by interested parties, prompting a debate about the effects of such partial editing on the quality of articles. Software projects, such as the Wikiscanner, have sought to out anonymous editors, and as such have succeeded in identifying particularly egregious cases of self-interest over accuracy. Wikipedia has also been studied as a well-functioning bureaucracy, achieving stigmergy, or ant-like working efficiency. It also has a relationship with Google, where for years it benefited from being at the top of Google results for substantive queries (in one study some 95% of the time). Later, following the introduction of Google's knowledge graph, Wikipedia's relationship with Google's results flip-flopped. The knowledge graph displays thumbnail knowledge boxes (or panels) containing capsule summaries related to the particular query in Google's search engine results page. The panels' contents are borrowed from Wikipedia. Its introduction in various countries coincided with a decline in the amount of traffic to Wikipedia, generally, and specifically to Wikipedia via Google. Therefore, where Google once gave, it now takes away from Wikipedia.

Rather than regarding Wikipedia as a genealogical, epistemological, techno-authorial, bureaucratic or other object of study discussed above, with digital methods one is initially interested in taking stock of the natively digital objects embedded in Wikipedia and how its interface handles them. Wikipedia keeps its edit history, and the editors that made them, and when perusing a list of most active ones, bots are at the top. While they co-produce Wikipedia articles in numerous ways (e.g., interlinking), they also watch for vandalism. From a thought experiment (and an actual movie demo we made, where we turned off bot edits in an article), colleagues and I noted that turning off the bots would result in an unreadable encyclopedia, vandalized and rendered gobbledygook. 'Networked content' thereby became the term for considering how a network of bots holds together the content.

A second digital methods contribution again begins by looking at the interface and its objects and noting links to the 'same' article on other Wikipedia language versions (inter-wiki links). How to compare the articles? As other projects (such as Omnipedia and Manypedia) have discovered, the 'same' articles in different Wikipedia language versions may differ substantively. Tools may show the differences. For content comparison at a glance, there is a Wikipedia TOC Scraper, which allows the researcher to place side-by-side the table of contents of Wikipedia articles. For image comparison, there is the Wikipedia Cross-Lingual Image Analysis tool. For comparing references in two or more Wikipedia articles across language versions, there is the Triangulation tool. Of course, one is able to perform such work without these scrapers, but they provide means to document and study the meanings behind the 'diff's', as the computational term has it to describe the differences between two files. The seminal project in this regard is that of Srebrenica articles on Wikipedia. Srebrenica is a historic site in Bosnia and Herzegovina that witnessed the massacre, the genocide or the fall of the city, as the Serbian, Bosnian and Dutch Wikipedia articles respectively entitle their articles on the events of July 1995, when 6000–8000, 8000, or 7000–8000 Bosniaks were killed (again depending on the same respective articles at the time of analysis). With this 'cross-cultural reference' approach one examines the various Wikipedia elements in an article, some of which are standard (title), and others are specific to Wikipedia such as anonymous editors, revision history, talk pages and templates. Indeed, the image capturing tool also grabs the templates, so one is able to see at a glance which issues (such as NPOV) articles may have.

Platform studies

There is an urgent realization that the open web is threatened by platformization. In this rendering social media become sticky sites that attract and arguably entrap users, locking them in (for their departure, even if desired, would have considerable cost to one's social life). As the web is depopulated of users and content migrates to social media, it is worthwhile to take note of the new environment's publishing culture and vetting procedures.

Social media platforms as well as OS systems on the smartphone are not considered as 'writerly' as the web for they 'moderate' content and 'approve' apps. Social media have been the object of critique precisely for the choice of the notion of 'platform', which in a computing sense means 'writable'. It also connotes content neutrality, but platforms rather police content. There are multiple examples that one could mention, but the stream of banned apps on Apple's App Store is one category. For example, in one banned app the user is a drug dealer, and in another one (Me So Holy) the user replaces the Messiah with her/his own selfie. Yet another banned app portrays then US President Obama on a trampoline in the Oval Office. Another banned app stands out for it is a work of art; the 'I am rich' app, a shiny bauble that one can open and show to others, has no other function than as a display of ostentation, and thus has been called a Veblen good. It sold for the maximum price allowed on the App Store at the time, $999.99, and was soon banned.

Among the social media platforms under study, X/Twitter, Facebook and Instagram stand out, however much what I would call 'secondary social media' are also of interest for the alternatives they provide to the others in terms of research affordances. Twitter studies held steady over the years, arguably because Twitter data were abundant and accessible, and could be put to use in a variety of research contexts, from marketing through to media and social research. In the context of academic research, a number of questions are often raised that could be placed in the web's 'good data' debate. For example, when making a tweet collection, does one obtain 'all' the tweets or not? In fact, this was one of the first controversies in Twitter studies when a Twitter researcher was quoted as saying that one has to work at Twitter in order to have access to all the tweets, as cited in early 'big data' critique. Relatedly, it has been argued that researchers rarely clean Twitter data, meaning that most tweet collections and the studies based upon them have in their midst false positives and undisambiguated tweets. Twitter data are thus incomplete and messy (or even dirty). A third issue is that published Twitter studies rarely mention any ethical considerations in storing, analysing and publishing Twitter user data.

Debanalizing X/Twitter and studying engagement on Facebook

What is one studying when studying X/Twitter data? To begin, there have been at least five Twitters, beginning with the early 'What are you doing?' Twitter that was considered banal. One would study remote intimacy, ambient friend-following and, above all, phatic communication, for people were arguably 'only connecting' with each other rather than communicating substantively. The second Twitter arrived in 2009, with the new tagline, 'What's happening?' This is the event-following, newsworthy Twitter. It is also the revolutionary Twitter, the 140-character micro-blogging platform (which later doubled its character space size) that became associated with movement mobilization and aid pointers during the Iran election crisis and the Arab Spring. A more recent Twitter, the third, simply stated,

'Compose new tweet', as Twitter commodified (after the stock market capitalization) and sold more data for more generic research purposes. Twitter data were mobilized for celebrity award, election and stock market prediction. As these studies began to proliferate, questions arose about the demographics of users, and whether it could stand in for some measure of 'public opinion'. Or should it be considered a more elite, professional space? Twitter returned to its most successful tagline, in the sense once related by Jack Dorsey, its co-founder, when discussing how Twitter 'does well at' events, elections and disasters. Indeed, digital methods have been developed to take advantage of the 'What's happening?' Twitter. For 'remote event analysis' one may capture the top retweeted tweets per day and place them in chronological order (as opposed to the reverse chronological of a blog), so as to transform Twitter into a story-telling machine. Digital methods also have been developed for the study of issue spaces, or how issue professionals follow each other and contribute substantive tweets around global health and development, human rights and other issue spaces. Critical analytics measure dominant voice, concern, commitment, positionality and alignment in these spaces. Co-hashtag analysis result in networks (with clusters) that can be interpreted with the visual network story-telling routine. Though the 'What's happening?' tagline remains, a fifth Twitter has emerged with the change in ownership in 2022. With Elon Musk at the helm, X/Twitter has become a space to study its (lack of) content moderation, asking whether the toxicity and conspiracy theory circulating on X/Twitter only has increased since the new management's apparent disregard for that aspect of the enterprise (Alba and Wagner, 2023).

The main means to study Facebook described above – most engaged-with content – is quite far afield from the social network analysis once heralded, and the postdemographics approach, where one studies the preferences and tastes of public figures' friends (such as Donald Trump's and Joe Biden's) and inquires into the extent to which they may be compatible, thereby allowing for a reinterpretation of the culture wars. Since an API 'update' by Facebook in 2015, tastes and ties research as well as the postdemographics variation have become less probable, given the end of that data stream, though the availability of CrowdTangle spelled some relief as an alternative means to collect Facebook (and Instagram) Pages data. Facebook most recently has been one of the main staging areas for the fake news and Russian disinformation campaign debacle, where researchers have found high volumes of interactions of both hyperpartisan and Russian propaganda content, the most engaging of which were often memes. At least that is one empirical question put forward above, where Facebook is considered to be a so-called fake news machine, beyond its other guises as social networking site and ad-serving platform.

YouTube's ranking mechanisms

The erstwhile amateur video site has given way to commercialization as well as the rise of the 'native' YouTuber and micro-celebrity, although all three types of content-makers and their output continue to co-mingle in the massive repository. Popular instructional genres such as 'the walkthrough', 'unboxing' as well as 'how to fix it' inform the 'tear down' approach put forward. There are at least three modes of watching in YouTube, via the related videos, search and channel subscriptions, each of which may be 'torn down' or its recommendations laid bare by capturing the outputs for further study. In the methods built into the YouTube data tools, the researcher is able to put on display 'relatedness', or the carousel of recommended videos 'up next', ranking cultures from YouTube's own engine results as well as the networks of channel subscriptions and those that feature each other. In each technique, the question of authority is measured, or who is privileged by the platform (and when). Here one undertakes both medium and social research, asking whether native content providers (YouTubers or micro-celebrities) are becoming subject matter authorities given their standing on the platform. As may also be asked for Instagram influencers, how well do they use their 'platform'? May they be considered socially responsible?

TikTok's memetic infrastructure

TikTok, the Chinese platform which exploded upon the international social media scene in 2018, is known for its stickiness, given the time-on-app as well as user retention said to be driven by its 'For You Page' recommendations, which is also notable, compared to other platforms, for its primacy, filling the entire front page or screen. When released it had just merged with Musical.ly, incorporating features that make TikTok distinctive from other short-form video platforms that came before it, as Vine. These include duetting and stitching, where users react to and embed in theirs other videos on the platform. The feature of particular interest in the digital methods approach discussed above is the sound repository, where users can choose a sound to accompany their video, whereupon these videos become linked by virtue of deploying the same song. That the platform (and its users) additively make collections of associated videos gives it its memetic character.

TikTok's special affordances may be repurposed in order to study how they organize users, or publics. Building TikTok's memetic infrastructure, 'imitation publics', as they have been called (Zulli and Zulli, 2022), reuse the latest trending sounds and effects (and often insert the hashtags #fyp and #foryou) in an effort to gain greater visibility for their creative work. One may pursue this thesis through a sound-hashtag relational analysis, asking whether trending sounds are associated a broad range of subject matter hashtags, or whether sounds organize distinctive hashtag publics.

Not so unlike other platforms, TikTok is undergoing a transformation as a scholarly object of study, away from its original association of a 'playful, silly platform where teenagers share 15-second videos of crazy stunts or act out funny snippets from popular culture' (Vijay and Gekker, 2021: 712) to one that takes seriously its information culture, across user demographics, be it for pandemic vaccines, election misinformation as well as self-harm prevention. Thus, critical inquiries into the quality of information contained at the top of TikTok search results, but also generally in the FYP recommendations remain of interest.

Network discovery for data journalism research

The tracker analysis method and project extend from the study of Russian information campaigning both around the US presidential election of 2016 and beyond. In identifying website code and using reverse look-up software, one seeks to discover 'networks' of disinformation purveyors and other questionable sources and interpret content dissemination strategies. The 'Russians' – often referring to the work of the Internet Research Agency but it also could be called a style – adapted their content strategy of stirring conflict with the West to fomenting it *within* the West.

Google Analytics and AdSense IDs have been used to map websites (and groups of websites) onto owners. The owners may be 'media groups', such as an entity that owns a variety of channels from lifestyle to hard news, and plants stories worthy of study in all of them. Other tracker work also was presented, especially of interest to (data) journalists, such as the existence of Google Analytics and other Western analytics software on websites authored by ISIS sympathizers and other terror-recruitment groupings.

Conclusion: Prompting as query design for AI-driven platform critique

Doing digital methods, as the early chapters detail, relies on foundational skills referred to collectively as 'query design' and 'search as research' where one makes lists of keywords (or hashtags) and queries them in engines or platforms to demarcate a space of study and note trends and hierarchies in it. Making source lists, within which to query the keywords (or hashtags), is another foundation.

With the rise of natural language processing and generative AI, based on large language models, another form of query design research is called for: prompting. It is a common term, already employed in vulnerability-seeking and content moderation critique. For example, entering keywords or short sentences in Google Web Search prompts its autocompletions or predictions. How discriminatory or offensive are the autocompletions (Rogers, 2023)? For a systematic approach, one would make a list of categories, and for each a list of terms, and prompt an engine or another platform for its responses (Leidinger and Rogers, 2023).

The questions posed contribute to scholarship in the two areas discussed throughout: media or platform studies as well as social and cultural research. For the study of AI platforms as media, these are privileging critiques, teasing out hierarchies of concern. Which social groups are associated with offensive terms per platform, and which languages and cultures are well or under moderated? As such digital methods techniques are extended to AI platforms.

REFERENCES

Abbate, Janet (2000) *Inventing the Internet*. Cambridge, MA: MIT Press.

Abidin, Crystal (2014) '#In$tagLam: Instagram as a repository of taste, a burgeoning marketplace, a war of eyeballs', in Marsha Berry and Max Schleser (eds) *Mobile Media Making in an Age of Smartphones*. New York: Palgrave Pivot, pp. 119–128.

Abidin, Crystal (2016) 'Visibility labour: Engaging with influencers' fashion brands and #OOTD advertorial campaigns on Instagram', *Media International Australia, 161*(1): 86–100.

Abidin, Crystal (2021) 'Mapping internet celebrity on TikTok: Exploring attention economies and visibility labours', *Cultural Science Journal, 12*(1): 77–103. https://doi.org/10.5334/csci.140.

Aday, Sean, Farrell, Henry, Freelon, Deen, Lynch, Marc, Sides, John and Dewar, Michael (2013) 'Watching from afar: Media consumption patterns around the Arab Spring', *American Behavioral Scientist, 57*(7): 899–919.

Agar, John (2001) 'Review of James Gillies and Robert Cailliau, *How the Web was Born*. Oxford: Oxford University Press, 2000', *British Journal for the History of Science, 34*(3): 370–373.

Aggarwal, Anupama (2016) *'Detecting and mitigating the effect of manipulated reputation on online social networks', Proceedings of the 25th International Conference Companion on World Wide Web*. New York: ACM, pp. 293–297.

Aiello, G. and Parry, K. (2020) *Visual Communication: Understanding Images in Media Culture*. London: Sage.

Akrich, Madeleine and Latour, Bruno (1992) 'The de-scription of technical objects', in Wiebe Bijker and John Law (eds) *Shaping Technology / Building Society: Studies in Sociotechnical Change*. Cambridge, MA: MIT Press, pp. 205–224.

Alba, Davey and Wagner, Kurt (2023) 'Twitter cuts more staff overseeing global content moderation', *Bloomberg*, 7 January.

Albright, Jonathan (2017) 'Itemized posts and historical engagement – 6 now-closed FB pages', *Tableau Public*, https://public.tableau.com/profile/d1gi#!/vizhome/FB4/TotalReachbyPage.

Albright, Jonathan (2018) Personal conversation.

Alexa (2018) 'wikipedia.org traffic statistics', *Alexa.com*, www.alexa.com/siteinfo/wikipedia.org.

Alexander, Lawrence (2015) 'Open-source information reveals pro-Kremlin web campaign', *Global Voices*, 13 July, https://globalvoices.org/2015/07/13/open-source-information-reveals-pro-kremlin-web-campaign/.

Allan, Stuart (2015) '"iPhone-wielding amateurs": The rise of citizen photojournalism', in Chris Atton (ed) *The Routledge Companion to Alternative and Community Media*, London: Routledge, pp. 357–366.

Allen, Matthew (2013) 'What was Web 2.0? Versions as the dominant mode of internet history', *New Media & Society*, *15*(2): 260–275.

Alt-Right Open Intelligence Initiative (2017) 'Mapping the alt-right: The US alternative right across the Atlantic', Digital Methods Winter School, Amsterdam, https://digital methods.net/Dmi/AltRightOpenIntelligenceInitiative.

Amoore, Louise (2011) 'Data derivatives: On the emergence of a security risk calculus for our times', *Theory, Culture & Society*, *28*(6): 24–43.

Anderson, Chris (2009) *Free: The Future of a Radical Price*. New York: Random House.

Anderson, Ian (2012) 'Time for a World AIDS Day Google Doodle', *poz.com*, 19 November.

Andrejevic, Mark (2005) 'The work of watching one another: Lateral surveillance, risk, and governance', *Surveillance & Society*, *2*(4): 479–497.

Angwin, Julia, Varner, Madeleine and Tobin, Ariana (2017) 'Facebook enabled advertisers to reach "Jew Haters"', *ProPublica*, 14 September.

Apple (2017) *Environmental responsibility report*. Cupertino, CA: Apple, Inc.

Arnal, Timo (2014) 'Internet machine', film, https://vimeo.com/95044197.

Arthur, W. Brian (1989) 'Competing technologies, increasing returns and lock-in by historical events', *Economic Journal*, *99*: 106–131.

Aula, Pekka (2010) 'Social media, reputation risk and ambient publicity management', *Strategy & Leadership*, *38*(6): 43–49.

Baccarne, Bastiaan, Briones, Angeles, Baack, Stefan, Maemura, Emily, Joceli, Janna, Zhou, Peiqing, and Ferre, Humberto (2015) 'Does love win? The mechanics of memetics', *Digital Methods Summer School 2015*, https://wiki.digitalmethods.net/Dmi/SummerSchool2015DoesLoveWin.

Baio, Andy (2011) 'Think you can hide, anonymous blogger? Two words: Google Analytics', *Wired*, 15 November.

Baker, Nicholson (2008) 'The charms of Wikipedia', *New York Review of Books*, 20 March.

Baker, Paul and Potts, Amanda (2013) '"Why do white people have thin lips?" Google and the perpetuation of stereotypes via auto-complete search forms', *Critical Discourse Studies*, *10*(2): 187–204.

Balduini, Marco, Della Valle, Emanuele, Dell'Aglio, Daniele, Tsytsarau, Mikalai, Palpanas, Themis and Confalonieri, Cristian (2013) 'Social listening of city scale events using the streaming linked data framework', *ISWC 2013: The Semantic Web*, Heidelberg: Springer, pp. 1–16.

Bao, Patti, Hecht, Brent, Carton, Samuel, Quaderi, Mahmood, Horn, Michael and Gergle, Darren (2012) 'Omnipedia: Bridging the Wikipedia language gap', *Proceedings of the SIGCHI Conference on Human Factors in Computing Systems*. New York: ACM, pp. 1075–1084.

Barbaro, Michael and Zeller Jr., Tom (2006) 'A face is exposed for AOL searcher no. 4417749', *New York Times*, A1.

Bardak, Batuhan and Tan, Mehmet (2015) 'Prediction of influenza outbreaks by integrating Wikipedia article access logs and Google Flu Trends data', *Proceedings of 2015 IEEE 15th International Conference on Bioinformatics and Bioengineering (BIBE)*. Piscataway, NJ: IEEE.

Barnes, Susan B. (2006) 'A privacy paradox: Social networking in the United States', *First Monday*, *11*(9). https://doi.org/10.5210/fm.v11i9.1394.

Barthes, Roland (1967) *The Death of the Author*, trans. A. Leavers. New York: Smith & Hill.

Bartlett, Jamie, Birdwell, Jonathan and Littler, Mark (2011) *The New Face of Digital Populism*. London: Demos.

Basch, Corey H., Fera, Joseph, Pierce, Isabela and Basch, Charles E. (2021) 'Promoting mask use on TikTok: Descriptive, cross-sectional study', *JMIR Public Health and Surveillance*, 7(2): e26392.

Bastos, Marco (2021) 'This account doesn't exist: Tweet decay and the politics of deletion in the Brexit debate', *American Behavioral Scientist*, 65(5): 757–773.

Battelle, John (2003a) 'The "creeping Googlization" meme', *BusinessWeek Online*, 16 December.

Battelle, John (2003b) 'The database of intentions', *John Battelle's Searchblog*, 13 November, https://battellemedia.com/archives/2003/11/the_database_of_intentions.

Baughman, Jill (2010) 'Google picks Rosa Parks over World AIDS Day', *Cafemom.com*, 1 December.

Bauman, Zygmunt (2013) *Does the Richness of the Few Benefit Us All?* Cambridge: Polity.

Baym, Nancy (2015) 'Connect with your audience! The relational labor of connection', *The Communication Review*, 18(1): 14–22.

Baym, Nancy (2018) *Playing to the Crowd: Musicians, Audiences and the Intimate Work of Connection*. New York: New York University Press.

Bazzell, Michael (2016) *Open Source Intelligence Techniques: Resources for Searching and Analyzing Online Information*. North Charleston, SC: CreateSpace Independent Publishing Platform.

BBC Academy (2013) 'Israel and the Palestinians', in BBC Academy (ed) *Journalism Subject Guide*. London: BBC. www.bbc.co.uk/academy/journalism/article/art20130702112133696.

Bechmann, Anja (2017) *'Keeping it real: From faces and features to social values in deep learning algorithms on social media images', Proceedings of the 50th Annual Hawaii International Conference on System Sciences*. New York: IEEE Computer Society, pp. 1793–1801.

Beer, David (2008) 'Social network(ing) sites… revisiting the story so far: A response to danah boyd and Nicole Ellison', *Journal of Computer-Mediated Communication*, 13(2): 516–529.

Ben-David, Anat (2016) 'What does the web remember of its deleted past? An archival reconstruction of the former Yugoslav top-level domain', *New Media & Society*, 18(7): 1103–1119.

Ben-David, Anat (2020) 'Counter-archiving Facebook', *European Journal of Communication*, 35(3): 249–264. https://doi.org/10.1177/0267323120922069.

Benkler, Yochai, Faris, Robert, Roberts, Hal and Zuckerman, Ethan (2017) 'Study: Breitbart-led right-wing media ecosystem altered broader media agenda', *Columbia Journalism Review*, 3 March, https://www.cjr.org/analysis/breitbart-media-trump-harvard-study.php.

Bennett, Daniel (2009) 'The myth of the Moldova Twitter revolution', *Frontline Club* blog, 8 April, www.frontlineclub.com/the_myth_of_the_moldova_twitter_revolution-2/.

Bennett, W. Lance and Segerberg, Alexandra (2012) 'The logic of connective action: Digital media and the personalization of contentious politics', *Information, Communication & Society*, 15(5): 739–768.

Bergman, Michael K. (2001) 'The deep web: Surfacing hidden value', *Journal of Electronic Publishing*, 7(1). https://doi.org/10.3998/3336451.0007.104.

Berman, Ari (2009) 'Iran's Twitter revolution', *The Nation*, 15 June, www.thenation.com/article/irans-twitter-revolution/.

Berners-Lee, Tim (2014) 'Tim Berners-Lee on the Web at 25: The past, present and future', *Wired*, 23 August.

Bertelsmann Lexikon Institut (2008) *Das Wikipedia Lexikon in einem Band*. Gütersloh: Mohn Media.

Beurskens, Michael (2014) 'Legal questions of Twitter research', in Katrin Weller, Axel Bruns, Jean Burgess, Merja Mahrt, and Cornelius Puschmann (eds) *Twitter & Society*. New York: Peter Lang, pp. 123–136.

Bhandari, Aparajita and Bimo, Sara (2022) 'Why's everyone on TikTok now? The algorithmized self and the future of self-making on social media', *Social Media + Society*, 8(1): 20563051221086241.

Bielka, Nathalie, Buhl, Helena and dos Santos, Monica (2017) 'Wikipedia as object of study: A cross-cultural research on the German, Polish and Portuguese versions of the Wikipedia article, "Auschwitz concentration camp"', *course paper*, University of Mannheim.

Bird, S. Elizabeth (2011) 'Are we all produsers now? Convergence and media audience practices', *Cultural Studies*, 25(4–5): 502–516.

Bishop, Sophie (2018) 'Anxiety, panic and self-optimization: Inequalities and the YouTube algorithm', *Convergence*, 24(1): 69–84.

Bødker, Henrik and Brügger, Niels (2017) 'The shifting temporalities of online news: The *Guardian's* website from 1996 to 2015', *Journalism*, 7 February.

Bogers, Loes, Niederer, Sabine, Bardelli, Federica and De Gaetano, Carlo (2020) 'Confronting bias in the online representation of pregnancy', *Convergence*, 26(5–6): 1037–1059.

Borgman, Christine (2009) 'The digital future is now: A call to action for the humanities', *Digital Humanities Quarterly*, 3(4): 1–30.

Börner, Katy and Polley, David E. (2014) *Visual Insights: A Practical Guide to Making Sense of Data*. Cambridge, MA: MIT Press.

Borra, Erik and Rieder, Bernhard (2014) 'Programmed method: Developing a toolset for capturing and analyzing tweets', *Aslib Journal of Information Management*, 66(3): 262–278.

Bossen, Christina Bucknell and Kottasz, Rita (2020) 'Uses and gratifications sought by pre-adolescent and adolescent TikTok consumers', *Young Consumers*, 21(4): 463–478.

Bosworth, Andrew (2009) 'What's the history of the awesome button (that eventually became the like button) on Facebook?' *Quora*, www.quora.com/Whats-the-history-of-the-Awesome-Button-that-eventually-became-the-Like-button-on-Facebook.

Bouma, Joep, de Groot, Jos, de Groot, Mathijs, Lievisse Adriaanse, Mark, Polak, Sara, Zorz, Silvana, Stevenson, Michael, Gekker, Alex, and Colombo, Gabriele (2017) 'Bottom-up filter bubble mapping based on Trump and Clinton supporters' tweets', Digital Methods Winter School, University of Amsterdam, https://wiki.digitalmethods.net/Dmi/WinterSchool2017BeyondTheBubbleInside.

Bounegru, Liliana, Gray, Jonathan, Venturini, Tommaso and Mauri, Michele (2017) *A Field Guide to Fake News*. Amsterdam: Public Data Lab.

Bowker, Geoffrey (2005) *Memory Practices in the Sciences*. Cambridge, MA: MIT Press.

Boy, John D. and Uitermark, Justus (2017) 'Reassembling the city through Instagram', *Transactions of the Institute of British Geographers*, *42*(4): 612–624.

boyd, danah (2013) 'White flight in networked publics? How race and class shaped American teen engagement with MySpace and Facebook', in Lisa Nakamura and Peter A. Chow-White (eds) *Race after the Internet*. New York: Routledge, pp. 203–222.

boyd, danah and Crawford, Kate (2012) 'Critical questions for big data', *Information, Communication & Society*, *15*(5): 662–679.

boyd, danah and Ellison, Nicole (2007) 'Social network sites: Definition, history and scholarship', *Journal of Computer-Mediated Communication*, *13*(1), article 1.

boyd, danah and Hargittai, Esther (2010) 'Facebook privacy settings: Who cares?' *First Monday*, *15*(8). https://doi.org/10.5210/fm.v15i8.3086.

boyd, danah, Golder, Scott, and Lotan, Gilad (2010) *'Tweet, tweet, retweet: Conversational aspects of retweeting on Twitter'*, *Proceedings of the 43rd Annual Hawaii International Conference on System Sciences*. Los Alamitos, CA: IEEE Computer Society, pp. 1–10.

Bozzi, Nicola (2020) '#Digitalnomads, #solotravellers, #remoteworkers: A cultural critique of the traveling entrepreneur on Instagram', *Social Media + Society*, April–June: 1–15.

Brandtzaeg, Petter Bae and Haugstveit, IdaMaria (2014) 'Facebook likes: A study of liking practices for humanitarian causes', *International Journal of Web Based Communities*, *10*(3): 258–279.

Bratton, Benjamin H. (2016) *The Stack: On Software and Sovereignty*. Cambridge, MA: MIT Press.

Bridle, James (2010) 'On Wikipedia, cultural patrimony, and historiography', *Booktwo.org* blog, 6 September, http://booktwo.org/notebook/wikipedia-historiography/.

Brin, Serge and Page, Larry (1998) 'The anatomy of a large-scale hypertextual web search engine', *Computer Networks and ISDN Systems*, *30*(1–7): 107–117.

Brock, André (2005) '"A belief in humanity is a belief in colored men": Using culture to span the digital divide', *Journal of Computer-Mediated Communication*, *11*(1), article 17.

Broderick, Ryan (2016) 'This is how Facebook is radicalising you', *Buzzfeed News*, 16 November.

Brown, Andrew (2015) 'Wikipedia editors are a dying breed. The reason? Mobile', *Guardian*, 25 June.

Brügger, Niels (2008) 'The archived website and website philology: A new type of historical document?' *Nordicom Review*, *29*(2): 151–171.

Brügger, Niels (2012) 'When the present web is later than the past: Web historiography, digital history and internet studies', *Historical Social Research*, *37*(4): 102–117.

Bruno, Christopher (2002) 'The Google AdWords happening', *The Dadameter*, christophebruno.com, April.

Bruns, Axel (2007) 'Methodologies for mapping the political blogosphere: An exploration using the IssueCrawler research tool', *First Monday*, *12*(5). https://doi.org/10.5210/fm.v12i5.1834.

Bruns, Axel (2009) 'From prosumer to produser: Understanding user-led content creation', paper presented at Transforming Audiences, London, 3–4 September.

Bruns, Axel (2012) 'Ad hoc innovation by users of social networks: The case of Twitter', ZSI Discussion Paper 16, www.zsi.at/object/publication/2186.

Bruns, Axel (2019) 'After the 'APIcalypse': Social media platforms and their fight against critical scholarly research', *Information, Communication & Society, 22*(11): 1544–1566.

Bruns, Axel and Burgess, Jean (2011) *'The use of Twitter hashtags in the formation of ad hoc publics', Proceedings of the 6th European Consortium for Political Research (ECPR) General Conference*, Colchester: The European Consortium for Political Research (ECPR), pp. 1–9.

Bruns, Axel and Burgess, Jean (2015) 'Twitter hashtags from ad hoc to calculated publics', in Nathan Rambukkana (ed) *Hashtag Publics: The Power and Politics of Discursive Networks*. New York: Peter Lang, pp. 13–28.

Bruns, Axel and Eltham, Ben (2009) 'Twitter free Iran: An evaluation of Twitter's role in public diplomacy and information operations in Iran's 2009 election crisis', *Communications Policy & Research Forum*. Sydney: University of Technology, pp. 298–310.

Bruns, Axel and Highfield, Tim (2012) 'Blogs, Twitter, and breaking news: The produsage of citizen journalism', in Rebecca Ann Lind (ed) *Produsing Theory in a Digital World: The Intersection of Audiences and Production in Contemporary Theory*. New York: Peter Lang, pp. 15–32.

Bruns, Axel and Highfield, Tim (2015) 'From news blogs to news on Twitter: Gatewatching and collaborative news curation', in Stephen Coleman and Deen Freelon (eds) *Handbook of Digital Politics*. Cheltenham: Edward Elgar, pp. 325–339.

Bruns, Axel and Weller, Katrin (2016) 'Twitter as a first draft of the present, and the challenges of preserving it for the future', *Proceedings of WebSci16*, New York: ACM, pp. 183–189.

Bruns, Axel, Burgess, Jean and Highfield, Tim (2014) 'A "big data" approach to mapping the Australian twittersphere', in Paul Longley Arthur and Katherine Bode (eds) *Advancing Digital Humanities*. Basingstoke: Palgrave Macmillan, pp. 113–129.

Bruns, Axel, Moon, Brenda, Paul, Avijit and Münch, Felix (2016) 'Towards a typology of hashtag publics: A large-scale comparative study of user engagement across trending topics', *Communication Research and Practice, 2*(1): 20–46.

Bruns, Axel, Bechmann, Anja, Burgess, Jean et al. (2018) 'Facebook shuts the gate after the horse has bolted and hurts real research in the process', *Internet Policy Review*, 25 April, https://policyreview.info/articles/news/facebook-shuts-gate-after-horse-has-bolted-and-hurts-real-research-process/786.

Bucher, Taina (2013) 'Objects of intense feeling: The case of the Twitter API', *Computational Culture: A Journal of Software Studies*, 4. http://computationalculture.net/objects-of-intense-feeling-the-case-of-the-twitter-api/

Bucher, Taina (2017) 'The algorithmic imaginary: Exploring the ordinary affects of Facebook algorithms', *Information, Communication & Society, 20*(1): 30–44.

Budge, Kylie (2020a) 'Visually imagining place: Museum visitors, Instagram, and the city, *Journal of Urban Technology, 27*(2): 61–79.

Budge, Kylie (2020b) 'Remember me: Instagram, selfies and libraries', *Journal of the Australian Library and Information Association, 69*(1): 3–16.

Burgess, Jean (2006) 'Hearing ordinary voices: Cultural studies, vernacular creativity and digital storytelling', *Continuum, 20*(2): 201–214.

Burgess, Jean (2016) *'Twitter is the last of Web 2.0', personal communication, AoIR conference,* Berlin, 5 October.

Burgess, Jean and Baym, Nancy K. (2020) *Twitter: A Biography*. New York: New York University Press.

Burgess, Jean and Green, Joshua (2009) 'The entrepreneurial vlogger: Participatory culture beyond the professional–amateur divide', in Pelle Snickars and Patrick Vonderau (eds) *The YouTube Reader*. Stockholm: National Library of Sweden, pp. 89–107.

Burgess, Jean and Green, Joshua (2018) *YouTube: Online Video and Participatory Culture*. Cambridge: Polity Press.

Burns, Alex and Eltham, Benjamin (2009) 'Twitter free Iran: An evaluation of Twitter's role in public diplomacy and information operations in Iran's 2009 election crisis', Record of the Communications Policy & Research Forum (CPRF), Sydney, Australia, pp. 298–310.

Burrington, Ingrid (2014) 'The cloud is not the territory', *Creativetime Reports*, 20 May, http://creativetimereports.org/2014/05/20/ingrid-burrington-the-cloud-is-not-the-territory-wnv/.

Butler, Brian, Joyce, Elisabeth and Pike, Jacqueline (2008) 'Don't look now, but we've created a bureaucracy: The nature and roles of policies and rules in Wikipedia', *CHI'08: Proceedings of the SIGCHI Conference on Human Factors in Computing Systems*. New York: ACM, pp. 1101–1110.

Bychowski, Steve (2016) 'The Internet Archive Wayback Machine: A useful IP litigation tool, but is it admissible?' *Trademark and Copyright Law Blog*, 16 May, www.trademarkandcopyrightlawblog.com/2016/05/the-internet-archive-wayback-machine-a-useful-ip-litigation-tool-but-is-it-admissible/.

Cadwalladr, Carole (2016) 'Google, democracy and the truth about internet search', *The Guardian*, 4 December.

Caliandro, Alessandro and Graham, James (2020) 'Studying Instagram beyond selfies', *Social Media + Society*, April–June: 1–7.

Callahan, Ewa S. and Herring, Susan C. (2011) 'Cultural bias in Wikipedia content on famous persons', *Journal of the American Society for Information Science and Technology, 62*(10): 1899–1915.

Campbell, Matthew T. (2003) 'Generic names for soft drinks by county, The Pop vs. *Soda page'*, www.popvssoda.com/countystats/total-county.html.

Carr, Constance, Bast, Desmond, Madron, Karinne and Syrus, Ahmad Mafaz (2022) 'Mapping the clouds: The matter of data centers', *Journal of Maps*. http://dx.doi.org/10.1080/17445647.2022.2088304

Carr, Nicholas (2007) 'From contemplative man to flickering man', *Encyclopaedia Britannica* blog, 13 June, http://blogs.britannica.com/2007/06/from-contemplative-man-to-flickering-man/.

Carr, Nicholas (2009) 'All hail the information triumvirate!', *Roughtype* blog, 22 January, www.roughtype.com/archives/2009/01/all_hail_the_in.php.

Casey, Edward S. (1996) 'How to get from space to place in a fairly short stretch of time: Phenomenological prolegomena', *Senses of Place, 27*: 14–51.

Castro, Jenna M. Lo (2021) 'Framing the impact of pseudo-influencers via communication ethics', in Brandi Watkins (ed) *Research Perspectives on Social Media Influencers and Brand Communication*. Lanham, MD: Lexington Books, pp. 145–160.

Chao, Jason (2021) Memespector GUI: Graphical User Interface Client for Computer Vision APIs (Version 0.2), *Software*, https://github.com/jason-chao/memespector-gui.

Chancellor, Stevie, Pater, Jessica A., Clear, Trustin A., Gilbert, Eric and Choudhury, Munmun De (2016) '#Thyghgapp: Instagram content moderation and lexical variation in pro-eating disorder communities', *Proceedings of the 19th ACM Conference on Computer-Supported Cooperative Work & Social Computing*. New York: ACM, pp. 1201–1213.

Chen, Adrian (2015) 'The Agency', *New York Times*, 2 June.

Chen, Edwin (2012) 'Soda vs. pop', *Edwin Chen's Blog*, 6 July, http://blog.echen.me/2012/07/06/soda-vs-pop-with-twitter/.

Chen, Xu (2019) 'TikTok is popular, but Chinese apps still have a lot to learn about global markets', *The Conversation*, 1 April, https://theconversation.com/tiktok-is-popular-but-chinese-apps-still-have-a-lot-to-learn-about-global-markets-113039.

Chen, Xu, Kaye, Bondy Valdovinos and Zeng, Jing (2020) '#PositiveEnergy Douyin: Constructing "playful patriotism" in a Chinese short-video application', *Chinese Journal of Communication*, 14(1): 97–117.

Chesney, Thomas (2006) 'An empirical examination of Wikipedia's credibility', *First Monday*, 11(11). https://doi.org/10.5210/fm.v11i11.1413.

Chiber, Kabir (2014) 'American cultural imperialism has a new name: GAFA', *Quartz*, 1 December.

Chikofsky, Elliot J. and Cross, James H. (1990) 'Reverse engineering and design recovery: A taxonomy', *IEEE Software*, 7(1): 13–17.

CHM Tech (2017) 'I'm feeling lucky', video, www.youtube.com/watch?v=4qeGFMP-Ahw.

Chonka, Peter, Diepeveen, Stephanie and Haile, Yidnekachew (2023) 'Algorithmic power and African indigenous languages: Search engine autocomplete and the global multilingual internet', *Media, Culture & Society*, 45(2): 246–265. https://doi.org/10.1177/01634437221104705.

Chotiner, Isaac (2019) 'The underworld of online content moderation', *New Yorker*, 5 July.

Chouliaraki, Lilie (2013) *The Ironic Spectator: Solidarity in the Age of Post-humanitarianism*. Cambridge: Polity.

Chowdhury, Abdur (2009) 'Top Twitter trends of 2009', *Twitter Blog*, 15 December, https://blog.twitter.com/official/en_us/a/2009/top-twitter-trends-of-2009.html.

Christensen, Henrik Serup (2011) 'Political activities on the internet: Slacktivism or political participation by other means?' *First Monday*, 16(2). https://doi.org/10.5210/fm.v16i2.3336.

Chun, Wendy Hui Kyong (2008) 'The enduring ephemeral, or the future is a memory', *Critical Inquiry*, 35(1): 148–171.

Chun, Wendy Hui Kyong (2013) *Programmed Visions: Software and Memory*. Cambridge, MA: MIT Press.

Chun, Wendy Hui Kyong (2018) 'Queerying homophily', in Clemens Apprich, Wendy Hui Kyong Chun, Florian Cramer, and Hito Steyerl (eds) *Pattern Discrimination*. Lüneburg: Meson Press, pp. 59–98.

Cinelli, Matteo, Quattrociocchi, Walter, Galeazzi, Alessandro, Valensise, Carlo Michele, Brugnoli, Emanuele, Schmidt, Ana Lucia, Zola, Paola, Zollo, Fabiana, and Scala, Antonio (2020) The COVID-19 social media infodemic, *Scientific Reports*, *10*: 16598.

Cirio, Paolo (2012) 'Street ghosts', digital art, streetghosts.net.

Cohen, Daniel J. and Rosenzweig, Roy (2006) *Digital History: A Guide to Gathering, Preserving, and Presenting the Past on the Web*. Philadelphia, PA: University of Pennsylvania Press.

Cole-Lewis, Heather, Pugatch, Jillian, Sanders, Amy, Varghese, Arun, Posada, Susana Yun, Christopher, Schwarz, and Augustson, Erik (2015) 'Social listening: A content analysis of e-cigarette discussions on Twitter', *Journal of Medical Internet Research*, *17*(10): e243.

Colombo, Gabriele (2018) *The Design of Composite Images: Displaying Digital Visual Content for Social Research*, PhD thesis, Politecnico di Milano.

Colombo, Gabriele and De Gaetano, Carlo (2020) 'Dutch political Instagram: Junk news, follower ecologies and artificial amplification', in Richard Rogers and Sabine Niederer (eds) *The Politics of Social Media Manipulation*. Amsterdam: Amsterdam University Press, pp. 147–168.

Commons Select Committee (2018a) 'Evidence from Christopher Wylie, Cambridge Analytica whistle-blower', UK Parliament, 28 April.

Commons Select Committee (2018b) 'Dr Aleksandr Kogan questioned by Committee', UK Parliament, 24 April.

Confessore, Nicholas, Dance, Gabriel J.X., Harris, Richard, and Hansen, Mark (2018) 'The follower factory', *New York Times*, 27 January.

Confessore, Nicholas and Wakabayashi, Daisuke (2017) 'How Russia Harvested American Rage to Reshape U.S. Politics', *New York Times*, 9 October.

Cookson, Robert (2016) 'Jihadi website with beheadings profited from Google ad platform', *Financial Times*, 17 May.

Costanza-Chock, Sasha (2014) *Out of the Shadows, Into the Streets! Transmedia Organizing and the Immigrant Rights Movement*. Cambridge, MA: MIT Press.

Couldry, Nick (2001) 'The hidden injuries of media power', *Journal of Consumer Culture*, *1*(2): 155–177.

Couldry, Nick (2012) *Media, Society, World: Social Theory and Digital Media Practice*. Cambridge: Polity.

Counter-extremism Project (2018) 'The eGLYPH Web Crawler: ISIS Content on Youtube', *New York: Counter-extremism Project*, www.counterextremism.com/sites/default/files/eGLYPH_web_crawler_white_paper_July_2018.pdf.

Cox, Joseph (2017) 'This is how Twitter blocks far-right tweets in Germany', *Motherboard*, 13 June.

CR+DS (2022) 'A people's guide to finding algorithmic bias', *Center for Critical Race and Digital Studies, New York University*, www.criticalracedigitalstudies.com/peoplesguide.

Crampton, Jeremy W., Graham, Mark, Poorthuis, Ate, Shelton, Taylor, Stephens, Monica, Wilson, Matthew W. and Zook, Matthew (2013) 'Beyond the geotag: Situating "big data" and leveraging the potential of the geoweb', *Cartography and Geographic Information Science*, *40*(2): 130–139.

Crawford, Kate and Paglen, Trevor (2019) 'Excavating AI: The politics of training sets for machine learning', 19 September, https://excavating.ai.

Crescia, Stefano, Pietrob, Roberto Di, Petrocchi, Marinell, Spognardi, Angelo, and Tesconi, Maurizio (2016) 'Fame for sale: Efficient detection of fake Twitter followers', *Decision Support Systems, 80*: 56–71.

Critchlow, Will (2007) 'Search Google without Wikipedia – a Firefox search plugin', *Distilled* blog, 10 July, www.distilled.net/blog/seo/search-google-without-Wikipedia-a-firefox-search-plugin/.

Critical Art Ensemble (1998) *Flesh Machine: Cyborgs, Designer Babies, and New Eugenic Consciousness.* New York: Autonomedia.

CrowdTangle (2021) 'Agence France-Presses' strategy for using CrowdTangle search and meme search to report misinformation', CrowdTangle Help, https://help.crowdtangle. com/en/articles/4153905-agence-france-presse-s-strategy-for-using-crowdtangle-search-and-meme-search-to-report-misinformation.

Cush, Andy (2014) 'Who's behind this shady, propagandistic Russian photo exhibition?' *Gawker*, 10 October.

Cutts, Matt (2005) 'How to write queries', *Matt Cutts: Gadgets, Google, and SEO*, 11 August, www.mattcutts.com/blog/writing-google-queries/.

Cutts, Matt (2006) 'Indexing timeline', *Matt Cutts: Gadgets, Google, and SEO*, 16 May, https://www.mattcutts.com/blog/indexing-timeline/.

d'Andrea, Carlos and Mintz, André (2019) 'Studying the live cross-platform circulation of images with computer vision API: An experiment based on a sports media event', *International Journal of Communication, 13*: 1825–1845.

Datta, Amit, Tschantz, Michael Carl, and Datta, Anupam (2015) 'Automated experiments on ad privacy settings', *Proceedings on Privacy Enhancing Technologies, 2015*(1): 92–112.

Davenport, Coral (2017) 'With Trump in charge, climate change references purged from website', *New York Times*, 20 January.

Davies, William (2015) *The Happiness Industry: How Government and Big Business Sold Us Well Being.* London: Verso.

De Amicis, Giulia, De Gaetano, Carlo, Saulière, Saya, Bardelli, Federica, Rogers, Richard, Waardenburg, Thijs, den Tex, Emile, Kok, Saskia, and Roginsky, Sandrine (2013) 'Gezi Park life: From trees to cops', *Digital Methods Summer School 2013*, 11 July, https://wiki. digitalmethods.net/pub/Dmi/GeziParkLife/PP_GreenpeaceProject_Final.pdf.

De Geuzen (2006) 'Global anxiety monitor', www.geuzen.org/anxiety.

De Keulenaar, Emillie, Kisjes, Ivan, Smith, Rory, Albrecht, Carina and Cappuccio, Eleonora (2023) 'Twitter as accidental authority: How a platform assumed an adjudicative role during the COVID-19 pandemic', in Richard Rogers (ed) *The Propagation of Misinformation in Social Media: A Cross-Platform Analysis.* Amsterdam: Amsterdam University Press, pp. 109-138.

Dean, Brian (2016) 'Google's 200 ranking factors: The complete list', *backlink.io*, 5 November, http://backlinko.com/google-ranking-factors.

Dean, Jodi (1998) *Aliens in America: Conspiracy Cultures from Outerspace to Cyberspace.* Ithaca, NY: Cornell University Press.

Dean, Jonathan (2019) 'Sorted for memes and gifs: Visual media and everyday digital politics', *Political Studies Review*, *17*(3): 255–266.

Dekker, Annet and Wolfsberger, Annette (2009) *Walled Garden*. Amsterdam: Virtual Platform.

Delkic, Melina (2022) 'Leg Booty? Panoramic? Seggs? How TikTok is changing language', *New York Times*, 21 November, www.nytimes.com/2022/11/19/style/tiktok-avoid-moderators-words.html.

Depoorter, Dries (2019) Quick fix: Machine selling likes and followers, artwork, https://driesdepoorter.be/quickfix/.

Dewey, Caitlin (2014) 'Google will eat itself: A Q&A with the creators of a subversive, oddly timeless piece of conceptual art', *Washington Post*, 21 March.

Dharapak, Charles (2012) 'White House: Obama misspoke by referring to "Polish death camp" while honoring Polish war hero', *Washington Post*, 29 May.

Digital Methods Initiative (2007) *RFID Imagery: Wet and Dry Associations Compared*. Amsterdam: Digital Methods Initiative.

Digital Methods Initiative (2009) 'For the ppl of Iran – #iranelection RT', video installation, https://movies.issuecrawler.net/for_the_ppl_of_iran.html.

DiResta, Renee, Shaffer, Kris, Ruppel, Becky, Sullivan, David, Matney, Robert, Fox, Ryan, Albright, Jonathan, and Ben Johnson (2019) 'The tactics & tropes of the internet research agency', *White Paper, New Knowledge*.

Dohmen, Joep (2007) 'Opkomst en ondergang van extreemrechtse sites', *NRC Handelsblad*, 25 August.

Donttrack.us (2017) 'Google trackers are lurking on 75% of websites', donttrack.us.

Dorsey, Jack (2006) 'twttr sketch', image, *Flickr*, 24 March, www.flickr.com/photos/jackdorsey/182613360.

Dorsey, Jack (2008) 'Twitter trends & a tip', Twitter blog, 5 September, https://blog.twitter.com/official/en_us/a/2008/twitter-trends-a-tip.html.

Dougherty, Meghan and Meyer, Eric T. (2014) 'Community, tools, and practices in web archiving: The state-of-the-art in relation to social science and humanities research needs', *Journal of the Association for Information Science and Technology*, *65*(11): 2195–2209.

Dougherty, Meghan, Meyer, Eric T., Madsen, Christine, van den Heuvel, Charles, Thomas, Arthur and Wyatt, Sally (2010) *Researcher Engagement with Web Archives: State of the Art*. London: JISC.

Dowd, Maureen (2015) 'The Google art heist', *New York Times*, 12 September.

Duportail, Judith, Kayser-Bril, Nicolas, Richard, Edouard and Schacht, Kira (2020) 'The skin bias in Instagram', Voxeuropa, 15 June, https://voxeurop.eu/en/the-skin-bias-in-instagram/.

Elali, Louise, Keiser, Danielle, and Odag, Özen (2012) 'Logomorphism and liquid logos: An analysis of Google doodles', in Gisela Gonçalves (ed) *The Dialogue Imperative*, Covilhã, Portugal: LabCom Books, pp. 183–206.

Elliott, Mark (2016) 'Stigmergic collaboration: A framework for understanding and designing', in Ulrike Cress, Johannes Moskaliuk, and Heisawn Jeong (eds) *Mass Collaboration and Education*. Cham: Springer, pp. 65–84.

Elmer, Greg (2003) *Profiling Machines*. Cambridge, MA: MIT Press.

Elmer, Greg and Langlois, Ganaele (2013) 'Networked campaigns: Traffic tags and cross platform analysis on the web', *Information Polity*, *18*(1): 43–56.

Eltgroth, Deborah R. (2009) 'Best evidence and the Wayback Machine: Toward a workable authentication standard for archived internet evidence', *Fordham Law Review*, *78*(1): article 5.

Engelberts, Lernert and Plug, Sander (2009) 'I love Alaska: The heartbreaking search history of AOL user #711391', Minimovies documentary, Amsterdam: Submarine Channel, https://submarinechannel.com/minimovie/minimovie-i-love-alaska/.

EPIC (2017) 'Investigations of Google Street View', https://epic.org/documents/ investigations-of-google-street-view/.

Ericson, Matthew and Cox, Amanda (2009) 'What's cooking on Thanksgiving', *New York Times*, 26 November.

Eriksson Krutrök, Moa (2021) 'Algorithmic closeness in mourning: Vernaculars of the hashtag #grief on TikTok', *Social Media + Society*, *7*(3): 20563051211042396.

Esfandiari, Golnaz (2010) 'The Twitter devolution', *Foreign Policy*, 8 June.

Eslami, Motahhare, Rickman, Aimee, Vaccaro, Kristen, Aleyasen, Amirhossein, Vuong, Andy, Karahalios, Karrie, Hamilton, Kevin, and Sandvig, Christian (2015) '"I always assumed that I wasn't really that close to [her]": Reasoning about invisible algorithms in news feeds', *CHI 2015, Crossings, Seoul, South Korea*. New York: ACM.

EU DisinfoLab (2020) 'COVID-19 and 5G: A case study of platforms content moderation of conspiracy theories', April, EU DisinfoLab, www.disinfo.eu/wp-content/ uploads/2020/04/20200415_5G-blogpost.pdf.

Facebook (2016) 'Facebook platform changelog', Facebook for Developers, https://developers.facebook.com/docs/apps/changelog.

Facebook Liberation Army (2015) *Directives*. Amsterdam: Waag Society, http://fla.waag. org/downloads/FLA-Infographic.pdf.

Faife, Corin (2021) 'In Georgia, Facebook's changes brought back a partisan news feed', *The Mark Up*, 5 January, https://themarkup.org/citizen-browser/2021/01/05/in-georgia-facebooks-changes-brought-back-a-partisan-news-feed.

FairSearch (2011) 'Fact Sheet', https://fairsearch.org/wp-content/uploads/2011/06/ FairSearch_Fact_Sheet.pdf.

Farhi, Paul (2009) 'The Twitter explosion', *American Journalism Review*, April/May, http:// ajrarchive.org/article.asp?id=4756.

Ferenstein, Greg (2015) 'Google's end game is a single perfect search result, As Eric Schmidt explains (in one quote)', *Medium*, 20 April.

Fernie, Eric (1995) *Art history and its Methods: A Critical Anthology*. London: Phaidon.

Fehrmann Gisela, Linz, Erika, Schumacher, Eckhard and Weingart, Brigitte (2010) 'Original copy: Secondary practices', in Ludwig Jäger, Erika Linz and Irmela Schneider (eds) *Media, Culture, and Mediality: New Insights into the Current State of Research*. Bielefeld: transcript Verlag, pp. 77–86.

Feuz, Martin, Fuller, Matthew, and Stalder, Felix (2011) 'Personal web searching in the age of semantic capitalism: Diagnosing the mechanisms of personalisation', *First Monday*, *16*(2). https://doi.org/10.5210/fm.v16i2.3344.

Finkelstein, Joel, Donohue, Jack, Goldenberg, Alex, Jussim, Lee, Vasko, Collin, Ramos, Cristian, Glover, Tayler and Jagdeep, Anisha (2023) '#Twittertakeover: How the Musk Acquisition Became a Launchpad for Gen-Z Neo-Nazis, Ye, and Widespread Antisemitism', Network Contagion Research Institute, https://networkcontagion.us/wp-content/uploads/CAM_Musk-Ye-Groypers_1.26.23_v2.pdf.

Fisher, Adam (2013 'Google's road map to global domination', *New York Times*, 11 December.

Fishkin, Rand (2019) 'Less than half of Google searches now result in a click', *Sparktoro Blog*, 13 August, https://sparktoro.com/blog/less-than-half-of-google-searches-now-result-in-a-click/.

Floridi, Luciano, Kauffman, Sylvie, Kolucka-Zuk, Lidia, La Rue, Frank, Leutheusser-Schnarrenberger, Sabine, Piñar, José-Luis, Valcke, Peggy and Wales, Jimmy (2015) *The Advisory Council to Google on the Right to be Forgotten*, final report, 6 February. Mountain View, CA: Google.

Flusser, Vilém (2000) *Towards a Philosophy of Photography*. London: Reaktion Books.

Fratti, Karen (2014) 'No Google Doodle for World AIDS Day?' *Adweek*, 1 December.

Gaffney, Devin (2010) '#iranelection: Quantifying online activism', *Proceedings of the WebSci10: Extending the Frontiers of Society On-Line*, Raleigh, NC, USA.

Gallagher, Silvia Elena and Savage, Timothy (2013) 'Cross-cultural analysis in online community research: A literature review', *Computers in Human Behavior*, 29(3): 1028–1038.

Gallucci, Maria (2017) 'Google's data center raises the stakes in this state's "water wars"', *Mashable*, 23 April, http://mashable.com/2017/04/23/google-data-center-south-carolina-water-wars/.

Gazaryan, Karén (2013) 'Authenticity of archived websites: The need to lower the evidentiary hurdle is imminent', *Rutgers Computer and Technology Law Journal*, 39(2): 216–245.

Geboers, Marloes and Van De Wiele, Chad Thomas (2020) 'Machine vision and social media images: Why hashtags matter', *Social Media + Society*, April–June: 1–15.

Geboers, Marloes, Heine, Jan-Jaap, Hidding, Nienke, Wissel, Julia, van Zoggel, Marlie, and Simons, Danny (2016) 'Engagement with tragedy in social media', *Digital Methods Winter School 2016, Amsterdam*, https://wiki.digitalmethods.net/Dmi/WinterSchool2016EngagementWithTragedySocialMedia.

Geboers, Marloes, Stolero, Nathan, Scuttari, Anna, van Vliet, Livia, and Ridley, Arran (2020) 'Why buttons matter: Repurposing Facebook's reactions for analysis of the social visual', *International Journal of Communication*, 14: 1564–1585.

Gehl, Robert (2009) 'YouTube as archive. Who will curate this digital Wunderkammer?' *International Journal of Cultural Studies*, 12(1): 43–60.

Geiger, R. Stuart (2011) 'The lives of bots', in Geert Lovink and Nate Tkacz (eds) *Critical Point of View: A Wikipedia Reader*. Amsterdam: Institute of Network Cultures, pp. 78–93.

GeneralLudd (2011) 'Casually butterfly everything', Reddit /r/pics, 22 November, www.reddit.com/r/pics/comments/mkvd1/casually_butterfly_everything/.

Generous, Nicholas, Fairchild, Geoffrey, Deshpande, Alina, Del Valle, Sara Y., and Priedhorsky, Reid (2014) 'Global disease monitoring and forecasting with Wikipedia', *PLoS Computational Biology*, 10(11): e1003892.

Gerlitz, Carolin and Helmond, Anne (2013) 'The like economy: Social buttons and the data-intensive web', *New Media & Society*, *15*(8): 1348–1365.

Gerlitz, Carolin and Rieder, Bernhard (2013) 'Mining one percent of Twitter: Collections, baselines, sampling', *M/C Journal*, *16*(2). https://doi.org/10.5204/mcj.620.

Gerrard, Ysabel (2020) 'Social media content moderation: Six opportunities for feminist intervention', *Feminist Media Studies*, *20*(5): 748–751.

Gibbs, Martin, Meese, James, Arnold, Michael, Nansen, Bjorn, and Carter, Marcus (2015) '#Funeral and Instagram: Death, social media, and platform vernacular', *Information, Communication & Society*, *18*(3): 255–268.

Gibson, Angela (2016) 'URLs: Some practical advice', MLA Style Center, 2 November, https://style.mla.org/2016/11/02/urls-some-practical-advice/.

Gieck, Robin, Kinnunen, Hanna-Mari, Li, Yuanyuan, Moghaddam, Mohsen, Pradel, Franziska, Gloor, Peter A., Paasivaara, Maria, and Zylka, Matthäus P. (2016) 'Cultural differences in the understanding of history on Wikipedia', in Matthäus P. Zylka, Hauke Fuehres, Andrea Fronzetti Colladon, and Peter A. Gloor (eds) *Designing Networks for Innovation and Improvisation*. Cham: Springer, pp. 3–12.

Giles, Jim (2005) 'Internet encyclopedias go head to head', *Nature*, *438*: 900–901.

Gillespie, Tarleton (2010) 'The politics of platforms', *New Media & Society*, *12*(3): 347–364.

Gillespie, Tarleton (2012) 'Can an algorithm be wrong?' *Limn*, 2.

Gillespie, Tarleton (2017) 'The platform metaphor, revisited', *HIIG Science Blog*, 24 August, www.hiig.de/en/blog/the-platform-metaphor-revisited/.

Gillespie, Tarleton (2018) *Custodians of the Internet*. New Haven: Yale University Press.

Ginsberg, Jeremy, Mohebbi, Matthew H., Patel, Rajan S., Brammer, Lynnette, Smolinski, Mark S., and Brilliant, Larry (2009) 'Detecting influenza epidemics using search engine query data', *Nature*, *457*: 1012–1014.

Glasner, Peter and Rothman, Harry (2017) *Splicing Life? The New Genetics and Society*. London: Routledge.

Goel, Vindu (2015) 'Instagram to offer millions of current events photos', *New York Times*, 23 June.

Goggin, Gerard and McLelland, Mark (2017) 'Introduction: Global coordinates of internet histories', in Gerard Goggin and Mark McLelland (eds) *The Routledge Companion to Global Internet Histories*. New York: Routledge, pp. 1–19.

Gonzalez, Robbie (2018) 'Facebook is giving scientists its data to fight misinformation', *Wired*, 29 May.

Googlecache (2007) '96.6% of Wikipedia pages rank in Google's top 10', *Google Cache* blog, 26 June, www.thegooglecache.com/white-hat-seo/966-of-Wikipedia-pages-rank-in-googles-top-10/.

Graham, Mark (2011) 'Mapping Wikipedia's augmentations of our planet', *Mark Graham Blog*, www.zerogeography.net/2011/11/mapping-wikipedias-augmentations-of-our.html.

Graham, Rosie (2023) *Investigating Google's Search Engine*. London: Bloomsbury.

Graham, Mark, Hogan, Bernie, Straumann, Ralph K., and Medhat, Ahmed (2014) 'Uneven geographies of user-generated information: Patterns of increasing informational poverty', *Annals of the Association of American Geographers*, *104*(4): 746–764.

Gray, Joanne Elizabeth (2021) 'The geopolitics of platforms: The TikTok challenge', *Internet Policy Review, 10*(2): 1–26.

Grønstad, Asbjørn and Vågnes, øyvind (2006) 'An interview with W.J.T. Mitchell', *Image and Narrative, 15*. https://doi.org/10.4324/9781315664400-21

Grosfoguel, Ramán (2004) 'Race and ethnicity or racialized ethnicities? Identities within global coloniality', *Ethnicities, 4*(3): 315–336.

Gruber, Christiane (2013) 'The visual emergence of the Occupy Gezi movement, Part One: Oh Biber!' *Jadaliyya*, 6 July, www.jadaliyya.com/Details/28971/The-Visual-Emergence-of-the-Occupy-Gezi-Movement,-Part-One-Oh-Biber.

Grusin, Richard (2015) 'Radical mediation', *Critical Inquiry, 42*(1): 124–148.

Hagen, Sal and Jokubauskaitė, Emilija (2020) 'Dutch junk news on Reddit and 4chan/pol/', in Richard Rogers and Sabine Niederer (eds) *The Politics of Social Media Manipulation*. Amsterdam: Amsterdam University Press, pp. 169–215.

Hagey, Keach and Horwitz, Jeff (2021) 'Facebook tried to make its platform a healthier place. It got angrier instead', *Wall Street Journal*, 15 September.

Halavais, Alex (2004) 'The Isuzu Experiment', *Alex Halavais: A Thaumaturgical Compendium Blog*, 29 August, http://alex.halavais.net/news/index.php?p=794.

Halavais, Alexander and Lackaff, Derek (2008) 'An analysis of topical coverage of Wikipedia', *Journal of Computer-Mediated Communication, 13*(2): 429–440.

Halfaker, Aaron, Geiger, R. Stuart, Morgan, Jonathan, and Riedl, John (2013) 'The rise and decline of an open collaboration system: How Wikipedia's reaction to sudden popularity is killing it', *American Behavioral Scientist, 57*(5): 664–688.

Hardt, Michael and Negri, Antonio (2000) *Empire*. Cambridge, MA: Harvard University Press.

Hargittai, Ester and Shaw, Aaron (2015) 'Mind the skills gap: The role of internet know-how and gender in differentiated contributions to Wikipedia', *Information, Communication & Society, 18*(4): 424–442.

Hassine, Tsila (2005) 'Shmoogle', artwork, missdata.org/shmoogle/shmoogle_art.html.

Hautea, Samantha, Parks, Perry, Takahashi, Bruno, and Zeng, Jing (2021) 'Showing they care (or don't): Affective publics and ambivalent climate activism on TikTok', *Social Media + Society, 7*(2). https://doi.org/10.1177/20563051211012344.

Hay, James and Couldry, Nick (2011) 'Rethinking convergence/culture: An introduction', *Cultural Studies, 25*(4/5): 473–486.

Hecht, Brent and Gergle, Darren (2010) 'The Tower of Babel meets Web 2.0: User-generated content and its applications in a multilingual context', *Proceedings of CHI '10*. New York: ACM, pp. 291–300.

Heine, Jan-Jaap, Hidding, Nienke, Wissel, Julia, van Zoggel, Marlie, Simons, Danny, and Geboers, Marloes (2016) 'Engagement of tragedy on social media: The visual language of Instagram and Twitter in two case studies', *Digital Methods Winter School 2016*, Amsterdam, https://wiki.digitalmethods.net/Dmi/WinterSchool2016EngagementWithTragedySocialMedia.

Helmond, Anne (2013) 'The algorithmization of the hyperlink', *Computational Culture, 3*, http://computationalculture.net/the-algorithmization-of-the-hyperlink/.

Helmond, Anne (2015) 'The platformization of the web: Making web data platform ready', *Social Media + Society*, July–December: 1–11.

Helmond, Anne (2016) *The Platformization of the Web*. PhD dissertation, University of Amsterdam.

Helmond, Anne (2017) 'Historical website ecology: Analyzing past states of the web using archived source code', in Niels Brügger (ed) *Web 25: Histories from the First 25 Years of the World Wide Web*. New York: Peter Lang, pp. 139–155.

Helmond, Anne, Huurdeman, Hugo, Samar, Thaer, Steinfeld, Nili, and van der Velden, Lonneke (2012) 'Traces of the trackers', *Digital Methods Summer School 2012*, 29 June, https://wiki.digitalmethods.net/Dmi/TracingTheTrackers.

Helmond, Anne, Gerlitz, Carolin, van der Vlist, Fernando, and Weltevrede, Esther (2016) 'AoIR 2016 Digital Methods Workshop – tracking the trackers', *Slideshare.net*, 5 October, www.slideshare.net/cgrltz/aoir-2016-digital-methods-workshop-tracking-the-trackers-66765013.

Hermens, Eelke (2011) 'The New York Times – A web historiography', screencast documentary, Amsterdam: University of Amsterdam, https://vimeo.com/32319207.

Herrman, John (2016) 'Inside Facebook's (totally insane, unintentionally gigantic, hyperpartisan) political-media machine', *New York Times*, 24 August.

Highfield, Tim and Leaver, Tama (2016) 'Instagrammatics and digital methods: Studying visual social media, from selfies and GIFs to memes and emoji', *Communication Research and Practice*, *2*(1): 47–62.

Hilfing, Linda (2007) 'Misspelling generator', misspelling-generator.org.

Hindman, Matthew (2008) *The Myth of Digital Democracy*. Princeton, NJ: Princeton University Press.

Hine, Christine (ed) (2005) *Virtual Methods: Issues in Social Research on the Internet*. Oxford: Berg.

Hochman, Nadav (2014) 'The social media image', *Big Data & Society 1*(2). https://doi.org/10.1177/2053951714546645.

Hockx-Yu, Helen (2014) 'Access and scholarly use of web archives', *Alexandria*, *25*(1): 113–127.

Hogan, Bernie (2014) 'A comment on Fuchs' social media', *Bernie Hogan blog*, Oxford Internet Institute, 10 October, https://blogs.oii.ox.ac.uk/hogan/2014/10/10/a-comment-on-fuchs-social-media/.

Holt, Kristoffer, Figenschou, Tine Ustad and Frischlich, Lena (2019) 'Key dimensions of alternative news media', *Digital Journalism*, *7*(7): 860–869.

Honeycutt, Courtenay and Herring, Susan C. (2009) '*Beyond microblogging: Conversation and collaboration via Twitter*', *Proceedings of the Forty-Second Hawaii International Conference on System Sciences (HICSS-42)*. Los Alamitos, CA: IEEE Press, pp. 1–10.

Howard, Philip N. (2020) *Lie Machines*. New Haven: Yale University Press.

Howard, Philip N., Ganesh, Bharath, Liotsiou, Dimitra, Kelly, John, and François, Camille (2019) 'The IRA, social media and political polarization in the United States, 2012–2018', Computational Propaganda Project, Oxford University, https://demtech.oii.ox.ac.uk/wp-content/uploads/sites/12/2018/12/The-IRA-Social-Media-and-Political-Polarization.pdf.

Howe, Daniel C., Nissenbaum, Helen, and Toubiana, Vincent (2011) 'Track me not', software, http://cs.nyu.edu/trackmenot/.

Howell, Beryl A. (2006) 'Proving web history: How to use the Internet Archive', *Journal of Internet Law, 9*(8): 3–9.

Hu, Lixia, Min, Qingfei, Han, Shengnan, and Liu, Zhiyong (2020) 'Understanding followers' stickiness to digital influencers: The effect of psychological responses', *International Journal of Information Management, 54*: 102169.

Huberman, Bernardo A., Romero, Daniel M., and Wu, Fang (2009) 'Social networks that matter: Twitter under the microscope', *First Monday, 14*(1). https://doi.org/10.5210/fm.v14i1.2317.

Hund, Emily (2023) *The Influencer Industry: The Quest for Authenticity on Social Media.* Princeton: Princeton University Press.

HypeAuditor (2021) 'Instagram audit & fake follower check', HypeAuditor, https://hypeauditor.com/free-tools/instagram-audit/.

Internet Archive (2016) 'FAQ', https://archive.org/about/faqs.php#265.

Ito, Mizuko (2008) 'Introduction', in Kazys Varnelis (ed) *Networked Publics*. Cambridge, MA: MIT Press, pp. 1–14.

Jack, Caroline (2017) 'Lexicon of lies: Terms for problematic information', New York: Data & Society Research Institute, https://datasociety.net/pubs/oh/DataAndSociety_LexiconofLies.pdf.

Jacobsen, Grethe (2008) 'Web archiving: Issues and problems in collection building and access', *LIBER Quarterly, 18*(3–4): 366–376.

Jacomy, Mathieu, Venturini, Tommaso, Heymann, Sebastien, and Bastian, Mathieu (2014) 'ForceAtlas2, a continuous graph layout algorithm for handy network visualization designed for the Gephi software', *PLoS ONE, 9*(6): e98679.

Jansen, Bernard J. and Spink, Amanda (2006) 'How are we searching the World Wide Web? A comparison of nine search engine transaction logs', *Information Processing and Management, 42*: 248–263.

Jansen, Bernard J., Zhang, Mimi, Sobel, Kate, and Chowdury, Abdur (2009) 'Twitter power: Tweets as electronic word of mouth', *Journal of the American Society for Information Science and Technology, 60*(11): 2169–2188.

Java, Akshay, Song, Xiaodan, Finin, Tim, and Tseng, Belle (2007) *'Why we Twitter: Understanding microblogging usage and communities'*, Joint 9th WEBKDD and 1st SNA-KDD Workshop '07. New York: ACM, pp. 56-65.

Jeanneney, Jean-Noël (2008) *Google and the Myth of Universal Knowledge: A View from Europe.* Chicago, IL: University of Chicago Press.

Jeffries, Adrianne and Yin, Leon (2020) 'Google's top search result? Surprise! It's Google', *The Markup*, 28 July, https://themarkup.org/google-the-giant/2020/07/28/google-search-results-prioritize-google-products-over-competitors.

Jemielniak, Dariusz (2014) *Common Knowledge? An Ethnography of Wikipedia.* Palo Alto, CA: Stanford University Press.

Jenkins, Henry (2006) *Convergence Culture.* New York: New York University Press.

Jenkins, Henry (2009) *Confronting the Challenges of Participatory Culture.* Cambridge, MA: MIT Press.

Jenkins, Henry (2011) 'Transmedia 202: Further reflections', *Henry Jenkins blog*, 1 August, http://henryjenkins.org/2011/08/defining_transmedia_further_re.html.

Jenkins, Henry, Purushotma, Ravi, Clinton, Katie, Weigel, Margaret, and Robison, Alice (2005) *Confronting the Challenges of Participatory Culture: Media Education for the 21st Century*, White Paper, Chicago, IL: MacArthur Foundation, www.newmedialiteracies. org/wp-content/uploads/pdfs/NMLWhitePaper.pdf.

Jensen, Jens F. (1998) 'Interactivity: Tracking a new concept in media and communication studies', *Nordicom Review*, 1: 185–204.

Jerslev, Anne (2016) 'In the time of the microcelebrity: Celebrification and the YouTuber Zoella', *International Journal of Communication*, 10: 5233–5251.

Johansson, Anna, Eriksson, Maria, Vonderau, Patrick, Snickars, Pelle, and Fleischer, Rasmus (2019) *Spotify Teardown*. Cambridge, MA: MIT Press.

Joinson, Adam (2008) *'Looking at, looking up or keeping up with people? Motives and use of Facebook'*, CHI '08 *Proceedings of the SIGCHI Conference on Human Factors in Computing System*. New York: ACM, pp. 1027–1036.

Kao, Evelyn (2017) 'Making search results more local and relevant', *Google blog*, 27 October, www.blog.google/products/search/making-search-results-more-local-and-relevant/.

Karkın, Naci, Yavuz, Nilay, Parlak, İsmet and İkiz, Özlem Özdeşim (2015) 'Twitter use by politicians during social uprisings: An analysis of Gezi Park protests in Turkey', *dg.o '15: Proceedings of the 16th Annual International Conference on Digital Government Research*, New York: ACM, pp. 20–28.

Karsgaard, Carrie and MacDonald, Maggie (2020) 'Picturing the pipeline: Mapping settler colonialism on Instagram', *New Media & Society 22*(7): 1206–1226.

Kaye, D. Bondy Valdovinos, Chen, XU and Zeng, Jing (2021) 'The co-evolution of two Chinese mobile short video apps: Parallel platformization of Douyin and TikTok', *Mobile Media & Communication*, *9*(2): 229–253.

Kayser-Bril, Nicolas (2021) 'AlgorithmWatch forced to shut down Instagram monitoring project after threats from Facebook', Algorithm Watch, https://algorithmwatch.org/en/ instagram-research-shut-down-by-facebook/.

Keegan, Jon (2016) 'Blue feed, red feed: See liberal Facebook and conservative Facebook, side by side', *Wall Street Journal*,18 May.

Kennedy, Helen and Hill, Rosemary Lucy (2016) 'The pleasure and pain of visualizing data in times of data power', *Television & New Media*, 7 September.

Kennedy, Melanie (2020) '"If the rise of the TikTok dance and e-girl aesthetic has taught us anything, it's that teenage girls rule the internet right now": TikTok celebrity, girls and the Coronavirus crisis', *European Journal of Cultural Studies*, *23*(6): 1069–1076.

King, Gary and Persily, Nathaniel (2019) 'A new model for industry-academic partner- ships', *PS: Political Science and Politics*, *53*(4): 703–709.

King, Gary and Persily, Nathaniel (2020) 'Unprecedented Facebook URLs dataset now available for academic research through Social Science One, *Social Science One blog*, 13 February, https://socialscience.one/blog/unprecedented-facebook-urls-dataset-now- available-research-through-social-science-one.

Kist, Reinier and Zantingh, Peter (2017). 'Geen grote rol nepnieuws in aanloop naar verkiezingen', *NRC Handelsblad*, 6 March, https://www.nrc.nl/nieuws/2017/03/06/ fake-news-nee-zo-erg-is-het-hier-niet-7144615-a1549050.

Klein, Martin, Van de Sompel, Herbert, Sanderson, Robert, Shankar, Harihar, Balakireva, Lyudmila, Zhou, Ke and Tobin, Richard (2014) 'Scholarly context not found: One in five articles suffers from reference rot', *PLoS ONE*, *9*(12): e115253.

Klug, Daniel, Qin, Yiluo, Evans, Morgan and Kaufman, Geoff (2021) *'Trick and please. A mixed-method study on user assumptions about the TikTok algorithm'*, *13th Web Science Conference*, New York: ACM, pp. 84–92.

Knobel, Michele and Lankshear, Colin (2007) 'Online memes, affinities, and cultural production', in Michele Knobel and Colin Lankshear (eds), *A New Literacies Sampler*. New York: Peter Lang, pp. 199–227.

Kohs, Gregory (2014) 'Google's knowledge graph boxes: Killing Wikipedia?', wikipediocracy.*com*, 6 January, http://wikipediocracy.com/2014/01/06/googles-knowledge-graph-killing-wikipedia/.

Kok, Saskia and Rogers, Richard (2017) 'Rethinking migration in the digital age: Transglocalization and the Somali diaspora', *Global Networks*, *17*(1): 23–46.

Kokolakis, Spyros (2017) 'Privacy attitudes and privacy behaviour: A review of current research on the privacy paradox phenomenon', *Computers & Security*, *64*: 122–134.

Kovalev, Alexey (2017) 'Russia's infamous 'troll factory' is now posing as a media empire', *Moscow Times*, 24 March.

Kramer, Adam D.I., Guillory, Jamie E. and Hancock, Jeffrey T. (2014) 'Experimental evidence of massive-scale emotional contagion through social networks', *Proceedings of the National Academy of Sciences of the USA*, *111*(24): 8788–8790.

Krause, Till and Grassegger, Hannes (2016) 'Inside Facebook', *Süddeutsche Zeitung*, 15 December [in German].

Kruitbosch, Gijs and Nack, Frank (2008) *'Broadcast yourself on YouTube – really?'* HCC '08 *Proceedings of the 3rd ACM international workshop on Human-centered computing*, Vancouver, British Columbia, Canada, 31 October, pp.7–10.

Kücklich, Julien (2007) 'Homo deludens: Cheating as a methodological tool in digital games research', *Convergence: The International Journal of Research into New Media Technologies*, *13*(4): 355–367.

Kulish, Nicholas (2012) 'Twitter blocks Germans' access to neo-Nazi group', *New York Times*, 18 October.

Kurt, Serhat a.k.a. Hogg, Jon (2016) Ruin My Search History, software, http://ruinmysearchhistory.com/.

Kwak, Haewoon, Lee, Changhyun, Park, Hosung and Moon, Sue (2010) 'What is Twitter, a social network or a news media?', *Proceedings of WWW 2010*. New York: ACM.

Langelaar, Walter (2012) 'Web 2.0 suicide machine', Presentation at Unlike Us #2: Understanding Social Media Monopolies and Their Alternatives, Network Cultures, Amsterdam, 9 March.

Langreiter, Christian (2017) 'Google.com and Google.cn results compared', *langreiter.com, 2004–2006*, www.langreiter.com/exec/google-vs-google.html.

Lardinois, Frederic (2016) 'A look inside Facebook's data center', *TechCrunch*, 13 July, https://techcrunch.com/gallery/a-look-inside-facebooks-data-center/.

Latour, Bruno (2005a) 'From realpolitik to dingpolitik or how to make things public', in Bruno Latour and Peter Weibel (eds) *Making Things Public: Atmospheres of Democracy*. Cambridge, MA: MIT Press, pp. 14–41.

Latour, Bruno (2005b) *Reassembling the Social*. New York: Oxford University Press.

Laufer, Paul, Wagner, Claudia, Flöck, Fabian and Strohmaier, Markus (2015) '*Mining cross-cultural relations from Wikipedia: A study of 31 European food cultures*', *Proceedings of the ACM Web Science Conference WebSci '15*, New York: ACM, pp. 1–10.

Laursen, Cæcilie (2017) 'What is a data sprint? *An inquiry into data sprints in practice in Copenhagen*', *Ethos Lab blog*, 15 February, https://ethos.itu.dk/2017/02/15/caecilie-laursen/.

Lavigne, Sam (2017) 'Taxonomy of humans according to Twitter', *The New Inquiry*, 5 July.

Lawrence, Steve and Giles, C. Lee (1998) 'Searching the world wide web', *Science*, *280*(5360): 98–100.

Lawrence, Steve and Giles, C. Lee (1999) 'Accessibility of information on the web', *Nature*, *400*(6740): 107–109.

Lazer, David, Pentland, Alex, Adamic, Lada, et al. (2009) 'Life in the network: the coming age of computational social science', *Science*, *323*(5915): 721–723.

Le, Huyen, Maragh, Raven, Ekdale, Brian, High, Andrew, Havens, Timothy and Shafiq, Zubair (2019) 'Measuring political personalization of Google News Search', *Proceedings of the World Wide Web Conference (WWW '19)*, New York: ACM, pp. 2957–2963.

Leaver, Tama, Highfield, Tim and Abidin, Crystal (2020) *Instagram: Visual Social Media Cultures*. Cambridge: Polity.

Lecher, Colin and Keegan, Jon (2021) 'Biden and Trump voters were exposed to radically different coverage of the Capitol riot on Facebook', *The Markup*,14 January, https://themarkup.org/citizen-browser/2021/01/14/biden-and-trump-voters-were-exposed-to-radically-different-coverage-of-the-capitol-riot-on-facebook.

Leftintherain (2011) 'Wikipedia is the new Google', image, Photobucket, http://media.photobucket.com/image/Wikipedia%20icon/leftintherain/google-Wikipedia.png?o=16.

Leidinger, Alina and Rogers, Richard (2023) 'Which stereotypes are moderated and under-moderated in search engine autocompletion?' *FAccT '23: Proceedings of the 2023 ACM Conference on Fairness, Accountability, and Transparency*, New York: ACM, pp. 1049–1061.

Lenssen, Philipp (2006) *55 Ways to Have Fun with Google*, 55fun.com.

Lessig, Lawrence (2004) *Free Culture*. New York: Penguin.

Leszczynski, Agnieszka (2018) 'Digital methods II: Digital-visual methods', *Progress in Human Geography*, *43*(6): 1143–1152.

Levy, Steven (2012) 'Google throws open doors to its top-secret data center', *Wired*, 17 October.

Lewis, Kevin, Kaufman, Jason and Christakis, Nicholas (2008a) 'The taste for privacy: An analysis of college student privacy settings in an online social network', *Journal of Computer-Mediated Communication*, *14*(1): 79–100.

Lewis, Kevin, Kaufman, Jason, Gonzalez, Marco, Wimmer, Andreas and Christakis, Nicholas (2008b) 'Tastes, ties, and time: A new social network dataset using Facebook.com', *Social Networks*, *30*(4): 330–342.

Light, Ben (2018) 'Ashley Madison: Introduction to the walkthrough method', in Jeremy Wade Morris and Sarah Murray (eds) *Appified*. Ann Arbor: University of Michigan Press, pp. 31–42.

Lih, Andrew (2009) *The Wikipedia Revolution*. New York: Hyperion.

Lindgren, Simon and Lundström, Ragnar (2011) 'Pirate culture and hacktivist mobilization: The cultural and social protocols of #WikiLeaks on Twitter', *New Media & Society*, *13*(6): 999–1018.

Lindquist, Johan (2018) 'Illicit economies of the internet: Click farming in Indonesia and beyond', *Made in China Journal*, October–December.

Ling, Chen, AbuHilal, Ihab, Blackburn, Jeremy, De Cristofaro, Emiliano, Zannettou, Savvas, Stringhini, Gianluca (2021) 'Dissecting the meme magic: Understanding indicators of virality in image memes', *Proceedings of 24th ACM Conference on Computer-Supported Cooperative Work and Social Computing*, New York: ACM.

Lippmann, Walter (1922) *Public Opinion*. New York: Macmillan.

Lippmann, Walter (1927) *The Phantom Public*. New York: Macmillan.

Livingstone, Randall M. (2010) 'Let's leave the bias to the mainstream media: A Wikipedia community fighting for information neutrality', *M/C Journal*, *13*(6). https://doi.org/10.5204/mcj.315.

Livio, Maya, Mataly, Jules and Schuh, Mathias (2012) 'TheKnot.*com – a website historiography', screencast documentary, Amsterdam: University of Amsterdam*, www.youtube.com/watch?v=5cxVXJthETA.

Lomborg, Stine and Bechmann, Anja (2014) 'Using APIs for data collection on social media', *The Information Society*, *30*(4): 256–265.

Losh, Liz (2009) 'The Googlization of the BNF', *virtualpolitik.blogspot.com*, 2 September.

Lotan, Gilad, Graeff, Erhardt, Ananny, Mike, Gaffney, Devin, Pearce, Ian and boyd, danah (2011) 'The revolutions were tweeted: Information flows during the 2011 Tunisian and Egyptian revolutions', *International Journal of Communication*, *5*: 1375–1405.

Loveland, Jeff and Reagle, Joseph (2013) 'Wikipedia and encyclopedic production', *New Media & Society*, *15*(8): 1294–1311.

Lovink, G (2008) *Zero Comments*. New York: Routledge.

Lury, Celia and Wakeford, Nina (2012) 'Introduction: A perpetual inventory', in Celia Lury and Nina Wakeford (eds) *Inventive Methods: The Happening of the Social*. London: Routledge, pp. 1–24.

Magnus, P.D. (2008) 'Early response to false claims in Wikipedia', *First Monday*, *13*(9). https://doi.org/10.5210/FM.V13I9.2115.

Maheshwari, Sapna (2017) 'On YouTube Kids, startling videos slip past filters', *New York Times*, 4 November.

Maheshwari, Sapna and Holpuch, Amanda (2023) 'Why countries are trying to ban TikTok', *New York Times*, 16 March.

Mandiberg, Michael (2015) 'Print Wikipedia', art project, printwikipedia.com.

Manovich, Lev (2007) 'Cultural analytics: Analysis and visualization of large cultural data sets. *A proposal from Software Studies Initiative*', *CALIT2*, 30 September.

Manovich, Lev (2011a) 'Style space: How to compare image sets and follow their evolution', Manovich.*net*, http://manovich.net/content/04-projects/073-style-space/70_article_2011.pdf.

Manovich, Lev (2011b) What is visualisation? *Visual Studies*, *26*(1): 36–49.

Manovich, Lev (2016) 'The science of culture? Social computing, digital humanities and cultural analytics', *Journal of Cultural Analytics*, 23 May.

Manovich, Lev (2017) *Instagram and Contemporary Image*. Manovich.net, http://manovich.net/index.php/projects/instagram-and-contemporary-image.

Manovich, Lev (2020) *Cultural Analytics*. Cambridge, MA: MIT Press.

Markham, Annette and Buchanan, Elizabeth (2012) 'Ethical decision-making and internet research: Recommendations from the AoIR Ethics Working Committee (version 2.0)', *Association of Internet Researchers*.

Marres, Noortje (2015) 'Why map issues? On controversy analysis as a digital method', *Science, Technology and Human Values*, *40*(5): 655–686.

Marres, Noortje (2017) *Digital Sociology*. Cambridge: Polity.

Marres, Noortje (2018) 'Why we can't have our facts back', *Engaging Science, Technology, and Society*, *4*: 423–443.

Marres, Noortje and Weltevrede, Esther (2013) 'Scraping the social? Issues in live social research', *Journal of Cultural Economy*, *6*(3): 313–335.

Marsh, Jackie (2016) '"Unboxing" videos: Co-construction of the child as cyberflâneur', *Discourse: Studies in the Cultural Politics of Education*, *37*(3): 369–380.

Marwick, Alice and boyd, danah (2011a) 'I tweet honestly, I tweet passionately: Twitter users, context collapse, and the imagined audience', *New Media & Society*, *13*(1): 114–133.

Marwick, Alice and boyd, danah (2011b) 'To see and be seen: Celebrity practice on Twitter', *Convergence*, *17*(2): 139–158.

Massa, Paolo and Scrinzi, Federico (2011) 'Exploring linguistic points of view of Wikipedia', *Proceedings of the 7th International Symposium on Wikis and Open Collaboration*, New York: ACM, pp. 213–214.

Massey, Philip M., Kearney, Matthew D., Hauer, Michael K., Selvan Preethi, Koku Emmanuel, and Leader, Amy E. (2020) 'Dimensions of misinformation about the HPV vaccine on Instagram: Content and network analysis of social media characteristics', *Journal of Medical Internet Research*, *22*(12): e21451.

Matthews, David (2016) 'Do academic social networks share academics' interests?' *Times Higher Education*, 7 April.

Matthews, Rob (2009) 'Wikipedia, 5000 pages, fully printed', artwork, www.rob-matthews.com/index.php?/project/wikipedia/.

McCown, Frank and Nelson, Michael L. (2009) 'What happens when Facebook is gone?' *Proceedings of JCDL'09*. New York: ACM, pp. 251–254.

McCullagh, Declan (2006a) 'AOL's disturbing glimpse into users' lives', *cnet.com*, 9 August.

McCullagh, Declan (2006b) 'Politicians lash out at tech firms over China', *cnet.com*, 16 February.

McGill, Andrew (2016) 'Can Twitter fit inside the Library of Congress?' *The Atlantic*, 4 August.

McIver, David J. and Brownstein, John S. (2014) 'Wikipedia usage estimates prevalence of influenza-like illness in the United States in near real-time', *PLoS Computational Biology*, *10*(4): e1003581.

McKeon, Matt (2010) 'The evolution of privacy on Facebook', Mattmckeon.*com*, April, http://mattmckeon.com/facebook-privacy/.

McMillan, Sally J. (2000) 'The microscope and the moving target: The challenges of applying content analysis to the World Wide Web', *Journalism and Mass Communication Quarterly*, 77: 80–98.

Mediative (2011) 'Eye tracking and click mapping Google Places', Toronto: Mediative.

Medina Serrano, Juan Carlos, Papakyriakopoulos, Orestis and Hegelich, Simon (2020) 'Dancing to the partisan beat: A first analysis of political communication on TikTok', *Proceedings of the 12th Conference on Web Science*, New York: ACM, pp. 257–266.

Memri (2012) 'Special dispatch: The list of flagged videos', Middle East Media Research Institute, www.memri.org/publicdocs/youtube_flagging_9.11_list.pdf.

Merrill, Jeremy B. and Oremus, Will (2021). 'Five points for anger, one for a "like": How Facebook's formula fostered rage and misinformation', *Washington Post*, 26 October.

Merritt, Harry C. (2013) 'Sharecropping in the Cloud', *Jacobin*, 7 November, https://jacobinmag.com/2013/11/sharecropping-in-the-cloud/.

Mesgari, Mostafa, Okoli, Chitu, Mehdi, Mohamad, Nielsen, Finn Årup and Lanamäki, Arto (2015) '"The sum of all human knowledge": A systematic review of scholarly research on the content of Wikipedia', *Journal of the Association for Information Science and Technology*, 66(2): 219–245.

Messina, Chris (2007) 'Groups for Twitter; or a proposal for Twitter tag channels', Factory Joe blog, 25 August, http://factoryjoe.com/blog/2007/08/25/groups-for-twitter-or-a-proposal-for-twitter-tag-channels/.

Metahaven (2013) 'Data / Saga, digital models and sketches', Amsterdam: Metahaven.

Metcalf, Jacob and Crawford, Kate (2016) 'Where are human subjects in Big Data research? The emerging ethics divide', *Big Data & Society*, January–June: 1–14.

Meyer, Michelle N. (2015) 'Two cheers for corporate experimentation: The A/B illusion and the virtues of data-driven innovation', *Colorado Technology Law Journal*, 13(2): 273–332.

Michel, Jean-Baptiste, Shen, Yuan Kui, Aiden, Aviva P., et al. (2011) 'Quantitative analysis of culture using millions of digitized books', *Science*, 331(6014): 176–182.

Miller, Claire Cain (2014) 'LeanIn.org and Getty aim to change women's portrayal in stock photos', *New York Times*, 9 February.

Miller, Claire Cain (2017) 'From sex object to gritty woman: The evolution of women in stock photos', *New York Times*, 7 September.

Miller, Vincent (2008) 'New media, networking and phatic culture', *Convergence*, 14(4): 387–400.

Milligan, Ian (2016) 'Lost in the infinite archive: The promise and pitfalls of web archives', *International Journal of Humanities and Arts Computing*, 10(1): 78–94.

Milne, David and Witten, Ian H. (2013) 'An open-source toolkit for mining Wikipedia', *Artificial Intelligence*, 194: 222–239.

Miltner, Kate M. (2018) 'Internet memes', in Jean Burgess, Alice Marwick and Thomas Poell (eds), *The SAGE Handbook of Social Media*. London: Sage, pp. 412–428.

Mitchell, William J.T. (1994) *Picture Theory: Essays on Verbal and Visual Representation*. Chicago: University of Chicago Press.

Mohr, John W., Wagner-Pacifici, Robin and Breiger, Ronald L. (2015) 'Toward a computational hermeneutics', *Big Data & Society*, *2*(2). https://doi.org/10.1177/2053951715613809.

Montaño, Celeste and Slobe, Tyanna (2014) '#DoodleUs: Gender & Race in Google Doodles', Waterville, MA: SPARK Movement.

Moretti, Franco (2005) *Graphs, Maps, Trees: Abstract Models for a Literary History*. London: Verso.

Moretti, Franco (2013) *Distant Reading*. London: Verso.

Morlin, Bill (2016) 'The Anti-Defamation League added the popular Pepe the Frog meme to its Hate on Display database', *Hatewatch, Southern Law Poverty Center*, www.splcenter.org/hatewatch/2016/09/28/pepe-joins-echoes-new-hate-symbols.

Morozov, Evgeny (2009) 'Iran: Downside to the "Twitter Revolution"', *Dissent*, *56*(4): 10–14.

Morozov, Evgeny (2010) 'Why the internet is failing Iran's activists', *Prospect Magazine*, *166*, 5 January.

Morozov, Evgeny (2011) *The Net Delusion: The Dark Side of Internet Freedom*. Philadelphia, PA: Perseus.

Mostaghim, Ramin and Daragahi, Borzou (2009) 'Iran election anger boils; Ahmadinejad defends results', *Los Angeles Times*, 15 June.

Mueller, Robert S. (2019) Report on the Investigation into Russian Interference in the 2016 Presidential Election, Washington, DC: US Department of Justice.

Murgia, Madhumita, Criddle, Cristina and Murphy, Hannah (2021) 'Investigating Facebook: A fractious relationship with academia', *Financial Times*, 6 December.

Murphy, Jamie, Hashim, Noor Hazarina and O'Connor, Peter (2007) 'Take me back: Validating the Wayback Machine', *Journal of Computer-Mediated Communication*, *13*(1): 60–75.

Myers West, Sarah (2018) 'Censored, suspended, shadowbanned: User interpretations of content moderation on social media platforms', *New Media & Society*, *20*(11): 4366–4383.

Napoli, Philip M. (2014) 'Automated media: An institutional theory perspective on algorithmic media production and consumption', *Communication Theory*, *24*: 340–360.

Nemoto, Keiichi and Gloor, Peter A. (2011) 'Analyzing cultural differences in collaborative innovation networks by analyzing editing behavior in different-language Wikipedias', *Procedia – Social and Behavioral Sciences*, *26*: 180–190.

Newton, Casey (2020) 'Why no one knows which stories are the most popular on Facebook', *The Verge*, 22 July.

Niederer, Sabine (2016) *Networked Content Analysis: The Case of Climate Change*. PhD dissertation, University of Amsterdam.

Niederer, Sabine (2018) *Networked Images: Visual Methodologies for the Digital Age*. Amsterdam: Hogeschool van Amsterdam.

Niederer, Sabine and Colombo, Gabriele (2019) 'Visual methodologies for networked images: Designing visualizations for collaborative research, cross-platform analysis, and public participation', *Diseña*, *14*: 40–67.

Niederer, Sabine and Colombo, Gabriele (2023) 'The earnest platform: Coverage of the US presidential candidates, COVID-19, and social issues on Instagram', in Richard Rogers (ed) *The Propagation of Misinformation in Social Media: A Cross-Platform Analysis*. Amsterdam: Amsterdam University Press, pp. 139–164.

Niederer, Sabine and van Dijck, José (2010) 'Wisdom of the crowd or technicity of content? Wikipedia as a socio-technical system', *New Media & Society*, *12*(8): 1368–1387.

Nieva, Richard (2022) 'In the age of TikTok, YouTube Shorts is a platform in limbo', *Forbes*, 20 December, www.forbes.com/sites/richardnieva/2022/12/20/youtube-shorts-monetization-multiformat/.

Nissenbaum, Helen (2009) *Privacy in Context: Technology, Policy, and the Integrity of Social Life*. Stanford, CA: Stanford University Press.

Nissenbaum, Helen (2011) 'A contextual approach to privacy online', *Daedalus*, *140*(4): 32–48.

Noble, Safiya Umoja (2018) *Algorithms of Oppression*. New York: New York University Press.

Nye, David E. (1994) *American Technological Sublime*. Cambridge, MA: MIT Press.

Oates, Sarah (2017) 'Kompromat goes global? Assessing a Russian media tool in the United States', *Slavic Review*, *76*(S1): S57–S65.

OccupyWallStreet (2011) 'Forum Post: Proposed list of demands for Occupy Wall St movement!' 25 September, http://occupywallst.org/forum/proposed-list-of-demands-for-occupy-wall-st-moveme/.

OILab (2019) '4chan's YouTube: A fringe perspective on YouTube's great purge of 2019', *OILab Blog*, 17 June, https://oilab.eu/4chans-youtube-a-fringe-perspective-on-youtubes-great-purge-of-2019/.

Omena, Janna Joceli (2021) *From Regimes of Functioning to Digital Research*. PhD dissertation, Universidade NOVA de Lisboa.

Orbe, Mark (2015) '#AllLivesMatter as post-racial rhetorical strategy', *Journal of Contemporary Rhetoric*, *5*(3/4): 90–98.

O'Reilly, Tim (2005) 'What is Web 2.0: Design patterns and business models for the next generation of software', *blog post, Sebastopol, CA: O'Reilly Media*, www.oreilly.com/pub/a/web2/archive/what-is-web-20.html.

O'Reilly, Tim and Milstein, Sarah (2009) *The Twitter Book*. Sebastopol, CA: O'Reilly Media.

Osterberg, Gayle (2013) 'Update on the Twitter archive at the Library of Congress', *Library of Congress blog*, 4 January, http://blogs.loc.gov/loc/2013/01/update-on-the-twitter-archive-at-the-library-of-congress/.

Osterberg, Gayle (2017) 'Update on the Twitter Archive at the Library of Congress', *Library of Congress blog*, 26 December, https://blogs.loc.gov/loc/2017/12/update-on-the-twitter-archive-at-the-library-of-congress-2/.

Ostrow, Adam (2009) 'Twitter reschedules maintenance around #iranelection controversy', *Mashable*, 15 June, https://mashable.com/2009/06/15/twitter-iran-election/.

Ozduzen, Ozge and McGarry, Aidan (2020) 'Digital traces of 'Twitter revolutions': Resistance, polarization, and surveillance via contested images and texts of occupy Gezi', *International Journal of Communication*, *14*: 2543–2563.

Paglan, Trevor (2016) 'Deep web dive: Behind the scenes', creators project, www.youtube.com/watch?v=h7guR5ei30Y.

Panda Buddy (2020) 'Social Media in China: Top 9 Platforms in 2021', Panda Buddy, https://pandabuddy.net/social-media-in-china/.

Papacharissi, Zizi (2012) 'Without you, I'm nothing: Performances of the self on Twitter', *International Journal of Communication*, 6: 1989–2006.

Papacharissi, Zizi (2015) *Affective Publics*. New York: Oxford University Press.

Paquet-Clouston, Masarah, Bilodeau, Olivier and Décary-Hétu, David (2017) 'Can we trust social media data? Social network manipulation by an IoT botnet', *Proceedings of the 8th International Conference on Social Media & Society*, New York: ACM, pp. 1–9.

Pariser, Eli (2011a) *The Filter Bubble*. New York: Penguin.

Pariser, Eli (2011b) 'Beware "online filter bubbles"', *Ted Talk*, March, www.ted.com/talks/eli_pariser_beware_online_filter_bubbles.

Parker, Ashley (2011) 'Twitter's secret handshake', *New York Times*, 10 June.

Pear Analytics (2009) 'Twitter study', Pear Analytics, August.

Pearce, Warren (2018) 'Approach with care: Research within and beyond APIs', lecture, University of Southampton, 30 April, www.youtube.com/watch?v=DaIRdyMIzeA.

Pearce, Warren, Niederer, Sabine, De Gaetano, Carlo, Christ, Katharina, Liao, Han-Teng, Foxton, Holly, Klang, Mathias, Jacomy, Mathieu, Lorenzen, Soenke, Wang, Zijia, Qing, Shenglan (2019a) 'Changing visual vernaculars of climate', Digital Methods Summer School 2019, University of Amsterdam, https://wiki.digitalmethods.net/Dmi/ChangingVisualVernacularsOfClimate.

Pearce, Warren, Niederer, Sabine, Özkula, Suay Melisa, Sánchez Querubín, Natalia (2019b) 'The social media life of climate change: Platforms, publics, and future imaginaries', *WIREs Climate Change*, 10:e569.

Pearce, Warren, Özkula, Suay M., Greene, Amanda K., Teeling, Lauren, Bansard, Jennifer S., Omena, Janna Joceli, and Rabello, Elaine Teixeira (2020) 'Visual cross-platform analysis: Digital methods to research social media images', *Information, Communication & Society*, 23(2): 161–180.

Peeters, Stijn and Hagen, Sal (2022) 'The 4CAT capture and analysis toolkit: A modular tool for transparent and traceable social media research', *Computational Communication Research*, 4(2): 571–589, https://doi.org/10.5117/CCR2022.2.007.HAGE.

Perrow, Charles (1984) *Normal Accidents: Living with High-risk Technologies*, New York: Basic Books.

Pink, Sarah (2008) 'An urban tour: The sensory sociality of ethnographic place-making', *Ethnography*, 9(2): 175–196.

Poell, Thomes and Borra, Erik (2012) 'Twitter, YouTube, and Flickr as platforms of alternative journalism', *Journalism*, 13(6): 695–713.

Pon, Bryan, Seppälä, Timo and Kenney, Martin (2014) 'Android and the demise of operating system-based power: Firm strategy and platform control in the post-PC world', *Telecommunications Policy*, 38(11): 979–991.

Portwood-Stacer, Laura (2013) 'Media refusal and conspicuous non-consumption: The performative and political dimensions of Facebook abstention', *New Media & Society*, 15(7): 1041–1057.

Poster, Mark (1990) *The Mode of Information*. Chicago: University of Chicago Press.

Prada, Piotr (2007) 'On occasion', par-don.com/piotr/google/.

Purba, Kristo Radion, Asirvatham, David, Murugesan, Raja Kumar (2020) 'Classification of Instagram fake users using supervised machine learning algorithms', *International Journal of Electrical and Computer Engineering*, 10(3): 2763–2772.

Puschmann, Cornelius (2017) 'How significant is algorithmic personalization in searches for political parties and candidates?', *Digital Society Blog*, Humboldt Institute for Internet and Digitalisation.

Puschmann, Cornelius and Bozdag, Engin (2014) 'Staking out the unclear ethical terrain of online social experiments', *Internet Policy Review*, 3(4). https://doi.org/10.14763/2014.4.338.

Puschmann, Cornelius and Burgess, Jean (2014) 'The politics of Twitter data', in Katrin Weller, Axel Bruns, Jean Burgess, Merja Mahrt, and Cornelius Puschmann (eds) *Twitter & Society*. New York: Peter Lang, pp. 43–54.

Raehsler, Lisa (2012) 'What people search for – most popular keywords', *Search Engine Watch*, 18 April.

Rambukkana, Nathan (2015) 'Hashtags as technosocial events', in Nathan Rambukkana (ed) *Hashtag Publics: The Power and Politics of Discursive Networks*. New York: Peter Lang, pp. 1–10.

Rao, Adithya, Spasojevic, Nemanja, Li, Zhisheng and Dsouza, Trevor (2015) 'Klout score: Measuring influence across multiple social networks', *2015 IEEE International Big Data Conference – Workshop on Mining Big Data in Social Networks*. New York: ACM.

Rauchberg, Jessica Sage (2022) 'A different girl, but she's nothing new: Olivia Rodrigo and posting imitation pop on TikTok', *Feminist Media Studies*, 22(5): 1290–1294.

Raymond, Matt (2010a) 'How tweet it is! Library acquires entire Twitter archive', *Library of Congress blog*, 14 April, https://blogs.loc.gov/loc/2010/04/how-tweet-it-is-library-acquires-entire-twitter-archive/.

Raymond, Matt (2010b) 'The Library and Twitter: An FAQ', *Library of Congress blog*, 28 April, https://blogs.loc.gov/loc/2010/04/the-library-and-twitter-an-faq/.

Read, Brock (2006) 'Can Wikipedia ever make the grade?' *Chronicle of Higher Education*, 53(10): A31.

Reagle, Joseph M. (2008) *In Good Faith: Wikipedia and the Pursuit of the Universal Encyclopedia*. PhD dissertation, New York University.

Reagle, Joseph M. (2015) *Reading the Comments: Likers, Haters, and Manipulators at the Bottom of the Web*. Cambridge, MA: MIT Press.

Rector, Lucy Holman (2008) 'Comparison of Wikipedia and other encyclopedias for accuracy, breadth, and depth in historical articles', *Reference Service Review*, 36(1): 7–22.

Remaker, Phillip (2015) 'What's the story behind the 'I'm Feeling Lucky' button on the Google home page?', quora.*com*, 5 August.

Renner, Nausicaa (2017) 'Memes trump articles on Breitbart's Facebook page', *Columbia Journalism Review*, 30 January.

Rettberg, Jill Walker (2014) *Seeing Ourselves Through Technology: How We Use Selfies, Blogs and Wearable Devices to See and Shape Ourselves*. Houndmills: Palgrave Macmillan.

Rettberg, Jill Walker (2017) 'Hand signs for lip-syncing: The emergence of a gestural language on musical.ly as a video-based equivalent to emoji', *Social Media + Society*, 3(4): 2056305117735751.

Rhizome (2014) 'Amalia Ulman: Excellences & Perfections', web project, New York: Rhizome, http://webenact.rhizome.org/excellences-and-perfections.

Rieder, Bernhard (2012) 'What is PageRank? A historical and conceptual investigation of a recursive status index', *Computational Culture*, 2.

Rieder, Bernhard (2013) 'Studying Facebook via data extraction: The Netvizz application', *Proceedings of WebSci13*, New York: ACM Press.

Rieder, Bernhard (2015a) 'The end of Netvizz (?)', *The Politics of Systems blog*, 23 January, http://thepoliticsofsystems.net/2015/01/the-end-of-netvizz/.

Rieder, Bernhard (2015b) 'Social media data analysis', lecture delivered at the University of Amsterdam, December.

Rieder, Bernhard (2016) 'Closing APIs and the public scrutiny of very large online platforms', *The Politics of Systems blog*, 27 May, http://thepoliticsofsystems.net/2016/05/closing-apis-and-the-public-scrutiny-of-very-large-online-platforms/.

Rieder, Bernhard (2018) 'Facebook's app review and how independent research just got a lot harder', *The Politics of Systems blog*, 11 August, http://thepoliticsofsystems.net/2018/08/facebooks-app-review-and-how-independent-research-just-got-a-lot-harder/.

Rieder, Bernhard, Abdulla, Rasha, Poell, Thomas, Woltering, Robbert and Zack, Liesbeth (2015) 'Data critique and analytical opportunities for very large Facebook Pages: Lessons learned from exploring "We are all Khaled Said"', *Big Data & Society*, 2(2). https://doi.org/10.1177/2053951715614980.

Rieder, Bernhard and Hofmann, Jeanette (2020) 'Towards platform observability', *Internet Policy Review*, 9(4): 1–28.

Rieder, Bernhard, Matamoros-Fernández Ariadna and Coromina, Òscar (2018) 'From ranking algorithms to "ranking cultures": Investigating the modulation of visibility in YouTube search results', *Convergence: The International Journal of Research into New Media Technologies*, 24(1): 50–68.

Riesewieck, Moritz and Block, Hans (2018) *The Cleaners*, documentary film, Cologne: Gebrueder Beetz Filmproduktion.

Roberts, Sarah T. (2016) 'Commercial content moderation: Digital laborers' dirty work', in Safiya Umoja Noble and Brendesha M. Tynes (eds), *The Intersectional Internet: Race, Sex, Class and Culture Online*. New York: Peter Lang, pp. 147–160.

Robinson, Piers (2002) *The CNN Effect: The Myth of News, Foreign Policy and Intervention*. London: Routledge.

Robinson, Sue (2009) '"If you had been with us": Mainstream press and citizen journalists jockey for authority over the collective memory of hurricane Katrina', *New Media & Society*, 11(5): 795–814.

Robinson, Sue and DeShano, Cathy (2011) '"Anyone can know": Citizen journalism and the interpretive community of the mainstream press', *Journalism*, 12(8): 963–982.

Rogers, Richard (2000) 'Introduction', in Richard Rogers (ed) *Preferred Placement: Knowledge Politics on the Web*. Maastricht: Jan van Eyck Editions.

Rogers, Richard (2009a) *The End of the Virtual: Digital Methods*. Amsterdam: Amsterdam University Press.

Rogers, Richard (2009b) 'The Googlization question, and the inculpable engine', in Felix Stalder and Konrad Becker (eds) *Deep Search: The Politics of Search Engines*. Edison, NJ: Transaction Publishers, pp. 173–184.

Rogers, Richard (2018c) 'Social media research after the fake news debacle', Partecipazione e Conflitto (PaCo), 11(2): 557–570.

Rogers, Richard (2009c) 'Post-demographic machines', in Annet Dekker and Annette Wolfsberger (eds) *Walled Garden*. Amsterdam: Virtual Platform, pp. 29–39.

Rogers, Richard (2013a) 'Debanalizing Twitter: The transformation of an object of study', *Proceedings of WebSci13*. New York: ACM.

Rogers, Richard (2013b) *Digital Methods*. Cambridge, MA: MIT Press.

Rogers, Richard (2014) 'Political research in the digital age', *International Public Policy Review*, 8(1): 73–87.

Rogers, Richard (2018a) 'Otherwise engaged: From vanity metrics to critical analytics', *International Journal of Communication*, 12: 450–472.

Rogers, Richard (2018b) 'Periodizing web archiving: Biographical, event-based, national and autobiographical traditions', in Niels Brügger and Ian Milligan (eds) *SAGE Handbook of Web History*. London: Sage, pp. 42–56.

Rogers, Richard (2019). *Doing Digital Methods*. London: Sage.

Rogers, Richard (2020) 'The scale of Facebook's problem depends on how "fake news" is classified', *HKS Misinformation Review*, 1(6). http://dx.doi.org/10.37016/mr-2020-43.

Rogers, Richard (2023) 'Algorithmic probing: Prompting offensive Google results and their moderation', *Big Data & Society*, 10(1), https://doi.org/10.1177/20539517231176228.

Rogers, Richard and Ben-David, Anat (2010) 'Coming to terms: A conflict analysis of the usage, in official and unofficial sources, of 'security fence', 'apartheid wall', and other terms for the structure between Israel and the Palestinian Territories', *Media, Conflict & War*, 2(3): 202–229.

Rogers, Richard and Govcom.org (2008) 'Google and the politics of tabs', screencast documentary, Amsterdam: Govcom.*org*, https://movies.digitalmethods.net/google.html.

Rogers, Richard and Niederer, Sabine (eds) (2020) *The Politics of Social Media Manipulation*. Amsterdam: Amsterdam University Press.

Rogers, Richard and Sendijarevic, Emina (2012) 'Neutral or national point of view? A comparison of Srebrenica articles across Wikipedia language versions', *Proceedings of Wikipedia Academy: Research and Free Knowledge*, June 29–July 1, Berlin, Germany.

Rogers, Richard, Jansen, Fieke, Stevenson, Michael and Weltevrede, Esther (2009a) 'Mapping democracy', *Global Information Society Watch 2009*, Association for Progressive Communications and Hivos.

Rogers, Richard, Sanchez-Querubin, Natalia and Kil, Aleksandra (2015) *Issue Mapping for an Ageing Europe*. Amsterdam: Amsterdam University Press.

Rogers, Richard, Weltevrede, Esther, Borra, Erik, van Dijk, Marieke and the Digital Methods Initiative (2009b) 'For the ppl of Iran: #iranelection RT', in Gennaro Ascione, Cinta Massip and Josep Perello (eds) *Cultures of Change: Social Atoms and Electronic Lives*. Barcelona: Actar and Arts Santa Monica, pp. 112–115.

Rogers, Richard, Weltevrede, Esther, Niederer, Sabine and Borra, Erik (2013) 'National web studies: The case of Iran online', in John Hartley, Axel Bruns and Jean Burgess (eds) *A Companion to New Media Dynamics*. Oxford: Blackwell, pp. 142–166.

Romm, Tony (2020) 'Justice Department sues Google, alleging multiple violations of federal antitrust law', *Washington Post*, 20 October.

Roose, Kevin (2020) 'What if Facebook is the real 'silent majority'?' *New York Times*, 27 August.

Roosendaal, Arnold (2012) 'We are all connected to Facebook… by Facebook!' in Serge Gutwirth, Ronald Leenes, Paul De Hert and Yves Poullet (eds) *European Data Protection: In Good Health?* Dordrecht: Springer, pp. 3–19.

Rose, Gillian (2016) *Visual Methodologies*. London: Sage.

Rosenzweig, Roy (2003) 'Scarcity or abundance? Preserving the past in a digital era', *American Historical Review, 108*(3): 735–762.

Rosenzweig, Roy (2006) 'Can history be open source? Wikipedia and the future of the past', *Journal of American History, 93*(1): 117–146.

Roth, Daniel (2009) 'The answer factory: Demand media and the fast, disposable, and profitable as hell media model', *Wired*, 19 October.

Rouvroy, Antoinette and Berns, Thomas (2013) 'Algorithmic governmentality and prospects of emancipation', *Réseaux, 1*(177): 163–196.

Rubinstein, Daniel and Sluis, Katrina (2008) 'A life more photographic: Mapping the networked image', *Photographies, 1*(1): 9–28.

Russell, Edmund and Kane, Jennifer (2008) 'The missing link: Assessing the reliability of Internet citations in history journals', *Technology and Culture, 49*(2): 420–429.

Ryan, J. (2011) *A History of the Internet and the Digital Future*. London: Reaktion.

Sanchez-Querubin, Natalia, Couturier, Anna, Invernizzi, Michele, Jimenez, Carlos, Profeta, Giovanni and Werner, Nadine (2018) 'YouTube as an archive for the end of life', *Digital Methods Summer School, Amsterdam*, https://digitalmethods.net/Dmi/SummerSchool2018YouTubeArchiveEndOfLife.

Sanchez-Querubin, Natalia, Wang, Shuaishuai, Dickey, Briar and Benedetti, Andrea (2023) 'Political TikTok: Playful performance, ambivalent critique and event-commentary', in Richard Rogers (ed) *The Propagation of Misinformation in Social Media: A Cross-platform Analysis*, Amsterdam: Amsterdam University Press, pp. 187–206.

Sandvig, Christian, Hamilton, Kevin, Karahalios, Karrie and Langbort, Cedric (2014) *'Auditing Algorithms: Research Methods for Detecting Discrimination on Internet Platforms'*, paper presented at the 64th Annual Meeting of the International Communication Association, Seattle, WA.

Sandvig, Christian, Hamilton, Kevin, Karahalios, Karrie and Langbort, Cedric (2016) 'When the algorithm itself is a racist: Diagnosing ethical harm in the basic components of software, *International Journal of Communication, 10*: 4972–4990.

Sarno, David (2009a) 'Twitter creator Jack Dorsey illuminates the site's founding document. Part I', *Los Angeles Times*, 18 February.

Sarno, David (2009b) 'Twitter creator Jack Dorsey illuminates the site's founding document. Part II', *Los Angeles Times*, 19 February.

Savic, Milovan (2021) 'Research perspectives on TikTok & its legacy apps | from Musical.ly to TikTok: Social construction of 2020's Most downloaded short-video app', *International Journal of Communication, 15*(22). https://ijoc.org/index.php/ijoc/article/view/14543.

Schneider, Steve and Foot, Kirsten (2004) 'The Web as an object of study', *New Media & Society, 6*(1): 114–122.

Scholz, Trebor (2008) 'Market ideology and the myths of Web 2.0', *First Monday, 13*(3). https://doi.org/10.5210/fm.v13i3.2138.

Scholz, Trebor (2016a) 'Platform Cooperativism: Challenging the Corporate Sharing Economy', New York: Rosa Luxemburg Foundation.

Scholz, Trebor (2016b) *Uberworked and Underpaid: How Workers Are Disrupting the Digital Economy*. Cambridge: Polity Press.

Schur, David (1998) 'An introduction to close reading', Cambridge, MA: Harvard University, http://sites.fas.harvard.edu/~lac14/texts-resources/SchurCloseReading99.pdf.

Schwartz, Barry (2016) 'Google's Paul Haahr: We don't fully understand RankBrain', *seroundtable.com*, 8 March.

Schwarz, Jonas Andersson (2017) 'Platform logic: An interdisciplinary approach to the platform-based economy', *Policy & Internet*, 9(4): 374–394.

Scott, Mark (2017) 'Google fined record $2.7 billion in EU antitrust ruling', *The New York Times*, 27 June.

Scuttari, Anna, Stolero, Nathan, Ridley, Arran, Teernstra, Livia, van de Wetering, Denise, Invernizzi, Michele and Geboers, Marloes (2017) 'Emotional clicktivism: Facebook reactions and affective responses to visuals', *Digital Methods Summer School 2017*, University of Amsterdam, https://digitalmethods.net/Dmi/EmotionalClicktivism.

Sen, Indira, Aggarwal, Anupama, Mian, Shiven, Singh, Siddharth, Kumaraguru, Ponnurangam and Datta, Anwitaman (2018) 'Worth its weight in likes: Towards detecting fake likes on Instagram', *Proceedings of the 10th ACM Conference on Web Science*, New York: ACM, pp. 205–209.

Senft, Theresa (2013) 'Microcelebrity and the branded self', in John Hartley, Jean Burgess and Axel Bruns (eds) *A Companion to New Media Dynamics*. London: Wiley, pp. 346–354.

Senft, Theresa and Nancy Baym (2015) 'What does the selfie say? Investigating a global phenomenon', *International Journal of Communication*, 9: 1588–1606.

Shelton, Taylor (2011) 'The (expanded) pop vs. *soda debate*', *Floating Sheep blog*, 3 October, www.floatingsheep.org/2011/10/expanded-pop-vs-soda-debate.html.

Shifman, Limor (2013) *Memes*. Cambridge, MA: MIT Press.

Shirky, Clay (2010) 'The Twitter Revolution: More than just a slogan', *Prospect Magazine*, *166*, 6 January.

Siddiqui, Faiz (2022) 'Twitter brings Elon Musk's genius reputation crashing down to earth', *Washington Post*, 24 December.

Silverman, Craig (2016) 'Hyperpartisan Facebook pages are publishing false and misleading information at an alarming rate', *Buzzfeed News*, 20 October.

Silverman, Matt (2013) 'Wikipedia is losing editors, but why?', *Mashable*, 8 January, http://mashable.com/2013/01/08/wikipedia-losing-editors/.

Simpson, Ellen and Semaan, Bryan (2021) 'For You, or For 'You'? Everyday LGBTQ+ Encounters with TikTok', *Proceedings of the ACM on Human-Computer Interaction*, 4(CSCW3): 1–34.

Sinders, Caroline (2020) 'Feminist data set', University of Denver: Clinic for Open Source Arts.

Smart Metrics (2016) *Rebooting Ranking Factors: Google.com*. San Mateo, CA: Smart Metrics.

Smith, Thomas, Obrist, Marianna and Wright, Peter (2013) 'Live-streaming changes the (video) game', *Proceedings of the 11th European Conference on Interactive TV and Video (EuroITV '13)*. New York: ACM, pp. 131–138.

Software Studies Initiative (2011) ImagePlot software v. 1.1, http://lab.softwarestudies.com/p/imageplot.html.

Sottimano, Dave (2013) 'Google ccTLDs and associated languages & codes reference sheet', distilled.net, 13 December, www.distilled.net/blog/uncategorized/google-cct-lds-and-associated-languages-codes-reference-sheet/.

Spohr, Dominic (2017) 'Fake news and ideological polarization: Filter bubbles and selective exposure on social media', *Business Information Review*, 34(3): 150–160. https://doi.org/10.1177/0266382117722446.

Srinivasan, Ramesh (2014) 'What Tahrir Square has done for social media: A 2012 snapshot in the struggle for political power in Egypt', *The Information Society*, 30(1), 71–80.

Statistica (2017) 'Number of Facebook users by age in the US as of January 2017', Hamburg: Statistica.

Steinberg, Marc and Li, Jinying (2017) 'Introduction: Regional Platforms', *Asiascape: Digital Asia*, 4(3): 173–183, https://doi.org/10.1163/22142312-12340076.

Stepnik, Agata, Martin, Alejandro, Benedetti, Andrea, Karsgaard, Carrie, Yee Ting Ng, Cynthia, Major, Daniela, Garcia-Mingo, Elisa, Granzotto, Francesca, Maia, Gabriel et al. (2020) 'Black squares as (in)authentic behaviour: Displays of solidarity on Twitter, Instagram and Facebook', *Digital Methods Summer School*, University of Amsterdam, https://wiki.digitalmethods.net/Dmi/SummerSchool2020BlackSquares.

Stevenson, Michael (2007) 'Whatever button', erikborra.net/portfolio/whatever-button/.

Stevenson, Michael (2016) 'Rethinking the participatory web: A history of HotWired's 'new publishing paradigm', 1994–1997', *New Media & Society*, 18(7): 1331–1346.

Steyerl, Hito (2009) 'In defense of the poor image', *e-flux Journal*, 10.

Stone, Biz (2010) 'Tweet preservation', *Twitter Blog*, San Francisco: Twitter, Inc., 14 April, https://blog.twitter.com/2010/tweet-preservation.

Stone, Linda (2008) 'Continuous partial attention', Lindastone.*net blog post*, http://lindas-tone.net/qa/continuous-partial-attention/.

Studio Moniker (2012) 'State of the queries', *video artwork*, studiomoniker.com/projects/state-of-the-queries.

Stutzman, Fred, Ralph Gross and Alessandro Acquisti (2013) 'Silent listeners: The evolution of privacy and disclosure on Facebook', *Journal of Privacy and Confidentiality*, 4(2), article 2.

Stvilia, Besiki, Al-Faraj, Abdullah and Yi, Yong Jeong (2009) 'Issues of cross-contextual information quality evaluation: The case of Arabic, English, and Korean Wikipedias', *Library & Information Science Research*, 31(4): 232–239.

Sullivan, Andrew (2009) 'The revolution will be Twittered', *The Atlantic*, 13 June.

Sun, Max (2012) 'Twitterverse map shows what Australians are tweeting about', *The Advertiser*, 23 May, www.cci.edu.au/node/1358.

Sun, Tianze, Lim, Carmen C.W., Chung, Jack, Cheng, Brandon, Davidson, Lily, Tisdale, Calvert, Leung, Calvert, Gartner, Coral E., Connor, Jason, Hall, Wayne D. and Chan, Gary C.K. (2023) 'Vaping on TikTok: a systematic thematic analysis', *Tobacco Control*, 32(2): 251–254.

Surowiecki, James (2004) *The Wisdom of Crowds*. New York: Doubleday.

Swartz, Aaron (2006) 'Who writes Wikipedia?' *Raw Thoughts blog*, 4 September, www. aaronsw.com/weblog/whowriteswikipedia/.

Sweeney, Latanya (2013) 'Discrimination in online ad delivery', *Communications of the ACM, 56*(5): 44–54.

Sysomos (2009) 'A look at Twitter in Iran', *Sysomos blog*, 21 June, https://blog.sysomos. com/2009/06/21/a-look-at-twitter-in-iran/.

Tanash, Rima S., Chen, Zhouhan, Thakur, Tanmay, Bronk, Chris, Subramanian, Devika and Wallach, Dan S. (2015) 'Known unknowns: An analysis of Twitter censorship in Turkey', *Proceedings of WPES'15*, New York: ACM.

Tandoc, Edson (2019) *Analyzing Analytics: Disrupting Journalism One Click at a Time*. London: Routledge.

Tech Transparency Project (2020) 'Facebook leans on states to spot voter interference', Tech Transparency Project, 23 September, https://www.techtransparencyproject.org/ articles/facebook-leans-states-spot-voter-interference.

Terranova, Tiziana (2003) 'Free labor: Producing culture for the digital economy', *Electronic Book Review*, 20 June.

Testa, Jessica (2013) 'How the 'lady in red' became Turkey's most inspiring meme', *Buzzfeed News*, 4 June.

Thelwall, Mike, Vaughan, Liwen, and Björneborn, Lennart (2005) 'Webometrics', *Annual Review of Information Science and Technology, 39*: 81–135.

Thielmann, Tristan, van der Velden, Lonneke, Fischer, Florian and Vogler, Robert (2012) 'Dwelling in the Web: Towards a Googlization of Space', HIIG Discussion Paper Series No. 2012-03, Berlin: Alexander von Humboldt Institute for Internet and Society.

Thornhill, John (2022) 'Elon Musk's free speech absolutism may endanger fragile democracies', *Financial Times*, 25 November.

Thornton, Pip (2017) 'What is Orwell's 1984 really worth?' https://pipthornton. com/2017/08/28/what-is-orwells-1984-really-worth/.

Tifentale, Alise and Manovich, Lev (2015) 'Selfiecity: Exploring photography and self-fashioning in social media', in David M. Berry and Michael Dieter (eds) *Postdigital Aesthetics*. Cham: Springer, pp. 109–122.

Timberg, Craig (2017) 'Russian propaganda may have been shared hundreds of millions of times, new research says', *Washington Post*, 5 October.

Timberg, Craig and Dwoskin, Elizabeth (2016) 'Facebook takes down data and thousands of posts, obscuring reach of Russian disinformation', *Washington Post*, 12 October.

Time Magazine (2006) '*Person of the year: YOU*', http://content.time.com/time/cov-ers/0,16641,20061225,00.html.

Toler, Aric (2015) 'Inside the Kremlin troll army machine: Templates, guidelines, and paid posts', *GlobalVoices*, 14 March, https://globalvoices.org/2015/03/14/russia-krem-lin-troll-army-examples/.

Toor, Amar (2013) 'How a 'lady in red' became the symbol of Turkey's unrest', *The Verge*, 7 June.

Torres, Guillen (2023) 'Problematic information in Google Web Search? Scrutinizing the results from US election-related queries', in Richard Rogers (ed) *The Propagation of Misinformation in Social Media: A Cross-platform Analysis.* Amsterdam: Amsterdam University Press, pp. 33–46.

Torres, Guillen and Rogers, Richard (2020) 'Political news in search engines: Exploring Googles susceptibility to hyperpartisan sources during the Dutch elections', in Richard Rogers and Sabine Niederer (eds) *The Politics of Social Media Manipulation.* Amsterdam: Amsterdam University Press, pp. 97–122.

Tran, Khoi-Nguyen, Christen, Peter, Sanner, Scott and Xie, Lexing (2015) 'Context-aware detection of sneaky vandalism on Wikipedia across multiple languages', in Tru Cao, Ee-Peng Lim, Zhi-Hua Zhou, Tu-Bao Ho, David Cheung and Hiroshi Motoda (eds) *Advances in Knowledge Discovery and Data Mining,* Cham: Springer, pp. 380–391.

Truby, Jon, Brown, Rafael Dean, Dahdal, Andrew and Ibrahim, Imad (2022) 'Blockchain, climate damage, and death: Policy interventions to reduce the carbon emissions, mortality, and net-zero implications of non-fungible tokens and Bitcoin', *Energy Research & Social Science, 88*: 102499.

Tufekci, Zeynep (2008) 'Can you see me now? Audience and disclosure regulation in online social network sites', *Bulletin of Science, Technology & Society, 28*(1): 20–36.

Tufekci, Zeynep (2017) *Twitter and Tear Gas.* New Haven, CT: Yale University Press.

Tunc, Asli (2013) 'Turkish mainstream media's mask has finally slipped', *The Conversation,* 14 June, https://theconversation.com/turkish-mainstream-medias-mask-has-finally-slipped-15187.

Turow, Joseph (2006) *Niche Envy.* Cambridge, MA: MIT Press.

Turow, Joseph (2008) 'Introduction: On not taking the hyperlink for granted', in Joseph Turow and Tsui Lokman (eds) *The Hyperlinked Society: Questioning Connections in the Digital Age,* Ann Arbor, MI: The University of Michigan Press, pp. 1–18.

Tuters, Marc (2019) 'LARPing & liberal tears: Irony, belief and idiocy in the deep vernacular web', in Maik Fielitz and Nick Thurston (eds) *Post-Digital Cultures of the Far Right.* Bielefeld: Transcript, pp. 37–48.

Tuters, Marc and Hagen, Sal (2020) '(((They))) rule: Memetic antagonism and nebulous othering on 4chan', *New Media & Society, 22*(12): 2218–2237.

Twitter (2017a) 'Twitter terms of service', San Francisco: Twitter, Inc., 2 October, https://twitter.com/en/tos.

Twitter (2017b) 'Twitter privacy policy', San Francisco: Twitter, Inc., 18 June, https://twitter.com/en/privacy.

Twitter (2017c) 'Twitter developer agreement & policy', San Francisco: Twitter, Inc., 18 June, https://dev.twitter.com/overview/terms/agreement-and-policy.

Twitter (2021) 'Permanent suspension of @realDonaldTrump', Twitter blog, 8 January, https://blog.twitter.com/en_us/topics/company/2020/suspension.

Twitter (2022) 'Using hashtags on Twitter', Help Center, San Francisco, CA: Twitter, Inc., https://support.twitter.com/articles/49309.

Twitter (n.d.) How to get the blue checkmark on Twitter, Twitter Help Center, https://help.twitter.com/en/managing-your-account/about-twitter-verified-accounts.

Ubermorgen, Ludovico, Alessandro and Cireo, Paolo (2005) 'Google will eat itself', gwei.org.

Ubermorgen, Ludovico, Alessandro and Cireo, Paolo (2006) 'Amazon noir', amazon-noir.com.

Ubermorgen, Ludovico, Alessandro and Cireo, Paolo (2011) 'Face to Facebook', face-to-facebook.net.

Udell, Jon (2005) 'Heavy metal umlaut', screencast documentary, http://jonudell.net/udell/2005-01-22-heavy-metal-umlaut-the-movie.html.

Upshot Staff (2014) 'The Thanksgiving recipes googled in every state', *New York Times*, 25 November.

Upworthy (2012) 'How to make that one thing go viral', Slideshare.*net*, 3 December, www.slideshare.net/Upworthy/how-to-make-that-one-thing-go-viral-just-kidding/9.

US Centers for Disease Control and Prevention (2014) 'CDC Announces Winner of the "Predict the Influenza Season Challenge"', press release, Washington, DC: US Center for Disease Control, 18 June, www.cdc.gov/flu/news/predict-flu-challenge-winner.htm.

US Senate (2020) Russian Active Measures Campaigns and Interference in the 2016 US Election, Senate Report 116-290, Washington, DC: US Government Publishing Office.

Vaidhyanathan, Siva (2011) *The Googlization of Everything*. Berkeley, CA: University of California Press.

Van Couvering, Elizabeth (2007) 'Is relevance relevant? Market, science, and war: Discourses of search engine quality', *Journal of Computer-Mediated Communication*, *12*(3), article 6.

Van de Poel, Ibo (2009) 'The introduction of nanotechnology as a societal experiment', in Simone Arnaldi, Andrea Lorenzet and Federica Russo (eds) *Technoscience in Progress: Managing the Uncertainty of Nanotechnology*. Amsterdam: IOS Press, pp. 129–142.

Van Den Berg, Eric (2019) 'Opnieuw misser bij Forum voor Democratie: Persoonlijke advertentie Thierry Baudet offline gehaald', NPO3, 30 July, https://www.npo3.nl/brandpuntplus/opnieuw-misser-bij-forum-voor-democratie-persoonlijke-adver-tentie-thierry-baudet-offline-gehaald.

Van Den Hoogen, Juul (2019) *The Engineering of the Self Online*, MA Thesis, Utrecht University.

Van der Velden, Lonneke (2012) 'The third-party diary', blog, http://thirdpartydiary.net/.

Van der Velden, Lonneke (2014) 'The third-party diary: Tracking the trackers on Dutch governmental websites', *NECSUS. European Journal of Media Studies*, 3(1): 195–217.

Van Dijck, José (2009) 'Users like you? Theorizing agency in user-generated content', *Media, Culture & Society*, *31*(1): 41–58.

Van Alphen, Ernst (2018) *Failed Images: Photography and Its Counter-Practices*. Amsterdam: Valiz.

Van Ess, Henk (2005) 'Google Secret Lab, Prelude', *Henk van Ess's Search Engine Bistro*, 1 June, www.searchbistro.com/index.php?/archives/19-Google-Secret-Lab,-Prelude.html.

Varnali, Kaan and Gorgulu, Vehbi (2015) 'A social influence perspective on expressive political participation in Twitter: The case of #OccupyGezi', *Information, Communication & Society*, *18*(1): 1–16.

Venturini, Tommaso (2019) 'From fake to junk news: The data politics of online virality', in Didier Bigo, Engin Isin and Evelyn Ruppert (eds) *Data Politics: Worlds, Subjects, Rights*. London: Routledge, pp. 123–144.

Venturini, Tommaso, Baya Laffite, Nicolas, Cointet, Jean-Philippe, Gray, Ian, Zabban, Vinciane and De Pryck, Kari (2014a) 'Three maps and three misunderstandings: A digital mapping of climate diplomacy', *Big Data & Society*, *1*(2). https://doi. org/10.1177/2053951714543804.

Venturini, Tommaso, Cardon, Dominique and Cointet, Jean-Philippe (2014b) 'Présentation – Méthodes digitales: Approches quali/quanti des données numériques', *Réseaux*, *188*(6): 9–21.

Venturini, Tommaso, Bounegru, Liliana, Jacomy, Mathieu and Gray, Jonathan (2017) 'How to tell stories with networks', in Mirko Schaefer and Karin van Es (eds) *The Datafied Society*. Amsterdam: Amsterdam University Press, pp. 155–170.

Venturini, Tommaso, Munk, Anders and Meunier, Axel (2018) 'Data Sprint: A public approach to digital research', in Celia Lury, Patricia T. Clough, Una Chung, Rachel Fensham, Sybille Lammes, Angela Last, Mike Michael and Emma Uprichard (eds) *Routledge Handbook of Interdisciplinary Research Methods*. London: Routledge, pp. 158–163.

Venturini, Tommaso and Rogers, Richard (2019) '"API-based research" or how can digital sociology and journalism studies learn from the Facebook and Cambridge Analytica data breach', *Digital Journalism*, *7*(4): 532–540, https://10.1080/21670811.2019.1591927.

Veronin, Michael A. (2002) 'Where are they now? A case study of health-related Web site attrition', *Journal of Medical Internet Research*, *4*(2): e10.

Vijay, Darsana and Gekker, Alex (2021) 'Playing Politics: How Sabarimala Played Out on TikTok', *American Behavioral Scientist*, *65*(5): 712–734.

Vilain, Pascal, Larrieu, Sophie, Cossin, Sébastien, Caserio-Schönemann, Céline and Filleul, Laurent (2017) 'Wikipedia: A tool to monitor seasonal diseases trends?' *Online Journal of Public Health Informatics*, *9*(1): e52.

Visual Computing (2018) ImageSorter, software, HTW Berlin - University of Applied Sciences, https://visual-computing.com/project/imagesorter/.

Vosoughi, Soroush, Roy, Deb and Aral, Sinan (2018) 'The spread of true and false news online', *Science*, *359*(6380): 1146–1151.

Walczer, Jarrod W. (2021) *Un-boxing Toy Un-boxing: Analysing YouTube's Toy Unboxing Creator Culture*. PhD dissertation, Queensland University of Technology.

Wall, Melissa (2015) 'Citizen journalism: A retrospective on what we know, an agenda for what we don't', *Digital Journalism*, *3*(6): 797–813.

Wall, Melissa and El Zahed, Sahar (2015) 'Syrian citizen journalism: A pop-up news ecology in an authoritarian space', *Digital Journalism*, *3*(5): 720–736.

Warncke-Wang, Morten, Uduwage, Anuradha, Dong, Zhenhua and Riedl, John (2012) 'In search of the ur-Wikipedia: Universality, similarity, and translation in the Wikipedia inter-language link network', *WikiSym '12 Proceedings*, article 20, New York: ACM.

Wardle, Claire (2017). 'Fake news: It's complicated', First Draft, 16 February, https://first-draftnews.org/latest/fake-news-complicated/.

Watters, Audrey (2011) 'How recent changes to Twitter's terms of service might hurt academic research', *ReadWriteWeb blog*, 3 March, https://readwrite.com/2011/03/03/how_recent_changes_to_twitters_terms_of_service_mi/.

Watts, Duncan (2007) 'A twenty-first century science', Nature *445*: 489.

Weaver, Matthew (2009) 'Oxfordgirl vs Ahmadinejad: The Twitter user taking on the Iranian regime', *Guardian*, 18 September.

Webb, Eugene J., Campbell, Donald T., Schwartz, Richard D. and Sechrest, Lee (1966) *Unobtrusive Measures: Nonreactive Research in the Social Sciences*. Chicago: Rand McNally.

Weimann, Gabriel and Masri, Natalie (2020) 'Research note: Spreading hate on TikTok', *Studies in Conflict & Terrorism*, https://doi.org/10.1080/1057610X.2020.1780027.

Weltevrede, Esther and Borra, Erik (2016) 'Platform affordances and data practices: The value of dispute on Wikipedia', *Big Data & Society*, *3*(1). https://doi.org/10.1177/2053951716653418.

Werbin, Kenneth C., Lipton, Mark and Bowman, Matthew J. (2017) 'The contextual integrity of the closet: Privacy, data mining and outing Facebook's algorithmic logics', *Queer Studies in Media & Popular Culture*, *2*(1): 29–47.

Weskamp, Marcos (2004) 'Newsmap', mashup, newsmap.jp.

Whitford, Troy and Prunckun, Henry (2017) 'Discreet, not covert: Reflections on teaching intelligence analysis in a non-government setting', *Salus Journal*, *5*(1): 48–61.

Whitlinger, Claire (2011) 'From countermemory to collective memory: Acknowledging the 'Mississippi Burning' murders', *Sociological Forum*, *30*(S1): 648–670.

Wikimedia (2010) 'An appeal from Wikipedia founder Jimmy Wales', *Wikimedia*, https://wikimediafoundation.org/wiki/Appeal17/en.

Wikimedia (2011) 'From Wikipedia founder Jimmy Wales', *Wikimedia Foundation*, https://wikimediafoundation.org/wiki/Keep_Wikipedia_Free.

Wikipedia Contributors (2014) 'Computing platform', *Wikipedia, the Free Encyclopedia*, article, https://en.wikipedia.org/w/index.php?title=Computing_platform&oldid=592679632.

Wikipedia Contributors (2018a) 'Twitter revolution', *Wikipedia, the Free Encyclopedia*, article, https://en.wikipedia.org/w/index.php?title=Twitter_Revolution&oldid=817942935.

Wikimedia Contributors (2018b) 'What is a troll?' *Wikimedia Meta-Wiki*, https://meta.wikimedia.org/w/index.php?title=What_is_a_troll%3F&oldid=17543718.

Wikipedia Contributors (2018c) 'Wikipedia: Featured article criteria', *Wikipedia, the Free Encyclopedia*, article, https://en.wikipedia.org/w/index.php?title=Wikipedia:Featured_article_criteria&oldid=766263132.

Wikipedia Contributors (2018d) 'Wikipedia: Neutral point of view', *Wikipedia, the Free Encyclopedia*, article, https://en.wikipedia.org/w/index.php?title=Wikipedia:Neutral_point_of_view&oldid=820289964.

Williams, Raymond (1975) *Keywords: A Vocabulary of Culture and Society*. London: Fontana.

Woo, Jesse (2023) 'How to legally scrape EU data for investigations', *The MarkUp*, 23 August, https://themarkup.org/levelup/2023/08/23/how-to-legally-scrape-eu-data-for-investigations.

Woodruff, Andy (2011) 'Web cartography, or putting things on top of other things', *andywoodruff.com*, 9 June, http://andywoodruff.com/blog/web-cartography-or-putting-things-on-top-of-other-things/.

Woolgar, Steve (ed) (2003) *Virtual Society? Technology, Cyberbole, Reality*. New York: Oxford University Press.

Yaman, Alev (2014) *The Gezi Park Protests*. London: English PEN.

Yasseri, Taha, Spoerri, Anselm, Graham, Mark and Kertész, János (2014) 'The most controversial topics in Wikipedia: A multilingual and geographical analysis', in Pnina Fichman and Noriko Hara (eds) *Global Wikipedia: International and Cross-Cultural Issues in Online Collaboration*, Lanham, MD: Rowman & Littlefield, pp. 25–48.

Zachte, Erik (2015) 'Wikimedia traffic analysis report – Google requests', Wikimedia Statistics, http://stats.wikimedia.org/wikimedia/squids/SquidReportGoogle.htm.

Zheng, David X., Ning, Anne Y., Levoska, Melissa A., Xiang, Laura, Wong, Christina and Scott, Jeffrey F. (2021) 'Acne and social media: A cross-sectional study of content quality on TikTok', *Pediatric Dermatology*, *38*(1): 336–338.

Zimmer, Michael (2008) 'More on the 'anonymity' of the Facebook dataset – it's Harvard College', *Michael Zimmer blog*, 3 October, http://michaelzimmer.org/2008/10/03/more-on-the-anonymity-of-the-facebook-dataset-its-harvard-college/.

Zimmer, Michael (2010a) '"But the data is already public": On the ethics of research in Facebook', *Ethics and Information Technology*, *12*(4): 313–325.

Zimmer, Michael (2010b) 'Is it ethical to harvest public Twitter accounts without consent?' *Michael Zimmer blog*, 12 February, www.michaelzimmer.org/2010/02/12/is-it-ethical-to-harvest-public-twitter-accounts-without-consent/.

Zimmer, Michael (2015) 'The Twitter Archive at the Library of Congress: Challenges for information practice and information policy', *First Monday*, *20*(7). http://dx.doi.org/10.5210/fm.v20i7.5619.

Zimmer, Michael and Proferes, Nicholas John (2014) 'A topology of Twitter research: Disciplines, methods, and ethics', *Aslib Journal of Information Management*, *66*(3): 250–261.

Zizek, Slavoj (1998) *The Interpassive Subject*. Traverses, Paris: Centre Georges Pompidou.

Zuckerman, Ethan (2011) 'The first Twitter revolution?', *Foreign Policy*, 15 January.

Zuckerman, Ethan (2021) 'I read Facebook's Widely Viewed Content Report. It's really strange', *Ethan Zuckerman blog*, 18 August, https://ethanzuckerman.com/2021/08/18/facebooks-new-transparency-report-is-really-strange/.

Zulli, Diana and Zulli, David James (2022) 'Extending the Internet meme: Conceptualizing technological mimesis and imitation publics on the TikTok platform', *New Media & Society*, *24*(8): 1872–1890. https://doi.org/10.1177/1461444820983603.

Zunger, Jonathan (2018) 'Computer science faces an ethics crisis. The Cambridge Analytica scandal proves it', *Boston Globe*, 22 March.

INDEX